Beyond Charity

Lindberg

SPIRITUAL THEOLOGY

A SYSTEMATIC STUDY OF THE CHRISTIAN LIFE

SIMON CHAN

InterVarsity Press
Downers Grove, Illinois

InterVarsity Press
P.O. Box 1400, Downers Grove, IL 60515
World Wide Web: www.ivpress.com
E-mail: mail@ivpress.com

InterVarsity Press® is the book-publishing division of InterVarsity Christian Fellowship/USA®, a student movement active on campus at hundreds of universities, colleges and schools of nursing in the United States of America, and a member movement of the International Fellowship of Evangelical Students. For information about local and regional activities, write Public Relations Dept., InterVarsity Christian Fellowship/USA, 6400 Schroeder Rd., P.O. Box 7895, Madison, WI 53707-7895.

Cover photograph: Erich Lessing/Art Resource, N.Y.

ISBN 0-8308-1542-2

Printed in the United States of America ♻

Library of Congress Cataloging-in-Publication Data

Chan, Simon.
  Spiritual theology : a systematic study of the Christian life / Simon
Chan.
    p.   cm.
  Includes bibliographical references.
  ISBN 0-8308-1542-2 (pbk. : alk. paper)
  1. Christian life. 2. Spirituality.   I. Title.
BV4501.2.C4754   1998
248.4—dc21   98-11316
                                                                                              CIP

21	20	19	18	17	16	15	14	13	12	11	10	9	8	7	6	5	4	3	2	1
16	15	14	13	12	11	10	09	08	07	06	05	04	03	02	01	00	99	98		

IN MEMORY OF DARRELL (1955-1995)
WHO TAUGHT ME THE ART OF DYING WELL

Acknowledgments

Most of the material of this book began as lectures delivered at several seminaries in India, the Philippines, Malaysia and Singapore over a number of years. I have learned much from the students of these seminaries—perhaps more than they realized. I thank Trinity Theological College for giving me a year of sabbatical leave. The project could not have been undertaken otherwise, given the tyically heavy teaching and administrative load of seminary teachers in Asia. I am grateful to the Global Research Institute of Fuller Theological Seminary, which provided the facilities for me to work in comfort and with minimal distraction. Dr. Walter Hansen, the director of GRI, not only offered many helpful suggestions but also made our stay in Pasadena quite unforgettable. Rare indeed is the gift of such friendship! My colleague Dr. Roland Chia read an earlier draft and gave me many provocative ideas. To my own regret, I did not always follow them up. Any deficiencies, therefore, are entirely my own. Finally I want to thank my students Kwa Kiem Kiok and Kuzipa Nalwamba, who shared out the task of proofreading under severe time contraints. Ms. Kwa also helped prepare the indexes. *Deo gloria!*

Preface

This work seeks to introduce evangelicals to spiritual theology as a systematic discipline. It differs from traditional works of spiritual theology in three ways. First, it attempts to give the study a wider contextual basis by discussing the various issues from both a Western and an Asian perspective. Second, it looks at the spiritual life from an evangelical perspective. By *evangelical* is meant a life created by the Christian story and distinguished by a conscious, personal relationship with God through Jesus Christ. Third, it considers the life of grace as having a charismatic dimension that is open to surprises from God.

The twelve chapters of this book are divided into two parts. Part one develops the flip side of some major loci of systematic theology. The aim is not to reflect on Christian doctrines per se but on their implications for the Christian life. For this reason I have not developed these loci systematically or in any detail. For example, chapter two presupposes some knowledge of classical and contemporary theological discussions about the Trinity. My primary concern is to show that the different ways of configuring the relationship between divine immanence and divine transcendence into different trinitarian concepts inevitably affects the way the Christian life is lived.

The scope of the theological loci and the particular emphasis given to them needs some explanation. Man is discussed primarily from the standpoint of man-the-sinner. The basic accent of the Christian spiritual tradition is on overcoming the hindrances to man's becoming the person God wants him to be, not on developing his natural, creaturely potential. Spiritual progress is viewed primarily from the perspective of restoring the image of God rather than from the perspective of developing innate human potential. This is not to say that spiritual progress simply means going back to the "original" image.

Rather, any attempt at realizing the human potential must take the person through the redemptive path. In other words, focusing on man-the-sinner is the more logical way of conceptualizing spiritual progress.

Similarly, we have not given eschatology the same emphasis that some modern theologians have given it. The historically conditioned is subsumed within the larger category of Christian perfection. It might be argued that the traditional concept of perfection lacks the historical dimension—a dimension that many modern theologians have come to see as most determinative. My response is twofold. First, theologically, if some form of incarnational theology lies behind the heavy historical accent, it could be argued on the same basis that the Incarnation is as much a doctrine of divine transcendence as of divine immanence. The Word became flesh is as much an affirmation of the preexistence of the Word as an affirmation of its historical presence. Second, if the doctrine of creation is what lies behind the emphasis on divine immanence, again it could be argued that creation is a free act and that God is who God is even before there was any creation.[1]

The accent of the Christian tradition has fallen a bit more heavily on God's transcendence than it has on God's immanence. Christian progress is not just a forward movement into God's historical future, as Moltmann or Pannenberg envisions it, but also an upward movement on Jacob's ladder, as the Christian spiritual tradition has consistently affirmed. Although the Christian life is firmly grounded in history, it certainly is not confined to it. This view is well summed up by Orthodox theologian John Zizioulas: "The fact that man in the Church is the 'image of God' is due to the *economy* of the Holy Trinity, that is, the work of Christ and the Spirit in *history*. This economy is the *basis* of ecclesiology, without being the *goal* of it. The Church is built by the historical work of the divine economy but leads finally to the vision of God 'as He is,' to the vision of the Triune God in his eternal existence."[2] In this connection, it can be added that eschatology as it is conceived in the Orthodox Church contains a strong metahistorical dimension because of its close link with the Spirit who is "the *beyond* history."[3]

My second consideration is on contextual grounds. If we place Christianity within the larger global context, the transcendent or eternal dimension of existence found in Asian religiosity must be given its due weight. This does not mean that we are surrendering the normative witness of Scripture to the cultural context; it means that the scriptural witness to divine immanence and transcendence has a wider contextual application than is recognized by certain modern historically oriented theologies, which have essentially collapsed divine transcendence into divine immanence.

Part two of this work discusses the spiritual exercises by which the

Christian life conceived in part one is to be actualized. The Christian life is from beginning to end a work of divine grace. Actual progress in that life, however, comes through diligent exercise of the means of grace. Acts are utterly basic, small acts, which over time form the Christian character. Without this ascetical base the practical implications noted in part one remain theoretical at best. I call this approach an "asceticism of small steps," of which the first is prayer. Prayer is the first ascetical principle because all the other spiritual exercises depend on it. Unless the various exercises are integrated into a rule of life, however, they remain incoherent and ineffective (chap. 10). Progress in the Christian life is not always smooth and straightforward. There are problems and dangers, unexpected twists and turns, choices to be made between several alternative paths. All these call for discernment (chap. 11). Those who want to discern God's will for their own lives and want to implement an effective rule of life need a spiritual director (chap. 12).

Regarding the issue of inclusive language, for good theological reasons, I would not have hesitated to use the masculine pronoun.[4] As a concession to the times, however, I have used all three genders indifferently whenever it is aesthetically suitable. I make no apologies for this on either contextual or moral grounds. As an Asian living in a culture that does not make an issue of inclusive language (even where English is extensively used), I do not feel obliged to be consistent one way or the other. Existentially and irreducibly, human beings are either male or female. Systematically avoiding gender-specific terms for the sake of political correctness can only reduce personhood and bring an end to any meaningful personal conversation.[5]

I have used the term *West* and its cognates primarily as an ideal type distinguished by a number of characteristics such as individualism, rationalism and egalitarianism, not as a strictly geographical designation. It is virtually equivalent to *modernity*. Quotations from premodern works have been modernized.

Part One
THE THEOLOGICAL
PRINCIPLES OF
SPIRITUAL
THEOLOGY

· ·

1
CHRISTIAN SPIRITUAL THEOLOGY

Its Nature & Criteria

. . . .

THE LAST FEW DECADES HAVE SEEN A FLOOD OF LITERATURE ON SPIRITUALITY. Its popularity may be gauged by the use of the term in a wide variety of contexts. In the past it was usually applied to the religious life. Nowadays, a sociocultural movement, an interest group or a particular cause or concern can be described as a "spirituality," for example, small group spirituality, marriage spirituality and single-life spirituality.[1] Calling any cause or movement a spirituality seems to bestow a certain respectability on it. In many of these contexts the term refers to an intense attitude or feeling that accompanies personal commitment toward the concern. Spirituality, in this sense, denotes the human subjective response to whatever is regarded as the "real."[2] Calling liberationism or feminism a spirituality may simply mean, "We feel deeply about our cause; therefore we expect you to take it seriously too!"

But if Christian spirituality is to be understood in terms of personal (but not individualistic or private, since the Christian life is always defined by a person's concrete existence within a community) relationship with God, we must question the adequacy of a merely subjective definition. We are not primarily concerned about a phenomenological description of spirituality but about truth—as faithfulness to the "given" that defines the Christian community, not as the correspondence of a statement to some object "out there." This given is the Christian story revolving around the life, death and resurrection of Jesus of Nazareth. It is this story that gives shape to our lives and defines the nature of our existence as a Christian community.[3]

What kind of life does the Christian story give rise to? This question is important, since the answer to it determines the shape of our spirituality. If the Christian community is a colony of "resident aliens," it is still a colony existing in a larger sociopolitical context. The shape of our spirituality, therefore, must be true to both the context in which we live and the Christian story. Christians can only realize this by taking into consideration certain material norms or resources. I would like to suggest three interconnected criteria or resources that meet these two requirements: the global-contextual, the evangelical and the charismatic. But first I need to clarify some concepts and consider some formal criteria of spiritual theology.

The Nature of Spiritual Theology

The term *spirituality* is used more frequently than the term *spiritual theology*. Generally, spirituality refers to the kind of life that is formed by a particular type of spiritual theology. Spirituality is the lived reality, whereas spiritual theology is the systematic reflection and formalization of that reality. Spiritual theology can be defined both broadly and narrowly. In the broad sense it refers to a certain way in which all theological reflections ought to be undertaken. In the narrower sense it refers to a distinct branch of theological studies concerned with the principles and practices of the Christian life. In the latter sense it takes its place next to other theological disciplines.

The division of theology (as spiritual, dogmatic, biblical and so on) was quite unknown before the rise of rationalistic philosophy in the eighteenth century, a period commonly known as the Enlightenment. Before then theologians conceived of their task as a profoundly spiritual exercise, even when they used scholastic methods. This explains why Anselm's *Proslogion,* a theological treatise that plumbs the mystery of God's existence, was set in the form of a deeply moving prayer.[4] Theology was known as "the queen of the sciences" because it promotes the highest end of humanity: knowing God and possessing eternal life. Thus all theology is or ought to be spiritual.

A merely "academic" theology would have been quite foreign to them, since theology is simply the rational and precise expression of the believer's reflection of God. This reflection is not a disinterested observation but a personal engagement with God and with God's glory. According to Diadochos of Photiki, a fifth-century Greek bishop, theology is "an exact tracing of the glory of God."[5] Similarly, the Puritan theologian William Ames defines theology as "the doctrine of living unto God" *(theologia est doctrina Deo vivendi).*[6] The early pietists were fond of saying that theology is a practical discipline *(theologia habitus practicus est).* In short, true theology arises from personal experience of God in Jesus Christ, and reflecting on that experience leads to a deeper experiential knowledge of God. The one who is engaged in "an exact tracing of the glory of God" will be affected by that glory, which inevitably elicits praise. True theology is always doxological.

Only by overcoming the disconnectedness of subdisciplines and specializations so characteristic of modern theological endeavors can theologians achieve the integration that modern theology so desperately needs.[7] This is the sort of spiritual theology that the Anglo-Catholic spiritual theologian Martin Thornton has in mind when he defines ascetical theology as "a practical and synthetic approach to all other branches of theology."[8] True ascetical theology, according to Thornton, breaks down the division between "dogmatic" and "affective" theology. It finds even the most academic theology useful for the Christian life because all truth concerning God is grounded in the fact that God has entered our human sphere.[9]

Spiritual Theology as a Theological Discipline
In focusing on spiritual theology as a distinct branch of theology, we are conceding to a certain failure in our modern situation. Ideally, there should be no separation between dogmatic theology and spiritual theology. But since the division of theology into disparate branches is a fait accompli, we can only recover the real function of theology, which is to lead us to godliness by giving the spiritual life a distinct focus. The logic of spiritual theology as a distinct activity, then, may be compared to the logic of festivals. The church sets aside certain days of the year specifically to remember the great verities of the faith. Some Christians, especially those from the free church tradition, justify the scant attention they pay to the liturgical year by saying that every day is a holy day and every week is an Easter. But such a stance renders no single day a holy day at all. If every week is an Easter, then no week is Easter. If the unique events of the Christian faith are not regularly called to mind, they will lose their poignancy and will fail to evoke a fresh vision. This study of spiritual theology as a distinct theological discipline can be justified on the same principle. By giving distinct focus to the spiritual life, spiritual theology may contribute to developing an appreciation of the spiritual nature of all theology eventually. But that must be regarded as a goal, not the starting point of our theological undertaking.

As a distinct branch of theological study, spiritual theology has been variously defined. Joseph de Guibert suggests that it "can be defined as the science which deduces from revealed principles what constitutes the perfection of the spiritual life and how man can advance towards and obtain it."[10] A more elaborate definition can be found in the work of the Anglo-Catholic

K. E. Kirk, *Some Principles of Moral Theology*. The scope of what Kirk calls moral theology corresponds closely with what we would call spiritual theology. It deals with "the ideal of Christian character . . . the internal dispositions of that character without which its virtues cannot flower . . . the means and motives by which its growth can be best fostered . . . the hindrances that threaten to spoil the work and the ways in which they can be met and neutralized."[11] Jordan Aumann, whose *Spiritual Theology* belongs very much to the traditional genre of Catholic spiritual theologies, gives us a good working definition:

Spiritual theology is that part of theology that, proceeding from the truths of divine revelation and the religious experience of individual persons, defines the nature of the supernatural life, formulates directives for its growth and development, and explains the process by which souls advance from the beginning of the spiritual life to its full perfection.[12]

Aumann's definition consists of three parts. First, spiritual theology defines the nature of the supernatural life and is concerned with the life renewed in Jesus Christ. It includes questions concerning the nature of Christian perfection, the life of grace and the operation of infused virtues and the gifts of the Holy Spirit (Is 11:8) or, in Protestant parlance, the work of salvation and sanctification. Second, it formulates directives for the growth and development of that supernatural life, for example, how to deal with sin and temptation and how to cultivate various spiritual disciplines that advance the spiritual life. Third, it explains the entire process by which souls advance from the beginning to the perfection of the Christian life. The Christian life is an intentional process aimed at a goal that is variously called union with God (Catholic), deification (Orthodox) and glorification (Protestant). John Cassian (360-435), whose works exerted considerable influence on Western monasticism, underscores its intentionality when he says, "There is no arrival unless there is a definite plan to go."[13]

Spiritual theology seeks to understand spiritual growth from beginning to end, making use of biblical and experiential data. Thus many ancient spiritual writers trace the development of the spiritual life as stages of growth. Perhaps the best known is the "three ways" of purgation, illumination and union, a scheme that crops up repeatedly in spiritual writings throughout history. Thomas has three classes of Christians: beginners, proficients and perfect. Bernard sees growth as four degrees of love and as twelve steps of humility. Teresa of Ávila speaks of seven grades of prayer.[14] In traditional Protestant theology, the Christian life is understood as progressing according to a certain "order of salvation" *(ordo salutis)*: justification, sanctification and glorification.

Spiritual Theology and Other Theological Disciplines

As a branch of the theology, spiritual theology may be distinguished from other branches. In the Catholic tradition definitions of moral, ascetical and mystical theology differ considerably.[15] The nature and scope of spiritual theology can be clarified by comparing it with some other branches of theology. The term *ascetical* needs some clarification, since it almost always has a pejorative connotation in popular usage and since it is a key concept in our study. It is derived from the Greek *askein*, "to train," and was originally applied to the training of athletes *(askesis)*. To describe spiritual theology as ascetical implies that systematic and disciplined spiritual exercises constitute the primary means of spiritual development.

Spiritual theology differs from systematic theology in both subject matter and approach. Systematic theology covers a wider range of subjects that are usually organized around broad loci such as God, creation, Christ, salvation, man and so on. The subjects of spiritual theology concern the development of the spiritual life. In terms of method, spiritual theology builds on the findings of systematic theology and draws out their practical implications. For example, while systematic theology may seek precise terms such as *persons, being, perichoresis* and so on to articulate an understanding of God as triune, spiritual theology asks how this understanding of God affects our understanding of the nature and goal of the Christian life. In other words, systematic theology concentrates on the concepts and the rational formulations of Christian experience, while spiritual theology concentrates on the experience behind those formulations. The systematic theologian seeks a clear understanding of the Christian faith and uses precise terms and definitions to achieve it. The mystery of the faith remains in the background as rational formulations are put forward. The spiritual theologian reverses this scenario by focusing on the mystery of the faith or of Christian life and leaving the theological formulations to provide the backdrop.[16]

A failure to distinguish between spiritual theology and practical theology has plagued Protestantism. In the narrow sense, spiritual theology is concerned with life in relation to God (the supernatural life), whereas practical theology is more broadly concerned with action in the world. In the broad sense, spiritual theology seeks to discover the transcendent within every sphere of life and every area of experience, whereas practical theology concerns the practical application of theology. For example, in practical theology the doctrine that God is love may provide the motive for loving others and practicing charity. But in spiritual theology, the doctrine that God is love is felt as an experiential reality, defining the basic character of our union with God (as can be seen, for example, in Bernard). Practical acts of charity flow from such experience. Thus spiritual theology stands between systematic theology and Christian praxis. The importance of the place that spiritual theology occupies between systematic theology on one end and practical theology on the other cannot be overemphasized. Without the mediation of spiritual theology, Christian praxis is reduced to mere activism. The result is what Richard Lovelace calls "the sanctification gap," which he identifies as a major failure in Protestantism.[17]

Types of Spirituality

Phenomenologically, spirituality can be described as a way of life that grows out of the structure of two basic components: the spirit and the word. The "spirit" component consists of the nonrational, experiential reality often expressed in the sense of transcendence—the "holy" or the "real." The "word" component is the rational conceptualization of the transcendent experience expressed in theological formulations and dogmas. Reflections on religious experience are often organized into a coherent framework that we call systematic theology. Each distinctive framework in turn shapes religious experience, resulting in different types of spirituality. Thus we could speak of Christian, Islamic and Hindu spiritualities as representing different broad theological frameworks that mediate the different experiences of people *as* Christians, Muslims and Hindus.[18]

Within Christianity there are different spiritualities that are organized around different theological emphases. Jesuit, Carmelite, Protestant and Pentecostal spiritualities represent different ways of living out the Christian life based on what each perceives to be the most significant concerns within its own distinctive framework. For example, Jesuit spirituality is generally more "active," Carmelite more contemplative, Protestant more dynamically personal. Distinct emphases within Protestantism result in different spiritual experiences. Some offer a form of spirituality that focuses largely on the individual's experience with God; others emphasize the corporate life. Some are more enthusiastic, others more sacramental. Although Christians differ in their outward expressions of the inner dynamics of the spiritual life, it is not inappropriate to speak of one Christian spirituality based on the Christians' experience of God through Jesus Christ, since Christians are, at least in principle, united around the ecumenical creeds.[19]

To the extent that they complement each other, different spiritualities are not necessarily a bad thing. Different spiritualities may appeal to Christians of different temperaments or even to the same person at different times. Thus Thornton notes that the English temperament prefers domestic images of the spiritual life (God's servant and handmaiden) to the military ones of Ignatius

Loyola. It favors the Cistercian and Augustinian monastic life over the more austere Carmelite and Carthusian.[20] A melancholic personality will naturally gravitate toward a more contemplative type of spirituality. If the apostle Paul were alive today, he would probably not be drawn to the Carmelite order. No single type of spirituality satisfies everyone. In fact, diverse Christian spiritualities are a gift of Christ to his church. According to Paul, God has endowed the members of the body of Christ with different gifts and functions (Rom 12:4-6). The effective exercise of gifts such as leadership, hospitality and teaching calls for different personality types and therefore different spiritualities. Aumann sums up the matter very well:

> The schools of spirituality are thus an indication of the diversity of the ways of the Spirit, a proof of the Church's respect for personal freedom in following the impulses of the Spirit, and a corporate witness to the variety of ways in which the mystery of Christ is imaged in the Mystical Body of the Church.[21]

But to affirm the existence of different types of spiritualities raises two common objections. The Protestant principle of laicization abrogates the distinction between "religious" life and "secular" life. Taken to extremes, it has sometimes been used to reduce the Christian life to a single stereotype. Allowing for different spiritualities is thought by some to be opposed to the biblical teaching that all Christians have one standard of perfection, namely, conformity to the image of Christ. But Christlikeness has to do with the development of virtues that can occur in any personality type, while spirituality has to do with living out the spiritual life in accordance with each person's makeup, nature and gifts. An extrovert may have no less love than an introvert but may express the virtue differently.

Another objection asks how any type of spirituality can be considered adequate if, by definition, one type excludes elements that are present in another type. Is a contemplative Carmelite nun missing something in life because her spirituality does not include direct involvement in the world? It is important to distinguish the spirituality that informs practical Christian living from the spiritual theology which undergirds that life. People's spiritual theology need not (in fact, should not) exclude any essential theological element, even if their spirituality demonstrates only certain aspects of it in practice. Thus the Carmelite nun's demonstrating the contemplative aspect of the Christian life does not mean that her spiritual theology necessarily excludes the "active" pole. Rather, she may see her contemplation less as withdrawal from the world and more as her unique engagement in the world, as contributing to the world in her own unique way.

Any "active" Christian who has an adequate spiritual theology will recognize the appropriateness of the contemplative's kind of worldly involvement. This kind of Christian will discover, as Thomas Merton obviously did, that "[h]e who attempts to act and do things for others and for the world without deepening his own self-understanding, freedom, integrity and capacity for love [through contemplation], will not have anything to give to others."[22] Thus, both the active Christian and the contemplative Christian may share the same broad theological framework while excluding or at least minimizing each other's *practical* emphasis from their respective spiritualities.

Another value of emphasizing different spiritualities is that each spirituality helps to highlight and preserve aspects of the totality of Christian life and belief that would be lost to a single superimposing spirituality. Even with an issue as controversial as infant versus believer's baptism, the different traditions help to preserve essential understandings of the nature of the church that have very different implications for the spiritual life. The believer's church highlights the need for individual responsibility in the community, while the inclusive church reminds us that the spiritual life of the church is also a corporate reality that includes natural associations like the family. In the believer's church faith is an intensely personal act (*my* faith), whereas in the inclusive church faith is, without denying the personal dimension, also an objective reality (*the* faith, as in Jude 3). The strengths and weaknesses of these spiritualities lead them to complement each other. The individualistic tendency of the former can be restrained by the corporate mindfulness of the latter, while the formalistic tendency of the latter can be inspired by the intense fervor of the former. But in the final analysis both concepts of faith have their roots in the Scripture.

Formal Criteria for an Adequate Spiritual Theology

To recognize the legitimacy of different Christian spiritualities, however, is not to say that one is as good as the other. There are certain formal criteria that determine the adequacy of any spirituality.

Comprehensiveness. An adequate spirituality should have a conceptual framework large enough to account for the various aspects of religious experience. For it to be comprehensive, it must be able to include experiences represented by different polarities, such as the immanent/transcendent, personal/corporate and natural/supernatural polarities. For example, some forms of spirituality are too historically oriented and gravitate too much toward the pole of divine immanence. Liberation spirituality is one such form. Other spiritualities are so transcendentally oriented that they leave little room for active social involvement. Conservative Christianity tends to fall into this category. In Asia, an extreme example of the second type is the spirituality of Watchman Nee.[23]

To be comprehensive, any spirituality must draw on all of the spiritual resources that are available to the church. These resources include Scripture and the Christian tradition, which is nothing but the church's humble reception and faithful embodiment of the primary revelation of God in Jesus Christ. We must be prepared to listen to the church existing in various contexts, not to whatever segment of it happens to have the loudest voice. We must be able to distinguish the living Tradition from the traditions, that is, what unites the churches in all places and times from what are the churches' necessary but conditional responses to changing situations in the world.[24] This does not mean that what belongs to the Tradition is timeless and what does not is time bound. Tradition, after all, exists in time and expands dynamically through time. What it does mean is that we must not be too quick to elevate a belief to the status of the Tradition when, over time, it may turn out to be only a passing fashion.

A comprehensive spirituality stresses a balanced approach to the cultivation of the spiritual life. It recognizes that true spiritual growth consists of rightly balanced opposing acts. The extent to which the human will is involved in spiritual progress is a problematic aspect of the Christian life. At one extreme is the Pelagian heresy, which makes the human will all-decisive; at the other extreme is the quietistic heresy, which counsels complete passivity. According to the seventeenth-century quietist Michael Molinos, "To will to operate actively is to offend God because He wishes to be the sole agent. Therefore one must relinquish one's whole self to him and thereafter remain as if dead. . . . By doing nothing the soul annihilates itself and returns to its beginning and its origin, the essence of God."[25] When we stress the need for *askesis,* we focus on activity while recognizing that any movement toward God is by grace. Similarly, when we stress the need for "self-surrender" (the parlance of Keswick spirituality) or "infused grace" (Catholic), we focus on being led while recognizing the cooperation of the will—the willingness to be led. Without such a balance we cannot hope to make real progress.

Coherence. Even as the rational framework should be comprehensive, it should possess its own internal consistency. The various parts must be meaningfully related to each other. This means that we need a coherent theology in order to develop a consistent spirituality. Coherence does not mean that every point in our theology must be rationalistically explained. A coherent framework must allow for mystery and paradox, which are central to Christianity.[26] Nothing is more inimical to the Christian life than attempts to explain away the mysteries of the faith. Yet these mysteries must not exist as "loose ends" but must be an essential part of a total structure. The Trinity in itself, however it is explained, will always remain a mystery. But it is a doctrine that makes sense of other doctrines and therefore must remain an intrinsic part or, as some believe, the foundation, of our framework.

One example of a lack of coherence is modern evangelicalism's inability to develop a consistent doctrine of the Christian life. Evangelical spirituality presupposes a doctrine of the means of grace when it enjoins prayer and other spiritual disciplines, yet it has not consciously developed a sacramental theology to undergird these practices. The reason for this neglect may be a fear that the means might become ends in themselves and might be turned into a form of works righteousness. Evangelicalism's strict adherence to the Reformation doctrine of justification by faith has not been brought into a meaningful relationship with the means of grace. The latter remains undeveloped, even though it is implicitly acknowledged. Consequently, evangelicalism's spirituality is often piecemeal and ad hoc, lacking in coherence instead of being systematic. People are told they should pray but are seldom shown how to pray in any systematic fashion.[27]

Evocability.[28] A spiritual theology that is intended to lead us in the way of godliness should be able to direct our attention beyond the rational formulations to the spiritual realities they express. Theological works should be as devotional as Anselm's *Proslogion,* and devotional works should be as theological as Thomas Merton's *Seeds of Contemplation.* Yet to a great extent, modern Christian literature continues to be plagued by the dichotomy between learned theological treatises in the style of (to borrow an expression from Austin Farrer) "Hegel with a hangover" and devotional works that are thin enough to pass under a steamroller unscathed. In a normative spirituality the line between dogma and devotion is no longer clearly drawn, and there is freedom of movement between the two. Theological reflection and prayer are no longer discrete activities but exist in a dynamic, ongoing relationship in which one activity enriches the other, stimulating the Christian to new insights and greater fervor.

Material Criteria for a Christian Spiritual Theology

The qualities of comprehensiveness, coherence and evocability are what we call formal criteria. They formally prescribe what must be included in *any* good spiritual theology. But what makes for a good *Christian* spiritual theology? What is the substance of Christian spiritual theology that makes it true in the respective contexts in which it exists and at the same time true to the Christian story? To address this question, we need to return to the three interconnected criteria mentioned at the beginning of this chapter: the global-contextual, the evangelical and the charismatic. The first criterion suggests that an adequate spiritual theology must be characterized by its sensitivity to contextual *difference(s)* in the world. It is global not because it has the character of a *theologia perennis,* which is appropriate in all places and at all times, but because it recognizes that the world is complex—made up of differing contexts that shape our behavior and thought in subtle and often unrecognized ways. Within this complexity the gospel can find its own authentic expression.[29] The failure to accept its complexity, as we shall see, is what renders many claims to universality invalid.

The evangelical criterion is also important for two reasons. First, it more or less reflects a persistent strain within the Christian tradition of telling the Christian story concerning the life, death and resurrection of Jesus Christ. While the specific Christian stories told in different traditions may not be all true—errors can and in fact have been perpetuated over long periods in Christian history—yet it is within the tradition itself that we have come to recognize these errors.[30] By sensitively listening to and reliving the Christian story, we begin to discern more clearly what belongs to the main story line and what does not. Faithfulness to the tradition also enlarges the global-contextual scope of our theology *through* time. If there is one error to which modernity predisposes us, it is historical pride, an overconfidence in the achievement of our own century. But if the true church exists in and through time, an openness to the diachronic scale of our existence may well be one way of rectifying the error of an overreliance on the synchronic scale. Second, the evangelical heritage contains resources that can be used to develop a more integrated and comprehensive spirituality. We believe that it is able to do this precisely because it is faithful to the Christian tradition.

The third criterion, the charismatic, is important because it too constitutes an essential component in the Christian spiritual tradition. The charismatic reality enlarges our doctrine of grace. It reminds us that the Christian life is not restricted to a predictable pattern of spiritual operations predicated on the Thomistic principle *gratia non tollit sed attolit naturam* (grace does not destroy nature but lifts it up). Sometimes God works in surprising and unpredictable ways. This is the freedom of God. Our doctrine of grace, so essential to spiritual theology, remains impoverished if it does not include this aspect of divine operation.

The global-contextual criterion. Nietzsche could not have been more correct when he said that the historical sense was modern man's sixth sense. Historical consciousness has become a deeply ingrained modern habit. This habit of thought is sometimes turned into a relativizing (or sacralizing) principle for all theological reflection, including spiritual theology.[31] But this historical awareness, ironically, is not always translated into a greater appreciation of the range of theological options arising from the distinctive Christian experiences in different contexts. The historical consciousness itself is taken to be a universal consciousness—a normative principle by which all contextual theologies must be judged. Sometimes, even more audaciously, a particular stance within the Western liberal tradition is assumed to be valid for the rest of the world. This is perhaps understandable, considering that Western scholars still constitute a vast majority of the global theological community. There is a tendency to assume that the predominant voice must be universally representative.

William Placher provides a recent example of this tendency. In *Narratives of a Vulnerable God* he seeks to give coherence to a doctrine that is becoming increasingly influential in the late twentieth century. Placher sees the emerging picture of the "vulnerable God" as an indication that "Christian theologians . . . [are] reclaiming their own birthright, for it is just such a God that is encountered in the biblical narratives."[32] Like many other recent theological writings, it is grounded in the doctrine of the Trinity. Although Placher recognizes that "cultural factors . . . might be at work in this theological development," it remains unclear to what extent the cultural factors that shape people's reading of the biblical narratives have been appreciated. Could it be that late twentieth-century Westerners, having grown skeptical of power and being incessantly challenged by various liberation movements, have now become aware of the suffering of oppressed and marginalized peoples? And as a consequence have found the vulnerable God particularly attractive? This is not to deny the validity of that particular biblical story line (which Placher, in fact, told quite admirably), but its universality cannot be assumed.

Could Asian Christians—many of whom encounter other spiritual powers in an animistic context or in the context of the "great religions" whose terms of reference are transcendent rather than historical—have discovered the vulnerable God in their reading of the biblical narratives? I doubt it. In fact, one of the main themes to come out of the stories or "testimonies" of ordinary Christians in China in recent years has been the *in*vulnerable God, the *Christus Victor,* a God who, like the God of the Old Testament, leads the church in triumph against incalculable odds.[33] Their testimonies are about overcoming temptations, finding strength in extreme suffering, receiving healing and deliverance. But this victorious spirit is a far cry from the triumphalism that the Western theologian fears.

It is a mistake to expunge certain kinds of language from our Christian discourse, as Placher and others have tried to do. One redeeming feature in Peter Wagner's "power encounter" type of thinking (even though much can be said against it)[34] is that it retains a language that continues to strike a resonant chord in much of Asia today. It addresses a situation that many Asians can readily identify with, namely, bondage to a fearsome spiritual power. Who in such a context would want a "vulnerable God"? A vulnerable God or some such picture, which is so pervasive in current theological discourse, is no more universal than the invulnerable God of Israel and of the Chinese church. It is a highly stylized portrait painted by late twentieth-century academics, the paint and canvas having been supplied by various cause-specific movements made possible by a certain type of sociopolitical culture.

Perhaps no one else has more thoroughly developed this sort of theological project than Jürgen Moltmann. His political theology is highly influential in certain theological traditions in the Third World, especially Latin America.[35] Jon Sobrino, for instance, has developed a spirituality of liberation centering on the virtues of "honesty," "fidelity" to and "willingness" to be swept along by the "real," that is, the God in history who is especially present among the poor. The poor are "the 'place' where God is found in history."[36] Similarly, some Asian theologians have come to see Asian Christian spirituality as denominating a certain existential attitude expressed wholly in "historical struggle" and "resistance": a "spirituality for combat."[37] This is especially true of Christianity in the Philippines, a country that shares many features with Latin America. The Asian religiosity expressed in the sense of the eternal is simply ignored, often dismissed as "superstition"[38] or a hindrance to progress.[39]

Although the historically conditioned premises of Moltmann's theological project are often elevated to the level of universal or self-evident truths, a recent major critique by Arne Rasmusson has shown how Moltmann is very much a captive to modern Western culture.[40] For instance, Moltmann's main study on pneumatology, *The Spirit of Life*, is pretentiously subtitled *A Universal Affirmation*. His assertion is based on the doctrine of God as "immanent transcendence," that is, a God who reveals himself wholly within the historical processes, and on the belief that the modern historical consciousness is universal. And since the Spirit is a "cosmic Spirit," he can be experienced everywhere in the same way. But this is by no means the case. Can we simply assume that the Spirit that indwells the church also indwells a benevolent Taoist medium?[41] Further, in many Asian countries (such as India, China and Japan) that are dominated by what the Sri Lankan theologian Aloysius Pieris calls the "metacosmic" religions (Hinduism, Taoism and Buddhism respectively) the sense of the eternal rather than the purely historical is still pervasive.[42] It is this sense of the eternal that must be taken full cognizance of if our Christian spirituality is to be contextually meaningful.

The return to trinitarian theology in the West in recent years represents yet another example of a context-specific theology. Many theologians have found in the doctrine fresh resources for addressing some specifically modern perplexities. In a world starved of meaningful and intimate personal relationship, the truth of the eternally self-giving persons in the Godhead offers hope. In a guilt-ridden society with an acute sensitivity to racial and sexual inequalities, a doctrine that "implies that God is not about power and self-sufficiency and the assertion of authority but about mutuality, and equality and love"[43] provides a powerful theological vision for restructuring society.

And yet there is a real danger here of "over-trinitarianizing" the doctrine of God at the expense of the equally true monotheistic conception.[44] Moltmann represents just this sort of distortion when he equates monotheism with the structure of political and clerical domination.[45] When the truth of who God is gets distorted by an overemphasis on either God's oneness or God's threeness, its universality is bound in the end to be limited. Monotheism is particularly significant in a missionary context. To confess one God is to say that there are no other gods; that nothing else is worthy of our absolute allegiance; that we are to serve God and not mammon. As Walter Kasper has observed, in confessing the one God, the ultimate issue is a radical decision between faith and unbelief, a radical answer to the question of where alone and in all situations unconditional trustworthiness is to be found.[46] For instance, in the context of polytheism and pantheism there is still much to be said about Christian monotheism. Many Asian Christians still find the God of Israel[47] to be very important as they seek to carry out their witness in the midst of religions of chaotic immanence (such as folk animism) on the one hand and an impersonal transcendence (as in philosophical Hinduism) on the other.

There are, as the Asian Theological Conference in Sri Lanka in 1979 observed, two Asias revolving around two poles: religiosity and poverty or the transcendent and the historical.[48] Yet Asia is a multiplex reality that cannot be readily comprehended by this binary model. Between these two poles there are other situations requiring Christians to respond in unique ways. In one situation Christians form a small minority in a society dominated by Islam, another Semitic faith with a strong eschatological orientation. Here, Christians have found it necessary to express their faith in strongly historical terms and yet without the liberationist overtones and postures. Their context requires a different kind of social engagement. Effecting change by directly influencing or manipulating the existing power structures (so commonly assumed in the West and Latin America) is not available to them. Any such attempt will be perceived by their majority Muslim neighbors as a challenge to their political dominance.

One option open to these Christians is to engage their world as responsible citizens in the common quest of nation building. Christian academics from Singapore, Malaysia and Indonesia recently had a consultation concerning Christian-Muslim dialogue. The participants came to a conclusion expressed by Malaysian theologian Ng Kam Weng when he speaks of the need to "enter into the national debate about what common society we should work towards."[49] Indonesian Eka Darmaputera argues vigorously for the Christian church to uphold the state ideology *(Pancasila)* as a way of ensuring the full and fair participation of Christians in the national process as responsible citizens.[50] Their involvement in the sociopolitical context *as* Christians is no less serious than that of their Filipino or Latin American counterparts, but it does differ. For one thing, the language of liberation is conspicuously absent. The basic strategy is to foster consensus through negotiation and active participation in the political process rather than to confront the existing structure. The liberationist perspective may regard such a strategy as acquiescence to the prevailing status quo that is not sufficiently critical (read confrontational). But what is important for Christians in Muslim contexts is what is being aimed at, namely, to secure for Christians a rightful place as common citizens with their Muslim neighbors.

So far we have been looking at the need to expand the synchronic scale of spirituality. But if our spiritual theology is to lay claim to universality, we also need to develop the diachronic scale by incorporating the rich resources of the past—the Christian tradition. Far from condemning the church to a static existence, tradition actually helps the church find the necessary resources to wrestle with contemporary situations. As Stanley Hauerwas reminds us, the traditions of the church that encapsulate the Christian story "are the bearers of rationality and innovation."[51]

One of the most positive developments in recent years has been a willingness among Christians to tap the spiritual resources of other Christian traditions. Even evangelicals are exploring forms of spirituality once considered taboo, like the use of the rosary and auricular confession.[52] At the same time Roman Catholics are finding that the charismatic form of spirituality has added an important component to their own spiritual life. In acknowledging the role of tradition, we are simply extending into our theological endeavor what we have generally taken for granted in our worship and liturgy: the doctrine of the communion of saints in and through time ("with angels and archangels and all the heavenly hosts"). An openness to the Christian past is one important sign of a genuine Christian spirituality. Many modern Christians who have undertaken a serious pursuit of the spiritual life have found a deep affinity with the spiritual writers of the past that transcends time. This is because at the heart of spiritual theology is prayer, and it is in prayer that past and present are linked. Prayers, as A. M. Allchin puts it, "bring the world of time in touch with eternity."[53] It is in a prayer made famous by T. S. Eliot in "Little Gidding" that the fourteenth-century recluse Julian of Norwich was "rediscovered" in the twentieth century: "Sin is behovely, but all shall be well, and all shall be well, and all manner of thing shall be well."[54]

The late twentieth century has seen a number of high-profile, issue-related spiritual movements that have distinguished themselves by repudiating tradition or by making a highly selective use of it to suit their own purposes. These movements are conscious of being modern and of taking on an issue that has captured the imagination of a significant portion of modern humanity. One who is raising uncomfortable questions about the link with the past is Matthew Fox with his creation spirituality. In a highly skewed reading of history, Fox virtually writes off two thousand years of Western Christian tradition as the scourge of the modern world. All the fault lies with the influence of Augustine, whose emphasis on the redemptive motif (a Neo-Platonic heritage, according to Fox) led the West to centuries of denying the goodness of creation and the equality of all creatures. The consequences of this denial are seen in the present-day ecological crisis, the oppression of minorities and sexual discrimination.[55] Fox is simply trumpeting one of the latest theological fashions that have grown out of a number of deeply felt issues like ecology, sexism and racism.

Another movement that has become highly influential in the West is feminism. Like many other cause-specific movements, it has sought to consolidate itself by developing its own distinctive theology and spirituality. This task has elicited different responses. Some feminist theologians find the whole biblical and Christian tradition hopelessly patriarchal and have repudiated it, preferring to build afresh on other foundations.[56] Others choose to use the Christian tradition selectively or interpret it in feminist terms.[57]

Advocates of this movement often seem to be quite unaware of the contextual aspects of their cause and the severely limited assumptions on which they operate. Margaret Miles, a moderate feminist historian, for instance, often uses terms like *twentieth-century people* or *twentieth-century consciousness* when what she means is the Western/North American consciousness or people who are most gender conscious.[58] It is ironic that this

Western historical consciousness often is not translated into a larger spatial consciousness—consciousness of the larger world of the twentieth century that lies beyond the Western context. If the same "hermeneutic of generosity" that Miles uses could be applied to other cultures and civilizations, perhaps there would be less presumption about speaking on behalf of "twentieth-century people." For one thing, feminist individualistic egalitarianism itself is derived from the Western liberal tradition,[59] which many people from traditional societies outside the West do not share. The hierarchical, communal and consensual ordering of life in Asia, for example, is inherently incompatible with modern feminist assumptions. This does not mean that there are no transcending Christian moral values—in fact, they often challenge the sinful patterns in traditional Asian societies—but they also find expression within a distinctively Asian form that is quite different from the Western way of ordering society. This means that if there is to be a feminist theology in Asia, the concerns of Asian women will have to be advanced in ways that are compatible with the basic nature of Asian society.[60]

All of this is to say that a universally affirmative spiritual theology must be broad enough to take in the differing contexts of the world where the church exists both in time and through time. It may not be practically possible to take in every context, but we must at least be sensitive to the major nuances that exist between the poles of transcendence and history. The question is, Can these poles be brought together in an integrated spirituality? It is probably in Asia where the tension between these two poles is most acutely felt. Further, it is generally believed that the key to this problem lies in Christology, more specifically the doctrine of the Incarnation, which schematizes the central belief of the church that the Eternal has in some very real and decisive way entered our history.[61]

Dyrness has observed that most Asian theologians coming from the metacosmic contexts have tended to emphasize the transcendent pole. Consequently the historical significance of Christ's life, death and resurrection is downplayed.[62] There is a general tendency among them to turn Christ into a cosmic principle or ideal of salvation, the fulfillment of Asian religiosity.[63] On the other hand, the historically oriented theologies following Moltmann and the liberation theologians of Latin America have their own unique problems in Asia. First, by tending to identify God with present historical processes and movements, they have created an acute problem of discernment. How can we tell if a particular historical movement is from God?[64] Second, many Asian liberation theologians tend to operate under certain Western liberal assumptions that interpret the church's task in terms of confronting power structures and participating in political struggles. But as a minority faith, the church either is hampered by powerlessness or must strike some kind of power arrangement with other sociopolitical movements, whether secular or belonging to the dominant religion. As Levison and Levison have rightly put it, the "crux of the problem with a liberation Christology . . . is that it cannot eliminate poverty if it develops in isolation from the liberative steams of other Asian religions."[65] But the moment the church cooperates with other liberation movements it is then forced to take an inclusivist understanding of the Christian faith, which blunts the Christian mission as a community witnessing to the life, death and resurrection of Christ.

Third, there are emerging in Asia today situations to which the liberation model has no application. This is demonstrated in Peter Lee's attempt to understand the Hong Kong situation in liberational terms.[66] Lee's case study of Mr. Tan as a victim of an oppressive system shows up the ludicrousness of liberation hermeneutics in such a context.[67] Traditional Chinese understanding would consider Mr. Tan a classic example of Chinese entrepreneurial skills, for which Chinese are deservedly well known. This is aided by a society that abets such social mobility: from rags to riches (to a degree) in seven years. It shows that liberation theology has a limited vocabulary that cannot address situations like Hong Kong, which are becoming more and more prevalent in Asia. At one point Lee gives away his game (or shows the exhaustion of the liberation vocabulary) when he speaks of "a general orientation of values that keeps a large segment of society from *being satisfied*" or the "socially disadvantaged feel[ing] further dissatisfied."[68] There is a vast difference between *feeling dissatisfied* and being oppressed!

The failure to integrate the two poles is the basic failure of Asian theology. Levison and Levison, however, claim that two theologians, M. M. Thomas and Aloysius Pieris, have been more successful in bringing the historical and transcendent poles together by placing "their Christology within the context of a viable Asian ecclesiology."[69] But how viable is their ecclesiolgy? In the case of Thomas, it is a church whose institutional marks are reduced to a bare minimum because the Christian community and the human community are seen as having Christ at the same center:

> The gospel is world-renewing in Christ. Therefore the boundary between the church and the world is becoming a little too difficult to draw. Both the human community and the Christian community have the same centre—Christ . . . I would like to see that the circle be not drawn if possible.[70]

In other words, while the centrality of Christ is strongly affirmed, it is not distinguished from the larger human community, where human values are also central. Thomas's Christology must be appreciated for its recognition of the larger presence of Christ—a fact that some modern evangelicals are only beginning to come to terms with.[71] But a question we must still ask is, Could we still speak of Christ's presence in the church in a way that he is not present in the human community? By Thomas's reckoning the answer has to be no. And it is this negative response that raises the question of whether he has actually succeeded in integrating the two poles—religious and historical. In a word, Thomas has ultimately collapsed the religious into the historical by introducing a kind of "cosmic" ecclesiology even as others have resolved the historical into the transcendent by a cosmic Christology.[72]

The ecclesiology of Pieris grows out of a similar concern to bring together the poles of religiosity and poverty expressed in terms of three dichotomies: liturgy versus spirituality, spirituality versus secular involvement and secular involvement versus liturgy.[73] The first dichotomy is united in the "liturgy of life," meaning that liturgy is not something we do in the church, but following the Calvary model (the first liturgy), it must be enacted outside the temple. The celebration of the liturgy of life enacts the Paschal mystery in the world amid poverty, death and struggles.[74]

The terms of the second dichotomy, contemplation and action, are unified by the Ignatian principle of self-abnegation, which can be exercised as either a movement starting from God to the world (the Abraham model) or a movement starting from the world to God (the Moses model).[75]

> Seek God in total *self-abnegation* and you will touch the depths of the human, your own and that of others. Conversely, commit yourself to human liberation *without any self-seeking,* and you have already experienced God. Without self-abnegation, both prayer and action are delusions, with self-centred introversion parading as interiority, and restless extroversion parading as political commitment.[76]

The sort of spirituality that unites contemplation and action in the *theologia crucis* is commendable and, indeed, necessary. But Pieris makes no distinction between these two movements. Either way, he assumes that a spirituality ensues. I would like to suggest that primacy be given to the first movement. This, I believe, is the accent of the Christian tradition. It is possible to be selflessly committed to the world without being a Christian (or without being religious, for that matter). That is the difference between a moral person and a spiritual person. To say that both are essentially committed to God is to fail to take seriously the possibility of the former's explicitly *non-religious* moral claims.[77] By equating the two movements, Pieris is forced either to steal in some form of anonymous Christianity (a concept that he explicitly rejects) or to see Christianity and non-Christian religions in terms of a common center:

"the soteriological nucleus or the liberative core of various religions."[78]

Pieris also blurs the distinction between church and world in the way he resolves the third dichotomy by rejecting Vatican II's concept of the church liturgy as "source and summit" *(fons et culmen)* of the liturgy of life. Accepting such a formulation would mean giving primacy to "an institutionalized community with an institutionalized worship" rather than to "the humanity of the historical Jesus." Like Thomas, Pieris sees the true church as the church completely incarnate in the world of suffering humanity, where Christ is primarily present. The institutional church is only the "occasion to transubstantiate" this primary reality. But "by subordinating church liturgy to the liturgy of life" rather than letting church liturgy issue in (that is, function as the *fons* of) the liturgy of life, Pieris has considerably reduced the significance of the institutional (better, "visible") church. The question is, Could the church function effectively as that "occasion" if it is not in some essential way distinguished from the world that it serves—distinguished, in fact, by what Pieris disparagingly calls "a gnostic Christ"?[79]

The evangelical criterion. The general failure to come up with an integrated spirituality that does not resolve itself either into an ahistorical interiority or into an uncritical involvement in the historical (more often, sociopolitical) processes leads us to consider the second major criterion as possibly providing a way forward.

But first, a word of clarification is in order. The term *evangelical* here does not refer to certain movements in the West that explicitly identify themselves as such, for example, the National Association of Evangelicals and its various affiliates throughout the world. Over the years evangelicalism has come to represent a range of ideological positions characterized by a particular theory of Scripture, such as inerrancy, or a certain attitude toward politics, culture and learning. These characteristics have been severely criticized from within the movement itself in recent years.[80] But there are certain essential features that these movements hold in common with the larger Christian church, as evangelical theologian Donald Bloesch has pointed out.[81]

The essence of an evangelical spirituality is to be found in the particular way it understands the coming of God in Jesus Christ to the believer. The truth is contained in the evangel; the preaching of the evangel mediates the experience of that truth. Thus becoming a Christian is not just accepting certain Christian principles or propositions. It is not conversion to a "cosmic Christ" but an entering into a personal relationship with the risen Jesus of Nazareth ("accepting Jesus as your *personal* Savior"). Each conversion experience involves a living contact with the transcendent person of Christ in a concrete historical context. This is the "biblical personalism" that Bloesch sees as defining an evangelical mysticism in contradistinction to the impersonal mysticism of Neo-Platonism.[82] The church as a community of such believers is the locus of Christ's transcendent presence. This is not to deny that Christ is also present in the world. But he is present in the church in a way that he is not present in the world. Such a view is not just peculiar to those who call themselves "evangelical" Christians. It is very much the traditional Catholic view. It finds practical expression in the devotional exercises of Francis de Sales, who enjoins the exercitant to "place yourself in the presence of God" by recalling four different ways in which God is present. The aim is to move from the broader to the more focused divine presence.[83] This, in sum, is the essential element in evangelical spirituality.[84]

The experience of evangelical conversion differs as widely as personality types. But what unites persons like C. S. Lewis and Sadhu Sundar Singh (no two persons were more unlike each other) is their common evangelical conversion. Each had a personal encounter with the transcendent Christ. Lewis's more philosophical reflections on his journey toward Christianity are explained in terms of what he calls "the dialectic of Desire." It is an experience of "interior longing" triggered by some ordinary experience, yet the "object" of the desire is not found in those experiences. They always point to something beyond. It was this understanding that helped Lewis move beyond idealism and pantheism through theism to Christianity.[85]

In the case of the Sadhu, it was described as "some new power from outside" that entirely changed his perception of the world, namely, that God is *not* present in everything.[86] The experiences of Lewis and Sundar Singh exemplify a pattern of spirituality in which the transcendent and historical dimensions of the Christian faith are brought together without watering down either one or the other. This is possible because, first, the transcendent is experienced in terms of an intimately personal relationship with the living Christ. Salvation is experienced as communion and not as an impersonal deliverance from some impending disaster (which is the case whenever an inclusivist concept of salvation is presupposed; how else could we speak of the salvation of those who do not know Christ explicitly, except in terms of some grand divine rescue plan that affected them without their actually knowing it?). Second, the Christian's commitment to history is preserved because he or she has met Christ in precisely such a manner. If the eternal has entered our time to meet with us, how can we ignore the historical medium by which he has revealed his glory to us? The kind of piety that forsakes the world in order to cultivate an otherworldly experience is in fact a false and sub-Christian piety. It is a piety that is preoccupied with self. It lacks the quality of "self-abnegation" that comes inevitably from a true personal relationship with the transcendent Christ. Where such a relationship exists there is true ecstasy, a coming out of one's self to follow Christ into the world.

Evangelical spirituality entails an ecclesiology that distinguishes itself sharply from the world, which many fear will lead to a world-denying faith. Such a fear is not altogether groundless. But the real problem is that for much of Christian history, the church operated on a monolithic understanding of engagement with the world that was based on the Constantinian model. The church has to take out citizenship in the world in order to exercise influence in it. Then, as a respectable world citizen, the church has to play by the rules set by the world. Stanley Hauerwas put this model of Christian engagement under deep probing and found it wanting.[87] He offered an alternative model for Christian engagement based on the Anabaptist concept of the church as an alternative polis, the church as a colony of "resident aliens" on earth whose real citizenship is in heaven.[88] Hauerwas believes that such a church, far from being irrelevant to the world, can actually challenge the world by offering a "real option" to the world through its own disciplined life (a "community of character"). The church is called back to pursue its biblical mandate of being salt and light of the world. Its smallness in relation to the world is not a liability; rather, it gives sharper focus to its distinctive way of life.

Hauerwas's vision of the church has important implications for the church in Asia. First, Hauerwas places spirituality at the very center of the church's life and mission. For the kind of church that he envisions to make an impact on society, it has to be a community of *character,* a people marked by discipline and cross bearing. Such a church influences the world by its very life, its individual and collective virtues, its "politics."[89] In contrast, in liberation theology, for all its recent accent on spirituality,[90] the qualities that the church cultivates are in the final analysis functional rather than intrinsic, aimed at pursuing a freedom and justice that is largely a carryover of the type envisioned in modern liberal democracies. This justice, as Hauerwas has noted, turns out to be "the name for the procedural rules necessary to secure enough fair play so that everyone will be able to pursue their private goods."[91] In short, the end of liberation spirituality is the cultivation of virtues in order to sustain the *vice* of individual self-interest!

Second, the nature of the alternative polis fits better the de facto smallness of the church in Asia. It means that the size of the church does not limit its ability to make an impact on society. The church can be a positive influence on the larger society without having to forge unholy alliances and manipulate power structures that historically have only weakened the church. Third, the emphasis on community ethics resulting from the church's telling and living out the Christian story is more consonant with the Asian sense of community. Methodologically, too, refocusing on a narrative theology for creating the church's identity has strong affinities with the Asian penchant for storytelling, which is still prevalent in many non-Western educated churches.[92] Hauerwas's vision of the church has provided strong theological underpinnings for the evangelical character of the church's spirituality. The church, therefore, need not fear being marginalized. On the contrary, it can be confident that the one indispensable distinguishing mark—its evangelical heritage—is what helps to maintain its integrity as the church of Jesus Christ in the midst of the shifting poles of religious transcendentalism and historical immanentism.[93]

The charismatic criterion. For much of Christian history enthusiasm has been treated as an aberration instead of being recognized as an essential component of spirituality.[94] But the sheer size and extent of the Pentecostal-charismatic renewal in the twentieth century has forced the church to reevaluate its position.[95] Its gradual acceptance in the mainline churches means that there is a need for a radical rethinking of spirituality as traditionally conceived. If the Pentecostal-charismatic reality is an important part of the spiritual life, what part does it actually play in relation to the ascetical dimension of the spiritual life? How is the direct working of God's Spirit related to his indirect working in nature?

Traditional Roman Catholic spirituality has been built almost exclusively on a concept of grace as working *nobiscum* (with us, lifting up nature). While it does acknowledge a doctrine of grace as operating *sine nobis* (apart from us), it has never really played a significant role in the development of the spiritual life. This is because what is "infused" (for example, the *gratia gratis data*) implies an element of passivity in the recipient. It can intensify a person's acts but does not actually make anyone more perfect. Actual perfection depends on "actual grace," which is acquired by acts of the will.[96] Traditional Protestantism, often lacking an awareness of the its own enthusiastic heritage, has generally manifested a high degree of polarization between enthusiasm on the one hand and rationalistic theology on the other.

But the Pentecostal reality among us has made the questions posed above more urgent. By and large it is to the credit of catholic charismatics that such questions are being systematically addressed. Donald Gelpi, for example, has called for the development of a "theology of transmuting grace" as opposed to the traditional Catholic doctrine of "thematic grace." Thematic grace sets to order something that is already predisposed to that order—it "thematizes" nature. It tends to see transformation of life within the individual and relation to God as primarily a matter of intellect and will. Transmuting grace, on the other hand, recognizes the possibility of the "radically new" in Christian experience. It embraces nonrational apprehension and intuition as well as intellect and will. In short, Gelpi shows the need to have an adequate theology of grace that includes the dimension Jonathan Edwards calls "the surprising work of God."[97] Gelpi's concept of grace comes surprisingly close to the Protestant view. Among Protestants, however, there is little systematic integration of the enthusiastic and ascetical aspects of spirituality, although in some popular devotions certain charismatic elements are being incorporated into traditional forms.[98]

Pentecostal spirituality is characterized by an awareness of and an openness to the "surprising work of God." It seeks the intimate presence of God, which usually involves an initial "baptism in the Spirit." This baptism represents a sort of quantum leap in spiritual consciousness, evidenced by, among other things, glossolalia and a new boldness and urgency to engage in the mission of God.[99] Pentecostal spirituality embodies a principle that has found support from an unexpected quarter. Stanley Hauerwas has observed that people in power, especially, are uncomfortable if they are not in control, because they see it as their destiny to make things turn out right. But the church as an eschatological community witnesses to the "peaceable kingdom" by "living without control," that is, in a manner that does not "exclude the possibility of miracles, of surprises, of the unexpected." As a people of *God's* kingdom, they know that God is in control, and because God is in control, they learn "to make the unexpected [their] greatest resource."[100] If what Hauerwas has described is the ethics of the kingdom, it could just as well be called Pentecostal ethics. This means that the Pentecostal component is a central feature of the Christian life.

There are important consequences when the Pentecostal-charismatic component is taken into consideration in any spiritual theology. Within Catholicism it opens up the awareness that God works directly for the ordinary Christian right from the beginning of the Christian life, not just for the contemplative at the top of the spiritual ladder receiving the grace of "infused contemplation." Within Protestantism it forces a rethinking on the nature of mystical union.[101] Typically, Protestants have understood mystical union in relational and ethical terms, following John Calvin, who locates it at the beginning of the Christian life.[102] But we need to reconsider Calvin's doctrine of mystical union in the light of the Pentecostal experience. Might it have other spiritual ramifications, since it is intimately connected with his doctrine of the Spirit, the *testimonium internum spiritus sancti?*[103] According to Calvin, union is effected by "the secret energy of the Spirit, by which we come to enjoy Christ and all his benefits."[104]

Unfortunately, contemporary Reformed thinking has not always acknowledged the enthusiastic implication of Calvin's doctrine of the Christian life. A recent book introducing Reformed spirituality, for example, does not even refer to Calvin's doctrine of the Spirit![105] Yet it is of interest to note that at least one group of seventeenth-century Puritans used Calvin's pneumatology as a major source for their understanding of the spiritual life, an understanding that at times bordered on enthusiasm. The Puritan theologian John Cotton constantly appealed to Calvin for his doctrine of the *direct* witness of the Spirit in bringing assurance to believers. In fact, he was accused of antinomianism by the "preparationists," who believed that assurance was derived from the Spirit's working mediately by the use of various preparatory signs of conversion.[106] Cotton might be considered an extreme case, but his understanding of the Spirit as a *practical* option for the Christian life was actually preceded by another Puritan, Richard Sibbes, and later was systematically developed by John Owen.[107]

The point I wish to make here is that Pentecostal spirituality is not just a twentieth-century reality that has to be reckoned with because it has become so widespread. Rather, it encapsulates an essential component of the Christian tradition that the mainstream largely ignored in the past. It must take its place as an essential part of a comprehensive spiritual theology. But Pentecostal-charismatic spirituality, if it is to have long-term viability, must be incorporated into the larger Christian tradition. An enthusiastic spirituality that is developed in isolation from an ascetical spirituality cannot be sustainable for long, nor can it have universal applicability. This explains why Quakerism, the most consistent outworking of enthusiasm, appeals only to a limited group of people. It may also explain why the charismatic dimension tends to be only a passing phase in the spiritual journey of some Christians who began their Christian life as Pentecostals.[108] Ideally, then, there should be no distinction between charismatic and noncharismatic Christians; every Christian should be both a charismatic and an ascetic.

The relationship between the three criteria may be stated as follows: The global-contextual scope of spirituality, expressed primarily in terms of the poles of transcendence and history, can best be developed by taking seriously the church's evangelical resources. The elements of spiritual theology will be enriched by a larger concept of grace if the charismatic component is included. The theology of the spiritual life that I hope to develop subsequently will seek to appropriate these three criteria. They will provide the general backdrop against which the specific contents of the spiritual life are explicated. If our spiritual theology meets these three criteria, it will stand the textual and contextual test of adequacy.

2

THE CHRISTIAN
DOCTRINE
OF GOD AS
THE FOUNDATION
OF CHRISTIAN
SPIRITUALITY

· · · · · · · · · · · · · · · · · · ·

CENTRAL TO ANY SPIRITUALITY IS ITS CONCEPTION OF WHAT IS ULTIMATELY REAL. This ultimate reality may be nonreligious, for example, an absolute ethical principle that determines all human conduct and all interpersonal relations. Confucianism espouses this conception of reality and shapes its nonreligious spirituality accordingly.[1] Pantheism conceives of ultimate reality as a nonpersonal, singular reality. The spirituality that is shaped by this pantheistic conception sees the goal of life as harmony with the universe rather than personal communion. A popular form of this spirituality can be seen in the New Age movement. Similarly, the Christian knowledge of who God is determines the character of Christian spirituality. Several years ago J. B. Phillips wrote a little book entitled *Your God Is Too Small,* in which he shows how our concepts of God relate directly to the way the Christian life is perceived and lived. Some see their God as a heavenly police officer, and consequently their Christian life consists of cringing compliance to a set of rules. Clearly, a proper conception of God—a theology that is faithful to God's self-revelation—is essential to the development of an adequate Christian spirituality.

One way to do this is to explore the many facets of the nature of God as described in the Scriptures. Each facet adds on to and enriches our experience of God. This is what Kenneth Leech, for example, has done.[2] Thus the mobile God of the Old Testament, the God of the desert, the God of suffering and justice (and so on) all add up to a fuller understanding of God and encourage a larger spirituality. All these facets of theology can be systematically explored in the light of the distinctively Christian doctrine of God as Trinity.

Trinitarian theology has undergone something of a revival since Karl Barth. It is not our purpose to retrace these modern trinitarian conceptions but to draw out some of the main emphases that have important implications for spirituality.[3] The doctrine of the Trinity is not a literal description or picturing of some kind of divine mathematics that defies human logic; rather, it is the Christian way of schematizing the basic self-revelation of God. It is "shorthand" for the nature and working of God that is revealed to us in the Old and New Testaments. God is truly the one God of Israel's confession, the Shema (Deut 6:4), and yet this same God is revealed in the flesh in Jesus Christ and continues to be present in the church by the Holy Spirit. The Christian church experiences him not only as the One, the creator and source of all things, but also as the Three. The church qualifies the three as persons, suggesting that it is in the realm of personhood and personal relationship that this threeness must be understood. The threeness of God makes sense only in the context of his revelation as the supremely personal being as Father, Son and Holy Spirit. The trinitarian doctrine brings together a number of polarities in the Christian understanding of God. God is not only "wholly other" he is also the God "for us," not only transcendent but also immanent, not only the one who unifies all things but also the source of all real diversity in creation.

The Problem of Divine Immanence and Transcendence

The return to trinitarian theology has been, on a whole, positive. It offers a needed corrective to the Platonizing tendency, present in the Western church since Augustine, which sees the undifferentiated being of God as constituting the larger category under which the threeness is subsumed.[4] The God of the Bible is a personal God working intimately in his creation, unlike the passionless, nameless one of Platonism, who is far removed from the world and only remotely related to it by a hierarchy of intermediaries. But the modern overreaction to this Platonic influence runs the risk of distorting the trinitarian doctrine in two ways, first by an overemphasis on the threeness of God at the expense of his unity, and second by collapsing the immanent Trinity into the economic Trinity.[5] The overall effect of these modern emphases is to weaken the doctrine of divine transcendence. This has serious implications for the spiritual life.[6]

We have already noted this distortion in Moltmann's rejection of monotheism as a symbol of domination and in his doctrine of "immanent transcendence," which explains God's relation to the world.[7] Modern theology is reticent to speak of the otherness or transcendence of God for fear of propagating a view of God as a sort of "super object" whose relationship to the world is "interventionist." According to Newlands, modern people simply find such concepts "unpalatable."[8] They prefer to see God's transcendence as hidden in his immanence "in a manner which is in important respects unique and inexplicable."[9] This transcendence-in-immanence, for Christians, gives to certain historical experiences their uniquely religious character, since "Christians find the central clue to God as the loving God in the historical events relating to Jesus." Is this all that Christians everywhere experience of God's transcendence?

We must fully appreciate the difficulty of referring to divine action in the world, since God is not a "super object" among objects.[10] God does not "cause" things to happen that can be explicated according to Newtonian laws of physics. Is there *any* sense in which God's objectivity can be affirmed without reducing it to either a super object or a subjective feeling? To call God a "super object" is to use an analogy that may not suit the twentieth-century Western mentality, but that does not rule out the possibility that *some such* analogy may be appropriate. Our analogies of God depend largely on how we experience God in our lives, which varies in different places and times. Christians in each context need to find their own suitable analogy. The Old Testament God *intervened* in human history through mighty acts. God is revealed in Jesus through the central event of the cross. And Jesus was revealed as Son of God, according to the early church's understanding, through signs and wonders and mighty works (Acts 10:38). Isn't that an interventionist model?[11]

Sometimes speaking of God's hiddenness in human history makes the mystery of God into a correlative of the mystery of evil.[12] Evil is then turned into a general problem to which no human responsibility can be attached. Although there is a certain metaphysical hiddenness in God *(deus absconditus)*, the hiddenness of God in Scripture is tied to the Christian understanding of sin. "Your sin has separated between you and your God." The cry "My God, my God, why hast thou forsaken me?" was a cry from one who "became sin for us." The hiddenness of God is related to the mystery of iniquity. Only when we are prepared to accept individual and collective responsibility for the evil in the world can we speak meaningfully of God's hiddenness. To situate the hiddenness of God in a context of diminished responsibility, in which sin is replaced by some mysterious evil, exaggerates the problem of evil. AIDS is commonly portrayed as a difficult and dangerous *problem* that concerns everyone but cannot be blamed on anyone.[13] Viewed from that perspective, AIDS is a mystery—how could it have happened? Actually, it is an issue that should challenge our collective and individual sense of responsibility or even culpability. Seeing AIDS in terms of human sin does not solve the problem of evil, but often the problem is exaggerated and is used to obscure our own human failure to face up to our responsibility.

Outside the so-called Christian West, the traditional doctrine of immanence *and* transcendence carries a number of important spiritual implications. First, it implies that God is both relational and distinct from creation. It presupposes separation between God and creation and recognizes that God's working in the world can be such that at times an "interventionist" model may well be the only appropriate way to speak of divine action. Consequently it allows for a more direct, personal kind of spirituality that is, as we have previously noted, characteristic of evangelical spirituality. It is this otherness that Moltmann's doctrine has virtually eliminated.

Second, it implies the freedom of God, the idea that creation and redemption are the free acts of God. Modern trinitarian theologies, especially those associated with Moltmann and Pannenberg, involve the temporalizing of God so that history becomes constitutive of the divine life.[14] If this is so, in what sense can we still speak of creation as a free act? If creation is a free act, then God is God even without creation. How then can creation be said to "constitute" the divine nature? The doctrine of divine freedom implies that God cannot be tied to a completely predictable pattern of behavior. It does not mean that God acts arbitrarily; rather, it means that there is a sense in which God always remains unknowable, a depth into which none can plumb. He is still "the blessed and only Ruler, the King of kings and Lord of lords, who alone is immortal and who lives in unapproachable light, whom no one has seen or can see" (1 Tim 6:16). But making God dependent on creation for his "fulfillment" confines God's working to historical processes and dismisses any transcendent religious experience outside that process. The "surprising works of God" are minimized or even eliminated altogether, even though this is not a necessary consequence.[15]

Third, the "otherness" of God is essential if we are to distinguish between what is of God and what is not of God. This is particularly true in contexts where there are "gods many and lords many" (1 Cor 8:5). The oneness of God is important for the Christian's own self-definition, and a doctrine that sees history as constituting God's nature leaves us without a criterion for discerning the spirits. In the various liberation theologies, the liberation of the poor constitutes a spiritual encounter with God. But in what way is the God who is revealed in all the "good" in creation, such as the poor, the liberation movements, the non-Christian religions and so on, also the trinitarian God revealed as Father, Son and Holy Spirit?

Some Asian liberation theologians have sought to discern the 'good' by the social criterion of whether it advances the good of society. This involves translating traditional spiritual concepts into sociological terms and reducing spiritual phenomena into social dynamics. This is what Korean Minjung theologians David Suh and Lee Chung Hee have done with shamanism. Just as shamans help the sick and pacify unhappy, wandering spirits, Minjung spirituality seeks to liberate those who cry out for justice out of a deep feeling of anger *(han)*. Shamanism, then, becomes spiritually significant only in its sociological dimension.[16] In Lee's words, "The subject, the energy, and the life force which lead the *dae-dong gut* [festival] are not the deity, the spirits of dead souls, or the shaman; it is the spirit of the minjung which lives amid the communal village."[17] The truth question of the spirits of the dead is simply ignored. Such a view may well satisfy a few Westernized intellectuals, but it will not satisfy countless millions of Asians for whom spirits are a life-and-death issue. This is not to promote accepting claims about the world of spirits at face value. But simply to demythologize them reveals a worldview that is just as uncritical as the so-called superstition that it rejects. Furthermore, it is a worldview that many people outside the constricted world of the Enlightenment do not share.

Theologians operating from a Western context assume a Christian universe of discourse in which the God of Christianity is assumed to be the immediate subject of any religious experience. Moltmann's social doctrine of the Trinity, for instance, borders dangerously on tritheism. He is not concerned about this because the real danger, for him, is monotheism, not tritheism.[18] But if the truth of a theological statement is tested by its adequacy for spiritual life, then the social doctrine of the Trinity cannot be accepted without further qualifications on contextual grounds.

There are many Christians outside the Western world for whom God's aseity (God's freedom and independence from creation) symbolizes order and hope in the midst of chaos, not alienation or domination.[19] A Moltmannian conception of the Trinity constitutes a temptation to polytheism and accentuates a long-standing stumbling block in Christian-Muslim dialogue. Thus a distinction must be made between the immanent Trinity and economic Trinity even if current explanations of their relationship are not fully adequate. Giving modern trinitarian thinking a broader contextual grounding would result in less readiness to jettison concepts like divine aseity and would temper the overeagerness to embrace relational and temporal concepts.[20] What is needed, to use Gunton's words, is "an account of relationality that gives due weight to both one and many, to both particular and universal, to both otherness and relation." Such an account can only be based on "a conception of God who is both one and three, whose being consists in a relationality that derives from the otherness-in-relation of Father, Son and Spirit."[21]

The Nature of Trinitarian Spirituality

Since an inadequate trinitarian theology engenders problems in Christian spirituality, it needs to be emphasized again that the doctrine of the Trinity is not about the threeness of God per se but about the mystery of the God who is both one and yet three, both a God-in-himself and a God-for-us in his trinitarian existence. A proper trinitarian spirituality can only be developed from a doctrine that gives equal place to unity and to plurality in God, both to transcendence and to immanence. In other words, contra Moltmann, monotheism should not be seen as a non-Christian accretion from Platonic metaphysics but as a true part of the Christian understanding of God. Because God is the *one* God who is above all, transcendence can be a source of the Christian's deepest assurance that there is nothing that is not ultimately related to God. Because God is the *triune* God who is intimately related to each other and to the world in love, God's transcendence is an open transcendence that fills us with a sense of purpose rather than meaninglessness and despair. As Kasper puts it, "Monotheism is the answer to the question raised at the natural level about the unity and meaning of all reality. It is precisely this ambiguous and open question that is defined in a concrete way by the trinitarian self-revelation of God so that the trinitarian confession is concrete monotheism."[22]

Viewing modern trinitarian thinking from a global context, it is clear that its tendency to deemphasize or even deny monotheism and to formulate the relationship of the persons consciously or unconsciously according to egalitarian principles creates as much of a problem as it solves. Notwithstanding this overall weakness, the focus on the threeness of God and the nature of their relationship, depending on how it is conceived, has important implications for Christian spirituality. It is to these that we now turn.

A fruitful—indeed, a necessary—way to begin our trinitarian reflection is in the context of the worshiping community.[23] Here we encounter the God who is Father, Son and Spirit in his concrete reality. The one universal prayer of the church begins with "Our Father" and ends "in Jesus' name." Trinitarian language pervades the entire liturgy (consider the Sanctus, the Benedictus and the doxology), yet few catch its practical implications. What we do have are ways of life—spiritualities—structured around one dominant person of the Trinity.[24] There is a certain incongruity between what we regularly profess in our worship and affirm in our creed (for example, in the Nicene Creed) and what we actually practice.

The spirituality of the Father. A spirituality focusing on God the Father and creator of all things has a number of distinctive characteristics. Ecologically, it affirms the value of creation. All creation belongs to God and reflects the glory of God (Ps 8; 19:1-6) and therefore ought to be cared for and used responsibly. (Of course, this has not always been the case.) Socially, it affirms our common humanity. Since we are all children of the Father, no one of us is to be treated more or less importantly than others. Thus all forms of racial and sexual discrimination are undercut as it pursues justice and peace for all. Soteriologically, the fact that all things come from God suggests that there is no ultimate disjunction between the physical world and the spiritual world. A spirituality of the Father values the sacramental nature of created things. It supports an ascetical theology that sees the physical as a means of grace, a "door of perception" opening to the spiritual world.[25] For some, the fatherhood of God carries universalistic implications: if God is the loving father of all, then all will eventually be saved.[26] Ecclesiastically, the spirituality of the Father tends toward an inclusive view of the church—the church as a *corpus mixtum* (a mixed body consisting of genuine and professing believers).

There are some admirable qualities in the spirituality of the Father. It encourages us to think holistically and to avoid positing a false dualism between the physical and the spiritual. It is at home in the world and is quite likely to encourage the cultivation of fine tastes like appreciation of music, art and architecture. It enshrines the principle of order and stability, which is often reflected in the Christian lifestyle and way of worship. But it also has some less attractive qualities. When divine fatherhood is understood in very strictly monotheistic terms, it is often perceived as cold, formalistic and aloof. There is little visible display of enthusiasm or emotion, but in our "sensate" world such reserve is not an attractive quality. It leaves little room for surprises; the Christian life goes on with measured predictability.

The spirituality of the Son. This spirituality focuses on the salvific work of Christ. Different spiritualities arise from stressing different aspects of the life and ministry of the Son. If the emphasis is on Christ as the liberator of the oppressed and the friend of publicans and sinners, the ensuing spirituality is likely to be one that stresses radical discipleship and commitment to sociopolitical justice. If Jesus is held forth as the model of patient endurance and suffering, then the Christian life is expressed largely in terms of the *imitatio Christi* and the *via dolorosa* (the way of suffering), which may result in an unquestioning acquiescence to the prevailing status quo.

In popular evangelicalism the christological focus is on Jesus, "the Savior of my soul." It has generated a spirituality centering in the gospel of forgiveness for personal sins, a warm personal piety and a church consisting of individuals who have made a personal profession of faith. A clearer distinction is made between the church and the world and between the supernatural and the natural. The strength of a christocentric spirituality is its stress on conversion to a lively, personal faith in Jesus Christ. In a world of depersonalization and loss of self-identity, this characteristic accounts for its tremendous appeal across cultures. Many do indeed experience the miracle of transformation that evangelical preaching promises. There is an implicit supernaturalism that lifts life out of its ordinariness and gives it a new depth and direction.

But there are dangers in a too narrowly defined christological spirituality. It can become too individualistic and can be turned into a system to support self-indulgence.[27] The corporate life could become a purely voluntary and dispensable matter. The all-important issue is "my own personal relationship with Jesus Christ." All other relationships become secondary. This explains why free churches are prone to schism, although such a tendency could be minimized by a more corporate conception of faith.[28] Furthermore, the legitimate distinction between the natural world and the supernatural world could widen into an unbridgeable chasm, so that the church's basic identity is defined in opposition to the world rather than as a transforming agent in the world. Thus the church is ghettoized, either in self-complacency (perceiving nothing out there in the world that could contribute to its spiritual well-being) or in fear (because the world is hostile to everything that the church holds dear).

The spirituality of the Spirit. If evangelicalism broadly represents the spirituality of the Son, the Pentecostal-charismatic movement represents the spirituality of the Spirit. In one respect Pentecostal spirituality can be seen as a transmutation of evangelical spirituality. If evangelical spirituality is the living out of the supernatural gift of new life in Christ, Pentecostal spirituality further qualifies it as a life of miraculous empowerment. The Spirit of God, who gives us new birth, enters into each believer as a mighty presence with visible demonstrations of spiritual gifts. Thus Pentecostal spirituality possesses a heightened sense of the divine presence. Its central experience, identified as "baptism in the Spirit," has come to be understood as "distinct from and subsequent to the new birth."[29] Sometimes it is described as a second work of grace.[30]

What is characteristic of this experience is that it represents a kind of quantum leap in spiritual consciousness, a "theophany."[31] Pentecostals have often explained their own experience as aimed at empowerment for service. But Catholic charismatic Peter Hocken has shown that it is infinitely much more—it is an experience of deep intimacy in which the one so "baptized" testifies to receiving a "revelation of the triune God in me."[32] At its best, Pentecostal spirituality forces us to recognize that the Christian life is more than just a predictable pattern subject entirely to human control, whether this control be exercised through the mechanism of sacramental ministrations or the new birth formula of "the four spiritual laws." Its expectation of the miraculous is not, to use an expression of H. H. Farmer, "the craving for portends to gape at, or for accommodations on the part of the universe to merely selfish desires, but for personality in God . . . a protest against an all-inclusive monism which leaves the soul choking for want of air."[33] God may yet do new things because God is personal and therefore never completely predictable. Life with God, for Pentecostals, is a journey into the unknown. God may take us through untrodden paths. This helps to instill in them a spirit of adventure and a sense of "holy boldness" that launches them "by faith" (which often means having little money or training) into the far-flung mission field.[34]

The weakness of Pentecostalism becomes apparent when Pentecostals try to routinize the extraordinary, that is, make it a regular part of day-to-day living. Sooner or later the adventurer must return to the reassurance of the homely and the familiar. If life were indeed one continuous adventure, the strain would be intolerable. The history of Pentecostalism can be seen broadly as a movement in which the strain of continuous adventure has been sublimated into continuous festivity. Any observer of the modern Pentecostal movement cannot fail to notice that the missionary thrust has weakened considerably in recent years. According to one Pentecostal academic in "hundreds of our USA churches (I am being conservative) there is no growth because there is no witness."[35] The emphasis now is on worship, praise and celebration in line with the charismatic renewal. But a perpetual holiday would soon become boring. Thus the strength of Pentecostal spirituality works to its own disadvantage in the long term. Its intense focus on one particular concern, while it holds, provides its definitive edge and identity. But such intensity either cannot be sustained for long or it turns into a fixation.

There are two discernible trends in the Pentecostal-charismatic movement today. One is a tendency to flit from one fashion to another, whether theological or liturgical. This gives the movement a reputation of being highly defined by popular culture.[36] The other is the fixation on power.[37] Pentecostalism has traditionally defined itself as a movement of power. Baptism in the Spirit according to the official teaching of the Assemblies of God is to endue the believer with power for service.[38] As long as this power is channeled constructively, its effects are generally positive. But when a centrifugal mission is replaced by a centripetal "praise and worship," the fixation on power, as demonstrated in John Wimber's "power encounters," can become destructive. The very nature of "power theology" as it is conceived among the so-called third wavers is that it has to be manifested in the here and now. Thus, coupled with "power encounters" is a practical "kingdom now" theology.[39]

A trinitarian spirituality. A spirituality that focuses exclusively on Father, Son or Spirit is not adequate, since it fails to take in the full range of God's self-revelation. For a spirituality to be holistic it must be trinitarian, at least implicitly. Trinitarian spirituality is characterized by, first, form and stability and a sacramental understanding of created things. Second, it seeks a personal relationship with God through the person of Jesus Christ. Third, it is open to the powerful workings of God the Spirit in signs and wonders as well as in "holy familiarity." In terms of the church's mission, trinitarian spirituality is oriented toward a critical and constructive engagement in the world, the preaching of the gospel of the grace of God and personal conversion to Jesus Christ, and "power encounters" in both the salvation of individuals as well as the created order. Liturgically, the preaching of the Word and lively worship are both part of an ordered worship that encourages the use of visible and tactile means of grace.

Trinitarian spirituality is not only modeled after the separate functions of the Father, Son and Spirit but also after the inner life of the Trinity itself. The term *perichoresis* designates the relationship between the persons in which their distinct identities are defined. The traditional way is to see the perichoretic relationship in terms of the Father by whom the Son is eternally begotten and from whom the Spirit proceeds. This implies a certain logical priority of the Father.[40] The original Nicene-Constantinopolitan Creed (A.D. 381), which does not include the *filioque* clause, implies mutuality between the Son and the Spirit. In light of this mutuality Yves Congar has called for the more familiar "christological pneumatology" to be balanced by a "pneumatological christology."[41] The first refers to the fact that Christ sends the Spirit and the Spirit glorifies Christ (Jn 16:12-15), while the second refers to the Spirit's anointing Christ and empowering him to fulfill his messianic mission. Understood in this way, our Christology and pneumatology must find their unity in God the Father.

In terms of the nature of the spiritual life, this perichoretic relationship implies that a basic ascetical structure underlies our life in Christ (the evangelical life) and in the Spirit (the charismatic life).[42] The ascetical structure defines the basic character of Christian spiritual life. Without it, evangelical life becomes insulated pietism and charismatic life is reduced to animistic superstition. Such a structure explains why spiritual theology may properly be called ascetical theology.[43]

The locus of trinitarian spirituality. Individual spiritualities tend to correspond to personality types. It is quite natural for different aspects of the Trinity to show through in different individuals. But everyone must be trinitarian in thought and be open to those with differing orientations. The real locus of trinitarian spirituality, therefore, is the church. The practical ramifications of this idea are almost limitless. If the church is to participate in the Trinity as the "many," it seems obvious that the unity of the church should not preclude a diversity of lifestyles, worship styles, liturgies, singing and so on. But frequently a strong leader imposes one particular order on an entire church. This is a practical denial of trinitarian confession. On the other hand thoughtless innovations in the church "for the sake of variety" will not do either. Variety must be consistent with the trinitarian pattern of thought, diversity existing in perichoretic harmony. Adding a few folk or rock songs to the weekly liturgy hardly qualifies a church as an "icon of the Trinity." The question is, What do these songs celebrate? The goodness of creation? The gospel of the grace of Jesus Christ? The freedom of the Spirit? Most importantly, how do such songs relate to the larger pattern of the church's participation in the trinitarian life?[44]

Implications of Trinitarian Theology

Often an attempt to draw implications for the Christian life from the Trinity appeals to particular aspects of the Trinity to support values that are culturally conditioned. Peters raises this criticism against certain social doctrines of the Trinity, in which the equality between Father, Son and Spirit serves as a *model* for human society. According to Peters, trinitarian formulations are not primary biblical symbols but "products of our intellectual context, which we shave and trim so they fit the needs dictated by evangelical explication."[45] To use them as a basis for our theory about society (such as social egalitarianism) looks suspiciously like reading modern values back into the Trinity. Trying to find female elements in the Trinity is another example of this. For some, the belief that the Spirit is the female principle creates a perfect trinitarian family in which "its members give themselves to one another with a totality of love that creates the identity of life they share from all eternity."[46] Moltmann, however, sees it differently. Such a concept means that "femininity [is] simply co-opted into a world of masculine concepts, without being able to change it,"[47] while for Rosemary Radford Ruether the very thought that only the Spirit is female implies that she is voted down two to one.[48]

But Peters's appeal to "a primary biblical symbol" like the kingdom of God as a preferred basis for nonabsolutism in human society[49] leaves open the question, When should a symbol be used "disjunctively" (that is, by way of contrast; if God holds absolute power, no power on earth is absolute) and when should it be used "conjunctively" (as a "model" to sanction the divine rights of kings)? In a situation like this cultural values will prevail. The "model-theory of morality" is not always wrong. The apostle Paul, for instance, uses it to appeal for a certain order or hierarchy in the worshiping community: "Now I want you to realize that the head of every man is Christ, and the head of the woman is man, and the head of Christ is God" (1 Cor 11:3).[50]

Nonetheless, the distinction between primary symbols and second-order symbols is helpful in distinguishing between what is primary—essential to the life of God and therefore more universally applicable to the human condition—and what is secondary—symbols that can be applied either "disjunctively" or "conjunctively" to particular cultural situations as long as these secondary symbols are not absolutized. Thus the "social analogy of the Trinity" may well be used as a model to legitimize an egalitarian society as long as egalitarianism is recognized as one legitimate, culturally conditioned way of ordering society.[51]

By the same token, Asians may find the ancient Eastern doctrine of generation of the Son and procession of the Spirit, in which the Father alone is "without origin" and hence has logical priority,[52] an appropriate model for their own understanding of society as hierarchical. In a Confucian society, the Father-Son relationship might even be pressed further to support a view of society that gives high priority to the father-son relationship.[53] Christians in such a society would insist on distinguishing between domination and hierarchy.[54] Confucianism includes a nondomineering hierarchy that is characterized by reciprocity; in fact, reciprocity is a prerequisite for the good ordering of a hierarchical relationship. Reciprocity in this context means that there are mutual obligations. The child's loving affection for the parents, for instance, is reciprocated by the parents' care for the child.[55] It is in maintaining reciprocity that we realize our true humanity.[56] It is not difficult to see how the Confucian concept can help to elucidate the trinitarian relationship between the Father and the Son as both mutual and hierarchical.[57] It is mutual in their self-giving to each other (they mutually constitute each other as persons), and it is hierarchical in that the Father sent the Son (Jn 20:21) and the Son in love fulfills the will of the Father by his perfect obedience (Phil 2:5-8).

A trinitarian theology has three major implications for Christian spirituality.

First, salvation is essentially personal union with God. If God is supremely a personal being, salvation must also be seen in relational terms: personal union with God. Herein lies one of the values of the Augustine's psychological analogy of the Trinity. It helps us appreciate the psychological depth of personal relationship with the Trinity. In this analogy, Christ and the Spirit are encountered as the word and love respectively coming from the Father. A contemplative character comes from listening to this indwelling word, while the outpouring of the Spirit inflames the soul with divine love, transforming the whole person.[58]

In the contemplative tradition and more recently in the Pentecostal-charismatic movement, the experience of intimacy is an important category for understanding personal relationship with God.[59] The contemplative tradition often uses the analogy of lovers to explain intimacy with God. The best-known exponent of this analogy is perhaps Bernard of Clairvaux in his commentary on the Song of Songs. The Pentecostal tradition understands the experience of personal intimacy with God in terms of a child's bombarding her parents with a stream of what seems to be meaningless prattle. Glossolalic utterances often express this childlike familiarity with the heavenly Father.[60] Far from being a childish activity that must be put aside when outgrown (an overeagerness to put away childish things may itself be a sign of youthful impulsiveness), this experience in fact recaptures a vital dimension of Christian spirituality: the yearning for the faith of a little child. Such a faith is beautifully captured in the prayer of François Fénelon:

I desire to find in the most secret place of my heart, an intimate familiarity with thee, through thy son Jesus, who is thy wisdom and thy eternal mind, become a child to humble our vain and foolish wisdom by his childhood and the folly of his cross. It is there that I wish, whatever it costs me, in spite of my foresight and my reflections, to become little, senseless, even more contemptible in my own eyes than in those of all the falsely-wise. It is there that I wish to become inebriate of Holy Spirit, as the Apostles were, and to be willing as they were to be the laughing stock of the world.[61]

Without being aware of it, Pentecostals have stumbled onto the same object of Fénelon's longing "to become inebriate of the Holy Spirit."[62] They just call it by a different name: baptism in the Spirit.

If personal relationship with the Trinity (of which the goal is intimacy or union with God) is what characterizes our life as Christians, those who accept an inclusivist paradigm of salvation face a certain inconsistency. In what sense can we describe the status of non-Christians as "saved" if a non-Christian by definition is one who does not know Christ explicitly or personally? I suspect that when an inclusivist like Hans Küng refers to an "ordinary" way of salvation for non-Christians,[63] the term *salvation* perhaps refers to no more than some form of freedom, release from pain or personal fulfillment. If those from the world religions are "pre-Christians, directed to Christ"[64] then the most that could be said of them is that they are only "pre-saved" or predisposed to salvation. True salvation from the Christian point of view must be trinitarian. It must partake of the trinitarian life itself, which can be nothing other than an explicit knowledge of Christ and a conscious personal relationship that progresses toward intimacy and union. An inclusivist theory of religions has to exclude, or at least cannot explicitly hold to, the trinitarian conception of life characterized by personal knowledge and intimacy.[65]

Second, spiritual life is essentially relational without ceasing to be particular. To be a Christian is to be "in Christ," that is, baptized into his body, the church, of which each person is a constituent member (1 Cor 12:12). This is the basis of Paul's appeal to the church in regard to ordering their lives and relationships with each other. There must be mutual dependence (the eye cannot dismiss the hand and the head cannot dismiss the feet, v. 21) and recognition of different gifts and support for the weaker ones (vv. 22-24). But individuals are not absorbed into a nameless, corporate entity. Here is where the social analogy of the Trinity provides us with rich resources for understanding the relational and particular nature of the spiritual life.

The perichoresis of the Trinity characterized by the distinct persons-in-relation offers a pattern for human relationship. It also provides a basis for Christians' participation in the trinitarian life.[66] Far from being just a model, perichoresis is the effective means by which the life of particularity-in-relationality can be realized. If humans are made in God's image, "the idea that human beings should in some way be perichoretic beings is not a difficult one to envisage."[67] Our relationship to each other and to nonpersonal creation is such that particularity is not lost in relationality. This perichoretic relationship extends even through time and is called tradition.[68] We are formed by the past just as we form each other in the present and for the future. Perichoresis holds also in the impersonal world—"everything in the universe is what it is by virtue of its relatedness to everything else."[69] The ecological implication is obvious. Yet because particularity-in-relationality is maintained, a trinitarian approach to ecology makes it distinctively different from that popularized by New Age thought, in which nature's balance can only be maintained by sacrificing human distinctiveness.

The dynamic between particularity and relationality has important implications for the world of the late twentieth century, threatened by what Samuel Huntington has vividly (if somewhat controversially) described as the "clash of civilizations."[70] One cultural fault line, which Huntington does not especially highlight but is relevant to our discussion, runs between the Western world, which stresses individual particularity to the point of social disintegration, and the emerging economic powers of Asia, which have a penchant for order through a system of carefully nurtured relationships, the consequence of which has been a lower priority given to individual human rights.[71] Extreme views on both sides could be moderated if a trinitarian theology of society takes more serious cognizance of the larger world of alternative civilizations. I am inclined to think that if this is done, the trinitarian society that emerges is not likely to be strictly of the kind envisioned by Western liberal democrats, but one in which particularity and relationality, individual freedom and communal order, and the best in egalitarianism and hierarchy are preserved.

The relational character of the intratrinitarian life also carries an important implication for a spirituality of the family. There is no question that where modernity dominates a society, whether in the West or in Asia, the family is placed under tremendous stress. The Trinity is in a most profound sense a family in which, according to Donald Gelpi, the Holy Spirit could be imaged as the mother.

> When Jesus addressed God as Papa, he invited his followers to relate to God with a new quality of intimacy and trust. Christians relate to Jesus with an analogous intimacy when they call him brother and friend. The time has come to include the Third Person of the Trinity in this circle of divine intimacy. We can begin to do that by imagining her as Mama, as the one who conceives divine life in us and like a loving mother nurtures us to the fullness of risen life in Christ.[72]

Some may feel uncomfortable with the idea of identifying the Spirit as Mother, but the analogy has the advantage of picturing a complete divine Family as a model for the human family.[73] It has the further advantage of imaging distinct identities and roles for earthly families.[74]

Third, life and work are inseparable. The Catholic and Orthodox traditions see the mission of the church in terms of participation in the trinitarian mission, in which the Father sent the Son and Spirit into the world.[75] The work of the Son and Spirit are united and correspond to the sacraments of baptism and confirmation. The Christian's movement to Christ at baptism is inextricably linked to his movement into the world at confirmation, which is also called "baptism in the Spirit."

The goal of the spiritual life is the indwelling of the holy Trinity through receiving the Son and the Spirit as they are sent into the world—visibly, in the incarnation and Pentecost, sacramentally, in baptism and confirmation, and experientially in new birth and baptism in the Spirit.[76]

What is significant in this conception is that the works of the Son and the Spirit are not separated, as often happens in Protestantism, whether of the evangelical or the Pentecostal-charismatic type. Perhaps in reaction to charismatic excesses evangelicals have sometimes tended to drive a wedge between gifts and life.[77] Pentecostals, on the other hand, by identifying baptism in the Spirit as a second work of grace but defining it narrowly as "enduement of power for service" have tended to exalt the charismata and to see the new birth as a preliminary stage to a higher life of power. But seeing the mission of the church in terms of the trinitarian life avoids such artificial separations. The mission of God is, first, the extension of the trinitarian life in which the Father sent the Son into the world. Second, the mission of the Son is carried out by the anointing of the Spirit. Third, the Spirit is in turn sent by the Son to continue the mission of the Father on earth (Jn 15:26; compare 14:26). The life, death and resurrection of Christ and Pentecost make up one continuous mission of the triune God.

Conclusion

The doctrine of one God in three persons is a foundational Christian belief that distinguishes the Christian concept of deity from other monotheistic concepts. It is basic to a distinctive Christian spirituality. Many modern trinitarian reflections have grown out of certain Western sociopolitical contexts that have limited their usefulness for Christians living beyond those contexts. The current preoccupation with "the social analogy of the Trinity" is just one example. Yet as Ted Peters reminds us, trinitarian talks are "second-order symbols" that grow out of specific contexts. Their truth is tested by how they function contextually. In situations outside the Western world where hierarchy (not necessarily domination and oppression) may be the basic structure of society;[78] where worldviews are characterized by "gods many and lords many"; where the summum bonum is an ordered community rather than individual rights (though the latter is not denied), we may need to return to the "primary symbol" of one God in three persons, a God who is both transcendent and immanent, beyond the world and yet within it.

Augustine's psychological analogy may be just as significant as the social analogy. In affirming these prereflective symbols, we are confessing divine mysteries (although some may suggest that this is anti-intellectual). But in so confessing, we hope to highlight the vast and complex world in which the Christian life is lived, a world that no single *theology* of the Trinity can adequately encompass.

3

SIN & HUMAN NATURE

. . . .

T HE SUBJECT OF HUMAN NATURE AND ITS CONDITION RAISES A NUMBER OF important issues for spiritual theology. This chapter considers how various views of human nature affect our understanding of the spiritual life and how different conceptions of sin carry different consequences for spirituality. Finally, it analyzes the depth of sin and the variety of sins and suggests viable solutions to both.

The Spiritual Life and Human Nature

Traditional approaches to theological anthropology (the doctrine of the human being) tend to focus on human nature as self-transcending being. A human being is a self-determining agent with freewill and other unique human qualities. Consequently, individuals tend to be treated in isolation. Modern approaches tend to focus on the relational nature of human beings as constitutive of their personal identity. The social sciences have made us more aware than ever that individuals are profoundly shaped by the sociolinguistic systems they inhabit. We cannot, therefore, think of individual agents apart from their interhuman relationality and their particular social world. Relationality rather than individual agency is regarded as basic to and constitutive of persons. The "human reality" is considered the more basic reality within which individuals can be understood.[1] There is also a tendency to view a person as an integrated unit or a holistic being rather than a being with composite parts or "faculties." The holistic view of the human being is an established fact of biblical theology.[2] Human acts cannot be isolated into purely physical, psychological or spiritual categories. An activity like eating has meaning only when viewed within the context of interhuman relationship (a candlelight dinner), social bonding (a village fiesta) or religious communities (the Lord's Supper).

The larger understanding of human nature is reflected in a larger conception of sin. Sins are not just acts of isolated individuals or isolated acts of individuals. They also pertain to interpersonal relations (such as alienation) and to the social order (such as structural evil—injustice and oppression). The spirituality (or more often spiritualities) that is developed to address this enlarged concept of sin cannot be confined to the cultivation of the individual's relationship with God; it must incorporate the interpersonal (for example, a spirituality of friendship) and the social (for example, a spirituality of some form of social engagement of which liberation spirituality is one).

There is a good reason, however, to begin with the individual agent as the locus of our spiritual theology. If spirituality primarily concerns our relationship with God,[3] then this relationship is fundamental to our understanding of the interpersonal and the social dimensions of life. But the converse is not necessarily true. Our interpersonal relationships and our social involvement do not necessarily add up to an encounter with God. (This is a point we shall return to later.) While recognizing the importance of anthropological holism, it is useful to begin with what might be called a biblical theology of human nature[4] or a psychology of human nature (compare the functional trichotomy of Viktor Frankl).[5] Significantly, this approach avoids reductionistic explanations. Human nature is so complex that it defies any attempt, ancient or modern, to reduce it to any single explanatory category.[6] Any explanation that is predicated on a "nothing but" view is almost certain to be wrong.

There are three major forms of reductionism. *Materialism* is the belief that everything about human nature can be reduced to some aspect of the physical world. Materialistic reductionism takes on many forms, from the ancient naturalism of Democritus, who reduced all realities into immutable atoms, to the modern identification of mind with cerebral chemistry. (Every twisted thought is the result of a twisted molecule.) *Psychologism* seeks ultimate explanations in the psychological dimension. The Freudian theory of human nature is a classic example. The human is "nothing but" a being driven by instinct or, more precisely, by the conflicting claims of id and superego finding an uneasy truce in the ego. Psychologism applies to many practical aspects of life. For example, physical problems are assigned a psychological explanation, giving a new twist to an old adage: a slip of the tongue *is* the fault of the mind! Spiritual problems are invariably seen as psychological. Demon possession is nothing but schizophrenia; conversion is nothing but infantile dependence; prayer, autosuggestion; sin, addiction. Christians sometimes practice *spiritualistic reductionism* by offering a spiritual explanation for every problem. The "spiritual warfare" school is often guilty of this.[7] Depression is caused by a "spirit of depression"; a habitual liar is possessed by a "lying spirit"; physical sickness is due to a "lack of faith."

Against all these forms of reductionism, Christianity since Augustine has formulated a view of the person that acknowledges the physical and rational aspects of human existence but rises beyond both to see the human being as bearing the image of God and having the capacity for "self-transcendence."[8] Such a view of human nature could be described as a functional trichotomy: a person *is* body, soul and spirit all at once.

These fundamental distinctions provide a framework for clarifying a number of pastoral issues. One common problem faced by many pastors in Asia is the relationship between sickness and sin. Is God punishing me for my sinful past? Am I suffering now because of what my parents did? These questions reflect the heart-wrenching experiences of many Asian Christians. They may explicitly repudiate the Hindu law of karma, but the karmic consciousness remains deeply rooted in the Asian soul. It reassures them to know that physical problems are not necessarily the result of sin. The relationship between the psychological and the spiritual dimensions also raises questions. Can a person who is right with God be chronically depressed? Can mentally retarded people have any meaningful relationship with God? True spirituality is determined by what becomes of the *person*, not the various physical and psychological components, which are subject to any number of mishaps. A mentally retarded person may well be a saint. As Viktor Frankl has observed, "Only God can know how many saints were concealed behind miens of idiots."[9] On the other hand, a psychologically "healthy," well-adjusted person may have a functionally dead conscience. Such a person has come to perfect terms with the id by killing off the superego![10]

A holistic view of human nature suggests that we need to seek wholeness in all aspects of life, not just the spiritual. Contrary to popular thinking, the major Christian spiritual traditions promote this. Just as the body is not to be neglected, it is not to be pampered. The wise spiritual master counsels moderation in all things. The counsel of Francis de Sales concerning moderation is significant in that he claimed the backing of Jerome and Bernard:

I have learned by experience that the little Ass [the body] being weary in his journey, seeketh to go out of the way; I mean that young folk being brought low through excess of fasting, do fall willingly to rest and delicateness. The deer run ill in two seasons, when they are charged with overmuch fat, and when they become over lean. We are likewise most subject to temptations, when our body is too much pampered with dainty fare, and when it is over weakened: for the one maketh it insolent with ease, and the other maketh it desperate with affliction. . . . The lack of this moderation in fasting, in disciplining in hairclothes, and other austerities, make the best years of many to be unprofitable in the chief work of charity.[11]

Both body and mind have a part to play in spiritual development and must not be neglected in favor of the spirit. Genuine Christian asceticism never polarizes body and spirit. Voices that accuse the ancients of emphasizing the spirit to the neglect of the body usually come from moderns who themselves lack the spiritual and mental discipline to resist overindulging themselves.

God can and does work through the body and mind to the heart. Communion with God is not merely a matter of spirit with Spirit. Body and mind can become avenues of grace. Such practices as worship and prayer must involve all three dimensions. Protestantism is sometimes guilty of confining life with God to cerebral operations: preaching and hearing the Word, analytical Bible study and so on. But life in the Spirit can be enriched considerably through visual (postures, gestures and dance), olfactory (incense and candles) and tactile (beads and anointing oil) routes.

The Problem of Sin in Spiritual Theology

In most standard Catholic spiritual theologies sin is treated as an aspect of growth in the Christian life and is understood largely in terms of the cultivation of Christian virtues. Conversion is part of the process of virtue formation. Thus Aumann discusses conversion from sin as essentially a matter of changing various predispositions from evil to good, all of which eventually form our character.[12] In Garrigou-Lagrange the discussion of virtues precedes the discussion of sin. Sin is discussed under mortification or the process of purification.[13] The traditional Catholic view of sin sees it, first, in ontological rather than relational terms.[14] Sin is a sort of spiritual pollutant rather than an attitude or stance that the sinner takes in relation to God. Second, the Catholic view locates sin more in the will than in the heart. It exists in the actions themselves rather than as a condition that predetermines the sinner's action. The Catholic doctrine of grace working in nature and uplifting it means that sin is not understood in all its radicalness. The sinner is described as having "a fallen nature, deprived of grace and wounded," and the sinful nature is characterized as "disorder and weakness of the will."[15] It mostly addresses sins as contrary acts instead of addressing sin as a fallen condition. The basic thrust of the spiritual life is dealing with the aftereffects of original sin.

More recent developments in the Catholic theology of sin and grace, however, have tended to move away from the older conception of sins as acts to sin as a basic condition. According to Mark O'Keefe, "sin and grace must be understood not primarily in terms of individual acts for good or evil but in the light of the person's basic life orientation or direction."[16] This new understanding is expressed in the theory of "fundamental option." By fundamental option is meant the choices that affect the basic direction of one's life. Thus a negative fundamental option is choosing a life whose basic direction is away from God, while a positive fundamental option is choosing a life lived under grace. In this context, sin is defined (following Augustine) as "a turning away from God and a turning toward creatures *(aversio a Deo per conversionem ad creaturam)*.

The actualization of the positive fundamental option is not recognized as a one-time isolated act. It "requires the lifelong effort of integrating all of one's choices and attitudes into this fundamental choice for God."[17] This means exerting continuous effort at developing the virtues and the progressive integration of the self. The three ways—purgation, illumination and union—are not three discrete steps but "the basic dynamism of the Christian life—a life of ongoing or continual conversion."[18] This newer view has the advantage of taking sin and grace in their more radical sense and also giving an essential place to ascetical theology. But it still does not open the door to the characteristically evangelical doctrine of conversion as altering one's relationship with God *positionally*. This is because a crisis experience of conversion is more likely to be considered an act of "categorical freedom" rather than an act of "transcendental freedom." The former refers to the ordinary, conscious choices that we make every day. The latter is a more basic kind of choice that is not open to our consciousness and yet is realized through our everyday choices.[19]

The "fundamental option" theory has not radically altered the general Catholic conception of sin and grace. If sin is no longer understood as isolated acts, it is still seen as rooted in the will. The relational character of sin tends to fade into the background. The Reformation doctrine of sin, in contrast, recovers the Augustinian and Anselmic concepts, which understand sin in relational terms as well as in all its radicalness. For Augustine, sin has completely disabled the human will.[20] For Anselm, sin is an infinite affront against God; for Luther, a willful rebellion rooted in unbelief.[21] The sinner who is cut off from God is totally depraved. This means that apart from prevenient grace the sinner is incapable of responding to God. In the language of Scripture, the sinner is "dead in trespasses and sins" (Eph 2:1). The Catholic view sees the heart as a garden overgrown with weeds that need to be uprooted. Rooting out the weeds is part of the larger work of cultivating a more perfect garden. In Protestantism the heart is a wilderness that needs to be radically transformed before cultivation can begin. Conversion is a prerequisite for character formation.

The Protestant account of sin reworks the essential nature of the Christian life. First, it entails its own view of conversion. Conversion is nothing less than a miracle of new birth. Because the sinner is totally helpless without the grace of God, each conversion is an exaltation of divine grace. Grace is experienced not just as a power at work in the soul but as a gift that transforms a relationship of hostility and alienation into one of reconciliation and peace. A deep appreciation of divine goodness follows the realization that it is a totally undeserved gift. Second, it recognizes the redeeming grace of God in Christ as distinct from, though not discontinuous with, God's creating grace. The redeemed life is more than just the transposition of human values to a higher key. Being a Christian is more than being human. We cannot overstress the importance of this point for Christian spirituality. Christian spirituality is Christian only to the extent that it retains its specifically Christian *religious* character—it partakes of a specific story about the life, death and resurrection of Jesus Christ. Without it, Christian spirituality becomes just another name for moral development, an instantiation of the natural life.[22]

If a relational understanding of sin is interpreted strictly within a juridical context, sin is understood as an infringement of divine law eliciting God's wrath. Then the Christian life is lived more out of fear of punishment than out of love. Within the Reformed tradition, this fear manifests itself in the nervous search for assurance of salvation. Since it is impossible for the human mind to penetrate God's inscrutable decree concerning personal salvation, the only alternative is to look for signs of the preparatory workings of grace within the soul leading to conversion. In the seventeenth century a whole "preparationist" tradition grew up within certain segments of Puritanism. Feeling beaten down by "a lively sense" of one's own sin was believed to provide a surer knowledge of salvation. As a result, Puritanism has since been caricatured as a joyless religion.[23] But the juridical view needs to be balanced by the relational view, which understands sin as an offense against the person of God. It is less a legal problem than a family problem (as expressed in the parable of the prodigal son). This relational concept is crucial to our overall understanding of the Christian life. Reformed theologian James Torrance asserts that if the Christian life is ultimately what *we* do,

> then God's grace would be conceived of in semi-Pelagian terms as simply "enabling grace," "infused" grace, an "invisible" thing we need, an efficacious impersonal cause (like gasoline to drive our cars!) that is there to make programs work. But in reality, are not mission, evangelism and social action also, like worship, activities in which we are called through the personal activity of the Holy Spirit to participate in Christ's ministry—in the work of the triune God as he establishes his kingdom? In the Bible, grace is always conceived of in personal terms. In grace, the triune God personally stands in for us, gives himself to us and draws us into his inner life.[24]

But when we think of God in trinitarian (that is, relational) terms, continues Torrance, God is no longer the object but the *agent* in our worship, mission and social action.[25] Worship becomes "the gift of participating through the Spirit in the (incarnate) Son's communication with the Father."[26] In other words, to understand the Christian life *as* relational is to acknowledge that "we pray, and yet it is not so much we who pray, but Christ and the Holy Spirit who pray for us and with us and in us (Rom. 8:26, 27, 34)."[27] Unfortunately, in the history of Protestant thought and life, this idea has been distorted into a doctrine of cheap grace, parodied by televangelists as "easy believism" and reduced by popular evangelicalism into a mere "crisis conversion." Despite these travesties the essential truth remains, that sin and grace must be seen in terms of relationship to the Trinity.

Protestantism stops short when it should go on to develop an ascetical theology to deal with the problem of inbred sin. In terms of the garden analogy, it rightly acknowledges that God the gardener has cleared the wilderness and has prepared the ground. But it has neither the comprehensive theory nor the technical know-how necessary to turn the barren plot into a garden. The Protestant is one who enjoys warm fellowship with the gardener but fails to work the garden afterward—not for lack of trying but for lack of what Thornton calls "proficiency."[28] Torrance may be right in asserting that biblically grace is always understood in personal terms. But there is every reason to accept the biblical extension of *charis* into *charisma*, a gift, and hence the operative power of grace.[29] The doctrine of critical conversion and the concept of continuous conversion are not mutually exclusive,[30] just as a doctrine of the forgiveness of sin should include a doctrine of the mortification of sins.[31]

To sum up, the different conceptions of sin have very different consequences for the cultivation of the spiritual life. The advantage of the Catholic view is that it produces a more systematic program for advancement in the spiritual life. It is no coincidence that ascetical theology became a highly developed theological science long before Protestants came to recognize its importance.[32] It is only in relatively recent times that Protestants, especially evangelicals, have revived some of the traditional spiritual disciplines, for example, Richard Foster's *Celebration of Discipline.*[33] The Catholic fundamental option theory should caution us against seeing every "decision for Christ" as a genuine conversion. Both Scripture and experience militate against such a hasty judgment.[34] The weakness of the Catholic view lies in not fully appreciating the radical nature of sin. This is seen most clearly in the Roman Catholic "new morality," which equates being Christian with cultivating human values. But even the fundamental option theory fails to fully appreciate the relational character of sin. But if we accept the Reformation conception of sin as a radical evil that fundamentally alters our relationship with God, then the spiritual life is not conceivable without a strong awareness of the depth of sin. This is why Luther insists that "the first duty of the preacher of the gospel is to declare God's law and describe the nature of sin."[35] Dealing with sin, therefore, is not a part of the process of renewal but a "precondition of renewal."[36]

The Depth of Sin and the Variety of Sins

It is customary to discuss the sources of sin in terms of the "three enemies of the soul." But these three enemies—the flesh, the world and the devil—do not merely list three sources of sin. Taken together, they encompass the depth and extent of human evil. The flesh is the sin *within* us, the world designates the sin *around* us and the devil, the sin *beyond* us. Everywhere we turn we encounter *sin* as a pervasive human condition as well as *sins* in their vast and varied manifestation. The focus on sins as acts has been very much a part of moral theology and casuistry. The term *casuistry,* which may be defined as the science and art of bringing general moral principles to bear on specific moral or spiritual issues, is not a part of the typical Protestant vocabulary. So it may come as a surprise to many modern Protestants that in an earlier age casuistry was as much a Protestant as it was a Catholic concern. It was usually known as "cases of conscience"[37] or "spiritual direction,"[38] but that did not alter the fact that it represented essentially the same attempts at applying larger theological and moral principles to specific situations of life.

Casuistry is unavoidable when we think about specific sins in specific situations. Life in the real world forces us to come to decisions in regard to concrete situations of loving, hating, ignoring, informing, commanding or obeying persons A, B or C, who are related to us in situations x, y or z. The possibilities are so bewildering that most Christians need to seek "expert guidance" in order to identify the "right" course of action. In short, the moment Christians seek to advance spiritually, they can no longer ignore specific sins. Hazy notions about the general badness of our condition seldom motivate us to chart a path of spiritual growth. But when we come to a specific awareness of a sin ("I am an alcoholic," not "I'm pretty bad") we start down the road to change. The autobiographies of many famous Christians seem to confirm this observation. The first stirrings of life occur when the remembrance of a specific sin homes in powerfully on the heart. Richard Baxter recalled being convicted of "robbing an orchard or two with rude boys."[39] Perhaps this is the reason that Scripture furnishes long lists of sins. The apostle Paul, for example, does not just talk about the works of the flesh in general, he lists them in some detail: "sexual immorality, impurity and debauchery; idolatry and witchcraft; hatred, discord, jealousy, fits of rage, selfish ambition, dissensions, factions and envy; drunkenness, orgies and the like" (Gal 5:19-21; compare Mk 7:21-23; 1 Cor 6:9-10; Rom 1:29-31; Col 3:5-9).

Comparing these lists reveals some interesting facts about the biblical conception of sin. First, the Bible makes no distinction between "venial" and "mortal" sins. The sins of slander and envy, for example, are mentioned along with sins of murder and adultery because they all come from an evil heart (Mk 7:21). Second, all the lists except Mark's warn of God's wrath. This underscores the relational character of sin. Third, some sins are referred to more frequently than others (such as sexual immorality and greed). This probably means that these sins were pervasive in the world of the first century.[40] This point underscores the biblical contextual approach to sins.[41] Fourth, there is a wide variety of sins: sins of the mind (evil thoughts), sins of attitude (envy, hatred), sins of speech (slander, gossip, filthy language) and sins of action (theft, swindling). Sin affects every aspect of life. The theological term for this is *total depravity*.

The traditional approach to sin, which analyzes its depth and variety and suggests specific "cures," shows itself to be wise. It is only by such an approach that practical mortification and systematic advance are made possible. Sin, in both its intensity and extensity, is well portrayed in contemporary discussions on the subject. Patrick McCormick describes sin as

> a spiral in which the individual actions and habits of persons are expressions of a viral cancer within them, a cancer which is communicated not only from person to person but from generation to generation, sustained by the ongoing cooperation of various members and groups

and ever deepening and hardening against the will and salvific love of God.[42]

Ted Peters in his book *Sin: Radical Evil in Soul and Society* shows how the path to radical evil leads downward in seven steps: anxiety, unfaith, pride, concupiscence, self-justification, cruelty and finally blasphemy.[43]

Scriptures underscore the dynamic nature of sin with expressions like "hardening the heart" (compare Ps 95:8; Heb 3:8) and the "searing of conscience" (1 Tim 4:2). Paul describes sin as a debilitating power that prevents the will from carrying out its good intentions (Rom 7:18-24). James pictures it as a restless agitation deep within the heart that breaks out in external conflicts.

> What causes fights and quarrels among you? Don't they come from your desires that battle within you? You want something but don't get it. You kill and covet, but you cannot have what you want. You quarrel and fight. You do not have, because you do not ask God. When you ask, you do not receive, because you ask with wrong motives, that you may spend what you get on your pleasures. You adulterous people, don't you know that friendship with the world is hatred toward God? . . . Submit yourselves, then, to God. Resist the devil, and he will flee from you. (Jas 4:1-4, 7)

These inner conflicts are themselves symptoms of a more primary sinful nature seen in a covetous spirit (*epithymia,* Jas 4:2), in false motives that lurk behind religious acts and in an insatiable lust for pleasure. People who live in the grip of sin are powerless against the devil. The only way to resist the devil is to submit to God and to repent (vv. 7-10). This passage, incidentally, brings together the three enemies of the soul. But the real enemy is the flesh—the enemy within. Without it the other two are powerless.

The flesh (the sin in us). To recognize the primacy of the flesh is to acknowledge the ultimacy of personal accountability. This point is deeply etched in the writings of the later Hebrew prophets. The idea that "what I am is a result of what my forebears did" was so widely held in Israel that it became a proverb: "The fathers eat sour grapes, and the children's teeth are set on edge" (Ezek 18:2). Ezekiel, however, calls this a moral cop out: "The soul who sins is the one who will die" (v. 4). Joey may be born into an abusive family, may grow up in a gang-infested neighborhood and so forth, but ultimately Joey must accept responsibility for what he does if he is to make any real change. This is not to deny the extenuating circumstances that helped shape his attitude and behavior. But if he goes through life blaming the world, the devil or bad genes, his moral and spiritual development will be blocked. Real change can begin when he comes to terms with his own sinfulness before God and prays with the publican: "God, have mercy on me, a sinner" (Lk 18:13). As he confesses that *he* is a sinner, he becomes a recipient of the grace of God.

The problem of lust is especially acute in our modern sensate culture and perhaps deserves special mention. Traditional spiritual theology has identified the flesh almost exclusively with sensuality or lust.[44] While recognizing that the flesh expresses itself very poignantly in *epithymia* ("lust" or "concupiscence"), it is a deeply rooted condition that manifests itself in other ways as well. All of the seven deadly sins are rooted in the flesh. But unlike Buddhism, which sees desire itself as the root of all evil, Christianity has never identified desire itself as sin. It is inordinate and excessive desire expressing itself compulsively that is seen as sinful. Natural pleasures like food and sex, being part of our true humanity, are good. We must guard against the implicit dualism that easily creeps into our avoidance of sensible pleasure. At the same time we must remember that pleasures, though good, are not ends in themselves. Every sensible pleasure is directed ultimately to a higher end: We are to "eat and drink to the glory of God" (1 Cor 10:31).

A great challenge for Christianity is to present its doctrine of sin effectively to a system that does not have a strong sense of innate human evil, such as Confucianism.[45] If evil is simply "an improper development of the innate goodness of human nature" in accordance with the cosmic order,[46] then there is nothing to be "saved" from. Moral development or at most moral transformation is not the same as salvation from sin. Confucian spirituality is largely the path of self-improvement, a "do-it-yourself" spirituality. The relational concept of sin is confined to social relations; the more transcendental concept of sin is not understood in personal-relational terms. It is failure to conform to *li*, the universal moral ultimate. Since sin is usually understood as "crime" that can be corrected by legal means and by education, the idea of divine forgiveness is also quite alien to Chinese thought. Thus it comes as no surprise that Christianity has not been able to penetrate the Chinese intelligentsia.[47]

The chasm between the "Pelagianism" of Confucian orthodoxy and the Augustinianism of orthodox Christianity is wide indeed at the abstract level. But there is an important point of convergence at the spiritual level. The spiritual awakening described in Christian autobiographies begins with awareness of specific sins rather than agreement with an abstract idea like original sin. That awareness seems to be a universal experience that extends to Confucianism.[48] If Christians would try to establish contact with Confucianists at the level of lived realities rather than abstract thought, they could make a stronger case for their doctrine of sin and for a corresponding appreciation of God's amazing grace.[49]

The world (the sin around us). The Bible often uses the word *world* to refer to organized humanity in its opposition to God. John often puts "the world" in opposition to the people of God. "If the world hates you, keep in mind that it hated me first. If you belonged to the world, it would love you as its own. As it is, you do not belong to the world, but I have chosen you out of the world. That is why the world hates you" (Jn 15:18-19; compare 16:20; 17:14; 1 Jn 3:13; 5:19).

The social dimension of sin is demonstrated in "structural evils" such as racial and sexual discrimination. The evil within individuals contributes to a larger, deeply entrenched sinful social structure. If the flesh provides the occasion for external temptation in the world, the world in turn molds and shapes the flesh without our being fully conscious of it. When the fathers eat sour grapes, the children's teeth *are* set on edge. This realization of the larger reality of sin has led to a fresh appreciation of the doctrine of original sin.[50] What makes social sins so dangerous is that people are less aware of them and so do not feel personally responsible for them.[51] Yet they are more deeply entrenched and thus are more difficult to eradicate. The consequences of these "structural evils" are far more socially destructive than the consequences of individual sins.

The world is more than the sum of individuals who are indifferent to Christ, actively or passively opposed to Christ or even outwardly religious.[52] Such a superficial view of the world misses the radical nature of structural evil, as is the case with most traditional definitions of the world.[53] Kevin O'Shea calls the sin of the world "perdition history" as opposed to salvation history.

> The Sin of the World is a virus of evil which entered the world as a personal force through original sin and dynamically unfolds itself and tightens its grip on humanity and on the world in an escalating fashion down the ages of history. It is the hidden power which multiplies transgressions in the history of mankind. They are merely its symptoms; it is greater and deeper than all of them. It forms human history into what we might call "perdition history" (to coin the opposite of "salvation history").[54]

Just as salvation history moves to its consummation in Christ, "perdition history" is a downward spiral that moves to its own fulfillment in the eschatological symbol of the antichrist. When sin reaches its logical conclusion, it possesses a power all of its own. The Bible identifies this structural evil as *principalities and powers,* terms also associated with the demonic realm.[55]

> Sin acquires the powerful and elusive form of a spirit—the spirit of an age or a company or a nation or a political movement. Sin burrows into the

bowels of institutions and traditions, making a home there and taking them over. The new structure that is formed by the takeover is likely to display some combination of perversion, formlessness, or excessive rigidity. Law, for example, may be bent to end the freedom of selected pariah groups. Whole companies may dissolve in an orgy of intertwined deceit and neglect. Whole nations may join in lockstep with brutal dictators.[56]

Sin is so deceitful that even Christians miss discerning it in the world and often end up trivializing it. There was a time when conservative Christians saw worldliness quite unambiguously in things and places. Identifying the sin of worldliness in this way simplifies life considerably. Holiness is achieved by avoiding worldly places and abstaining from worldly things (anything from cinemas to bars, from cigarettes to coffee). But externalizing worldliness leaves people open to the real worldliness within—a self-righteous and condemnatory attitude toward those who happen to see worldliness differently or see it in a different set of things. Late twentieth-century conservative Christians have seen through the errors and hypocrisy of their forebears, but now they do not identify worldliness with anything at all. If money is not the root of all evil, only the love of it, then it does not matter how much I accumulate for myself. And if worldliness is not in things but in attitude, then it does not matter how I acquire the money as long as my motive is right, namely, to use it to preach the gospel or to support a good cause (such as prolife campaigns).

The cure for worldliness is seeing the world for what it really is: passing away (1 Cor 7:29-31). No human activity, however legitimate, such as marrying, buying and possessing, may become all-determinative. The Christian must adopt an "as if not" attitude toward things. This attitude of detachment can be cultivated, according to many ancient spiritual writers, by meditating on the vanity of the world, the shortness of life and, by contrast, the eternal life to come.[57] Everything in the world, including the lust of the flesh, the lust of the eyes and the pride of life, will pass away (1 Jn 2:16). And even if the world does not pass away immediately, we will.[58] Sometimes worldly detachment is expressed in stronger language, such as contempt for the world *(contemptus mundi)*. Some fear that such contempt leads to a gnostic dualism that pits spirit against matter.[59] That may or may not be true. What is certain is that if "world" is understood in the way defined above, then the Christian's response is quite unequivocal: "love not the world" (1 Jn 2:15).

Perhaps the traditional *contemptus mundi* motif is now unacceptable not because the ancients were wrong in principle but because we have come to identify the world by a different set of sins. For example, the Puritans were probably right in condemning "lewd" books and plays, even though by today's standards they were no more than the equivalent of comic books and soap operas. But to dismiss the Puritans' concern is simply to judge them by the criteria that define lewdness for us. (Most Christians today agree that pornography, however it is defined, is corrupting and soul destroying.) Or perhaps our historical pride (a particularly modern sin), displacing historical perspective, has prevented us from being more sympathetic toward the past.[60] The truth of the matter is that modern, sensate people have little to fear from the sin of gnostic renunciation.

Modern Christians are not lacking in "relevance." What they do lack is a disciplined life and a critical mind to resist the temptation to conform to what everybody thinks or does (Rom 12:1-3). What they sorely need is an in-depth spiritual renewal of the whole person in order to decide for God or for the world. Decisiveness is the mark of true discipleship. "If anyone would come after me, he must deny himself and take up his cross and follow me" (Mt 16:24). There is no "middle ground," according to Calvin: "either the world must become worthless to us or hold us bound by intemperate love of it."[61] This is also the burden of Bonhoeffer's *The Cost of Discipleship*.

The devil (the sin beyond us). When it comes to devils, C. S. Lewis identifies two errors to avoid. "One is to disbelieve in their existence. The other is to believe, and to feel an excessive and unhealthy interest in them. They themselves are equally pleased by both errors and hail a materialist or a magician with the same delight."[62] Our present world, unfortunately, seems to be polarized between these extremes. A rationalistic worldview has created a backlash of spiritualistic reductionism and Satan worship.

Christians need to avoid both fixating on spiritualistic phenomena and being indifferent to them. As the apostle Paul reminds us, we should not be ignorant of the devil's devices (2 Cor 2:11), nor should we become unduly curious over them. The Christian tradition has much to teach us regarding the discerning of spirits.[63] For example, one of the tasks of discernment is to recognize that the tempter can use our own sinful nature to tempt us to sin. Most of us experience such temptations often enough. As James puts it, "Each one is tempted when, by his own evil desire, he is dragged away and enticed" (Jas 1:14). But we can also experience temptation as a more direct attack. The devil injects vain and tumultuous thoughts into our imaginative faculty. Here it is important to distinguish between having involuntary thoughts and feelings and focusing intensely on certain objects. There is a world of difference between a passing glimpse of a woman that momentarily and perhaps involuntarily delights and the obsessive thought and intense gaze that Jesus said constitute adultery in the heart. From a spiritual director's point of view, understanding the difference helps overscrupulous Christians distinguish between temptation and sin and saves them from unnecessary self-condemnation.

It is also generally believed that the devil cannot directly attack the mind and will. He can only influence the mind through the imagination. Even though such a view is based on an outmoded faculty psychology, it helps draw a distinction between temptation and sin. Actual sins are committed by the consent of the will.[64]

Late Judaism, Christianity and Islam agree on the existence of the devil. Although scientific modernity banished the devil from serious discourse, a growing awareness of radical evil in the late twentieth century has again raised the subject to the status of a serious question. Scott Peck's own encounters with evil eventually led him to acknowledge that there are genuine cases of demonic possession, although they are rare.[65] J. B. Russell also came to the conclusion that the devil is a real person "with consciousness, will and intelligence."[66] Acknowledging the reality of radical evil is but one step from acknowledging the reality of the devil, for the devil can be defined as the principle and embodiment of deliberate evil. Even if the devil as a fallen spirit being were not to exist, there are enough candidates at the human level to fill his place. To recognize the reality of the demonic is to recognize at the same time the human capacity for superhuman evil. It is not just cruelty that human beings are capable of, but cruelty in the extreme. "So artistically cruel" is how Dostoevsky puts it. The vastness of the human moral potential, whether for good or for evil, is well captured in these words of C. S. Lewis:

> It is a serious thing to live in a society of possible gods and goddesses, to remember that the dullest and most uninteresting person you talk to may one day be a creature which, if you saw it now, you would be strongly tempted to worship, or else a horror and a corruption such as you now meet, if at all, only in a nightmare.[67]

Humans can become demonic. Perhaps this is the unpardonable sin. All the passages of Scripture that refer to this sin (Mt 12:31-32; Heb 6:4-6; 10:26-29; 1 Jn 5:16-17) mention its deliberateness. The human will has become so completely bent inward upon itself *(incurvatus in se)* that it would resist the strongest assault of grace. Kierkegaard calls it "despair," the sin of one who "wills . . . to be rid of the self which he is, in order to be the self he himself has chanced to chose [sic]."[68] The degree of deliberateness can reach the point of denying what is known to be true. Perhaps it was the failure to take this possibility seriously (which Barth decried in classical liberalism) that led to the failure to discern the radical evil in Hitler, Stalin and Mao until it was too late.

Contemporary discussions of the devil as a symbol of radical evil, however, have been more forward in identifying specific acts with radical evil. J. B. Russell, for example, sees it globally in "genocide, terrorism, and preparations for war" and individually in "actions of callousness and cruelty."[69] Peters's criterion for the satanic is "the request to shed innocent blood."[70] Chinese people invariably identify the most heinous evils as murder and arson. We need to objectify evil in order to identify it concretely. We must be galvanized to the presence of radical evil. It is equally important to avoid confusing a contextually defined understanding of sin with universal evil thus identifying radical evil with whatever we feel a strong revulsion toward.[71] A related, insidious danger is allowing such feelings to become a fixation and to see such evil where it does not exist, thus creating a perfect situation for a witch hunt.[72]

Radical evil cannot be answered in kind. Returning evil for evil creates a downward spiral into greater violence and cruelty. Evil can only be overcome when the evil person realizes that there is a greater power, the power of love that overcomes evil with forgiveness and the promise of life. The answer to the problem of evil is the Christian story, which actualizes love, forgiveness and the power of life. Elaborating the cardinal virtues does not make them ours and incessantly portraying the seven deadly sins does not make them go away. What we need is Christian spirituality. We need to access the spiritual resources available to us. Internalizing virtues drives away the vices. Peters is surely right:

> When we realize we are forgiven, we find we can borrow the goodness of the forgiver rather than working to manufacture the illusion of our own goodness. Similarly, the promise of life relieves us of the responsibility of finding immortality in our own accomplishments. We no longer need to rely strictly on ourselves or try to steal life from other creatures; we can rely on the giver of life.
>
> What these two things require, of course, is that we are loved by someone who has the power to forgive and the power to give life. This is the message that the symbols of God try to communicate.[73]

The operative word here is *realize*. We must realize that we are forgiven. To do this we need to understand the dynamics of love and repentance. We talk about loving the sinner and hating the sin. Only true love can tell the difference because love seeks to extricate the sinner from the sin. It never confuses the two and in fact resists doing so. This is why love looks like indifference or even hypocrisy to someone who refuses to repent. The sinner who fails to extricate himself from sin cannot properly respond to love. Every soul faces a stark alternative: repent or perish (Lk 13:3). Despite all the love

God can and will give, some will not repent. Does not radical evil require a more radical response than just love? Is love alone adequate in the face of a Hitler or a callous child abuser? To phrase the question in this way is to misunderstand the fundamental nature of love. First, to love a radically evil person does not eliminate the need to work toward the dismantling of evil structures or to take appropriate steps to minimize or even remove the effects of an evil person's actions. Second, if love forces the sinner to face the truth of his own sin, it will ultimately either transform him or force him to choose his own self-destruction. In the latter case, the sinner is so identified with the sin that he *becomes* the sin. In either case, the power of a discriminating love can eradicate evil.

The seven deadly sins. The seven deadly sins were codified as early as the fourth century by John Cassian (360-435).[74] The order in which they are normally listed comes from Gregory the Great (540-604). He identified pride as the root sin from which the other seven sins proceed: vainglory, envy, anger, melancholy *(tristitia)*, greed, gluttony and lust.[75] Eventually vainglory and pride were brought together, and *tristitia* was subsumed under acedia (sloth).

These sins are called deadly or capital because, as Thomas Aquinas explains, they are the head *(caput)*, the principle cause or root of other graver sins, not because they are worse than other sins such as murder of the innocent and genocide, for example.[76] They identify certain basic evil dispositions that determine one's basic orientation in life;[77] they are "characterological."[78] They are also universal. Practically every culture has its fair share of sloths and gluttons, even if what constitutes a sloth or glutton may be culturally defined. Singapore boasts a "Glutton Square," and people eat five meals a day (three big ones with two smaller ones in between). But this does not mean that gluttony is acceptable; it only means that what it takes to be guilty of that deadly sin has been raised.

The seven sins are the root of what is nowadays called radical evil, which is actually their culturally conditioned fruit.[79] This is why they serve as a useful point of departure in some contemporary discussions of evil. The seven deadly sins have been related to various modern contexts of personal life[80] and social conditions.[81] Chilling elaborations of them are included in descriptions of sins that are practiced in the modern world.[82] But not everybody is happy with the traditional list. Radical feminist Mary Daly charges that the traditional list reflects male dominance, which actually hides the "primary" deadly sin: "the deceptiveness of male-constructed 'morality.'"[83] Still, by analyzing contemporary sins in the light of the seven we put names to the sins and recognize them for what they are. Pride may be clothed in various cultural guises, but to recognize it in whatever form it appears contributes to a more critical stance toward culture. Perhaps an example each from the East and the West would help here. One of the major scourges of Chinese history is incessant infighting. Chinese folklore glorifies this scourge as the work of vengeance, variously called the protection of family honor or the vindication of the victim. But the humanist critic Bo Yang has rightly called it an "ugly Chinaman" syndrome.[84] In the final analysis it is a cultural evil rooted in raw anger and subtle pride. In the West, the same root sin, pride, "that blend of narcissism and conceit," manifests itself quite differently. Cornelius Plantinga has well portrayed both its usual and its more subtle forms in American culture.

> Of course, pride itself is still with us. Professors still leave faculty meetings feeling less enlightened by what they heard than by what they said. People still feel injured when admirers offer them the sort of sincere but moderate praise that limits their merit. What has changed is that, in much of contemporary American culture, aggressive self-regard is no longer viewed with alarm. Instead, people praise and promote it. This is a culture in which schoolchildren outrank Asian schoolchildren not in math ability but in self-confidence about their math ability; a culture in which prophets of the New Age and gurus of pop psychology (who are sometimes the same) package transcendence and sell it to consumers, advising them that they are superconscious beings, Higher Selves growing toward godhood, "one with the One," and thus in line for the ultimate job promotion.[85]

In moving from the "three enemies" to the seven deadly sins, we are moving from *sin* that denotes the human condition to *sins* in their varied and specific manifestations. Progressing in the spiritual life requires more than acknowledging the reality of our sinful condition and being able to analyze it in all its depth and extent. In real life we need to deal with specific sins, besetting sins, often one overpowering sin that dogs us throughout life. We need to be specific because the "naming of sins enables us to explore the dynamic roots of sin and to recognize that different sins have different effects on personality and character formation."[86] Scripture itself is quite specific about this:

> Put to death, therefore, whatever belongs to your earthly nature: sexual immorality, impurity, lust, evil desire and greed, which is idolatry. . . . But now you must rid yourselves of all such things as these: anger, rage, malice, slander, and filthy language from your lips. (Col 3:5-6)

Traditional spiritual theologies have provided the standard "cures" for these sins, and little more can be said to improve on them.[87] The manifold fruit of sin has been prodigiously illustrated in the more recent works. There is little that we can add to that here. Rather, we will focus on pride and its ramifications in some of the other deadly sins. Some of the sin's Asian fruit is worth looking into. The characteristic Asian reserve (euphemistically called modesty) may be loath to accept such exposés: nothing is more shameful (or unforgivable) than airing dirty linen publicly. But as Asian Christians, we need to deal with our besetting sins too if we are to make spiritual progress. How it is to be done, of course, is quite another matter.

Pride. Dorothy L. Sayers in her characteristically delightful way distinguishes between the "warm-hearted" (disreputable) sins like lust, anger and gluttony and "cold-hearted" (respectable) ones like covetousness, envy, sloth and pride.[88] Sayers's categories might be disputed. A Confucian culture always associates progress, whether moral or economic, with hard work. Thus sloth, at least the more common sort, is hardly respectable. Pride, on the other hand, is almost universally regarded as a respectable sin. Having one's pride injured is almost everywhere regarded as a just cause for retaliation.

How is it, then, that Christians have come to see pride as the first of the deadly sins? "Pride is the beginning of sin,"[89] according to Augustine. It is "undue exaltation, when the soul abandons Him to whom it ought to cleave as its end, and becomes a kind of end to itself."[90] By making the self supreme, pride perverts the truth of who we really are (only the creator can be supreme, not creature) and distorts *shalom*, "the universal flourishing, wholeness, and delight,"[91] based on it. Pride is the sin of the devil, who, according to John Milton, would rather rule in hell than serve in heaven.[92] Pride manifests itself in self-sufficiency, exaggerated ideas of one's own virtues, abilities or importance. It puts down others in order to exalt the self. It produces presumption (a false estimate of oneself, Rom 12:3), ambition (an inordinate love of honor or authority) and vanity (an inordinate desire to be thought well of).

The fruit of pride. Regardless of whether we are looking at the phenomenon from the perspective of the third-century desert fathers or late twentieth-century industrial societies, pride conceives and gives birth to all the other six deadly sins. Pride almost always elicits *envy* and resentment from other proud people. Envy is always directed against our fellow-creatures and consists in discontent with other people's good. The people who are objects of envy, however, are not spared the sin of envy themselves. Because they think too highly of themselves, they cannot bear to see others better than themselves. In order to put themselves ahead of others, the proud go on a relentless pursuit of things (*gluttony* and *greed*). The inevitable clash of interests between the proud results in "fights and quarrels" (Jas 4:1), sustained *anger,* hatred and cruelty.

Where does sloth come into the picture? According to Karl Barth, both pride and sloth reject God and put something else in God's place. One is active whereas the other is an "inactive action," but both stem from the same hatred of God.[93] In the New Testament sloth is condemned in no uncertain terms in the parable of the talents (Mt 25:28). Perhaps the servant's "inactive action" was so reprehensible because he did nothing but managed to produce a carefully contrived rationale for it. Doing nothing is, in a way, worse than doing wrong, "for it kills the potentiality of the personality and makes God's gift useless and barren, whereas doing wrong is at least still keeping the gift alive, and there always remains the chance of redirecting it aright."[94] In a modern industrial society, whether Western or Asian, overwork and not sloth would seem to be the more deadly sin.

But busyness may sometimes be an excuse for laziness. As Eugene Peterson observes, busy people are too lazy to take control of things, so they fit themselves into other people's demands.[95] Activities can be an excuse for spiritual inertia or *acedia,* an unwillingness to accept God as God, that is, his absolute claims on our lives. It is easier to be physically active in order to be spiritually indolent. A fast-paced life may also hide a pernicious boredom. According to Lyman, "the theater of industrial drama conceals a subtextual tragicomedy of grotesque *acedia*"[96] that gives rise to the overpowering demon of *lust.* Modern leisure (or the problem of what to do with it) is just as beguiling as the *daemon meridianus* (noontide demon) that hounded the desert monks.[97]

In Asia, sloth often takes the form of an ethic of easy acquiescence to the prevailing status quo. The consensual decision-making process, quite desirable in itself, can become an excuse for slothful thinking, slavish conformism and a means of manipulation for personal ends.[98] Tradition both in the church and in the larger culture is accepted uncritically and turned into sacrosanct traditionalism. Sloth would prefer to put up with the barely supportable burden of cultural dead weight than face the short-term pain of taking it to task in the interest of truth. In the Chinese context, the obligation of family ties has, under certain circumstances, managed to spawn a string of acedic and avaricious hangers-on. Overseas Chinese visiting relatives in mainland China are often flabbergasted by a greed that shows only the slightest pretense to modesty. From the mainlanders' point of view, the status their overseas relatives have risen to means that they are eternally obligated to help in every way, and their obligation to help is translated into "our right" to expect it.[99]

The cure for pride. If pride is the cardinal sin, humility is the only way forward. Scripture counsels humility (Jas 4:6; 1 Pet 5:5-6) and warns against having too high an estimate of oneself (Rom 12:3). Calvin underscores the importance of humility: "if you ask me concerning the precepts of the Christian religion, first, second, third, and always I would answer, 'Humility.'" Calvin realizes that the sinner does not willingly abandon his pride and seek after the true knowledge of God unless he is "overwhelmed by the awareness of his calamity, poverty, nakedness, and disgrace." Quoting Augustine, Calvin adds, "When anyone realizes that in himself he is nothing and from himself he has no help, the weapons within him are broken, the wars are over."[100] Similarly, for Luther, "the preacher's message must show men their own selves and their lamentable state, so as to make them humble and yearn for help."[101]

But it was left to the monastic tradition to specify how these counsels are to be carried out in practice. The Rule of Saint Benedict sets out systematically to teach monks the way of humility in twelve steps. Each step is associated with corresponding actions and attitudes. The first step is for the monk to "keep the fear of God before his eyes" by remembering all the commandments, meditating on the terrors of hell for the disobedient and constantly examining himself.[102] Some of the rules are still relevant today. For example, the rule on obedience (the third step) can help to draw us out of our self-centered world and overcome one of the more common forms of pride, namely, our modern narcissistic preoccupation.

Conclusion

The basic problem of spirituality is the problem of sin. But sin must be properly understood to be effectively combated. Understanding sin as both a relational problem and a most debilitating condition means that the resources needed for dealing with it are religious and not merely moral. We need more than an elaborate ascetical program; we need conviction concerning what God has done for the world and its sinful creatures. Only then will we have the spiritual resources to overcome "the sin which so easily besets us." What we need to do next is to elaborate on these resources, which are encapsulated in the Christian doctrine of salvation.

4

SALVATION &
THE LIFE
OF SPIRITUAL
PROGRESS

· · · · · · · · · · · · · · · · · · · ·

MANY EASTERN RELIGIONS UNDERSTAND SALVATION AS CONSISTING IN FOLLOW-
ing timeless precepts and principles.[1] Christianity, however, sees salvation as
a complex of events grounded in history. The truth of God is not esoteric
information, as it is in Gnosticism. As Rowan Williams has put it so poignantly,
"God 'utters' the life of Jesus, he 'speaks' an event, a human history; and so
he enters the fabric not merely of human verbal or conceptual exchange but
of human society, community, making it the *commixtio et communio Dei et
hominis.*"[2] Christian soteriology is set squarely within a historical framework
bounded on one side by historic covenant and on the other side by
eschatological fulfillment. The work of salvation is essentially God's work in
the history of a people: calling Abraham, delivering Abraham's descendants
from captivity and covenanting with them to be the people of Yahweh.

The ultimate fulfillment of the covenant is in Jesus Christ, whose coming
is the eschaton (Heb 1:2) and whose life of perfect obedience and self-sac-
rifice effectively brought deliverance from the captivity of sin, both for Israel
and for the rest of the world. Salvation history is the story of God's deliverance
within the historical process (although not confined to it). In all gnostic
religions salvation is deliverance from a transitory history to a timeless
eternity. In Neo-Platonism it is the freeing of the soul from bondage to the
material world to return to the bosom of the eternal, nameless One. In
Buddhism it is freedom from the cycle of karmic rebirths and entrance into

timeless nirvana. In these gnostic religions salvation is attained by manipulating certain spiritual techniques—ascetic disciplines such as contemplation and/or moral endeavor such as observing the eightfold path of Buddhism.

The wholeness that Christianity presents as the goal of life is quite different from wholeness in the gnostic religions. For the latter wholeness is essentially an ontological freedom that dissolves the self into some larger eternal reality. For Christianity it is an existential freedom understood strictly in personal terms: communion, love and fellowship. Personality rather than its extinction lies at the root of the Christian conception of the ultimately real. Christianity takes history with the utmost seriousness because the experience of personhood involves real continuity between the historical present and the reality beyond the present, which is traditionally called eternity. The term *eternity* needs to be carefully qualified in view of the distinctively Christian eschatological vision of the new creation, of which we are given an inkling in the resurrection of Jesus Christ.[3]

The Christian story is not primarily about how God in Jesus came to rescue sinners from some impending disaster. It is about God's work of initiating us into a fellowship and making us true conversational partners with the Father and the Son through the Spirit and, hence, with each other (1 Jn 1:1-4). Attaining heaven and avoiding hell represent just one aspect of the *koinonia* of God's extended family. This explains why heaven and hell do not receive any sustained focus in the Scriptures. The biblical writers avoid direct discussion of details about the hereafter (2 Cor 12:1-4). But they have bequeathed to us a rich vocabulary describing the nature of the life of fellowship (justification, regeneration, reconciliation and so on) and explaining it (as in the various hortatory sections of the Epistles). Above all, they furnish us with four Gospels, four related stories about Jesus, whose life and work made it all possible.

The task of spiritual theology is to describe and analyze the nature and effects of this story not just as facts but as the facts impinge on the person whose relationship with God has been fundamentally changed by the story. In the pursuit of this we will examine some key terms in the vocabulary of salvation that help clarify the story. In so doing we will answer a number of questions that are vital for spirituality. First, if Christians are people who are justified by faith, how is this spiritual reality translated into concrete historical existence? Second, if Christians are regenerated and sanctified, what specific shape does the regenerated and sanctified life take in daily living, interpersonal relationship and social life? In relation to this, the nature of the theological and cardinal virtues will have to be analyzed. Third, if the spiritual life is progressive, what is its goal? Finally, if life in Christ is received as a free gift (that is, by grace), what part does human effort play in furthering that life? The nature of grace is perhaps the most problematic issue for the development of a Protestant spiritual theology.

The Protestant Conception of Grace and the Problem of Ascetical Theology

Protestantism has encountered two related problems in developing a theology of the spiritual life, both of which go back to Augustine. Augustine had a rather bleak picture of humanity. He understood progress in Christian living in terms of God's ability to move people to act rather than in God's giving people the freedom to act, as did the Greek fathers: "Teach me so that I may act, not just know how I ought to act."[4] This doctrine is known as prevenient grace. From time to time it has been translated into some form of the quietist heresy, which teaches that the human will should not act in the absence of prior action by God. The second (and perhaps more serious) difficulty is Augustine's notion of grace as relational. Grace is not primarily a power that acts like a tonic to strengthen us—that would be Pelagianism—but the love and unmerited favor of God that comes preveniently, setting us free to respond in love. In Reformed theology the relational dimension of grace leaves no room for a concept of infused grace. Berkouwer, for instance, fears that any idea of infused grace might turn human beings into independent objects of interest.[5] Berkouwer sees regeneration in terms that are relational, not substantive. Grace refers to the restoration of interrupted fellowship with God. Following Kuyper, he argues that it is not the substance of human life that is changed but the direction.[6] (How a concept that relies on metaphors of seeds growing, rebirth and transformation of creation can be conceived of in purely relational terms is unclear.)

The problem of grace and work. The difficulty that this rather restricted concept of grace poses for spirituality can be clarified by an example. Helmut Thielicke in his *Theological Ethics* argues, rightly, that ethics must be grounded in right relationship with God, that is, justification by faith. Otherwise morality can become secularized and even "blasphemous."[7] But how is ethics related to the singular event of being declared righteous or of being given an "alien righteousness"? To pose the problem theologically, how is justification related to sanctification? At one level the relationship between justification and sanctification is quite straightforward: sanctification is a fruit of justification. The one who is in right relationship with God will bear the fruit of righteous living.

But this theological reality does not always transform itself into practical reality. As many Christians have learned (more often sooner than later), the changed relationship that justification brings about does not automatically translate into a changed life. Thus imputed righteousness could easily turn into legal fiction. Thielicke is fully aware of the difficulty. "[T]o say that works have to actualize and express the fact of justification is not to solve the ethical problem of Christian action, but in effect really to pose it for the first time."[8] Why are imperatives given in connection with good works if good works are the fruit of justification? Thielicke sees the relationship between the imperative and the "automatism" of the indicative in two ways. First, "the imperative . . . refers exclusively to the fact that I am set into a particular relationship to the Spirit, a relationship by virtue of which that automatic process itself is first set in motion."

Second, "there are certain conditions under which, in principle, the work of the Holy Spirit cannot take place . . . the action of man might well have some influence on these special conditions and on their removal, and therefore it could make sense to have an imperative which would demand such action."[9] It is Thielicke's view that the imperative is not the means to make us more holy (that takes place by grace alone). It puts in place the condition that makes it possible for grace to be fully operative. "If asceticism has any valid point at all, it can only be the fact that it enables me to sit loose to life and thereby makes me ready for new ventures in obedience."[10] Thielicke's approach to the problem has not eliminated a doctrine of the means of grace but has pushed it one step back by seeing imperatives not as means to make us better Christians or aid us in spiritual progress but as prerequisites for what is essentially God's work in us and for us. Psychologically, this takes the concept of merit out of our effort and retains more fully the doctrine of justification by faith: I don't do something in order to be more acceptable to God. But in the end what I do is still the means of grace. Unless I do these prerequisites, God's grace cannot be fully operative.

As another solution, Thielicke argues for the conjunction between divine action and human agency. The "automatic" fruit accruing from God's action does not cancel out human will; rather, God acts within human action.

Good works are not to be regarded simply as products of the renewed subjectivity, as though one whose heart was full now pressed on to action, as though he were "endowed" with a new dynamic and now sought to apply this dynamic and let it unfold. Possibly this latter process does play a role; but those strains within Pietism and the revival movements which find in it the essential connection between justification and sanctification are quite mistaken. The decisive process is something very different. It takes place in an objective relation to God, who in loving us becomes for us totally different. As the one who loves us he becomes, as far as we are concerned, the one who is loved by us. Our love and the acts which flow from it are not just a response to the preceding love of God (even if they take place promptly, spontaneously, and as a matter of course). They are not just a reaction, a second act. On the contrary, they are actually the reverse side of God's love. Or, to speak in terms of "active" and "passive," our love and good works—in short, our active ego—is the theater in which God does his acting. Luther says, "it is true to say concerning ourselves that, inasmuch as God works in us, we work—though 'work' here means actually that the one doing the acting is himself acted upon, moved, and led."[11]

The idea could not be more beautifully expressed, but what does it mean for spirituality? There are three possibilities. First, there is pietism, to which Thielicke gives only limited endorsement, which practically entails some felt "new dynamics" as a basis for action. Second, God's-action-in-our-action could be translated into a practical imperative: we need to act as proof that God is acting in us. Third, the imperative could be seen as God's appointed means of furthering the life of faith.

Some solutions. I have referred to Thielicke because he accentuates certain problems and offers solutions that are encountered again and again in the history of Protestant spirituality. The first solution is represented by the different enthusiastic movements. The Quakers would not act at all unless "moved" by the Spirit.[12] Proceeding along the spectrum of enthusiasm, we encounter spiritualities that stress varying degrees of passivity as the appropriate response to God's initiative. In the Higher Life and Keswick movements terms like *surrender* and *entire abandonment* feature prominently.[13] In early Pentecostalism the watchword was *tarrying*.

The second solution is represented best by John Calvin, whose understanding of the Christian life illustrates the outworking of what Thielicke calls the "motive of fruit." Calvin has much to say about the life of prayer and meditation.[14] But it is important to note the context in which he understood these disciplines. Book 3 of his *Institutes of the Christian Religion* begins with a question: "How do we receive those benefits which the Father bestowed on his only-begotten Son—not for Christ's own private use, but that he might enrich poor and needy men?" Calvin's answer is that we must be united with Christ if any of his benefits are to accrue to us. The benefits become truly ours by the "testimony of the Spirit." The "Holy Spirit is the bond by which Christ effectually unites us to himself."[15] Subjectively, we appropriate the benefits by faith, which is itself produced by the Spirit within us.[16]

But what is faith? Calvin defines it as "a firm and certain knowledge of God's benevolence toward the believers, founded upon the truth of the freely given promise in Christ, both revealed to our minds and sealed upon our hearts through the Holy Spirit."[17] (It is hard to miss the trinitarian dimension of the definition.) Faith denotes a certain kind of relationship with God. The life of prayer and meditation is but the living out of the life of faith. Faith directs believers' thoughts to God in prayer and in the contemplation of heavenly things. Thus growth in the Christian life may be said to be growth in the life of faith, which is the strengthening of the personal bond with God. It could not conceivably be a growth in grace, since grace is not a substantial reality within believers but a favorable disposition of God toward them.

The third solution is best exemplified by the Puritans. They produced sustained reflections on the theory and practice of the Christian life that were commonly known as "guides" to godliness.[18] They constantly appealed to the "use of means" as the way to advance the life of godliness. Theologically, they (following Calvin) give priority to faith. According to the influential Puritan theologian William Ames, faith is "the first act of spiritual life." Observance or duty is "the second act or operation flowing from that principle act." Faith and duty are set in a paradoxical relationship: "Although Faith always presuppose a knowledge of the Gospel, yet there is no saving knowledge in any . . . but what follows this act of the will, and depends upon it." In other words, faith is based on "a Divine Testimony . . . yet this testimony cannot be received without a pious affection of the will towards God." Faith, then, is both a cause as well as an effect of duty or the "means."[19] Another, Henry Scudder, observed that "if men will wait in the use of the means" such as "the Word, Sacrament, Prayer, Meditations, and holy conference, and communion of saints" then they will be able to "increase, strengthen, stir up, and inflame [the Spirit]."[20] The Puritan ascetic's position is perhaps best summed up by Richard Baxter:

> Some think, if they should thus fetch in their own comfort by believing and hoping, and work it out of Scripture promises, and extract it by their own thinking and studying, that then it would be a comfort of their own hammering out (as they say) and not the genuine joy of the Holy Ghost. A desperate mistake, raised upon a ground that would overthrow almost all duty, as well as this: which is, their setting the workings of God's spirit, and their own spirits in opposition, when their spirits must stand in subordination to God's. They are conjunct causes, cooperating to the producing of one and the same effect. God's Spirit worketh our comforts, by setting our own spirits awork upon the promises, and raising our thoughts to the place of our comforts.[21]

Grace as divine favor and power. Thornton calls ascetical theology "the technique of loving God" and observes that Augustine's emphasis on the priority of grace and the human response in love laid a sound foundation for spiritual theology but not necessarily its superstructure.[22] The same could be said about Calvin's doctrine of the Christian life, except that Calvin gives priority to the faith response[23] and sees love as the consequence of faith.[24] The Reformed tradition never developed an ascetical theology anything like "the technique of believing God," with the exception of certain Puritans. We must now inquire why no adequate superstructure followed the laying of a sound foundation.

When the Christian life is seen in terms of fostering a relationship, there is little concern with technical precision. In fact, techniques might even hinder the freedom, spontaneity and surprises that are thought to characterize an ideal personal relationship. There is no ascetical program for eliminating sins or cultivating virtues. When growth in the Christian life is seen as the cultivation of virtues, proper instruction in techniques of cultivation is essential.[25] Behind these two pictures of growth are two different conceptions of grace. The first presupposes a doctrine of grace as divine favor; the second, a doctrine of grace as endowment, an enabling gift.[26] Reformed theology has overemphasized the first and has treated the second with grave suspicion. But surely grace can be seen as both a favor and an infused quality in the soul. Relationships, after all, produce character, and character in turn is needed to sustain and enhance relationship. The two aspects of grace must be kept together, as indeed they are in Scripture. In Romans 5:1-4 the apostle Paul speaks of justification, peace with God and access to God (which are relational concepts) producing hope, which sustains the Christian in suffering. The end result is perseverance and character—objective virtues. And character in turn enables one to hope.

It is my position that any sustaining spiritual theology must keep the two aspects of grace together. We need a concept of grace as *God's* unmerited favor to undeserving sinners or the cultivation of virtues will be reduced to mere moralism. Without this concept the Christian saint cannot be distinguished from the Buddhist ascetic with his finely contoured physique or the Confucian gentleman. On the other hand, grace must also be understood as an empowering gift, or we cannot hope to develop any meaningful human response. It is in the second sense that Christian tradition distinguishes between a prevenient and a concomitant grace,[27] between a power that comes from without *(sine nobis)* and a power that works in us and with us *(in nobis et nobiscum)*—a distinction that lays the groundwork for ascetical theology. Their relationship is well summed up by Augustine: God "begins His influence by working in us that we may have the will, and He completes it by working with us when we have the will."[28]

The Protestant fear of virtues becoming an independent object of interest is valid only if virtues are abstracted from relationship. But if that happens, virtues are no longer virtues; they are the filthy rags of work righteousness. Such a fear is groundless when spiritual disciplines are recognized as the means of grace and virtues as the products of grace. The test of whether virtues are graces, not just good works, can be reduced to the question, Do they have their basis and goal in the theological virtues of faith, hope and charity, that is, in the fact that they are ultimately from God and to God? But in a practical sense, how do we tell the difference between the fruits of grace and legalistic striving? Thornton has once again applied the pastoral perspective to such a question.

> Pastorally, we are not concerned with grace *versus* free-will but with which comes first. How does one guide the habitual sinner? By an appeal to resist temptation, aided by hints from psychiatry, or by a prior stress on sacramental grace and co-operating prayer? What is our approach to one who has lost his faith? Is it in terms of rational argument or emotional appeal, or in terms of ontology, of the doctrine of Baptism, of the vicarious nature of the Church through which grace flows? What is the doctrine behind evangelistic preaching? Are we to stir up our hearers to make strong decisions or to respond to grace already given? Some of these questions are very difficult, but they cannot be answered in terms of expediency: they are questions of orthodoxy or heresy.[29]

It is not necessary to agree fully with Thornton concerning the exact "loci" of grace, but the principle is clear: the one condition that Christian spirituality must satisfy is that it must acknowledge the priority of grace in whatever way it comes, preveniently or concomitantly. In this connection, the theological virtues (as we shall see shortly) are crucial to any further discussion on the content of the spiritual life. But the theological virtues derive their specific character from the Christian story of salvation. That story has also produced a rich theological vocabulary that helps the church focus on the most important features of the story. It is to this rich language of Scripture and tradition that we now turn.

The Language of Salvation

Any attempt to deal with the variegated vocabulary of salvation must set certain limits. The apostle John tells us that if everything that Jesus said and did were recorded, the world's books would not be sufficient to contain it. We will focus on three key terms that sum up the basic contours of the Christian life when it is lived in faithfulness to the Christian story.[30] The three terms are *justification, sanctification* and *glorification,* chosen here because they are usually employed to define the three-part structure of a typical Reformed order of salvation *(ordo salutis)* that most Protestants are familiar with.[31] Taken together, they refer to the whole process in which a person turns from sin to God and progresses in holiness until attaining perfection in glory. The *ordo* suggests that salvation is not a single or punctiliar event. In Scripture salvation occurs in the perfect tense (that is, a completed action with continuing effects) as well as in the present (continuous) and future tenses.[32] Understanding salvation as progressive gives it a direction and a goal; understanding it as multifaceted gives it richness and depth. These understandings of salvation provide the conditions for a proper spiritual theology to develop. It is no wonder that popular evangelicalism, which overemphasizes the crisis conversion experience, continues to come up with ad hoc and piecemeal "spiritualities" but has yet to produce a systematic spiritual theology.

Justification. The Protestant doctrine of justification by faith, God's act of declaring the sinner righteous by virtue of the righteousness of Christ, is first and foremost a profound experiential reality.[33] Luther's own account of his experience is exemplary. He describes how the "righteousness of God" struck him with fear and provoked hatred at first because it was an impossible standard for anyone to attain, his own best efforts notwithstanding. But his understanding of the phrase changed as he meditated on it.

> I began to understand that "righteousness of God" as that by which the righteous person lives by the gift of God (faith); and this sentence, "the righteousness of God is revealed," to refer to a passive righteousness, by which the merciful God justifies us by faith, as it is written, "the righteous person lives by faith." This immediately made me feel as though I had been born again, and as though I had entered through open gates into paradise itself.[34]

Justification, for Luther, solves the problem of finding acceptance before a righteous God. God "reckons" the person righteous not on account of any righteousness that exists in the person but on account of Christ's righteousness. The "alien righteousness" of Christ provides a firm basis for personal assurance. Thus for Luther and the classical Protestant tradition in general the assurance of salvation is founded on a right relationship rather than on a virtuous life. Calvin is quite insistent on this: "For unless you first of all grasp what your relationship to God is, and the nature of his judgment concerning you, you have neither a foundation on which to establish your salvation nor one on which to build piety toward God."[35] Calvin further elaborated on the believer's justification by grounding it in his or her union with Christ, a union that is effected by the secret working of the Spirit.[36]

The problem lies in translating these theological realities into practical options for the Christian life. The conscientious Christian who asks, "How do I know that I am saved?" may already possess the correct theological answer. What that person is looking for is a personal assurance of salvation, a sense of being accepted in God's presence. Here the early Reformers were not of much help. They laid the theological foundation but left it to the next generation to build the superstructure. Calvin's internal testimony of the Spirit was developed into two major ramifications by the Puritans who claimed him as their forebear. One was an appeal to the hidden power (*arcana virtus*) of the Spirit as the direct source of assurance as well as the means for dealing with other practical concerns. This approach was exemplified by John Cotton (1584-1652), whose teaching led directly or indirectly to the Antinomian heresy in New England in 1636-1637. Understanding how Cotton converted the testimony of the Spirit into a practical option is important to achieving an appreciation of the essential nature of enthusiastic spirituality. In his work *The Way of Life* (1641) Cotton presents his version of the *ordo salutis*. The whole work of salvation centers in the "Spirit of grace" and is wholly predicated on the divine initiative: "First, if God be pleased to open thine eyes . . ."[37] But this does not imply complete passivity. Cotton repeatedly challenges the Christian to exercise faith, which is understood as a kind of power to receive "the quickning Spirit." But it is a faith that is expressed as a benign action rather than an active apprehending: one yields and gives way to the Spirit. This sort of reflex action reemerged centuries later in the Keswick movement.

Do but give way for the Lord Jesus Christ to dwell in us, then we receive a mighty power of a quickening spirit from him, quickening us with assurance of pardon of sin, and power of grace and consolation.[38]

With the possible exception of extreme enthusiasts like the Quakers, what is characteristic of enthusiastic spirituality generally is that the divine initiative is expressed in terms of passive action. This often entails giving more detailed attention to the workings of the Spirit and enjoining the appropriate passive response. Richard Sibbes (1577-1635), another Puritan in this tradition, constantly appeals to the intricate workings of the Spirit in enabling enjoyment of "the glorious feast of the gospel." The Spirit of illumination removes the veil from our eyes and "doth breed a taste in the soul" and "alters the taste and relish of the will and affections." For the one wishing to appropriate the benefits of the gospel personally, Sibbes counseled *letting* certain actions be done on oneself: "Let us labour to have this veil *taken* off; let us labour to have the eyes of our understanding *enlightened*, to have our hearts *subdued* to belief; let us take notice of our natural condition,"[39] more than active pursuit of certain duties.

The second ramification of Calvin's pneumatology was pursued by the Puritan ascetics, who recognized in principle the "inner operation of the Holy Spirit" but paid scant *direct* attention to it. They chose to focus on the means of grace and duties. Implied in this approach is that the Spirit works mediately in nature, so that someone who focuses on duties is in effect affirming the priority of grace.

> The less able we are to believe of ourselves, the more careful should we be to use the means that God hath ordained, that we might obtain it. Marriage was never held superfluous or unnecessary for the propagation of mankind, because the reasonable soul is not generated by our parents, but immediately created and infused by God. That faith is the sole gift of God, wholly infused, not partly acquired by us, should rather incite than anyway abate our endeavour for attaining it.[40]

Regarding assurance of salvation, the ascetics' approach is not to wait for the internal testimony of the Spirit but to obtain it indirectly by some external sign like contrition of heart, which can be generated by intensive meditation. Thomas Hooker defined contrition of heart as "nothing else, but namely, when a sinner by the sight of sin, and vileness of it, and the punishment due to the same, is made sensible of sin, and is made to hate it, and hath his heart separated from the same."[41] One is "made sensible of sin" through "daily and serious meditation and apprehension" of one's own sins until sin is seen "clearly," "convictingly" and "nakedly in its own proper colours."[42]

Modern Christians may disagree with much of the Puritan ascetical program, such as Hooker's. What the Puritan ascetics demonstrated is that an essentially Protestant doctrine of justification by faith, which brings a person into a relationship of acceptance before the righteous God, is not incompatible with a full-fledged asceticism. With regard to assurance of salvation, the works of the ascetic and the enthusiast are ultimately complementary. Whether assurance is experienced as a direct testimony of the Spirit or through some ascetical discipline that acknowledges the indirect working of the Spirit in the means of grace, what is finally borne out by both is that the Christian experiences salvation as an intimate relationship with God and discovers full acceptance by God on account of Christ.

Life with the Father through the Son is a far cry from a life spent calculating the impersonal and iron law of karma. It is at the level of spirituality that the doctrine of justification by faith often strikes a resounding chord in the heart of the ordinary Hindu, Buddhist and Confucianist. Ultimately all people long for the very reality that the doctrine so carefully elaborates and schematizes, namely, being accepted by God and by oneself.

These days the doctrine of assurance is hardly an issue with most

Christians, not because they understand the doctrine better but because the doctrine has been watered down. Modern Christians proclaim *their* acceptance of Christ rather than Christ's acceptance of them! Justification by faith has simply become a quick fix for a troubled conscience. When Christ is being ingested like health pills by people desperately searching for good feelings, someone needs to reissue the challenge: How can you be sure that you are accepted before a righteous God? It should force those accustomed to superficialities to reexamine the deeper religious basis of their faith.

The doctrine of assurance highlights a dimension of justification that Reformation theology has generally overlooked. It is quite apparent from the testimony of Luther and subsequent Christians troubled by a lack of assurance that what they were looking for was an assured basis on which to build an indubitable knowledge of who they were before God. Because justification is based on the imputed righteousness of Christ, which completely satisfies divine justice,[43] assurance has to be complete and absolute. This awareness of what assurance entails gave Puritans in the next century no small mental anguish. In their quest for assurance they were expressing a universal spiritual instinct that exists in all the children of God, namely, the instinct for perfection. Assurance, therefore, may be said to represent the perfectionistic instinct redirected to the intellect rather than the will. We will return to this subject later.

Sanctification. The order of salvation should be seen as a logical rather than a chronological order. Sanctification does not represent a "higher stage" than justification. Justification considers the Christian life from a relational point of view, while sanctification views it from the perspective of personal growth and development. Justification is instantaneous only in the sense that it involves a juridical act by God. In Calvin's words, the person "has God to witness and affirm his righteousness," that is, the imputed righteousness of Christ.[44] But the assurance of "the acceptance with which God receives us into his favor as righteous men" is an enduring state, not a steppingstone that leads to a second stage.

A problem in seeing the *ordo* as stages (as in the Wesleyan holiness, Keswick and Pentecostal movements) rather than as simultaneous, ongoing realities is the tendency to think of justification as a lower level of spiritual existence that is outgrown and left behind once the higher stage is reached. Groups that follow this thinking try to upstage each other by emphasizing their distinctives and demonstrating the deficiencies of the others. The overall result is truncated spiritualities incapable of looking beyond their narrowly defined self-identities. Thus the Christian and Missionary Alliance, which taught a doctrine of divine healing very similar to the Pentecostals' doctrine, became their most ardent opponents over the issue of tongues. Pentecostals, on the other hand, tend to look disdainfully at their holiness predecessors as having "not yet arrived."

Sanctification is traditionally referred to as both instantaneous and progressive. Instantaneous sanctification usually refers to the initial work of conversion, which reorients the person toward God. In the parlance of spiritual theology, this represents the infusion of habitual grace, which is defined as "a new principle of life transforming the soul and making it and its action godlike."[45] While many Christians can point to a particular moment when that "turnaround" event occurred, it is actually a continuing event of daily dying to self and being raised anew. From the human standpoint, it is the work of repentance, which is a "continuing discipline that we undertake at increasingly deeper levels, bringing more and more of ourselves to God in humility and trust."[46] It is not a work we can undertake by ourselves; it is always experienced as a response to a prior revelation that utterly humbles us as we see ourselves as we really are. In short, it is a work of grace.

Grace, as already noted, is both God's favorable disposition toward undeserving sinners and a transforming power in the soul. Sanctification primarily concerns grace in the second sense. It represents a progressive "more and more."[47] Real progress in sanctification depends on actual grace, which is "a supernatural and transitory power which God gives us to enlighten the mind and strengthen the will so that we may act according to his will."[48] Actual grace works in various ways. It works preveniently and concomitantly. It works directly and indirectly, miraculously and providentially. It is important for a comprehensive spiritual theology to recognize the workings of grace in all these ways.

The preponderance of emphasis today is on the conjunctive working of grace in creation. This is doubtlessly the result of a felt need in the church for deeper involvement in the world. Thus the papal encyclical *Evangelium Vitae* sees evangelization as the church's "deepest identity" with the world. It includes not just the proclamation of the gospel of life but also the celebration of all aspects of life in God as a witness to that gospel, including the "daily heroism" of taking care of the family, organ donations and such like.[49] On the other hand, grace must not become so diffused in the world that it loses its theological character—a problem that can be prevented by recognizing grace as a direct, prevenient and miraculous operation.[50]

Sanctification is an ongoing process of growth in conformity to the image of Christ. It has to do ultimately with the formation of virtues—replacing bad habits or vices with good ones. The idea that virtues are good habits does not mean that virtue is merely a matter of repeating an act over and over again. The key idea is growth toward an ideal, which, for Christians, is Christlikeness and deepening communion with God through Christ. Protestantism generally prefers to identify this process with the cultivation of the fruit of the Spirit (Gal 5:22-23). Catholicism treats it under the different categories of virtues.[51] But the singular emphasis of both is that the goal of sanctification is not the creation of an independent human quality, an object of admiration. That would be the most hideous form of pride, the exact opposite of the truly virtuous life. Virtues are indeed intrinsic values, but they cannot exist as qualities independent of relationship to God. As Augustine puts it, "Either virtue exists beyond the soul, or if we are not allowed to give the name of virtue to the habit and disposition of the wise soul, which can exist only in the soul, we must allow that the soul follows after something else in order that virtue may be produced in itself." This "something else" is none other than God himself.[52]

All virtues are ultimately theological. The cardinal virtues must be sanctified by the theological virtues. Together they offer an essential summary of the nature of the sanctified life. The theological virtues are faith, hope and charity. That they are usually mentioned in this order may reflect the greater familiarity with 1 Corinthians 13. The order is faith, love and hope in 1 Thessalonians 1:3, while in Colossians 1:4-5, faith and love are said to spring from hope, thus giving logical priority to hope (see also Rom 5:2-5; Gal 5:5-6; 1 Thess 5:8; Heb 10:22-24). Calvin, as noted previously, gives first priority to faith, while the medieval theologians see love as definitive. According to St. Thomas, "he who is perfect in charity is perfect in the spiritual life."[53] For St. Bernard, growth in the spiritual life is growth in love. One may begin with love of self for self's sake, proceed to love of God for self's sake, advance to love of God for God's sake and finally end in love of self for God's sake.[54]

A similar idea is found in John Wesley's doctrine of Christian perfection. To the question, What is Christian perfection? he gives this answer: "The loving God with all our heart, mind, soul and strength. This implies that no wrong temper, none contrary to love, remains in the soul; and that all the thoughts, words, and actions are governed by pure love."[55] There are good reasons for seeing love as the primary virtue just as pride is seen as the root sin. Loving God and neighbor are the two greatest commandments, according to Jesus in response to an inquirer (Mt 22:35-39). The apostle Paul regards love as the fulfillment or the summary of all other commandments (Rom 13:8-10). Furthermore, if the basic character of God is love, then the perfection of the Christian life must be defined in terms of that characteristic. But a vague concept of love is not adequate for spiritual life. Love is concretely expressed in the other virtues. Thus in 1 Corinthians 13, love is specified as being "patient . . . kind . . . does not envy . . . does not boast" (compare Rom 12:9-21).

The theological virtues are so called because they are God-directed virtues. Love clings to God as the "chief good," according to Augustine.[56] Faith holds on to the promises given by God in Jesus Christ, and hope lays hold on the future reality, the fullness of grace given at the revelation of Jesus Christ (1 Pet 1:13). All three are closely linked to the trinitarian economy of salvation. Thus love is commonly associated with the Father, faith with Jesus Christ and hope with the Spirit, who both inspires hope and guarantees it (Rom 8:23; 15:13; 2 Cor 1:22; 5:5). In the familiar language of John 3:16, the *love* of God is revealed in the gift of his Son, in whom Christians place their *faith*. Out of that faith relationship, they are given the *hope* of eternal life. The theological virtues specify in a concrete manner the essentially trinitarian nature of the Christian's relationship with God as the basis for Christian moral development.[57] Love, faith and hope are the key concepts for telling the Christian story, and they give to the moral life its distinct Christian signature. It would not be correct to assert that love, faith and hope do not exist in other religions, but they do not have the same significance. They may play a minor role in their stories or no role at all. The stories of other religions may be constructed around other virtues. In Buddhism perfection is schematized around rooting out the cardinal sin of ignorance and cultivating right knowledge.[58]

While the theological virtues are God-directed, the cardinal virtues—prudence, justice, fortitude and temperance—are directed toward the world. They are not distinctively Christian; in fact, they go back to the Stoics and were already well established by Plato's time. Christianity sanctified them with the theological virtues and gave them a new basis. This was what Augustine did when he interpreted the cardinal virtues as different expressions of the theological virtue of love.

As to the virtue leading us to a happy life, I hold virtue to be nothing else than perfect love of God. For the fourfold division of virtue I regard as taken from four forms of love. For these four virtues . . . I should have no hesitation in defining them: that temperance is love giving itself entirely to that which is loved; fortitude is love readily bearing all things for the sake of the loved object; justice is love serving only the loved object, and therefore ruling rightly; prudence is love distinguishing with sagacity between what hinders it and what helps it. The object of this love is not anything, but only God, the chief good, the highest wisdom, the perfect harmony. So we may express the definition thus: that temperance is love keeping itself entire and incorrupt for God; fortitude is love bearing everything readily for the sake of God; justice is love serving God only, and therefore ruling well all else, as subject to man; prudence is love making a right distinction between what helps it towards God and what might hinder it.[59]

Take, for example, the virtue of temperance. It is a moderating quality that discourages excessive indulgence, especially in the areas of taste and touch. No one would deny that it is a desirable quality in and of itself. From this root virtue have come other virtues like abstinence, sobriety, chastity, meekness, clemency, modesty and eutrapelia (moderation in recreation).[60] But for Augustine, what determines an intemperate enjoyment of a thing is whether it "turns us away from the laws of God and from the enjoyment of His goodness" and thus prevents us from totally cleaving to God in love.[61] Augustine had earlier defined love as cleaving to the object loved;[62] in this sense, nothing is to be loved except what can be loved for God's sake. Nothing must blur our vision of God as the "chief good" in himself (love), as the chief good for me (hope), and as the highest truth (faith).[63]

Thus, when it comes to cultivating the virtue of temperance, there is a marked difference between an approach that treats it merely as a moral quality and Augustine's, which treats it as a theological virtue. Someone who understands temperance as a moral quality might, for example, counsel self-denial and sublimation of sensible desires.[64] But for Augustine, "the whole duty of temperance . . . is to put off the old man and to be renewed in God . . . to turn the whole love to things divine and unseen." The object of the soul's gaze is not things that are seen but things that are unseen, "for the things which are seen are temporal, but the things which are not seen are eternal."[65]

Taking a cue from Augustine that prudence is "love making a right distinction between what helps it toward God and what might hinder it," it is something that goes far beyond the commonsense ability to distinguish between different courses of action in a given situation and then choose the one that is best. Rather, Christian prudence is a wisdom rooted in a distinctive life. This is why it comes in the form of a paradox: Be wise as serpents and innocent as doves (Mt 10:16). The paradox is necessary in the light of the exacting demands placed on those who bear the good news. They are to trust fully in God to provide for their basic needs (v. 10). They are to rely wholly on the Spirit of the Father speaking through them when they encounter opposition from those who by worldly standards are far wiser (vv. 17-20). They must implicitly hold on to the words of Jesus to protect them in the face of the dangers to which they will be exposed when they proclaim the good news (vv. 24-31). It is in these extreme situations they are called on to exercise a supernatural prudence that goes beyond commonsense discretion. This is wisdom rooted in the story of the cross which, paradoxically, reveals God's hidden wisdom even as it appears foolish to the world (1 Cor 1:18-31).

Augustine's point should not be passed over lightly. All too often discussions of the virtues, even among Christians, have tended to divorce them from the Christian story, either in the interest of "relevance" or on the false assumption that virtues can be objectively defined and that these definitions are universally valid. The theological virtues "ensure that the Christian moral life remains radically distinct from mere ethical culture."[66] We have already seen that a Western concept of justice tied to human rights has been severely criticized by "vision" ethicists for its assumed universality.[67] More significantly, unless the virtues are interpreted theologically, they will remain only tenuously connected to the Christian life, with disastrous consequence for Christian spirituality. If faith, hope and charity are only superfluous adornments for a far more exciting and down-to-earth ethic, then why retain them at all in our ethical program? Christian spirituality becomes only a pious cliché used to describe what is essentially moral development. The Augustinian connection between the theological virtues and the cardinal virtues means, at least as far as Christianity is concerned, that the cardinal virtues cannot become independent qualities. Only in the context of this connection can we speak of Christian formation as virtue formation and vice versa.

The Augustinian connection also implies that the theological virtues cannot be considered apart from the cardinal virtues. When the theological virtues are isolated, they become disconnected from the vital issues of our historical existence. Spirituality is turned into a sanctimonious longing for the pie in the sky. The sanctified life must be lived in the world, which demands the exercise of temperance, prudence, fortitude and justice. Further, if the cardinal and theological virtues are unified in the sanctified life, then no single virtue can exist apart from the others and still remain essentially Christian. In this connection, we must question the appropriateness of viewing Christian involvement in the world largely, if not exclusively, in terms of justice. Does not Christian prudence have something to say about how justice ought to be carried out? Are there not situations where issues like ecology are better served not by the naive identification of culprits and victims but by a more nuanced exercise in temperance in the interest of a more basic (that is, theological) concern, such as love of God's creation as well as creatures, including the culprits?[68] When virtues are no longer understood within the Christian story, they are in danger of being read in terms of other stories. Thus what is alleged to be universal justice may turn out to be a justice defined by liberal-democratic ideals.

Having considered the Augustinian connection between the theological and the cardinal virtues, we are now well placed to answer the question of how the virtues are formed. But first we need to consider two related issues. The first has to do with the specification of virtues in Christian character. Because the cardinal virtues do not grow independently but out of the theological virtues, it is perhaps not in the best interest of Christian spirituality to inquire too deeply into the names and number of virtues that make up the Christian moral life. This is because virtues do not have the same logic as vices. Any one vice is a work of the flesh and is sufficient to evidence the flesh (Gal 5:19) and therefore has to be dealt with specifically. But it does not follow that any one virtue or even a "bag of virtues" tells us anything about the Christian character. Christian character is not the sum total of so many virtues but is reflected in the quality of the virtues present in one's life and in the way they are brought together as part of a coherent life of virtue, a single "fruit of the Spirit" (Gal 5:22).

Situations and circumstances may call for a certain virtue as the appropriate response (like temperance at a sumptuous banquet), but it must be a response that is consistent with Christian character shaped by faith, hope and charity. It is conceivable that the circumstance in which a person is placed may determine the frequency or rarity of opportunities for certain virtues to develop or to remain relatively undeveloped. These differentials in and of themselves do not essentially affect the quality of the Christian's spiritual life.[69] For instance, a Christian living in an environment of persecution may be called on more frequently to exercise the virtue of fortitude and may have actually developed it to a high degree. But that virtue by itself does not necessarily make him or her more Christlike unless it is the avenue by which faith, hope and charity are exercised. The same fortitudinous person in a different environment (a "free" country) may find temperance sorely lacking. Thus what is expected of all Christians everywhere is living out the Christian life and responding Christianly to any given situation.

This means that the primary focus should be on the growth of the theological virtues and only derivatively on the cardinal virtues. But this is not to say that the cardinal virtues are of secondary importance. If the cardinal virtues are ultimately dependent on the theological virtues, they in turn are the means by which the theological virtues are developed. It may well be that through the avenue of abstinence (one form of temperance) one comes to see more clearly the dispensability of things seen and the far-surpassing value of things unseen and so detach oneself from the one to cling to the other. Similarly, through fortitude true Christian hope may emerge. Many Christians under persecution have testified to how patient endurance of suffering has deepened their hope. If Christian character is needed to produce virtue, acts of virtue in faith, hope and charity in turn form Christian character.

The circumstantial nature of virtue formation raises the second issue, namely, the relationship between Christian virtues and their cultural expressions. Just as sins find specific cultural expressions (see chap. 3), so do virtues. This is to be expected, since virtues do not exist as abstract principles but are found among people living in specific sociocultural contexts. Even *Christian* virtues, in the sense explained above, are sometimes expressed in widely divergent ways. As Bernard T. Adeney has amply illustrated, Christians from different cultural contexts seldom share the same understanding of what it means to apply such Christian virtues as justice and honesty.[70]

Take, for instance, the principle of justice. We may all agree on its formal definition as an abstract principle. Yet, in real life, it is not always understood or practiced in the same way. A society that employs the egalitarian principle often expresses the concept of a just society in terms of individuals rights. But a hierarchical society may see it in terms of reciprocal obligations. Perhaps a more concrete example might help us at this point. How is the virtue of justice to be concretely realized in a Confucian society? If we take the Confucian value of the five relationships (see p. 251, n. 53), the Christian virtue of justice in the family might well be expressed in the father's unmitigated responsibility to raise up his children "in the fear of the Lord" and the children's responsibility to render *lifelong* filial piety to their parents.[71] Similarly, the relationship between the ruler and the ruled requires that the ruler be *inherently* virtuous. Only in this way does a ruler possess the "mandate of heaven" to rule.[72] The ruled reciprocate by rendering obedience.

Confucian society recognizes no distinction between public and private morality in rulers, unlike the West, which does not see personal morality as absolutely essential to good public leadership. It becomes important only when it impinges on the ruler's ability to exercise effective leadership. Personal goodness alone does not ensure continuation in public office (as former U.S. president Jimmy Carter found out), whereas in the Chinese context a ruler's position is secure as long as his moral authority is intact, or at least not suspect in the public eye.

This predominantly Chinese way of ordering society has both a positive and a negative result. Positively, it requires a certain virtuous life—a spirituality—as the primary qualification if not the sine qua non for leadership. This is important in a world where the qualification for leadership is personal charisma rather than personal virtue. Christian organizations are sometimes tempted to do the same, which explains why morally discredited evangelists can continue to enjoy a successful ministry. On the negative side, it becomes a source of institutional stagnation and deep frustration for the younger leaders. In both the Asian state and the Asian church it is not uncommon for leaders to continue to exert considerable moral authority after they have formally retired from office and have lost their effectiveness as leaders. The deep irony is that usually the old leader himself would be the first to acknowledge the need for "new blood" in the institution. But the new blood is incapable of rejuvenating the institution as long as the old blood remains. In such a context the perfection of virtue would seem to require the cultivation of a certain kind of *kenosis,* the willingness to make oneself to become literally nothing, so that the ruled and the younger leaders would not be obliged to constantly defer to the moral authority of "the grand old sage."

We see, then, that Christian virtue and cultural values sustain a dialectical relationship to each other. While cultural values shape the way Christian virtues are expressed, Christian virtues, as a coherent pattern of living out the Christian story, must challenge values that contradict the Christian story. Only in maintaining this dialectic can the Christian be theologically and culturally authentic.

We must now return to our original question, How are the virtues formed so that they come to constitute one's character? The answer in Christian tradition has been quite consistent: virtues are formed by acts. This teaching found its fullest elaboration in Aquinas and has hardly been improved upon since.[73] Contemporary moralists often invoke this principle. C. S. Lewis once observed, "When you are behaving as if you loved someone, you will presently come to love him."[74] Similarly, M. Scott Peck tells us that his own way of overcoming shyness was a principle learned from Alcoholics Anonymous: "Fake it to make it."[75]

However, when it comes to virtue formation, not any action will do. All actions are habit forming or habit reinforcing, but to acquire a certain virtue that is not there requires courageous action, acting against a host of other contrary habits. This explains why many good intentions are never carried out or, if carried out, the actions are sporadic and quickly fizzle out. A vicious cycle is operating here. In order for actions to begin forming a virtue, there first needs to be a certain predisposition of the will to begin the action, that is, some kind of virtue to enable one to act. But this is what is precisely lacking. The cry of Paul, "Wretched man that I am! Who will deliver me?" (Rom 7:24 RSV), is certainly one with which most people can readily identify. His own answer is "through Jesus Christ" (v. 25). The Christian story tells us that even at the most basic level of human action, it is still by God's enabling that we can act. Catholicism identifies this grace as the gift of "infused virtue,"[76] while Protestantism (insofar as it has a concept of grace as enablement) might call it prevenient grace. St. Thomas is also quite clear that no single act is adequate to form a *habitus* or disposition.[77] It takes intentional, repeated actions of *growing* intensity for virtues to grow. The principle of virtue formation through acts is extremely important, since all ascetical practices must finally come to rest on it.

Glorification or Christian Perfection

If the Christian life is a life of progress, a question that naturally arises is how that life can be characterized as it progresses. Traditional Protestant theology, which emphasizes the relational character of the Christian life, has tended to treat growth with less precision and to see its completion in the consummation beyond history (glorification). Progress is simply progress of faith. "Perfection is not sanctity but faith," says P. T. Forsyth.[78] Progress is not clearly marked out into beginner, proficient and perfect stages, as in St. Thomas. The "more and more" is explained in terms of maturity or Christlikeness or some other ethical concept. In the Reformed tradition, which is mainly concerned with the assurance of faith, spiritual progress is seen more as the overcoming of doubt that stems from human frailty.[79] Within such a schema it is hardly surprising that ideas of perfection would meet with general suspicion.[80] Yet the doctrine of perfection remains within the larger Christian tradition; it is not a peripheral doctrine. It will not do, therefore, simply to dismiss it as a sectarian aberration. The conclusion that Flew came to so many years ago still bears quoting:

> The doctrine of Christian perfection—understood not as an assertion that a final attainment of the goal of the Christian life is possible in this world, but as a declaration that a supernatural destiny, a relative attainment of the goal which does not exclude growth, is the will of God for us in this world and is attainable—lies not merely upon the by-paths of Christian theology, but upon the high road. To this declaration some of the greatest theologians have set their seal.[81]

However perfection is defined, a number of common ideas can be clearly delineated. First, absolute or sinless perfection is not attainable in this life; it can never be a once-for-all, fixed accomplishment. On this side of eternity there cannot be any final arrival. Even the Quakers, at least in the later, more reflective phase of their history, did not advocate sinless perfection:

> Because we have urged the necessity of a perfect freedom from sin, and a thorough sanctification in body, soul, and sprit, whilst on this side the

grace, by the operation of the holy and perfect Spirit of our Lord Jesus Christ, according to the testimony of the holy scripture, we are made (i.e. represented as being) so presumptuous, as to assert the fullness of perfection and happiness to be attainable in this life: whereas we are not only sensible of those human infirmities that attend us, whilst clothed with flesh and blood; but know that here we can only "know in part, and see in part": the perfection of wisdom, glory, and happiness, being reserved for another and better world.[82]

Wesley is quite adamant that "neither love, nor the 'unction of the Holy One,' makes us infallible."[83] Similarly, Asa Mahan, one of the founders of the victorious life movement in 1874 (better known as the Keswick Convention), sums up his teaching on Christian perfection in this way:

Holiness, in a creature, may . . . be perfect, and yet progressive—progressive, not in its nature, but in degree. To be perfect, it must be progressive in the sense last mentioned, if the powers of the subject are progressive. He is perfect in holiness, whose love at each successive moment corresponds with the extent of his powers.[84]

Second, Christian perfection has to do with the perfection of love. Perfection, according François Fénelon, is total self-abandonment to God in love: "We must renounce ourselves, forget ourselves, lose ourselves, enter into thy interests, O my God, against our own. To have no will, no glory, no peace but thine. In a word, it is to love thee without loving ourselves."[85] And if self comes into consideration, it is always for God's sake. Here Fénelon harks back to a theme of Bernard, the fourth degree of love:

It is not that the man who loves without interest does not care for the reward. He cares for it in so far as it is of God, and not in so far as it is his own interest. He wants it because God wants him to want it. It is the order, not his own interest, that he seeks in it. He cares for himself, but he only cares for himself for love of God, as a stranger would, and for the sake of loving what God has made.[86]

Perfection, agrees Mahan, "implies the entire absence of all selfishness, and the perpetual presence and all pervading influence of pure and perfect love."[87] In the Wesleyan tradition the focus of perfection is more on the quality of Christian life. This is why perfection is equated with "entire sanctification."[88] But in the Catholic tradition purity of life is an important prerequisite; the real goal, however, is union with God or the beatific vision.[89] The pursuit of God in love is done with focused intention. There must be "simplicity . . . in intention" that "reaches out after God" and "purity in feelings" that "catches hold and tastes," says Thomas à Kempis.[90] The lover of God is never at rest until finally united with the Beloved.

We do not want merely to *see* beauty, though, God knows, even that is bounty enough. We want something else which can hardly be put into words—to be united with the beauty we see, to pass into it, to receive it into ourselves, to bathe in it, to become part of it.[91]

This is the singular reality that occupied the great mystics of the church.[92] We could perhaps do no better than quote, again from Fénelon, one of the most moving prayers in the mystical tradition:

O my God, O love, love thyself in me! In this way thou wilt be loved as thou art lovable. I only want to live to be consumed before thee, as a lamp burns ceaselessly before thine altars. I do not exist for myself at all. It is only thou who existest for thine own self. Nothing for me, all for thee. . . . Love on, O love! Love in thy weak creature! Love thy supreme beauty! O beauty, O infinite goodness, O infinite love: burn, consume, transport, annihilate my heart, make it a perfect holocaust![93]

Among Protestants who developed the mystical theme in their theology the most notable were the Puritan ascetics. From the "godly" bishop Joseph Hall to Richard Baxter, this theme became quite prominent in their later years. It is closely linked to their concept of heavenly meditation. The Christian, according to Hall, is one who is "heavenly-minded."

[He] walks on earth, but converses in heaven: having his eyes fixed on the invisible, and enjoying a sweet communion with his God, and Saviour. . . . The heaven of heavens is open to none but him; thither his eyes pierceth, and beholds those beams of inaccessible glory, which shines in no face but his.[94]

Hall counsels the devout soul drawing nearer to his final destination to strip his contemplation of all "materiality" and concentrate more and more on the divine essence itself.

Divest thyself therefore . . . of all materiality, both of objects, and apprehensions; and let thy pure, renewed, and illuminated intellect work only upon matter spiritual and celestial: And above all, propose unto thyself, and dwell upon that purest, perfectest, simplest, blessest Object the glorious and incomprehensible Deity. . . . Be thou, O my soul, ever swallowed up in the consideration of that self-being Essence, whom all created spirits are not capable sufficiently to admire. . . . Thou canst not hope yet to see him as he is, but lo, thou beholdest where he dwells in light inaccessible; the sight of whose very outward verge is enough to put thee into perpetual ecstacy.[95]

Baxter too believes that the work of "complacential contemplation" belongs to those who are more advanced in godliness. The Christian life is a process by which the soul grows "from the more troublesome (but safe) operations of fear, to the more high and excellent operations of complacential love, even as it hath more of the sense of the love of God in Christ and belief of the heavenly life which it approacheth."[96] In urging deeper contemplation, many Puritans often resorted to the language of Bernardine mysticism. One such was Nathaniel Ranew:

> Let meditation be carried up to admiration; not only should we be affected, but transported, rapt up, and ravished with the beauties and transcendencies of heavenly things. Act meditation to admiration, endeavour the highest pitch, coming the nearest to the highest patterns, the patterns of saints and angels in heaven whose actings are the purest highest ecstacies and admiration.[97]

The mystics claim that this intentional pursuit of God elicits a response from God that bathes the soul with inexpressible delight. The mystics often compare union with God to the consummation of love in marriage (sometimes in explicitly sensual terms). Sometimes the focus they give to that experience resembles selfish indulgence, but they are simply being true lovers. As C. S. Lewis puts it, "Marriage is the proper reward for a real lover, and he is not a mercenary for desiring it."[98] It would be a great mistake, therefore, to think that they are seeking spiritual experiences for themselves, looking for cheap thrills. The "greatest saints," observes Kenneth Kirk, "have always recognized that to make enjoyment, even though it be a communal enjoyment, the goal of life, is to import a motive less than the purest into ethics. . . . [Panhedonism] represented something in essence at once immoral and un-Christian."[99] The great Christian mystics never saw love as "a private affair between Christ and the individual, but that the real measure of our love for Christ is our love for others."[100] According to Bernard, a saint is one who has

> shown himself benevolent and charitable; who has lived humanely among men, keeping back nothing for himself, but using to the common advantage of all every grace that he possesses; who has regarded himself as a debtor to all men, to friend and foe, to wise and foolish alike. Such as these, being humble at all times, were useful to all.[101]

These characteristics of Christian perfection have always provided the spiritual resources from which fresh understandings of the Christian life have been built to this day. Thus, in a way, Moltmann's revisioning of modern society based on God's coming kingdom can be seen as extending this doctrine into the social reality. For example, the continuing quest for Christian perfection guards against any wild ideas about final earthly utopias of human origin, while the emphasis on love represents the center of human solidarity and social relationships, including international relations.[102]

The doctrine of Christian perfection completes the essential features of Christian spirituality. The life of faith that begins with our being accepted by God through Christ must continue to grow in love by means of various disciplines. Love of God is the only goal toward which all the ascetical disciplines are aimed. But this love of God always overflows to the neighbor. Mystical union, or whatever we choose to call it, is but the proper end of a life of fellowship with God that begins at justification. Without the idea of Christian perfection our spiritual theology would remain incomplete.

5

THE CHURCH
AS THE
COMMUNITY
OF SAINTS

· ·

CHAPTER FOUR DISCUSSES SALVATION AS A PROCESS OF GROWTH IN VIRTUE. THIS growth, which leads to union with God in love, can only be growth within the body of Christ. The saint is not one whose virtues stand out from the rest of the body. The saint is not "outstanding" in that sense. The more perfected in love the saint becomes, the greater the identification with the church. The closer the union with God the stronger the bond with Christ's body. Sainthood is perfected in communion with others, never apart from it. This has been the teaching, by word and deed, of all great saints—even the desert fathers, who were falsely accused of being rugged individualists. There were some individualists and dualists, but there were also others who offered strong correctives to both. When someone looking for solitude sought Abbot Lucius's advice, he was told: "If you have not first lived rightly with men, you will not be able to live rightly in solitude."[1] Out of the desert has come story after story of monks who, when faced with a conflict between service to neighbor and their own personal rule of life, unhesitatingly chose service to neighbor. For example, when someone went to see an anchorite and afterward apologized for upsetting his rule, the anchorite replied, "My rule is to refresh you and send you away in peace."[2] The most solitary of them saw their austere regimen as commando training to prepare them to fight the Lord's battle.[3]

The purpose of Christian formation is not developing a better self-image, achieving self-fulfillment or finding self-affirmation; nor is it the development of individualistic qualities that make singularly outstanding saints. Rather, it is developing certain qualities that enable us to live responsibly within the community that we have been baptized into. Virtues are ecclesially based.[4] The theological virtues of faith, hope and charity make the best sense (if not the only sense) for Christians when they are lived out in the Christian community as the "peaceable kingdom." Thus in the midst of a violent world the Christian community cultivates the virtue of hope (that violence has not the last word) and patience in view of the kingdom, which is already present, and in view of the certainty of its future consummation.[5]

A Theology of the Visible Church

Since the spiritual life is essentially life-in-relation patterned after and sustained by the Trinity[6] that assumes a definite shape within the church created by Christ, a theology of the visible church becomes crucial for understanding such a life. This is one of the least developed areas of Protestant thought, especially among evangelicals.[7] But if the problem of ecclesiology is serious in the West, it is catastrophic in Asia. Churches planted by denominational mission agencies simply reproduce after their kind and thus perpetuate the deep divisions in Western Protestantism. Their presence continues to be a major stumbling block to Christian witness in Asia. But a more serious defect is found in the nondenominational agencies that produce churches without any sense of history or tradition. These churches are no more than collectivities of individuals who profess Christ as savior. The primary reality is the individual's relationship with God. The church is just an ancillary entity that exists to serve the spiritual needs of individuals. The evangelical turned Catholic, Thomas Howard, has pointed out this particular weakness in evangelicalism.[8] There is little sense of the church as a corporate, spiritual reality existing in and through time, worshiping God with the apostles, prophets, saints and martyrs together with angels and archangels and all the heavenly host. A whole new perspective opens up when Christians begin to see themselves as participating in a much larger reality:

> There is a sacred and liberating anonymity here. I am not primarily conscious of my own agenda of troubles now. I am a Christian, bringing the sacrifice of adoration to the Most High, as all other Christians have done before me. It does not mean that I may pretend to ignore my troubles or the troubles of others. Indeed, those burdens form part of the offering that we lift to the Throne. But our attention is now on God Himself.[9]

The personal fervor that characterizes evangelicalism is commendable, but making it the determinative principle for ecclesiology is disastrous. The Asian church (and probably most churches in traditional societies outside the West) senses it more keenly because of its traditional sense of the community. It is no wonder that the call for fresh thinking on ecclesiology is more urgently sounded in Asia than in the West where an assumed "Christian universe" lulls many Christians into a laissez-faire existence.[10]

Recent thinking about the church stresses the need for small groups. But most of these groups reinforce a "feel good" spirituality through group dynamics. They hardly challenge individuals to make deeper commitments to objective and absolute norms apart from themselves.[11] Small group spirituality has come to mean no more than reorganizing the congregation into "cell groups" to make them serve the needs of individual members better. Most evangelical thinking, particularly in the area of church growth, has been along this line.[12] Something more promising has come along in the form of small groups organized as effective agents for change in the church and in society at large. They deepen spirituality, since they require from their members a high degree of commitment to an objective ideal.[13] Chastened liberation theologians have shown the way through their Ecclesial Base Communities (EBC).[14] While liberation theology has not changed its overall goal, the EBC movement has significantly altered the strategy for its accomplishment.

The Anabaptist vision of the church as a "contrast community" has been reinforced by the influential works of Hauerwas. The contrast community invokes the biblical model of the church as salt, lamp, leaven and mustard seed. These are small things that contain a disproportionately large potential or strong influence. They show that there are other, more effective ways of bringing about change than through pressure groups and power manipulation—even where the Moltmannian strategy remains a possible option. The strategy was envisaged by Elton Trueblood some thirty years ago:

> We are far more effective if we know that the Gospel will never be entirely acceptable, and that the Christian Movement will continue to be a minority movement. The Gospel must seek to penetrate the world and all of its parts, but it cannot do so unless there is a sense in which it is in contrast to the world.[15]

Eugene Peterson takes a similar approach when he describes the work of the minister (and the church) as "subversion" of the alien surrounding community. It requires *being there* in a place, altering the situation by small degrees rather than direct confrontation.[16] In places like Asia, where "political theology" is not a viable option, we must take more seriously the idea of a "contrast community" as the way by which the church carries out its responsibility to proclaim the kingdom of God and bring about the desired changes in the larger society. Perhaps the word *subversion* is not the best way to describe the church's role, since it connotes a clandestine operation. But if it means a quiet, unobtrusive way of bringing about change through negotiation, consensus building, and, more importantly, a way of life that dares to be different, then the Asian church must be a subversive church.

The real problem is not the minority status of the Christian movement. Creating such a community requires a "committed Christianity"[17] that is always in short supply even within the "contrast community." The problem is further exacerbated by the Protestant principle of laicization. Historically, when Luther invoked the universal priesthood of all believers and abolished the monastic system, the idea of the church was radically reconceived. Theoretically, it should uplift all believers, but in actual fact it tends to reduce them to the lowest common denominator. We wanted to make everyone in the church into robust saints but succeeded only in making mostly mediocre ones. We expect everyone in the church to be the remnant reaching out to the world. But there is a whole body of people belonging to the visible church who are at best partially committed. Where do they fit in? We need a theology that makes sense of their presence. The Anabaptist model of the voluntary church that restricted membership to committed individuals offered one solution. But a small church of pure souls is at best a short-term solution. It will either become an exclusive club or won't be pure for long once it starts mass evangelization. The Anabaptist model can hardly be the answer to the depersonalization and unabashed commercialism of the modern megachurch.

What is conspicuously absent in much of the modern discussion on small groups is a theology of the visible church that makes sense of the small groups within the larger church. The Protestant doctrine of universal priesthood tends to subsume all distinctions in the church under a single spiritual entity (see figure 1). Thus they become incidental to the far more real spiritual singularity of the people of God.[18] Some evangelical theologians, however, are calling for the "remonasticization" of the church.[19] Such a call would involve a radical revamp of Protestant ecclesiology, but so far no evangelical body has responded to such a challenge. An adequate theology of the visible church needs, first, an understanding of the church as a corporate reality rather than a collectivity of individuals. Second, it needs to maintain some kind of *theological* distinction within the church. Mainline Protestantism retained the first requirement but failed because it abolished the second through laicization.

Anglo-Catholic Martin Thornton has suggested a different approach to local church renewal. It is patterned after the monastic model and focuses on a "remnant" in the church as the effective agent for spiritual development

Figure 1. The Protestant concept of the church

of the whole church.[20] Thornton's remnant concept is worth considering because it highlights a feature that is not clearly envisaged by those who advocate the "small group" concept. Thornton sees the local church as one organic unity, a microcosm of the church universal. The remnant are to the local parish what monasticism was to the larger church (see figure 2). They are not separate from the rest of the church but are organically one with them as their representatives.[21]

> The Remnant, far from being an amputated segment—the clique detached from the whole—is at the centre of the parochial organism and of power extending beyond it. It is the very heart which recapitulates and serves the whole; in fact the complete Body of Christ in microcosm, and its relation to this environment is the relation between Christ and the twelve, to their world. This palpitating heart pumps the blood of life to all the body as leaven leavens the lump or salt savours the whole.[22]

The remnant stands in vicariously for the larger whole. Thornton draws on an illuminating analogy. A "good cricket school" is not one where everyone is a good cricketer, "but one whose first eleven wins most of its matches." To make every student a cricketer is what Thornton calls "multitudinism." It "has reduced Christianity to a conventional mediocrity." But Thornton is not talking about a small group running the entire show for the rest. The work of the remnant is essentially ascetical: commitment to the corporate rule and prayer. "There is nothing so contagious as holiness, nothing more pervasive than Prayer. This is precisely what the traditional Church means by evangelism and what distinguishes it from recruitment."[23] Their relation to the minister is like that of the Twelve to Jesus. They are sustained less by the public teaching and preaching of the minister and more by the latter's spiritual direction, which helps them maintain their corporate rule.

Figure 2. Thornton's remnant concept

Thornton's theology of the visible church (which he calls "parochial theology") seems to offer a better alternative to the "small church" concept in that it introduces a truly spiritual principle in renewal quite apart from institutional changes. Renewal that is tied to such matters as reorganization or changes in the church's composition and size has tended to inflict severe but needless pain. Thornton's approach does require a radical reorientation in pastoral thinking and practice. It means that the pastor's *main* focus is not on large-scale public appeal but on prayer and the spiritual guidance of the small group of committed Christians within the church. It also requires greater emphasis on the objective character of the church, the factualness of the spiritual life. Far from making the spiritual life too cut-and-dried, recognizing its objective reality is what makes for greater spiritual proficiency in the Thomistic sense of the word. Our spiritual life is first and foremost not something of our own generating; it does not depend on our feelings but is a basic fact, a given. That is the meaning of being incorporated into the church. We were baptized passively into the body. How does this help us ascetically? The answer, according to Thornton, begins with the prayer of recollection.

> If by Baptism and Communion we live in Christ, he can hardly be other than with us. So an act of recollection can either emphasize the real presence of Christ beside us, or it can form an act of recognition of our membership of the Church. I do not think it matters very much which thought is uppermost in the life of a particular soul, both should play some part, but it is important to realize—especially in times of aridity or fatigue—that recognition of our Church membership is as valid an act of prayer as the most vivid sense of the divine presence: as always in all prayer, fact matters more than feeling.[24]

This act of recollection resembles the act of "reckoning" in the higher life movement but differs from it on a crucial point. The "reckoning" there is an individual's act of applying the truth to oneself, while recollection acknowledges that one is in fact part of an actual corporate reality—the church. Ascetically, reckoning or "letting go and letting God" entails a rather complex psychological process that only more spiritually proficient persons are able to perform.[25] The failure to provide an effective ascetical program may explain why the method of the higher life movement did not become widely accepted. The act of recollection, by contrast, is based on a broader ascetical structure, namely, the individual's participation in the life of the church, which is the life of Christ in the church. When we participate in the worship and events of Christmas, Easter or an ordinary Sunday worship, it is more than commemorative. We are involved in the very reality of these events. "The life of the Church, in these services, makes actual for us the mystery of the Incarnation."[26] Our participation makes us part of the story. There are, to be sure, different degrees of participation, from just "being there" to participating with some degree of spiritual fervor. And with participation (which Thornton calls "the technique of going to church") there is already some spiritual progress.[27]

We make further progress, become proficient, when we are able to recollect and recognize this solid fact of our spiritual existence. What we do as individuals, the mental and vocal prayers and the meditation (what we call "private prayers"), does not depend on ourselves but grows out of our participation in the corporate life. Protestant devotion begins by requiring too much, often acts involving inner intention, motive and fervor, in short, a high degree of individual finesse. These "affections" are important. But what is more basic—and on which the spiritual fervor and affections largely depend—is often left out: the simple acts of obedience, of going to church regardless of one's momentary disposition toward it. Growth in spiritual proficiency is hard work, but it is not as hard as trying to get into "the right state of mind" or cultivating certain "inner attitudes" of some considerable psychological complexity as a prerequisite to growth. These are a result of ascetical efficiency, not the cause of it.

To recognize the factuality of spiritual life is to recognize its communal nature and vice versa, since the Fact we participate in is something that others also have a share in. The spiritual life that depends on feelings can only result in subjective and individualistic piety because one has to make the Fact fit into one's individual existence and private concerns. This is not to say that corporate spirituality that recognizes the objective Fact is devoid of feelings. It can in fact uplift the soul to great heights of adoration. But it does not equate progress with feelings. In fact, feelings become the least important indicator of how far one has advanced in the spiritual life. Going to church despite the lack of feelings and despite the football game on TV may actually be doing us more good spiritually than going to church when all is well.

Emphasizing the factuality of the spiritual life is important because Protestantism gravitates toward the individualistic and subjective pole of spirituality. Its emphasis on the relational nature of the Christian life has meant that truth has to be internalized to be "real." The process of internalization is inevitable in any spirituality. But what usually happens is that the subjective begins to swallow up the objective. The Fact is then equated with "dead letter," which is set in direct antithesis to "spirit." We can see something of this process at work in the early Reformers who understood justification by faith as strictly denoting the individual's assurance of salvation. Again, this is not to deny the reality of the Christian experience of assurance.

But the Pauline doctrine of justification by faith has a more objective and communal character. It is not only about the individual's acceptance before a righteous God but is also concerned with the larger, corporate issue of Gentile participation in the covenant community. Justification by faith means that with the coming of Christ, the righteousness of God is made available for both Jews and Gentiles on the same basis—by faith—which is an objective, divine provision.[28] The objective character of justification explains why for Paul, the signs of justification are also objective, namely, the presence of the Spirit in the working of miracles (Gal 3:5) and the fruit of the Spirit (Gal 5:22-26).[29] Paul stands in stark contrast to the Reformed view in which assurance of justification is vouchsafed to the believer by the *internal* testimony and the *secret* working of the Spirit.[30] Its failure to fully appreciate the corporate and objective nature of the Christian life is one reason why Protestantism did not develop a viable theology of the visible church. Even though mainline Protestantism had a sacramental theology undergirding the corporate life, it was the "introspective conscience" rather than the corporate reality that dominated its spirituality.[31]

The Nature of the Visible Church

Present-day Protestantism must return to its sacramental heritage if it hopes to discover an authentic spirituality that goes beyond individualistic piety. To help in the recovery, the objective and communal character of the Christian life needs to be further elaborated so that it can be visibly expressed and not remain an abstraction. Two things may be said about the nature of the ecclesial life. First, it is a life created by God in Christ, and second, it is a sacramental life.

A community in Christ. There is a profound difference between the Christian community and the general human community. The human community satisfies the characteristic human desire for direct human contact, either in the form of direct union in love (as between husband and wife) or in the influence that a stronger person exerts on a weaker person or group.[32] The second kind is dangerous. Bonhoeffer, speaking in the context of Nazi Germany, warns:

> There is such a thing as human absorption. It appears in all the forms of conversion wherever the superior power of one person is consciously or unconsciously misused to influence profoundly and draw into his spell another individual or a whole community. Here one soul operates directly upon another soul. The weak have been overcome by the strong, the resistance of the weak has broken down under the influence of another person. He has been overpowered, but not won over by the thing itself. This becomes evident as soon as the demand is made that he throw himself into the cause itself, independently of the person to whom he is bound, or possibly in opposition to this person. Here is where the humanly converted person breaks down and thus makes it evident that his conversion was effected, not by the Holy Spirit, but by a man, and therefore has no stability.[33]

In the Christian community, by contrast, Christ stands *between* the lovers; union is never direct. No matter how loving a relationship, without Christ between the persons in love, it threatens to become an idol.[34] The book of Acts describes the life of the early Christians in terms of just such a community. It is a caring and sharing community but also a community where Christ is present through the worship and breaking of bread (Acts 2:42-47; 4:32). This historical description is reinforced in the rest of the New Testament in regard to the nature of the church as the *sanctorum communio*. To be a Christian is to be "in Christ," that is, to be baptized into the one body, the church (1 Cor 12:13). Our Christian life cannot properly exist apart from that body. Our fellowship is always "in Christ" and through Christ. "He is our peace" who makes fellowship between the most disparate elements a reality (Eph 2:14-18). Becoming a better Christian is not a matter of individual personal development. It is growing in the body with the other members of it. The "me and my God" mentality is contrary to the essence of the Christian life. Private prayers are important, but even in the most private enclosure we are always praying *as* a member of the body of Christ in communion with other members. No prayer is exactly "private" "since *all* prayer is but part of the total prayer of the Church" because of the sheer fact of our incorporation into Christ. But incorporation does not submerge the individual personality. Private prayers are "both the actual prayer *of* Christ to the Father, and our own personal prayer *to* Christ."[35]

Practically, "life together" means that we seek "the common good" (1 Cor 12:7) and live in fellowship with one another. Biblically, *koinonia* is a powerful term that means far more than what we are normally accustomed to calling "fellowship" nowadays: polite conversations around coffee tables with plenty of food to fill in the uncomfortable silences in between and casual gatherings in the social hall of the church for an hour of singing, "testimonies" and a short talk by an invited speaker on an ego-boosting theme. We kill the spirituality of fellowship by making it too spiritual! A community that exists for purely spiritual ends is in greater danger of letting unspiritual, carnal elements develop, since any minor infraction becomes an infringement of a spiritual reality that demands radical action often accompanied by a very uncharitable attitude. This explains why fellowships that seek to preserve the purity of the "New Testament church" are more likely to experience ugly schisms than are churches that have no such pretensions.

Fellowship in Christ includes ordinary structures like marriage, family and friends. In Christ, the ordinary becomes a channel of grace; to consign it to the realm of the secular is to surrender to dualism and to deny Christ's lordship over all things. A Christian community that recognizes the reality of ordinary fellowships of everyday life (albeit "in Christ") is better able to distinguish more clearly between the periphery and the core of the community and hence maintain both.[36] Where ordinary relationships are recognized as a part of true Christian community (as seen in the Reformed concept of the covenant with the family), the bond is usually stronger. Differences at the ordinary level can coexist in the community. The difference is recognized as a human difference, not a spiritual difference.

The type of community we have been describing could also be called a sacramental community—a community whose essential life is undergirded by the sacraments of baptism and the Lord's Supper. Some might understand this view as undermining a cherished Protestant principle that enthrones preaching and subordinates the sacraments. Calvin understood the relationship between Word and sacraments as marks of the church. The Word is always primary; the sacraments derive their significance from the Word. The sacraments are nonetheless "marks" of the church and occupy a place of a very high order next to the Word, although not the central place.[37] But modern Protestantism, especially the free church tradition, reduces the sacraments to minor appendices in the life of the church. Preaching occupies the central role in the church. The resultant spirituality is what Pannenberg calls "penitential piety," whose central focus is the spiritual well-being of individual souls. It generates a community of like-minded *individuals* concerned with their individual salvation.[38] The alternative is to return to a "Eucharistic piety" that sees the church as a symbolic community. As such, the church is an efficacious sign that carries in the present something of the reality of the future eschatological kingdom of God.[39]

The church is most truly the church as it celebrates baptism and the Eucharist. Baptism incorporates new members into the body of Christ and the Eucharist reveals the communal nature of the Christian life (Acts 2:42-47). It is there that "the essence of the church itself is alive, present, and effective."[40] The sermon must be seen within the larger context of the church's life, which is essentially Eucharistic. Preaching should point to and confirm that life, not take on a life of its own. In the case of modern preaching everything depends largely on the skill, personality and performance of the preacher.

If modern evangelicalism is to experience a paradigm shift from individualism to a vision of life-in-community, its whole ascetical apparatus will have to be remodeled. First, it must give greater emphasis to the objective mysteries of the faith embodied in baptism and the Lord's Supper as the visible expression of the life of faith. It must rethink preaching that gives the preacher an independent authority.[41] Preachers are not free to speak on any subject they desire or think relevant, even if it is from the Bible. Their main task is to tell the Christian story faithfully so that the community is constantly reinforced by it. Second, the family rather than the individual provides the model for understanding the factuality of the church's life: a family member *belongs* to that family, willingly or not. Within the family, members experience basic identity and belonging; it merits their commitment. It might be argued, however, that such a view of the family is derived from the traditional society, which understands such values as "family name" and "family honor." This view of the family, unfortunately, has been largely lost to modern society. But the Church is not called to model itself after modern society. It is to be an alternative society, a colony of "resident aliens" that poses a constant challenge to the larger society. When the church exists as the family of the triune God that includes families, it can be a powerful corrective to the individualism fostered by a "penitential piety."

Signs of a Sacramental Community

We cannot conceive of the church as a sacramental community without at the same time conceiving of it as an eschatological community. It is in the sacraments that the transcendent and historical poles of the church's being are brought into a dialectical relationship.[42] Baptism is incorporation into the *new* creation in Christ; the Eucharistic celebration is a constant reminder that

Christ is present and also still to come (1 Cor 11:26). The church is part of an unfolding story whose end has already been anticipated in the resurrection and whose historical finale will be, to borrow a term from Tolkien, a "eucatastrophe." Thus the signs of a sacramental community are also the signs of an eschatological community: a community on the move, whose life and mission are always directed toward the future, the *visio Dei*. This gives an eschatological seriousness to everything the church does. Thus the "fellowship of Jesus Christ" to which God calls the baptized (1 Cor 1:9) is not just a warm, cozy gathering but a most exacting community, a costly fellowship. This costliness will be apparent when we consider three signs that authenticate the Eucharistic community: suffering, celebration and solitude.

A community of suffering. At baptism we begin a journey with a suffering community in a world that is still groaning in the pangs of childbirth (Rom 8:22). Baptism is burial with Christ (Rom 6:4-6), which works itself out in painful dying and in sharing Christ's sufferings (Phil 3:10). Within the Eucharistic community we regularly share the broken body and the shed blood—powerful reminders that our basic identity is found in suffering together. In earlier times (as well as in some areas of the world today), fellowship in the Eucharistic community carried the possibility of physical martyrdom. Today the suffering is of a different kind but is no less painful. We feel pain when we share our material possessions with fellow believers who have few or none. We feel pain when we try to listen empathetically. C. S. Lewis was right on the mark when he said, "It's much easier to pray for a bore than to go and see him."[43] We may not be called to physical martyrdom, but it is just as much a suffering to suffer fools gladly. Our world glamorizes personal intimacy. But intimacy is more talked about than experienced because it is a painful process. It involves risks, possible misunderstanding, vulnerability, perhaps even losing something of oneself to the other person. Relating to the other as person means giving him or her the space to be truly a person.[44] It means foregoing the temptation to impose our own will on the other. There is joy in personal relationship, but the joy comes by way of death to self. Giving, listening and personal intimacy are painful processes, but they are also renewing processes that form our communal character. They teach us what it means to "bear one another's burdens and so fulfill the law of Christ."

In light of the suffering community we examine another feature of the sacramental community, namely, the ministry of healing. Kenneth Leech has observed that at "the centre of the Christian tradition are the sacraments, and at the centre of sacramental life is deliverance and healing." He adds that "the whole of the church's life of prayer and sacrament is concerned with healing."[45] Healing includes forgiveness, reconciliation, restoration of relationship within the body of Christ in the Eucharistic celebration (1 Cor 11:17-31) and prayers offered by the elders of the church for the sick (Jas 5:14-16).

Because those who exercise this charismatic ministry are in danger of falling victim to a power fixation, it is of the utmost importance to set it squarely within the context of the sacramental community of suffering. The church has suffered at the hands of self-proclaimed prophets and evangelists, who recognize no other authority except their own, undertaking ministries of healing and deliverance outside of the church's sacramental life. How different this is from the model of ministry we find in the apostle Paul! Paul's ministry can be described as charismatic in that through him the power of the Spirit was manifested (2 Cor 12:12). But it was a ministry exercised in suffering and weakness (2 Cor 6:3-10). As Hafemann observes, "Paul's revelatory function is grounded in the fact that *in his suffering* he preaches and acts *in the Spirit,* and that in the midst of his being led to *death* the Spirit is poured out on others to bring them to *life* in Christ."[46] The air of triumphalism so characteristic of many a modern prophet is totally absent in Paul. Paul indeed saw himself as a member of God's triumphal procession (2 Cor 2:14), but as "the captive slave of God who is constantly being led to death."[47]

A community of celebration. There is a serious and a glad side to the Christian life. It has Good Friday and Easter, fast days and feast days. Celebration, however, is not restricted to the so-called spiritual activities we do in church. (Some modern charismatics have even reduced it to praise.) Because the Christian community also consists of natural associations, celebration includes this-worldly activities like play. Play should not be the sort of thing that Christians have trouble with. But the issue is not really that simple, at least not in some contexts of Asia today. If there is one common sin among Christians from the so-called four little dragons of Asia (Korea, Hong Kong, Singapore and Taiwan), it is their obsession with work and the fierce competition underlying it. True, people may take vacations, but the reason is purely private and pragmatic, namely, to unwind in order to recondition the human machine for more work. They have lost their capacity for communal play, and with it the traditioning capacity.

Play may be understood as the ability to suspend temporarily the usual course of life to enter a different world, a world in which another dimension of relationship opens up to reveal a more profound meaning of living together.[48] Children at play are lost in a different world, and in the course of play friendships are forged. What we have forgotten is that the same principle applies throughout life and at all levels of relationship. Play is a powerful means by which the shared values of a Christian community are imbibed by God's sons and daughters. If the community does not learn to enjoy each other at play, it is doubtful that it truly understands what it means to "enjoy God forever," which is "man's chief end." Christians who do not play together do not worship well together either, since worship is a "religious form of play."[49] Both at play and at worship the Christian community enjoys its sabbath rest.[50]

Worship is the central focus of the Christian community because in worship it "anticipates and symbolically celebrates the praise of God's glory that will be consummated in the eschatological renewal of all creation in the new Jerusalem."[51] The church is constituted "a chosen people, a royal priesthood, a holy nation, a people belonging to God, that you may declare the praises of him who called you out of darkness into his wonderful light" (1 Pet 2:9). Worship here must be understood in its broadest sense: "to glorify God and enjoy him forever." To glorify God is to proclaim who God really is, and this act is always accompanied by a certain creaturely attitude of humility, wonder and awe. Glorifying God is not confined to church but extends to every circumstance of life, including eating and drinking (1 Cor 10:31).

Worship attains its sharpest focus in the Eucharistic celebration. It brings together all the significant events of revelation—who God is and what he has done—and celebrates "with angels and archangels and all the heavenly hosts . . . in songs of everlasting praise." Ultimately worship is a response to the glory of God that theology seeks to trace.[52] It has little to do with the histrionics that characterize the electronic church. It is not the art of creating the "right mood" with the help of media technology. Worship, in Scripture, is simply the flip side of theology. Theology tells us who God is and directs us to worship. In worship we encounter God personally; reflection on that encounter issues in theology. In one sense, worship is not something we *do* but something that *happens* to us in the face of the divine self-disclosure. This happened to Job when God answered him out of the whirlwind (Job 42:1-6), to Isaiah when he saw the glory of God (Is 6) and to John on Patmos when he saw Christ (Rev 1:17). Thus it is not surprising that some of life's deepest perplexities are resolved in worship (Ps 73:16-17).[53]

Worship is enabled by the triune God. We are enabled by the Spirit to worship God the Father, whose glory is revealed in the face of Jesus Christ (Jn 1:14). The Spirit does this in three ways. First, he glorifies Christ and reveals the things of Christ to us (Jn 14:26; 15:26; 16:14). Second, he joins us to the rest of creation through his intercession with "unutterable groanings," directing our thoughts to the future consummation of redemption (Rom 8:26).

Third, the Spirit is the Spirit of adoption that awakens the cry of intimate sonship, "Abba, Father!" and directs our vision to the eschatological fulfillment (Rom 8:15-18). In short, the work of the Spirit is both God directed and future directed. These are the two basic presuppositions of worship. True worship is always turned Godward and heavenward, to the final manifestation of the kingdom of God.

Worship includes a number of distinct acts such as singing (Eph 5:19; Col 3:16), praying (Mt 18:19) and the reading of the Word (1 Tim 4:13).[54] Different liturgical traditions configure these acts variously. But the three acts, corporate prayer, public reading and corporate singing, form the basic building blocks of corporate worship in all of the traditions. Thus their theological significance bears consideration.

For centuries the church has used the psalms as its prayer book. The psalter is in a very real sense Jesus' prayer book. The early church understood these prayers as uniquely *his* prayers. When the church prays the psalms, it is praying the prayer of Jesus; more precisely, it is Jesus praying through the church for all time.[55] Such a view puts a different perspective on our corporate prayers. They are not the sum total of individuals praying together. When the church is praying together, it is the body of Christ with Christ at the head praying. For where two or three are gathered in prayer in Christ's name he is in their midst as the head. Even "private" prayers, as we have already noted, are offered up in the church. This does not mean that a Christian is only to pray for others and is not to be concerned about personal needs. What it means is that my own personal needs are not strictly for myself alone. When we pray for ourselves ("give us this day our daily bread"), we are praying *as* a member of the body of Christ who is in need and not as an individual. The difference between personal and corporate prayer, therefore, is only a difference in arrangement and content, not in essence. In personal prayer, we may be praying specifically for our own needs and/or in solitude, but essentially it is still a corporate prayer.

When the church put together the sixty-six books into one book and called it the Bible, it declared that the corporate life is defined by one continuous story with many different subplots. The Bible is read as a whole by the whole community. Such reading keeps the story alive, just as the story keeps the community alive from one generation to another. In other words, reading the Scripture is not just a pretext for preaching a nicely crafted sermon; it is a traditioning process. The flip side of reading is listening, and listening is no less a communal activity. "Listening together to the word," according to Nouwen, "can free us from our competition and rivalry and allow us to recognize our true identity as sons and daughters of the same loving God and brothers and sisters of our Lord Jesus Christ, and thus of each other."[56] It is in reading and listening that the Word addresses us afresh and draws us into a living relationship with God and with one another. This is the basic theology of Scripture reading.

This communal activity of reading and listening that constitutes the traditioning process is largely lost in the modern world due mostly to the emergence of a literate culture. After six centuries of being immersed in the printed page, modern people have moved from the world of the oral-aural community to the private world of silent reading.[57] Reading has become a convenient way to shut out the world. Tragically, the modern Christian has come to relate to the Bible in much the same way. Reading the Scripture has become a private, information-gathering exercise assisted by charts, study Bibles and guidebooks. In some churches this is even encouraged. The Bible is regarded as a resource book that provides, no doubt, more enduring answers to meet our human needs than many other books on medicine, psychology and computers, but a resource book all the same, whose wealth of materials anyone with the requisite tools can mine privately. It is this basic misuse of the Bible that has prompted Hauerwas's (somewhat outrageous) call to "take the Bible out of the hands of individual Christians in North America."[58]

If we are to maintain the theological integrity of public reading, a few points must be observed. First, we need to say something about its relationship to the sermon, particularly in view of the predominance of what is largely the informational sermon in the modern evangelical church. We need to give priority to the public reading of Scripture. Not only must all the books be read, but preferably in the order they are found. For that is the way the church has understood the story of its own existence. That story has to be repeated and impressed on the church's collective memory. Thus does the church's basic identity come to be reshaped. Too often, the readings are highly selective and haphazard because they are worked around sermon topics, whereas the whole process ought to be reversed: the sermons should be derived from the continuous, orderly reading of Scripture. If the sermon follows some form of *lectio divina* (in which the whole of Scripture is read over a period of time), we are more likely to avoid the habit of reading from a few favorite books (usually the Epistles) and preaching from our favorite texts. Preaching is or should be essentially the unfolding of the story in a contemporary idiom. What we call the "exposition of the Scriptures" should be the clarification of the Story so that we can listen to it more attentively and relate to the events more fully. Yet all too often the modern sermon is singularly calculated at satisfying the consumer demands of the modern churchgoer.

Second, the modern church has to learn how to listen to the Scriptures being read. The Bible must be listened to, not for helpful hints or tips but to enable the hearers to participate communally in its story. Eugene Peterson has summed up this scriptural function very well:

> The primary reason for a book is to put a writer into relation with readers so that we can listen to his or her stories and find ourselves in them, listen to his or her songs and sing along with them, listen to his or her arguments and argue with them, listen to his or her answers and question them. The Scriptures are almost entirely this kind of book. If we read them impersonally with an information-gathering mind, we misread them.[59]

In order to train the ear to listen, reading must first be restored to its proper place in the church. I used to wonder why the Anglican and Orthodox churches spent what seemed like an unwarranted amount of time on reading (or chanting) the Scripture in their services. Such laborious readings made no sense to someone in a tradition whose only rationale for reading is to acquaint the congregation with the sermon text. But once reading is understood, listening follows. These traditions (and I include the Catholic tradition) were in fact training the people of God in listening and imbibing their heritage. In the Anglican Church the congregation always stands for the reading of the Gospel, and the implicit message is clear: "Now, children of the kingdom, please pay special attention to the story!"

Third, we need to recover the lost art of memorizing Scripture. Once reading and listening to Scripture was accompanied by memorizing and reciting Scripture (of which we will have more to say later). It is part of a whole system of spiritual training in the art of continual prayer (see chapter eight). Memorization was very much the foundation of learning in an oral-aural culture.[60] But in a world where information can be recalled almost instantly and just as quickly become obsolete, memorization has become a lost art. And so the Christian story no longer becomes deeply embedded in the communal memory. In its place are bits and pieces of the story distilled into simplistic principles and formulas for meeting life's various exigencies: the four spiritual laws for becoming a Christian, five biblical keys to a successful marriage and so on.

Scripture exhorts us to "sing and make melody in your heart to the Lord" (Eph 5:19). Singing underscores more strongly than any other act of worship our life in Christ as one community. Whether or not that unity is best conveyed by "unison singing," as Bonhoeffer suggests,[61] it is certain that the singing must be "together," that is, in harmony. In singing together the whole community can speak the same word and pray the same prayer.

Historically, corporate singing, according to Peter Brunner, grows out of the need to read the Scriptures.

There is no other means through which the proclamatory authority of this word, the extramundane origin of this voice, the sacredness of this text, and also the inviting, appealing nearness of its message could be witnessed to more distinctly in a symbol of sound than through the reciting tone. . . . In the reading of Scripture, the musical tone places itself at the feet of the sacred Word, as in a *proskynesis,* with the utmost humility and renunciation of any claim to importance of its own.[62]

Singing is not intended to display the artistry of the singer(s) but to let the subject of the Scripture—God—speak clearly through the words. Because God is the subject speaking, the one reading cannot personally identify with the words but must read it as one addressed by God,[63] and this is best done through singing. Through singing, the Word is proclaimed with one voice and the individual personality recedes into the background. Even when one person is praying or reading, the singing tone "serves to accentuate the community character" of the act, so that "the praying person is the spokesman for the others."[64]

If we follow strictly the criterion that our singing, praying and reading must reflect our corporate celebration and enhance our communal life, a number of significant changes will have to be made in our contemporary church life. For one thing, the bulk of egotistical, self-indulgent charismatic choruses will have to be jettisoned. The organist who uses the worship service as an opportunity to provide a display of musical artistry rather than to join with the rest of the saints in rendering praise to God will have to be reformed or removed. Even the reading of the Nicene Creed, which begins with "I believe," needs to revert to the original Greek text, which actually begins with "We believe."[65] There is a dire need for a radical revamping of the church's liturgical life among the very people who have always prided themselves in having done away with "dead liturgy," namely, the low church evangelicals and fundamentalists. "No liturgy" simply means bad liturgy formed by years of unwritten and unreflected ritual actions performed out of sheer habit. This liturgical impoverishment has driven some to the opposite end of the pendulum to discover Orthodoxy.[66]

A community of solitaries. Being in community does not mean that personal distinctiveness is lost to the group. The Christian in communion with others is not simply a face in the crowd. On the contrary, there is no community unless each member learns to live in solitude. It takes true solitaries to form a true community. For it is only in solitude that we discover a deeper bond that transcends time and place. This is perhaps what Paul means when he refers to "being absent from you in body but present with you in spirit" (Col 2:5). The communion of saints is far more than just their being physically present with each other.

Solitude is essential for community life because there we begin to discover a unity that is prior to all unifying actions. In solitude we become aware that we were together before we came together and that community life is not a creation of our will but an obedient response to the reality of our being united.[67]

In solitude we discover the prior fact of our corporate existence. When we come together, we take our places as responsible and responsive members of the community. This is the way it should be, according to the apostle Paul, whenever we gather at the Lord's table: "Let a man examine himself and so let him eat" (1 Cor 11:28). Only the one who has undertaken the responsible act of "discerning the Lord's body" can be said to be in true communion with others around the Lord's table. As Henri Nouwen reminds us, all real community is "solitude greeting solitude, spirit speaking to spirit, heart calling to heart."[68] But it is also true to say that without the community, there are no true solitaries. We can be in solitude precisely because we are already members of the transcendent community. Solitude and community are interdependent.

Let him who cannot be alone beware of community. . . . Let him who is not in community beware of being alone. . . . We recognize, then, that only as we are within the fellowship can we be alone, and only he that is alone can live in the fellowship.[69]

Two dangers arise when community and solitude are isolated. On the one hand, a person in community who never learns to be alone becomes dependent on the fellowship, a parasite that feeds on the community. In the community we must beware of the danger of being swallowed up. We get swallowed up by the community if we give up on our personal responsibility and let the community do the praying and other spiritual works for us. This is not an uncommon phenomenon in the modern church. People seem only to pray well in a mass meeting under the incessant sounds of soothing music and persuasive words but could not maintain ten minutes of solitude each day. The community becomes a crutch. But it does not even stop at being that. When the individual becomes part of a mass psyche, the end is disastrous.

Each individual in the mass is insulated by thick layers of insensibility. He doesn't care, he doesn't hear, he doesn't think. He does not act, he is pushed. He does not talk, he produces conventional sounds when stimulated by the appropriate noises. He does not think, he secretes clichés.[70]

On the other hand, the one who cultivates solitude without being in community no longer grows in the community or is accountable to or responsible for it. Such a person becomes ground for the most unimaginable heresies, easily mistaking his or her own voice for the voice of God. True solitude and community are only two sides of the same coin. Both should be motivated by the love of God. We retreat into solitude in order to serve God and neighbor better, for it is only when we learn to be alone that we can enter into real community with others instead of being borne along by the crowd "into the great formless sea of irresponsibility."[71]

Solitude was a standing habit of Jesus that his followers should emulate (Mt 14:13, 23; 17:1; 20:17; Mk 6:30), yet for many a modern Christian it remains an elusive ideal. There are, however, some practical principles that can help us maintain solitude and community.[72] First, we need to learn to be alone with God and cultivate the habit of personal reflection by taking personal retreats, including the simple daily retreat of praying alone. Here the various monastic orders have lessons to teach. Carthusian monks, for example, live in communities but retain their individual cells. The Benedictine rule, while putting the main stress on the communal "work of God" *(opus Dei)*, encourages individual monks to engage in private prayers.[73] Second, we need to learn to struggle with our personal situations and problems. Some never learn to do this. They take comfort in numbers and push their problems into the subconscious. They never take time to face themselves in self-examination before God. They are even afraid to face themselves. Third, we need to enter into community with a deep sense of responsibility. Paul tells the Corinthians, "When you come together, *everyone* has a hymn, or a word of instruction, a revelation, a tongue or an interpretation" (1 Cor 14:26). No one is to come together with others without bringing something to share. At the minimum, it means being *attentively* present with others.

Conclusion

The doctrine of the church completes our study of the foundational doctrines of spiritual theology by bringing the doctrine of God, sin and salvation to their logical conclusion. With regard to God, the life of the church is the extension of the trinitarian life. As the body of Christ and eschatologically as the bride of Christ, the church is united with God through the Spirit.

The problem of sin is resolved in the church. The Christian fighting the flesh, the world and the devil is not fighting alone, even in the case of private sins. He or she is fighting as a member of the Lord's army, the militant church, and it is in the church that each of us discovers the resources to fight well. In this sense, there is no salvation outside the church *(extra ecclesiam nulla salus)*. Conversely, every sin committed, however private, is not just my sin against God but also my sin against the church. The one who has an infection is infected as a member of the body. For the Christian, there are no strictly private sins. The only private sins are committed by heathens and heretics, the only two groups of people who are not "in Christ." One is not yet, the other will not.

Finally, the life of virtue finds its fullest expression in the church as ecclesial virtues. The virtues of individual Christians are meant to create a better church, not just better individuals. In sum, Christian spirituality can be nothing other than living the Christian life in union with the Trinity in the church.

Part Two
THE PRACTICE OF
THE SPIRITUAL LIFE
....

6

THE THEOLOGY
& LIFE OF
PRAYER

· · · · · · · · · · · · · · · · · · · ·

T HE CHURCH, AS DISCUSSED IN THE PREVIOUS CHAPTER, PROVIDES THE CONTEXT for exploring the spiritual exercises as means of grace. For example, the acts of worship, prayer, reading and so on grow out of an awareness of the church as a community of celebration. But there is a deeper sense in which *askesis* grows out of the church. The sheer fact of our incorporation into the body of Christ is what makes *askesis* possible in the first place. The recognition of this fact constitutes the first act of prayer or what Thornton calls recollection.[1] In other words, prayer is the first act that links doctrine to practice, and all the other exercises are simply elaborations of this primal act. These exercises, therefore, do not have an independent status but are profoundly shaped by a particular conception of God, humanity, salvation and the church. The exercises of reading, meditation and memorization described here make sense only in the light of our doctrine of the church as an objective reality and a traditioning community.

The purpose of this discussion is not to offer tips and techniques on how to undertake the spiritual exercises, since books of this kind are already plentiful.[2] Rather, it will focus primarily on the theology of these disciplines. The focus on spiritual *exercises* implies that the basic structure of the spiritual life is ascetical, but this does not preclude the evangelical and charismatic dimensions. This is as it should be if our spiritual theology is to remain authentically trinitarian.[3]

There are a few preliminary caveats that every neophyte exercitant needs to keep in mind. First, offering a number of helps is not to suggest that spiritual proficiency depends on being adept in as many of them as possible. It is only to suggest the variety and range of possibilities that are available for advancing spirituality. Not many people will find all of them helpful or necessary. Many will find their own spiritual lives progressing on one primary exercise. Such was the case of Brother Lawrence and Jean Pierre de Caussade. Their primary focus was on one method of prayer, the practice of the presence of God for Brother Lawrence and the duty of the present moment for de Caussade.[4] Many Christians beginning on a more systematic approach to the spiritual life may feel excited and then frustrated by too many helps. Discovering what is personally helpful is best. Being skillful in one primary means of grace is better than being mediocre in several. Usually the most suitable spiritual tool is determined by individual temperament, gifts and previous training.

Second, spiritual helps are like other skills that we acquire, say, through reading a book or serving an apprenticeship. Above all, they come through practice. They are means to an end, not ends in themselves. No one learns carpentry skills, the proper use of hammer, saw and plane and so on, in order to use these tools as such. The purpose in learning to use them is to turn out chairs, tables and cabinets. In matters spiritual, however, the end needs further clarification. As indicated in chapter four, the goal of the Christian life is not to turn out fine specimens of sainthood. It is union with God—glorifying God and enjoying God forever, fulfilling the ultimate purpose for which we were created. This is not an exclusive fellowship or a private enjoyment, but an affirmation of our ecclesial identity and responsibility in the created order. Modern, sensate culture uses skills for self-fulfilling goals. Thus we need to keep in view the true end of the Christian life when engaging in spiritual exercises.

Third, in the final analysis the exercises must be integrated into a larger pattern of living. This can be done by a rule of life that enlarges the framework of our Christian existence to include the world. Even if one predominant exercise distinguishes our spiritual lives, it must be carried out within the enlarged framework. For example, the focus of the work of self-examination is not limited to my condition and relationship with God but must include what Sobrino calls honesty and fidelity to and a "willingness to be swept along by the 'more' of Reality."[5] If self-examination does not seriously raise the question about our attitude toward the larger world, particularly the world of human need and suffering, then we are in real danger of mere introspection.

Finally, much depends on proficiency in the use of the tools. To press the analogy further, a few basic tools in the hands of a master carpenter produce works of fine craftsmanship. The same can be said of spiritual tools. It is not always the latest spiritual technologies that help make better Christians. There is no lack of sophisticated gadgets on the market at the present time, from Bible texts that glow in the dark to concordances on CD-ROM. But what counts, ultimately, is what use we make of them.

Books on prayer have been written from every conceivable angle and continue to be written. This chapter is not intended to lengthen the burgeoning list. The task of teaching prayer is an awesome one. P. T. Forsyth warned that "no one ought to undertake [writing about prayer] who has not spent more toil in the practice of prayer than on its principle."[6] This chapter makes no claim to teaching anyone how to pray but simply points out that such teachings are available. It focuses on prayer as it relates to ascetical theology. Prayer is the first principle of ascetical theology in that it is the one act on which all other spiritual exercises depend. Meditation is preliminary to prayer; self-examination leads us to confession; spiritual reading directs the soul to a listening posture. Prayer is also the first principle in that the theological principles discussed in part one are activated through prayer. In prayer one enters into relationship with the Trinity, undergoes mortification and grows in the virtues. One becomes a practicing Christian by practicing prayer. In order to appreciate this primary function of prayer in ascetical theology, we need to explore briefly the nature or theology of prayer. Prayers are the life signs of faith. They occur as naturally as the cries of newborn babies. This nearly instinctive reflex makes prayer the first rule of ascetical theology in the third sense: we can all pray because we already know how to pray. Prayer does not *begin* with our willing it, although progress in prayer does require deliberation and training—*askesis*. This characteristic of prayer helps us see why petitionary prayer, far from being embarrassing baggage that better-informed Christians should discard, is fundamental to the whole life of prayer.

Prayer as Act and Habit

The term *prayer* has a broad sense and a narrow sense that correspond to what is traditionally called habitual prayer and actual prayer, respectively. In the broad sense prayer refers to the Christian's fundamental attitude toward and relationship with God. The whole life of a Christian may be described as a life of prayer. This life of prayer is embodied in Paul's injunction to pray without ceasing. Growth in the life of prayer involves different degrees of intimacy with God. Just as a human relationship grows in greater degrees of love, trust, commitment and so on, relationship with God grows similarly.

Spiritual writers have distinguished different grades of prayer signifying different levels of intimacy with God. Teresa of Ávila identifies seven levels or mansions in the interior castle of prayer. The more a person prays, the more intimate she will be with God. Thus growth in the Christian life can be defined largely in terms of growth in prayer.

In the narrow sense prayer refers to specific acts of the soul in communion with God. Actual prayers can be distinguished by different ways of praying, such as set prayer, free prayer, ejaculatory prayer; different kinds of prayer, such as confession, petition, thanksgiving and adoration; and different contexts of prayer, such as public prayer and private prayer. Spiritual exercises such as meditation and self-examination are more like preliminaries to prayer[7] but are usually included under the category of prayer. Some forms of prayer are both habitual and actual. The practice of the presence of God (the technical term for it is the prayer of recollection) involves both the specific acts of recalling the presence of God and a habit of living in God's presence.

The relationship between actual and habitual prayer may be best explained through an analogy. In a successful marriage husband and wife live in a habitual state of love, which is the foundation of their relationship. As good lovers, they set aside special times for expressing their love, be it a holiday or a special meal together, and regular times of intimate fellowship and communion. Both actual and habitual prayers are necessary. Thus acts of prayer help develop a habit of prayer and ensure that the habit does not become formalistic. At the same time, the habit enables regular performance of the acts. Both are mutually sustaining.

Prayer by Divine Initiative

It is necessary to understand the theology of prayer if the practice is to have a lasting basis. Theory is no substitute for practice; rather, it supports practice inasmuch as it explains the significance of it. Prayer, like everything else about the Christian life, begins with the fact of our incorporation into Christ. Prayer, as Gregory of Sinai (mid-fourteenth century) puts it, is the manifesting of baptism.[8] It arises out of the basic fact that we have been baptized into the body of Christ and that we share the life of Christ and his Word in the body. Prayer is essentially the human response to the Word. We do not originate prayer; it is already going on in us. God's Word has the initiative; we are simply the listeners.

It is always God who calls men to keep company with him, never the other way about. His call may indeed sometimes come to us in the form of a desire for prayer and contemplation; but we shall not have got very far before he makes it clear that the initiative is still and always in his hands.[9]

This dynamic of prayer—divine initiative and human response—has been expressed in various ways. Thornton calls it the via media principle, meaning that devotion always grows out of doctrine, feelings out of fact.[10] The most sublime contemplative prayer begins with the simple recognition of the coming of the Word to us. The human race, says von Balthasar, was created to hear the Word, and only in responding to the Word rises to its full dignity.[11] In responding to the Word we discover our true innermost being, namely, our life in the Trinity, without which we are dead even while we live, unable to be fully the persons we are meant to be. We are what we are by virtue of this most intimate of relationships. In the words of von Balthasar,

> No relationship is closer, more rooted in being itself, than that between the man in grace and the Lord who gives grace, between the Head and the body, between the vine and the branches. But this relationship can only have full play . . . if the freedom of the word is answered by a corresponding readiness on the part of man to hear, to follow and to comply.[12]

If indeed prayer is human readiness to hear, to follow, to comply so that the utterly basic relationship with God can be more fully realized, it explains why prayer is regarded as the heart of religion, the very sword of the saints[13] and the mother and source of the ascent of the soul to God.[14] In prayer we begin to see ourselves as God sees us and we see God as he is. In prayer we acknowledge that we are not in control. This is simply acknowledging a basic fact of our existence. Not to pray is to take destiny into our own hands, to falsify our true self as dependent creatures and to deny God as the Sovereign One.

Praying Beyond Ourselves

When we see God as the center of all things, our prayer begins to have far-reaching social implications. We come to realize that all things are ultimately connected to God. Everything has a place in God's world: the trees and birds and clods of earth, bolts and nuts, gas pipelines and political parties, my next-door neighbor and her dog, demons and angels. We cannot really pray without seeing the interconnectedness of all things. The Greek theologians call knowledge arising from prayer "spiritual knowledge." "Consisting wholly of love," it "does not allow the mind to expand and embrace the vision of the divine unless we first win back to love even one who has become angry with us for no reason."[15] Prayer thus enlarges our vision. It is, according to Eugene Peterson, an "unselfing" process that reverberates into every social and political realm.[16]

People who pray find themselves involved both with the king who is establishing his rule in the cosmos and the priest who is setting persons right, before God. In prayer we participate from the center to the periphery of God's oscillating personal/political action.[17]

Prayer spiritualizes all aspects of life. Prayer makes every activity, whether work, thought or anything else, religious. Without prayer, the Golden Rule is mere ethical precept, championing the cause of the poor, mere social ethics. Yet prayer is no substitute for work or other things we ought to do:

It is not a lazy substitute for work and thought: fields are not plowed by praying over them. But let a man remember also that fields become a drudgery, or a botched labor, or even a greed and a bitterness, unless the plowing is done in prayer.[18]

Today's world is increasingly defined by the market economy. Thus work has become one of the most significant activities that people pursue. In prayer, work loses its self-serving character and aims at serving God: *ad maiorem Dei gloriam* (to the greater glory of God). When we pray, we no longer see work solely in terms of profit and productivity; we begin to see it in terms of its ultimate intention in creation—to further the blessings of creation and counter the effects of wickedness.[19] This view of work can only be achieved through prayer, which opens our vision to the interconnectedness of all things to God.

But what if we cannot envision such purposefulness in our work? It is a question that merits a minor digression because it underscores the critical function of ascetical theology. The typical Protestant response assumes that the Christian who has a grasp of the truth will somehow be able to carry it out in practice. Thus most sermons exhort their hearers to practice truth but do not explain how to do it. No consideration is given to the fact that a wide chasm exists between their present state and the final goal. Ascetical theology bridges this chasm by elucidating several steps that lead to the fulfillment of a true theology of work. Working for profit may be the first step taken toward the final end of work. But the true ascetic working for profit has motives that differ from those of someone who is merely motivated by profit. The ascetic's work is part of a charted path of growth toward the internalization of a full theology of work. Between the first step and the final goal there are a number of small intervening steps. The theology of work in the monastic rule of Basil does not embrace such grand concepts as participating in God's creative work but focuses on the intervening steps. Work is aimed primarily at keeping the demon of idleness at bay and making one useful to the community.

Everyone, therefore, in doing his work, should place before himself the aim of service to the needy and not his own satisfaction. Thus will he escape the charge of self-love and receive the blessing for fraternal charity from the Lord, who said, As long as you did it to one of these, my least brethren, you did it to me.[20]

The same ascetical concern lies behind Bernard's four degrees of love. Even the love of self for self's sake contributes a small beginning toward the highest degree of loving self for God's sake. Thus to realize the divine purpose for work, we need *askesis,* simply doing our work, if not faithfully, at least relentlessly—with prayer. This combination of work and prayer will begin to have a positive formative effect on our life. For this, we have the example of the Benedictine rule, which probably achieves the highest integration of *ora et labora* (prayer and work). The rule of the Benedictine community revolves around the two poles: prayer, also called the *opus Dei* (work of God), and manual labor. The rhythm of prayer and work is maintained within the rule so that prayer progressively sanctifies work.

In seeking to integrate prayer and work, we must avoid an ancient danger that has reasserted itself in our technological society: magic. Magic is trying to manipulate natural or supernatural powers to serve our purposes. The self stands at the center of the universe, not God. Modern technologists are the successors to pagan magicians.[21] The magical attitude exists among technologically minded Christians as well. If you have faith, they say, anything you ask in prayer will be yours. Prayer is a technique for twisting God's arm to get what they want. Such prayers are an abuse of relationship. And to abuse a friendship is to lose it.

Another way of abusing prayer is trying to make it work for us. Instead of unselfing ourselves, we use prayer to reinforce our egos. Jesus unmasked Pharisees who only pretended to pray (at busy street intersections) and used prayer to confirm their own self-righteousness in the parable of the Pharisee and the publican. The Pharisee in the parable prayed *to himself* (Lk 18:11), not God. This is why honesty is essential in prayer. It differentiates the selfish prayer of a novice Christian from the prayer of the Pharisee. If a young Christian's prayers are constantly taken up with *my* health, *my* family, *my* personal relationship with God, at least they are prayed in honesty. They are the beginning (but only the beginning) of true asceticism leading to union with God (which, no doubt, is still some distance away). But without honesty, we can all deceive ourselves into thinking that we are praying to God when we are only using prayer as a manipulative tool. As Buttrick reminds us, "sincere prayer will keep you from self-deception, or self-deception will keep you from your prayers."[22]

Perhaps we adults need to relearn prayer from little children, whose prayers, if they are not yet corrupted by so-called adult sophistication, are disarmingly simple and honest. When a rich man invited Francis of Assisi to stay for the night in hopes of learning the secret of his prayer, what he heard all night was a single outpouring from the saint: "My God and my all."[23] What the rich man learned was sincere prayer, simple and unembellished. Duplicity is not easy to unlearn. Despite the sure knowledge that nothing in all creation is hidden from God's sight and that everything is uncovered and laid bare before the eyes of him to whom we must give account (Heb 4:13), most of us seldom pray in complete honesty. Austin Farrer was right when he called self-deception "a school in which we could all of us take first class degrees."[24] We have honed self-deception to a fine art. The only way to purify our motive and get rid of self-deception in prayer is through prayer itself: "Search me, O God, and know my heart. Try me, and know my thoughts." We are back to prayer as the basic *askesis*, the first principle of ascetical theology.

Growth in Prayer

Intimacy with God is what characterizes a life of prayer. Intimacy is the gift of God's Spirit, who indwells believers and raises their consciousness of being children of God so that they instinctively cry, "Abba, Father!" (Rom 8:15-16). All prayer, because it is the gift of the quickening Spirit, is charismatic.[25] The Pentecostal doctrine of baptism in the Spirit with the accompanying sign of glossolalia is not wholly adequate to encapsulate this dynamic reality. It teaches that the life of prayer can *begin* with the familiar intimacy of a child who comes before its Father with unquestioning trust and total abandon.[26] But this is only one level of intimacy. It needs to grow.

    Growth in personal relationships is never easy, as anyone who has been married long will attest. Intimate association unmasks us and forces us to face the truth about ourselves. But the mask does not come off all at once; the unmasking is like peeling an onion one layer at a time. It is a painful process. "Humankind cannot bear very much reality," observed T. S. Eliot.[27] Intimacy with God is especially difficult because the faults are never mutual. We cannot point our finger at God and say, "It's all your fault," or even "It's partly your fault." When there is difficulty in our relationship with God, the fault always lies squarely with us. Even righteous Job had to learn that lesson (Job 42:1-6). Perhaps this is why prayer is hard work. It is hard, much as any *serious* human relationship is hard. But it is especially hard when each time we face an impasse, a dry stretch, a deathly silence, we discover something within ourselves causing that problem. Prayer is hard work because it is so humbling. We are never given the satisfaction of being able to turn to God and say smugly, "I am right this time."

But are we free to express the inner turmoil, the dark confusion and the *feeling* of being wronged? The psalmist did—more than occasionally. And so did Teresa of Ávila, the saint who has taught us some of the most profound lessons on prayer. Teresa knew hardship, but it was hardship honestly faced. The last straw came during a particularly difficult period when she had to cross a river while sick with a fever. She turned to her Lord and complained, "Lord, amid so many ills this comes on top of all the rest!"

The voice answered her:

"That is how I treat my friends."

"Ah my God! That is why you have so few of them!"[28]

Hard as the spiritual life may be, we have spiritual fathers and mothers who have gone before us. Their progress in prayer enabled them to chart a generally reliable path of growth for us. While we do not slavishly follow everything they say, we would do well to heed the tips and advice these more mature saints have passed down. Those who have truly learned to pray are the best guides for our own prayer life. George Buttrick's question is entirely apropos here: "Who can understand music but the musician, or prayer but the man who long has prayed?"[29]

It is important to understand two aspects of growth in prayer. First, growth in prayer, unlike physical growth, cannot be clearly separated into stages, although it is possible to distinguish characteristics that belong to beginners and proficients. Second, growth in prayer seems to follow a pattern of development similar to growth in marriage. In the beginning prayer tends to be more vocal and petitionary. Like a young lover, the young Christian loves out of selfish considerations and a need to fill up every moment with words. The young Christian loves God for her own sake, and this is reflected in prayers that concentrate on personal concerns, even though they may be legitimate, as the eighteenth-century Jesuit Jean Grou astutely observed:

Self-love has often a larger share than we imagine in the desire to keep our conscience clear, to correct our faults and to make progress in virtue; however small the share may be it is always too large, for self-love has no place in holiness which demands its complete destruction.[30]

The one who grows in prayer moves farther and farther away from self-interested prayers of petition to God-directed prayers of adoration and thanksgiving. Prayers become less vocal and more mental. Words and images become unnecessary as the soul draws deeper into the heart of prayer. The one praying engages God with a simple attention of the mind and an equally simple application of the will. The highest prayers are those in which God prays in us: "Pray thou thyself in me so that my prayer may be ever directed to thy glory."[31]

Grou's practical summary of the soul's progress in prayer encapsulates the essential teachings of the Christian spiritual tradition:

Here I will observe that almost all those who confine themselves to vocal prayer generally relate their prayers to themselves; that more spiritual Christians who practise meditation generally use it as a means to the amendment of life, so that their reflections and acts of affection and resolutions have no other aim than the correction of their faults and growth in virtue. It is the interior souls who are the only ones who make God the supreme object of their prayers, for they are entirely devoted to his glory, his love and his adorable will. This will not seem strange when we consider that it is God who prays in them, God who praises himself and glorifies himself through them, and that, rightly regarded, their prayer is a more or less perfect image of what he is doing perpetually in himself.[32]

The similarity between growth in prayer and growth in marriage is instructive for anyone seeking a deeper prayer life. The basic pattern is joy-sorrow-joy. The Eastern bishop Diadochos sums it up most aptly. "Initiatory joy is one thing, the joy of perfection is another. The first is not exempt from fantasy, while the second has the strength of humility. Between the two joys comes godly sorrow (2 Cor 7:10) and active tears."[33] Marriage usually starts with a honeymoon period. Many Christians who are converted as adults find that prayer seems to come easily at the beginning of the Christian life. There is little struggle. Temptations are easily overcome. Many obnoxious habits just fall away. Prayer is all enjoyment. Every petition receives an immediate answer. Faith soars. The young lover is experiencing the first flush of romance. To use another analogy, little does the new convert realize that God, like every good farmer, is taking special effort to protect the young seedling from the severe natural elements. Thornton notes that in the early stages of our prayer, the Lord gives us "pleasant experiences—little spiritual sweetmeats—which are withdrawn as soon as we have achieved some modicum of maturity."[34]

Romance gives way to reality in a period of painful discoveries and adjustments. When the seedling has sufficiently taken root to withstand the heat of the noonday sun, the protective shelter is quietly withdrawn and the props are removed. No more sweetmeats! Praying becomes a constant struggle with distractions. Despite an occasional uplift, one plods through a lifeless devotion. The sudden shower is all too short to quench the seemingly endless aridity. God is silent. It is unfortunate that many modern Christians are never taught such elementary lessons of spiritual progress. They expect their early excitement to continue uninterrupted throughout life. The end of the honeymoon disturbs them, and they seek desperately to rekindle their first flush of feeling. But the great spiritual writers are quite unanimous that this is a basic part of growth. The struggles we have to go through in prayer are part of progress in prayer. There must be purgation, pruning and lancing for certain qualities to develop in preparation for union with God. Masters of the art of prayer try to help us deal with this critical aspect of the prayer life. The most sustained treatment is found in *Ascent of Mount Carmel* and *The Dark Night of the Soul,* by St. John of the Cross.[35]

The phenomenon of the dark night, so central to the life of prayer, is little understood nowadays. Some modern Christians see it as a failure instead of a sign of spiritual progress. Their expectations are conditioned by modern sensate culture telling them that whatever is good and true must *feel* good. Christians ought to be joyful and victorious. If ever they feel down, they must be out of God's will. Thus many measure the effectiveness of ministry by the ability to motivate people and to maintain their enthusiasm at a certain level. Someone who is going through a dark night is likely to be told to snap out of it or to see a psychologist.

Against such a trivialization of the spiritual life, John's analysis of the dark night takes on special significance. He explains that the dark night begins with the soul who is progressing from the "beginner" to the "proficient" stage. It intensifies with further progress toward union with God. Thus John distinguishes two dark nights—"the night of the sense" and "the night of the spirit."[36] During the first night the soul experiences aridities that tempt it to rely on previous activities that brought joy, namely, meditation and spiritual reflections. But what worked earlier is of no use now. Meditation is done with great dislike and inward unwillingness (1.10.1). The soul must now learn to be quiet and restful, to be patient and to persevere in prayer and not be anxious about meditation, contenting itself with directing its attention lovingly and calmly toward God. The soul must not even try to feel and taste God's presence (1.10.5) as it is being led from meditation to contemplation.

The soul that passes through this first night emerges as a proficient. It now experiences a new, deeper kind of joy, the joy of infused contemplation, which John describes as "a secret, peaceful and loving infusion of God, which, if admitted, will set the soul on fire with the spirit of love" (1.11.8). The proficient experiences "abundant sweetness and interior delight" that come from the sensual part, which is now purified. Still, the purgation of the soul remains incomplete. It must pass through a deeper night, the night of the spirit (2.1.2). Here the soul undergoes further stripping. Sense and spirit are detached from all sweetness and from all imaginations, and the soul travels on the road of faith dark and pure (2.2.6). God denudes the faculties—the affections and feelings, spiritual and sensual, interior and exterior—"leaving the understanding in darkness, the will dry, the memory empty, the affections of the soul in the deepest affliction, bitterness and distress, withholding from it the former sweetness it had in spiritual things" (2.3.4).

For John, the dark night is not confined to one phase of the Christian life. It actually intensifies through life as one draws closer to God. But what differentiates a dark night from boredom with life? John makes it clear throughout his work that when one is going through a dark night, however little feeling one has, one continues to persist in prayer, traveling on "the road of faith dark and pure" (2.2.6). The less one depends on feelings, the more one is prepared for union with God. Jean Grou, typically, distills the wisdom of his predecessor. He explains that to "the soul that has made some progress, love is not a matter of feeling but rather a determination of the will to do everything and to suffer everything for God." The "more this love is deprived of feeling, the stronger and purer it is."[37]

Tragically, unrealistic expectations in regard to the Christian life have kept many modern Christians from accepting the cost of this maturation process. They are like the seeds that fall on stony places. They receive the word with joy—for a time—but when tribulation or persecution comes, they quickly fall away (Mt 13:20-21). But the soul that perseveres through the dark night comes to the dawn of a new day. A deeper, more mature love emerges. It enjoys a kind of intimacy in prayer that is comparable to the golden years of a marriage. Occasional dry spells persist, but they are experienced with aplomb. The growth of a young tree is fast and dramatic. An older tree continues to grow, but its growth is less dramatic. Similarly, a young Christian may grow by leaps and bounds in the beginning of the Christian life. Maturity brings growth that is more subtle but no less real. The mature Christian lives with less and less reliance on signs and feelings. Some Christians, failing to understand this principle of growth, have resorted to desperate measures such as frequent and severe—but quite fruitless—self-examinations.

Problems in prayer frequently mirror difficulties in human relationships. For example, if we have difficulty relating to people, it is small wonder that we have difficulty relating to God. Conversely, as we learn that some people can accept us in spite of ourselves, that is to say, we are recipients of their grace, similarly, we can accept God's free forgiveness and receive God's grace.[38] But the converse is also true. Learning to trust God and receive his grace freely leads to better relationships with people. Thus there are two sides to the problem of prayer. We need to be right with people in order to be right with God, and we need to be right with God in order to be right with people. But where to begin? Do we need to get right with people and then get right with God or vice versa? Jesus' teaching about leaving the gift at the altar and seeking reconciliation first suggests the priority of human relationships (Mt 5:23, 24). But the one who was told to go and to reconcile was *first* at the altar offering his gift; it was there that he remembered his offended brother. What is crucial is that the whole reconciling process began in prayer. We are inexorably driven back again to prayer as the first principle of ascetical theology.

Praying by the Rule

It is unnecessary to belabor the point that anyone who takes prayer seriously eventually encounters difficulty. Teresa of Ávila, who has taught us so much about prayer, knew it acutely.

> Very often I was more occupied with the wish to see the end of my hour for prayer. I used to actually watch the sandglass. And the sadness that I sometimes felt on entering my prayer-chapel was so great that it required all my courage to force myself inside.[39]

Yet, Teresa counsels, we need to persevere, to persist in prayer despite the contrary feelings. "And when I persisted in this way, I found far greater peace and joy than when I prayed with excitement and emotional rapture." What Teresa teaches us is a truth both simple and utterly basic: the only way to learn to pray is to pray. Real prayer does not come from discovering some esoteric technique, although acquiring some techniques of proper breathing and posture can help us pray better. But mastering these skills is not mastering prayer, any more than learning the skills of sailing will bring us to our destination. If prayer is the manifesting of baptism, then every Christian cannot help but pray. The "technique" of prayer is the same as the technique of going to church. The question is not, Do you know how to go to church? but, Do you *want* to go to church? Every drowning man knows how to pray. The real problem is what he does after the crisis has passed. Does he want to pray? The problem of will is the problem of *askesis,* and that is a problem for ascetical theology.

The task for ascetical theology, therefore, is to provide an efficient rule of life and a good rationale for it so that we are motivated to live by rule. A rule of life could be simply defined as "a schedule of the occupations and practices of piety an individual should perform during the day."[40] Living by rule (Latin *regula*) is what turns one into a regular Christian. A regular Christian is one whose basic orientation in life is to be a full-time Christian. A Christian lay regular, explains Thornton, "is one who intends and attempts to order his life of prayer in a particular way, according to some clear-cut model."[41] The rule addresses precisely the problem of will in prayer. Accepting the rule of prayer is not the same as drawing up a list of *rules* and promising to keep them. It is more like embracing a state of being, such as opting to become married. The rule of prayer ties one to a rhythm of living in which praying is a way of life. The rule induces the will to pray, much as being married induces a young man to love his spouse and checks his unbridled lust. The rule sets the basic tone for Christian living. Occasional slip-ups do not make one less of a regular Christian any more than a few missed targets turn a professional soldier into an irregular or occasional arguments make a couple less married.

Petitionary Prayer

Prayer arises out of the fact of our incorporation into Christ. It is a manifesting of baptism. It is always a response to the divine initiative. This basic theology of prayer comes into focus when the nature of petitionary prayer is examined. Far from being an unnecessary appendage to faith, prayers of petition are central and foundational to the life of prayer. Prayers are the life signs of those who are in Christ. Just as the first cries of newborn babies are probably petitionary (I'm hungry! or I'm wet!), the primal cries of the newly born again are spontaneously petitionary. Their baptism, their passage through the crisis of conversion from the kingdom of darkness to the kingdom of God's Son (Col 1:13), is manifested in childlike and unabashed requests. People in a crisis know how to pray, returning to their primal instinct.

> Petition is our native response when life is rent, when in some terror or glory we realize that the world is infinite. Our boat is little, the sea is vast, the Spirit is Everlasting—from these ingredients, age after age, petitionary prayer is compounded. . . . A saving realism will admit that petition seizes us despite all our safeguards and sophistications. It is as elementally human as a cry.[42]

All prayers begin with petition. At the heart of prayer is the simple, unsolicited faith that rises up to ask, "Give us this day our daily bread." Luther understood this fact well. "Man tells what he desires . . . he desires to get out of his misery, to be free of the evil thing; he begs for it; he is not abashed before exalted Majesty but speaks outright, help me, dear God!" Heiler, from whom this quotation is taken, goes on to observe, "The kernel of prophetic prayer is, like that of primitive prayer, the simple request for deliverance from an evil, or the granting of gifts and favour."[43] Our Lord promised, "Ask and it will be given to you, seek and you will find, knock and the door will be opened to you." With this teaching he laid the foundation for the whole superstructure of ascetical theology.

At bottom, we do in fact pray and are enabled to pray. Petition proves it. The newborn baby and the newly born again demonstrate it. So why does prayer cease to be spontaneous and natural? Why does it become an uphill task? The problem has to do partly with the necessary fact of growth and partly with the wholly unnecessary fact of human negligence. As children grow up, they begin to acquire greater linguistic skills, assimilate more and more of the surrounding culture and take on increasing responsibilities as members of the human community. In this process of growth they inevitably meet new challenges that require further refinement of their linguistic skills. Growth in prayer involves similar challenges. Petition, while necessary and foundational, is not everything. Our prayer language must develop to assimilate the larger knowledge of God that finds expression in the more developed language of colloquy, thanksgiving and adoration.[44] What used to come instinctually must now be done with some deliberation. *Askesis* and rule are needed to sustain prayer, but these disciplines, it must be stressed, are possible because the prayer instinct is already present.

Those who find meeting the challenges of growth in prayer too painful prefer to opt out. Their prayer language is arrested at the infantile level of constant petitions for their selfish needs. A few do not even attain that point. If nothing seems to happen when they pray, they stop praying altogether. The primal instinct that they received at conversion becomes squelched. It is impossible even to imagine the frightful consequences of the end of conversation with God. When progress stops, regression begins. The end of prayer may be self-imposed banishment from the human community and the end of all conversation. "They that have despised the Word of God, from them shall the word of man also be taken away."[45]

If petitionary prayer is foundational to Christian asceticism, there is a sense in which it is common to all prayers and to all of life. We elevate petitionary prayer to the status of an unsolvable mystery only because of a mechanistic mindset: How could God intervene to answer our prayer without upsetting thereby the other parts of his ordered universe? If God answers the prayers of one Christian farmer for rain, may he not have to withhold answering the Christian fisherman's prayer for sunshine to preserve his day's catch?[46] Although petition can raise problems when it involves requests affecting the physical world, yet every prayer is directly or indirectly petitionary. When we ask for God's name to be hallowed and for God's will to be done on earth as in heaven, are we not in effect asking for large-scale reordering? If God's will is to be done on earth, how is it to be done? Asking this question, we are immediately overwhelmed by a host of humanly insuperable requests. Every dictator will have to be cast down, every unnatural death will have to be eliminated, every empty stomach will have to be filled, and on and on. Perhaps the reason why we do not see petition on such a scale as problematic is that we do not expect much to happen in response to such a prayer. We eliminate the problem by not taking the prayer too seriously.

Or perhaps we do take our prayers seriously. But we find it more credible that God should answer a spiritual prayer for his will to be done on earth than that he should respond to a request for more sunshine to produce quality dried fish. There is something inherently wrong with such thinking. Besides its crude dualism, it fails to notice that the praying person is united with the God who is Lord over all things—including dried fish! There is really no ultimate distinction between the simplest petition for daily bread and the highest reaches of the prayer of transforming union of Teresa of Ávila. They are both directly or indirectly petitionary. What affects our inmost spirit also affects our world. "Christianity is a religion of spirit and flesh. Its truth shines through our earthy day."[47]

Petition makes perfectly good sense when it is understood in the context of friendship, not in the context of physical cause and effect. Petition is the extension of the gift God shares with us, the gift of subcreation, whereby he works things not apart from us but through us. In encouraging his children to ask, God chooses to work through our prayer. God gives us things through our prayers rather than apart from them. When God gives us what we ask, we come to understand communion with him better. Real asking, giving and receiving are deep interchanges between friends, not business transactions. What we call the fixed laws of nature and nature's variableness are both means by which God reveals his goodness to his children.

> The variabilities of earth are God's play of impromptu act, which some-
> times grants our childish askings and thereby serves our growth. The
> fixities likewise are filled with His presence: they are not belts of inertia,
> but assurances of His unwearied care.[48]

This brief theology of prayer has highlighted the nature of growth in prayer and the fundamental relationship that prayer bears to ascetical theology. The first concern charts the path of spiritual progress and the second reveals its possibility. The path of ascent on Mount Carmel is well trodden and clearly marked. Successful climbers are the ones who leave their well-placed equipment behind so that we too can make our own ascent. We thwart our own progress if we ignore their posted signs and their offers of help.

7

SPIRITUAL EXERCISES
FOCUSING ON
GOD & SELF

· ·

T HERE IS A GROWING CONVICTION AMONG MODERN CHRISTIANS THAT CHRISTI-
anity must be relevant to the workplace. Otherwise it ceases to have much
meaning and becomes an esoteric activity we engage in for an hour one day
a week. We need a theology to help us in "redeeming the routine" so that
every aspect of ordinary life is fully integrated with faith.[1] What brings such
a theology to life for people is a spiritual or ascetical theology that trains
Christians in the art of unceasing or habitual prayer. If Christians know what
it means to "pray without ceasing" (1 Thess 5:17), "be constant in prayer"
(Rom 12:12), "pray in the Spirit at all times in every prayer and supplication"
(Eph 6:18), "continue steadfastly in prayer" (Col 4:2) and "always . . . pray
and not faint" (Lk 18:1), then all aspects of life will be redeemed.

Prayer keeps God at the center of all things, and unceasing prayer brings
God into every aspect of our day-to-day existence. We begin to see God in
creation, in every creature, in every historic or mundane event, in every
encounter of consequence or seeming inconsequence. Unceasing prayer
helps us maintain spiritual poise—a constantly prayerful frame of mind in
the midst of hectic activities. But cultivating such spiritual composure takes
practice and discipline. Like any other *habitus,* it is formed by repeated acts.
We are dealing with a habit that comes with some measure of spiritual
proficiency. Even Christians of many years' standing (especially evangelicals)
have not attained even a modicum of the mental discipline necessary for

such a habit to develop.[2] Thus one of the aims of spiritual theology is to help us build a bridge from the simple tasks involving small changes of mental habits, such as learning to acknowledge God in all things, to the higher reaches of prayer in which God becomes all in all. The "practical" mindset of modern people makes it almost impossible for them to learn even the basic skills of solitude and silence except in small steps.

The principle of unceasing prayer goes back to Basil's monastic rule. Monks could pray and recite psalms while they worked. (Basil was adamant that prayer and psalmody were not a substitute for work.) Better still, they could pray and sing in their hearts.

Thus, in the midst of our work can we fulfill the duty of prayer, giving thanks to Him who has granted strength to our hands for performing our tasks and cleverness to our minds for acquiring knowledge, and for having provided the materials, both that which is in the instruments we use and that which forms the matter of the arts in which we may be engaged, praying that the work of our hands may be directed toward its goal, the good pleasure of God.

Thus we acquire a recollected spirit—when in every action we beg from God the success of our labors and satisfy our debt of gratitude to Him who gave us the power to do the work, and when, as has been said, we keep before our minds the aim of pleasing Him. If this is not the case, how can there be consistency in the words of the Apostle bidding us to "pray without ceasing," with those others, "we worked night and day."[3]

According to Jean Grou, unceasing prayer is "prayer of the heart" created by the Holy Spirit who indwells us. The intention of the Spirit is to pray in us always. It does not mean that "definite acts of prayer would be made every moment" but that "the heart would always be at the disposition of the Holy Spirit, to make such acts as often as he should please, and the germ of them would be preserved in the ground of the soul, ready to be developed as the occasion arose."[4]

Unceasing prayer is possible only if we see ourselves as members of Christ's body throughout the world. No matter how unceasing an individual's prayer may be, sleep is a necessity. But while one member of the body rests, other members can carry on praying. Thus in the final analysis the call to unceasing prayer is a call to be an active participant in the work of the church. We pray unceasingly only as a member of the Christ's church.

We can cultivate unceasing prayer by means of three related exercises: practicing the presence of God, conforming to God's will and maintaining fidelity to grace. These three exercises have God as the primary focus. They are more clearly distinguished as acts than as habits. As habits they are simply different aspects of unceasing prayer. As acts they offer practical ways of training in habitual prayer. When we focus on God, we begin to see ourselves as we really are. Knowing God is only the obverse side of knowing ourselves. Unceasing prayer and the practice of self-examination go hand in hand. We cannot have one without the other.

The Practice of the Presence of God

Also called the prayer of recollection, the practice of the presence of God consists in recalling as frequently as possible that God is present everywhere, especially in the depths of the soul. The most famous exemplar of this type of prayer is Brother Lawrence: "The time of business does not with me differ from the time of prayer; and in the noise and clatter of my kitchen, while several persons are at the same time calling for different things, I possess God in as great tranquillity as if I were upon my knees at the blessed sacrament."[5] As a simple, unlettered man Brother Lawrence did not reflect much on his own experience. His practice of the presence of God was told simply and recorded by someone else. He did not have much of a method; in fact, he tells us that he found formal methods of prayer unhelpful. For many years Brother Lawrence tried the usual forms of prayer and meditation taught in books, such as the meditation on the four last things, but he did not find these methods helpful.

> I have quitted all forms of devotion and set prayers but those to which my state obliges me. And I make it my business only to persevere in His holy presence wherein I keep myself by a simple attention, and a general fond regard to God; or, to speak better, an habitual, silent, and secret conversation of the soul with God, which often causes me joys and raptures inwardly, and sometimes also outwardly, so great that I am forced to use means to moderate them and prevent their appearance to others.[6]

Through long practice the Christian tradition has evolved a number of ways to help us engage in this exercise. We shall briefly consider a few of them, namely, recollection, the Jesus Prayer, the church calendar and the book of providence.

Recollection. The habit of being in the presence of God that Brother Lawrence knew so well can be reinforced by *acts* of recollection: "the habit of turning to God at regular times throughout the working day."[7] The acts of recollection are formalized in Francis de Sales's well-worn exhortation at the beginning of each set meditation: "Place thyself with reverence before God." Francis encourages us to visualize four levels of God's presence with us. First, God is present with us in his immensity or omnipresence. Second, he is present by the fact of his indwelling all believers. Third, Christ is especially present with believers who are in prayer, and fourth, we are to imagine that Christ is right by us as surely as he is locally present in the sacraments.[8] Engaging in any one of these acts of recollection predisposes the mind to proceed with meditation and prayer.

Recollection need not consist of formalized acts or be fixed in time, although scheduling regular times for these acts produces greater proficiency. Ejaculatory prayers are commonly used to help recollection.[9] These are short prayers—sometimes no more than just a mental note—that can be interspersed at various times throughout the day, such as when waking up, before meals, leaving for work, going home and retiring at the end of a day. Ancient writers compared ejaculation to arrows that are shot directly up to heaven. One Puritan writer vividly described the function of an "ejaculatory meditation" in this way:

> A holy heart, in heavenly mindedness, will get out of the throng of cares and business, will be often breaking off the thread of earthly thoughts, and interpose some heavenly dart up to heaven, make a short visit thither, refresh itself with some heavenly dainty . . . have a running banquet of heavenly sweetmeats, when it cannot sit down and feed at large by a fuller set meditation.[10]

Traditional spiritual directories, such as Lewis Bayly's *Practice of Piety,* are full of such ejaculatory prayers. They can serve as fixed points in our personal rule of life, thus sustaining us in continual prayer throughout the day. Ejaculatory prayers can be practiced as readily in the uncomplicated world of ancient Christians as in the far more complex world of present-day Christians.[11] They do not need to conform to any formal structure, for they represent diverse conditions under which we speak to God. An ejaculatory prayer can be an expression of gratitude or a desperate cry for help. Protestants who are more accustomed to "free prayers" may find their own ad hoc compositions more congenial, although memorizing some short, set prayers (such as the Collects in the Book of Common Prayer) may come in handy at times. Even a well-worn cliché like "Thank God it's Friday!" can constitute an appropriate ejaculatory prayer.

We often excuse our lack of spiritual dynamism and attribute it to the demands of modern living. If the pace of life were less hectic, if I had more time, then I could begin to practice Christianity more conscientiously. We take a break from our work and spend a few days in a country retreat, where we can pray better. We then conclude that rural life is more conducive to spiritual cultivation. Nothing is further from the truth. What makes it conducive is not the rural life but probably the change of routine, which provides the opportunity, however brief, of a new perspective. A rural existence would be dogged by the demon of acedia no less than an urban one. No one who has read the desert fathers has any illusion about the desert's being conducive to spirituality. The fight with the flesh, the world and the devil is actually fiercer in the desert than in the city. If some did turn out to be better Christians (many did not), it was because their minds were trained for tough combat, and the desert provided just such a training ground. The key to spiritual proficiency is having a mind for it. Ejaculatory prayers may offer a good beginning for the one who has such a mind.

The Jesus Prayer. The Jesus Prayer, which is highly recommended by the Eastern fathers, is a form of ejaculatory prayer.[12] It comes in many forms. The form used most commonly is "Lord Jesus Christ, Son of God, have mercy on me, a sinner." The monks were painfully aware that the path of spiritual progress is fraught with difficulties. Greater exertions to purify the inner life seem to stimulate "assaults of the passions" and many other temptations of the devil and the flesh. Praying the Jesus Prayer helps keep the mind focused and helps strengthen the will to resist all such temptations. In one of the earliest mentions of the use of the prayer, Diadochos of Photiki (mid-fifth century) highly commends it: "He who wishes to cleanse his heart should keep it continually aflame through practising the remembrance of the Lord Jesus, making this his only study and his ceaseless task."[13] According to another monk, Hesychios (ninth century?), when we invoke the name of Jesus continually and humbly, praying it rhythmically with the rhythm of the breath, we will be able to maintain watchfulness against the enemy's onslaught.

> Attentiveness is the heart's stillness, unbroken by any thought. In this stillness the heart breathes and invokes, endlessly and without ceasing, only Jesus Christ who is the Son of God and Himself God. It confesses Him who alone has power to forgive our sins, and with His aid it courageously faces its enemies. Through this invocation enfolded continually in Christ, who secretly divines all hearts, the soul does everything it can to keep its sweetness and its inner struggle hidden from men, so that the devil, coming upon it surreptitiously, does not lead it into evil and destroy its precious work.
>
> The more the rain falls on the earth, the softer it makes it; similarly, Christ's holy name gladdens the earth of our heart the more we call upon it.[14]

The possibilities of the Jesus Prayer are beautifully exemplified in *The Way of a Pilgrim,* the story of a nineteenth-century Russian peasant who discovered the meaning of Paul's exhortation to pray without ceasing in the recitation of the Jesus Prayer. The staretz (spiritual director) from whom the anonymous pilgrim first learned the prayer explained that the ceaseless Jesus Prayer is a continuous, uninterrupted call on the holy name of Jesus Christ with the lips, mind, and heart; and in the awareness of His abiding presence it is a plea for His blessing in all undertakings, in all places, at all times, even in sleep. . . . Anyone who becomes accustomed to this Prayer will experience great comfort as well as the need to say it continuously. He will become accustomed to it to such a degree that he will not be able to do without it and eventually the Prayer will of itself flow in him.[15]

What is most significant about the prayer is that it embodies both a theology of prayer and a practical method of praying. Theologically, "the holy name of Jesus Christ contains within itself all the truths of the gospel." It is "the abbreviated form of the gospel," so that in praying the Jesus Prayer one is seeking to internalize the entire gospel. It operates on the same principle as regular reading of the Gospels.[16] The pilgrim under the direction of the staretz discovered that he could begin with vocal recitation of the prayer. In time it became an interior prayer or "prayer of the heart." Three thousand recitations a day became six and then twelve thousand recitations as he grew more and more accustomed to it. Finally "it became so easy and delightful that my tongue and lips seemed to do it of themselves."[17]

Repeatedly invoking the name of Jesus may be similar to chanting a mantra in Hinduism, but its intention and content are wholly different. The aim of praying the Jesus Prayer is not to induce a certain psychological state but to bring one closer to the person of Jesus. For this reason it has to be a prayer that sums up the essence of the gospel. Any psychological benefit it brings is incidental. Functionally, the Jesus Prayer is similar to the short choruses that are sung in charismatic churches today. Perhaps without knowing it, Pentecostal-charismatics have stumbled on a practice with an impeccable lineage! I shall say more about chorus singing later.

The church calendar. There is a sense in which Christians who belong to the so-called high church tradition have an advantage when it comes to the practice of the presence of God. All they need to do is plug themselves in to the already existing cycles of the daily office and feasts, special events and saints' days in the church calendar. These ready-made patterns can provide an efficient framework for the individual to develop a personal rhythm of recollection. It may be asking too much of a busy office worker to observe the seven canonical hours of the monastic daily office. But Basil Pennington has suggested some helpful modern lay equivalents. For example, one can celebrate lauds and vespers in the "chapel of the car" when driving to and from work.[18]

The book of providence. Another way to practice the presence of God is to learn to read the book of providence: God is present in all things and in all events, and to sense his presence in a situation, thing or event can create a powerful impression. Brother Lawrence's pilgrimage began with such an experience.

> That in the winter, seeing a tree stripped of its leaves, and considering that within a little time the leaves would be renewed, and after that the flowers and fruit appear, he [Brother Lawrence] received a high view of the providence and power of God, which has never since been effaced from his soul. That this view had perfectly set him loose from the world, and kindled in him such a love for God that he could not tell whether it had increased during the more than forty years he had lived since.[19]

What Brother Lawrence experienced was neither unique nor new. Earlier writers who commended its practice called it "occasional meditation" or "meditation on the creatures."

Many present-day Christians find work to be one of the greatest hindrances to habitual prayer because it intrudes into practically all aspects of life. We bring home our work—and destroy family conversation. We try to get the last few loose ends tied up at the office before we go on vacation and end up cutting short our vacation time (or we feel better taking some work along). Our supposed "quiet time" with God is habitually drowned by the incessant clamor for more time from the office. Prayer time, "a place of quiet rest, near to the heart of God," is repeatedly invaded by the pager and cellular phone. Even when we are not actually at work, we find it hard to let go of it in our minds. One solution to this captivity to work is to set definite transitions from one activity to another during the day. "We need to work when we work; we need to stop when we stop" is a good principle to live by.

> Definite breaks help to divide the day, allow for stopping and new beginning. Clear change helps to regulate life. Those who do not have sharp change—a housewife, a farmer, or a person with an office at home—must take initiative to set patterns for work and relaxation. Clear transition from one part of a day to another may renew physical, emotional, and spiritual strength.[20]

These daily turning points cut small niches in an otherwise seamless schedule to create a space for nurturing the prayers of recollection. We can by small degrees inculcate a new frame of mind, a mind that is oriented toward God as the center of all things, to replace our modern mindset with its singular fixation on work and productivity.

Conformity to the Will of God

Many young Christians are preoccupied with the question of God's will for their lives. By "God's will" they are thinking of God's specific plans for their own personal future. While the desire to live in God's will is commendable, the motivation for knowing and the very concept of God's will itself are quite questionable. Some desire to know God's will hoping to avoid the need to make painful personal decisions. Knowing in advance and with certitude God's special blueprint for them would simplify their lives considerably, they think. Such people prefer to live by sight rather than by faith with its accompanying struggle and doubt. Part of the problem is that they entertain a very mistaken notion of God's will. God's will is equated with a piece of information, which once grasped, releases them from the responsibility for further discovery.

The biblical idea of knowing God's will is quite different. To conform to God's will is to unite our wills to his in love. Knowing what God wants heightens rather than diminishes our responsibility. We have to make an existential choice: follow him or reject him. It is impossible to choose to follow God unless we love him with the love with which he loves us. Thus to love God is already to be united to God and to be conformed to God's will. This is why Scripture equates loving God with knowing God (1 Jn 4:7-8). Augustine was right when he said, "Love God and do whatever you like." For no one can truly love God and be out of God's will. Everything we do out of love for God will be circumscribed by love and therefore cannot be out of God's will. It does not mean that we will not make any mistakes. Our love is imperfect, and our knowledge, on which we make decisions, is even more so. What it does mean is that even when we make mistakes, we cannot *ultimately* go wrong because love will redirect us to the right path.

Here again practical *askesis* requires us to ask how we can, by taking small steps, learn conformity to God's will.

Immersion in Scripture. The children of God are quite right in following their spiritual instinct to go to the Scriptures to discover the will of God. This is why every Christian must study Scripture diligently, listen to it read in the church and meditate on it day and night. But we need to understand in what sense Scripture reveals God's will. Finding God's will in Scripture is more than just locating specific chapters and verses that seem to support our "affirmative action." Much of Western ideological Christianity tries to locate chapter and verse or, to make an even more impressive case, employs an array of sophisticated hermeneutical tools to discover biblical motifs to support some ideology. Neither does it mean indulging in a practice that is surprisingly common among Christians—flipping open the Bible at random and taking whatever verse the finger happens to rest on.[21] While God in his sovereignty may sometimes accommodate himself to the ways of simplistic

Christians, playing Russian roulette with the texts of Scripture hardly seems a prudent method of identifying God's will.

Scripture reveals God's will in the sense that the whole of it is the narrative of God's dealings with his world. It tells the story of God's creation, God's plan and work of salvation, God's deepest intention and purpose for the world and everything in it. It is in this primary sense that Scripture reveals God's will. When we immerse ourselves deeply in the story through reading and listening, memorizing and meditating, we become a part of the story. We realize that we are not standing outside of Scripture but belong to a living tradition that continues into the present day. It is from this broad understanding of being in God's will that we can address the more specific question of God's will for my life and for this world.

Acknowledging God. We need to make a habit of acknowledging God in all circumstances and decisions. Proverbs 3:5-7 says, "Trust in the LORD with all your heart and lean not on your own understanding; in all your ways acknowledge him, and he will make your paths straight. Do not be wise in your own eyes; fear the LORD and shun evil." There is something straightforward and simple about these instructions. They are the sorts of things we would say to a frightened child: "Trust me, don't be afraid. There, take my hand and I'll lead you. Everything is going to turn out right." Our failure to do God's will is not due to a lack of objective knowledge but to an improper attitude. We spurn God's outstretched hand. We devise our own plans without so much as acknowledging him. We are ill at ease until we are in full control, until we feel that we have a handle on things. We place ourselves in the center of things and keep God safely on the sidelines.

One of the most important lessons we can learn from the spirituality of François Fénelon is total surrender to God's will. But total surrender means a radical reordering of all of life. We cannot serve God, he says, "by opening up a highway toward him." Serving God on our own terms, even when it is done with great religious zeal and virtue, is ultimately self-serving.[22] One must learn "to accustom oneself to live in a continual dependence on the Spirit of God, receiving from moment to moment whatever it pleases him to give us."[23] But overscrupulousness can be defeating. There must be a certain self-forgetfulness in what we do. Simplicity rather than scrupulosity marks the self-surrendered soul.

> This liberty of a soul which sees immediately before it as it goes forward, but which loses no time reasoning about its steps, studying them, constantly considering those which it has already made, this is the true simplicity.[24]

Spiritual simplicity expresses itself sometimes in just plain honesty in God's presence, as Grou reminds us: "Let your heart tell you what you wish to say to God and say it simply without bothering too much about the words; it is ridiculous to be eloquent in his presence and take a pride in prayers that are well composed, instead of using those that are more natural to you."[25] Inner simplicity makes outward simplicity or the simple lifestyle possible. When God is truly at the center, things assume their proper places at the periphery. We achieve simplicity by relating all things to their true center, who is God. All this takes time and practice. Simplification is a process that comes with what Basil Pennington calls "centering prayer," which is itself a process developing from reading *(lectio)*, meditation and prayer *(oratio)*.[26] But the first step is to form the habit of acknowledging God in every situation.

Learning obedience. The Protestant doctrine of the priesthood of all believers has sometimes been distorted into a me-and-my-God egocentrism. We think that because we have direct priestly access to God, we owe obedience to God and no one else. We forget that obedience to God may well come through freely embracing the yoke of human authority. The ancient monks taught us that learning to be under obedience to a human superior is one of the most effective ways of checking our self-will. And self-will, not ignorance, is what hinders us from perfect conformity to God's will. We could "of our own free choice gladly cut off our whole will through obedience," says Diadochos, and "we shall become to some degree tractable and free from self-will."[27] One of the sayings of the desert fathers is that "he who lives in obedience to a spiritual father finds more profit in it than one who withdraws to the desert."[28] The monks knew all too well from experience that all who wished to advance spiritually without coming under some higher authority (usually an abba or amma) succeeded only in deluding themselves. The rule of St. Benedict opens with a call to obedience:

> Hearken, my son, to the precepts of the master and incline the ear of thy heart; freely accept and faithfully fulfil the instructions of a loving father, that by the labour of obedience thou mayest return to him from whom thou hast strayed by the sloth of disobedience. To thee are my words now addressed, whosoever thou mayest be that renouncing thine own will to fight for the true King, Christ, dost take up the strong and glorious weapons of obedience.[29]

Obedience is utterly basic and radical. This is why the rule uses military language to describe the nature of obedience: "Therefore our hearts and bodies must be made ready to fight under the holy obedience of his commands." But such obedience is never understood as an end in itself. It is a means "for the amendment of evil habit or the preservation of charity."[30]

Modern Christians have much to learn from their ancient forebears regarding the discipline of obedience. We are quick to assert our independence from human (and especially ecclesiastical) authority. Many of the modern spiritual helps on the market are based on a do-it-yourself technology that appeals to our pride and sense of self-sufficiency and minimizes the need for accountability to another human being. Self-help books, tapes and videos discuss the latest techniques of prayer and uncover the seven secrets of successful living—as well as delude us into believing that we can become self-taught saints. In point of fact, when it comes to the spiritual life, we are our own worst teachers. As Bernard warns, "If anyone makes himself his own master in the spiritual life, he makes himself scholar to a fool."[31] Christians need to learn obedience just as their Lord did (Heb 5:8). The importance of spiritual direction will be taken up later.

Fidelity to Grace

The term *fidelity to grace,* as usually understood, refers to a specific act of obedience, namely, the humble response to the workings of actual grace. The classic illustration of this practice is found in Jean-Pierre de Caussade (1675-1751), a Jesuit who was for a time spiritual director to the Visitation nuns of Nancy, France. From his direction of these nuns he evolved an exercise that he called "the duty of the present moment." de Caussade explains it in this way:

> Something will prompt us to say: "At the moment I have a liking to this person, or to give away this or to make that." These stirrings of grace must be followed without relying for a single moment on our own judgement, reason or effort. It is God who must decide what we shall do and when, and not ourselves. When we walk with God, his will directs us and must replace every other guidance.
>
> Each moment imposes a virtuous obligation on us which committed souls faithfully obey. For God inspires them with a desire to learn one moment what, in the next, will uphold them in the practice of virtue.
>
> In all that these souls do, they are aware only of an urge to act without knowing why. All they can say is: "I have an urge to write, read, question or observe this. I obey this urge and God, who inspires it, supplies me with a store of knowledge which subsequently I am able to use to the advantage of myself and others." This is why they must always remain simple, pliant and responsive to the slightest prompting from these almost imperceptible impulses.[32]

Christians do experience, more often than they realize, moments when they "feel led" to do something. The name of a person whom we have not seen for some time suddenly comes to mind. We feel an urge to ring up someone.

Occasionally something like a burden descends on us, and we just feel a need to pray. At other times the "call" may come externally. We are told that dear old Mrs. Lee had a rather bad fall and is in the hospital. We bump into a tramp who requests a meal. The tasks that these situations call for may be weighty or trivial. But they require an obedient response. Sometimes it is the trivial and seemingly ridiculous task that creates the greatest difficulty for us. But as Fénelon reminds us, "Whoever goes forward in the presence of God in the most trivial matters ceases not to perform God's work, although he appears to do nothing important or serious."[33]

Incidents like these happen frequently. We can respond in one of the following ways: (1) ignore the promptings, (2) follow through on every one of them (which overscrupulous Christians often do) and end up exhausting and confusing ourselves or (3) learn to discern the genuine workings of grace. Anyone who wants to practice fidelity to grace cannot begin by taking the first alternative. Yet we often do. We are too busy to listen. Even if the inner voice of the Spirit is clearly heard, we rationalize it away. Then we wonder why God is silent. The one who errs by taking the second alternative has not erred badly. In fact most Christians begin that way. Christian proficiency, like any other skills, is learned through mistakes. What does it really matter if dear old Mrs. Lee is something of a hypochondriac or if the tramp we fed was no angel in disguise? Under proper spiritual guidance we eventually learn to tell the difference between promptings of grace and the compulsions of overscrupulosity.

Discernment is crucial, and I will say more about the art of discernment later. Here it is enough to say that while Christians do make mistakes, the mistakes of those who are willing to listen in humility are never fatal. Learning to listen is more a matter of being willing rather than of possessing intellectual acumen. Those who will to do God's will are already doing it. What we need, as Grou puts it, is to "be docile to the promptings of the Holy Spirit." A readiness to respond facilitates further movements of the Spirit and creates a "habitual obedience to grace," which is a prelude to higher things.[34]

Still, the fear of subjectivism and self-delusion is real and has to be addressed. It may be noted that de Caussade himself was in his day accused of teaching the quietistic heresy. Partly in response to the charge, his *Sacrament of the Present Moment* includes teachings that help to allay this fear. De Caussade distinguishes between God's "declared and defined will" and his "undefined will" or providence. In obeying the former we have to take certain courses of action, be attentive, observe certain precepts. In obeying his undefined will, we obey by "passive surrender." Christians who practice the sacrament of the present moment do not ignore the defined will.

The external religious practices lead them to passive surrender: "In short, they are active in everything needed for the fulfillment of their duty to the present moment, but passive and submissive and self-forgetting in everything else; only meekly waiting on the divine will."[35] In practical terms, it means that in seeking to listen to God's voice within, the Christian must not forsake the objective norms of faith found in Scripture and the teachings of the church. Nor should the counsels of other Christians, especially one's spiritual director, be ignored. Disobeying God's "defined will" makes it impossible to find God's "undefined will."

Self-Examining Prayer

Knowledge of God awakens a deep knowledge of self, but the reverse is also true, as seen in this Augustinian dictum: "Grant, Lord, that I may know myself and that I may know thee" *(noverim me, noverim te)*.[36] Thomas à Kempis well understood this principle when he said, "The humble understanding of yourself is a surer path to God than the deep inquiry into knowledge."[37] Earlier on, I spoke of the need for honesty and simplicity in prayer and the need to be watchful against self-deception. Only by examining ourselves can we be honest and simple. "Search me, O God, and know my heart; test me and know my anxious thoughts. See if there is any offensive way in me, and lead me in the way everlasting" (Ps 139:23-24). A prayer such as this can issue only from someone who has spent time in God's presence. Thus self-examination is not only the condition for but also the result of the three foregoing exercises. We need to examine ourselves in order to pray better, and yet we cannot engage in proper self-examination unless we are in prayer.

The need for self-examination. Some years ago, New Testament scholar William Barclay made this observation: "One of the great neglected duties of the Christian life is self-examination, and maybe self-examination is neglected because it is so humiliating an exercise."[38] We dare not remove the lid or rip off the mask for fear of what we might discover. Perhaps we are afraid to face ourselves because pop psychologists (including Christian ones) have convinced us that self-preoccupation is unhealthy, neurotic and symptomatic of a poor self-image. For many modern people, a poor self-image is something of a mortal sin, while a healthy self-image has acquired the status of a cardinal virtue.

The biblical message, however, is quite different. If we have sinned, the only way to come to a conscious knowledge of it and to be truly sorry for it is through self-examination. It is the beginning of self-responsibility. The apostle Paul, writing to the Corinthians about their unruly behavior at their agape feast, told them in no uncertain terms: "A man ought to examine himself before he eats of the bread and drinks of the cup" (1 Cor 11:28). We can commit the most outrageous acts without feeling any pangs of conscience until we are checked and asked to examine ourselves. Someone who participated in a mob scene starts to reflect on what the mob did (usually in the privacy of the home), and the awfulness of the deed begins to sink in for the first time. Perhaps something similar was happening in the Corinthian church. Their agape feast had sunk to the level of shameless mob behavior, and Paul had to put a check on it by enjoining self-examination.

Modern living with its constant pressure to compete, excel and produce has created a mindset not very different from the psychology of the mob. We are efficient to the extent that we perform by reflex action without giving much thought to what we do. Our basic lifestyle makes us not very different from a driver who tears along routinely at high speeds. Before long the humdrum of driving lulls her to inattention. She is not prepared for the surprises or emergencies that can accompany high-speed driving. This is why self-examination is essential. It provides the necessary speed check for those living in the fast lane. If the ancient pilgrim trudging along with staff in hand needed to examine the progress of his or her soul regularly, how much more does the modern pilgrim with steering wheel in hand need to take stock of the state of soul and body!

Self-examination forces us to face the real in the world as well as the real within. It is ironic that the pressure to compete in the world prevents many Christians from seeing the world as it really is. We are too trapped by market forces to see that we are actually its victims, incessantly driven by the demands of competition to get an ever-increasing share of the economic pie. It is only when we begin to question our participation in the "real," as liberation theologians have taught us, that we can begin to seek the true freedom that will enable us to engage the world critically and constructively.

The nature of self-examination. Self-examination is more than brooding over our faults and weaknesses. When we search our hearts, we are actually asking the Holy Spirit, the One who "searches all things, even the deep things of God" (1 Cor 2:10), to examine us. We read in Jeremiah 17:9 that "the heart is deceitful above all things and beyond cure. Who can understand it?" But the verse immediately following says, "I the LORD search the heart and examine the mind, to reward a man according to his conduct, according to what his deeds deserve." Only God can tell us the exact condition of our heart. Self-examination therefore must always be done *in the presence of God.* It is this characteristic of self-examination that distinguishes a saint from a neurotic. The saint sees himself in the light of God's revelation; the neurotic merely sees himself.

Among the early Protestants the Puritans were perhaps the masters of the art of self-examination. They recommended a daily self-examination that they called the reading of the "book of conscience." "Everyday we should be humbled for our sins," advised Richard Rogers.[39] But their method was not limited to being preoccupied with sins and failures, as is commonly thought. Rogers also urged that "we muse and think upon any good things, and ponder our words and actions we do, to see them done aright."[40] Self-examination is the occasion for humble confession of sins committed, certainly, but it is also the occasion for thanksgiving for the good things we receive from God's hand.

Most traditional spiritual guides differ concerning the frequency of self-examination. Ignatius Loyola's is perhaps the most rigorous. His work *The Spiritual Exercises* was originally intended for a specialized group seeking a vocation, not as a popular devotional manual.[41] He called for an "examination of conscience" three times a day, the last being a complete recapitulation of the first two. The exercitant was to keep an account of each lapse on paper, with one dot on a line representing one lapse.[42] At the end of the first week he was to make a "general examination of conscience."[43] The Puritans, on the other hand, usually recommended a daily self-examination, especially at the end of the day. Besides the daily examination, there were a weekly examination before the sabbath in preparation for the sacrament and a year-end inventory.[44]

The annual examination, according to Francis de Sales, is like giving the clock its annual overhaul.[45] The "clockman" takes the pieces of the clock apart so "that all faults and defect found out, may out of hand be redressed" and "with some delicate oil anointeth the wheels, junctures and gins of his clock that the motions may be more easy and the whole may be less subject to rust." Francis's vivid description, *mutatis mutandis,* provides an excellent reason for any Christian to take an annual retreat for the purpose of self-examination—just as many people have an annual medical checkup. What is ultimately important is not the frequency but the regularity of the exercise, if it is to become a standing habit. Someone who has already developed the habit of "daily devotions" could easily incorporate self-examination into it. It is very appropriate to begin our daily spiritual exercise, perhaps using the psalmist's prayer in Psalm 139, to initiate us into God's presence. We do not have to rack our brains to pick out a fault. If we truly pray for God to search our heart, it is highly unlikely that the Holy Spirit, who convicts the world of sin, righteousness and judgment (Jn 16:8), would fail to bring anything of consequence to our remembrance.

Self-examination and journaling. Self-examination can be further advanced by keeping a diary, recording the daily exercises and workings of grace in one's life. But journaling, as it is commonly known, has a much larger scope for many Christians (as well as non-Christians). Our primary concern is with journaling as a tool for self-examination.[46]

Journaling helps us examine ourselves systematically. It helps us trace what spiritual guides call the "workings of grace" in our lives over a period of time as well as for each day. Journaling is sometimes compared to setting up an accounting system.[47] The usefulness of accounting is not limited to what it does for us each day. It helps us know our financial state more accurately over a period of time. Similarly, by taking a long-term view of our life with God, we see more clearly where we have come from and where we are heading spiritually. It is amazing that many of us have meticulously worked out our life's plans to the smallest detail, including how far up the corporate ladder we hope to be in five years, what kind of family we wish to establish, what elite schools our children should go to (in the modern Asian family) and what career path they should pursue. Yet we have no goal whatsoever when it comes to the spiritual life.

If the spiritual masters of the past are any guide for us today, they testify with one voice that the Christian life has a definite goal that is worth our best effort. Union with God is a gift, but it does not come on the cheap. It belongs to pilgrims with a resolute vision of the Celestial City, not tramps who shuffle along aimlessly hoping that their minimalist religion will eventually get them somewhere. Keeping a personal or family account of spending helps develop a disciplined habit of spending. An account does not just inform. In the course of keeping tabs on how much we spend and where we spend it, we regulate our spending. Similarly, keeping tabs on our spiritual development through journaling will help us discipline our spiritual life and engender growth.

Another advantage of journaling is that it helps us view our life's situations more objectively. Very often at the time of going through a problem we are too emotionally involved to see it objectively. But writing it down objectifies it. Further, in the process of writing, we dialogue with ourselves and begin to see the situation in better perspective.[48] "The journal," as George Simons puts it, "is a word and a deed, a collection of words and deeds of a self in dialogue with itself seeking to articulate its inner word and to embrace it."[49] When situations arise that bear similarity to something that has already happened, we have the wisdom of our past to help us. By recalling what God did for us in times past, we can harness resources from the past to face the present and the future. As we journal we are creating our own history, forging our own identity in relation to God. This is a principle that we encounter repeatedly in Scripture. The record of what God did for Israel, the exodus, Israel's preservation in exile, the return to the land and scores of minor incidents and subplots are all woven into a tapestry of rich meaning that keeps the nation alive. They give the Israelite nation a sense of identity that preserves it through the darkest periods of its history. Israel of old was told repeatedly to remember. At the Last Supper Christ tells the church to remember. Unfortunately, modern-day people seem more capable of exercising abstract thought than remembering events. We have a short memory of history. This is why we never learn from it. Journaling is one way we can remember God's providential working in our lives. In so doing, we discover our own true identity in God that will help us face our own future, however happy or bleak it may be.

Conclusion

This chapter has focused on the ascetical principle of beginning with small steps, which will eventually lead us to unceasing prayer. Too often Christians are deterred from beginning a more systematic course of action because the program they are told to undertake overwhelms them before they even begin. A Christian who does not have the simple habit of reading, for example, is not likely to make much progress in the thirty-day Ignatian exercises, which require the intense engagement of the imagination. The four exercises that we have considered can be practiced throughout life, but they are also simple enough for a beginner to use.

8

SPIRITUAL EXERCISES FOCUSING ON THE WORD

. . . .

W E MUST NOT SUPPOSE THAT THE EXERCISES WE ARE ABOUT TO CONSIDER— reading and meditating on Scripture—are entirely distinct from the ones discussed in the last chapter. They are treated separately in order to clarify their respective functions. The practice of unceasing prayer, self-examination and meditating on God's Word are not readily separable in actual practice, neither should they be. A Puritan spiritual writer reminds us that "to read and not to meditate is unfruitful; to meditate and not to read is dangerous; to read and meditate without prayer is hurtful."[1] It is desirable to combine some of these exercises, such as meditation and journaling. Writing out our meditation on a text of Scripture as we let it speak to us combines the advantage of both exercises to further enhance our knowledge of self in the light of God's Word.[2] In this chapter, the progression from the simplest level of reading to the art of methodical meditation again illustrates the asceticism of small steps, or the principle of increment by small degrees. This is the only way of developing a viable spiritual theology. Beginners must be offered graded exercises that make for a sure footing as they begin to climb the "ladder of divine ascent."

Spiritual Reading
This chapter looks at reading from the standpoint of the individual rather than the corporate body (see chapter five). Theologically the two exercises are not very different from each other. Even in private reading we engage in

a process of assimilation into the Christian tradition instead of merely gleaning spiritual lessons for our own individual well-being.

Protestants are called the "people of the Word" for good reason. The Bible is central to their spirituality, and *sola Scriptura* is their watchword. Thus the exercise of spiritual reading is a good way to begin their spiritual theology. It can provide a foundation for higher things like systematic meditation. Most modern evangelical Christians, especially if their spiritual formation comes from a campus ministry such as InterVarsity Christian Fellowship or Campus Crusade for Christ, are likely to be more adept at Bible study than at spiritual reading. There is a fine distinction between the two operations that was illustrated by a question I was once asked at a meeting of college students: "Why do we need to meditate anyway? If we already understand the Scriptures, meditation is unnecessary; if we don't, it's useless."

This student thought that an understanding of Scripture comes through Bible study, a task for which she was well equipped with guidebooks that explained the background and meaning of a given text and included some leading questions and personal application at the end of each lesson. The first concern of Bible study is to explicate the meaning of the text and then apply it to life. Spiritual reading, on the other hand, is concerned with the Bible as the Word of God that calls us to God. With regard to specific texts, it implicitly asks, How does this particular text tell the Christian story of which I am a part? The spiritual reader intuitively grasps a biblical text as a part of the whole of Scripture. For centuries the church has assumed the unity of the Bible around a christological center. In the last century scholars have taken it apart, using various critical-historical methods to study it. Yet today we are once again seeing the importance of putting it together.[3] In *The Way of a Pilgrim* there is an interesting discussion on the relationship of prayer to the Bible that illustrates this principle in spiritual reading. The pilgrim asked his fellow traveler, "From which Gospel in particular can one learn about prayer?" and the latter replied,

> From all four Evangelists. . . . In a word, from reading the entire New Testament in order. After careful reading and rereading of the New Testament I discovered that the sacred writers present the teaching on prayer in a systematic way; that there is a gradual development and organic unity which begins in the writings of the first Evangelist and continues throughout the New Testament. For example, at the very beginning we have the introduction to prayer, then the form or the outward expression in words, then the necessary conditions for prayer. . . . Finally, the secret teaching about the interior and ceaseless prayer in the name of Jesus Christ is given and it is shown to be higher than formal prayer. . . . In a word

everything, complete and detailed knowledge about the exercise of prayer, is given in a systematic way from the beginning to end.[4]

Whether or not we agree with the assessment offered by the pilgrim's companion (from a critical-historical point of view it is probably not accurate), his perspective makes sense on the presupposition of the unity of the Scripture, which undergirds the centrality of prayer for Christian living ("prayer is both the first step and the crown of a devout life").[5] If the Bible is essentially one book that tells about God's work and God's relationship with his creatures, then prayer, which is looking at relationship with God from the human perspective, is indeed central to the Bible. On this presupposition, too, patristic and medieval theologians had no trouble reading the Bible allegorically and gleaning profound truths by it. We moderns with our historical perspective may have good reason to question their *method* of interpretation, but we are greatly mistaken if we think that we can better them in their understanding of what the Bible and its central message is meant to be. The presupposition of the ancients sets the necessary condition for spiritual reading. Spiritual reading begins with the realization that a text on prayer is not just related to its immediate context or historical circumstance but constitutes a part of a whole teaching on prayer that runs throughout the Bible. The part reminds us of the whole.[6] We cannot think of the Bible as a whole without at the same time seeing it as God's Word addressed to the community of which I am a part. This, according to James Barr, is what biblical authority signifies.

Biblical authority is part of a faith-attitude. And this means one thing above all: when a portion of scripture speaks to us, the question for us is not primarily "Is this in itself, as a piece of historical narrative perhaps, or as a piece of doctrine, or as a piece of moral wisdom, simply valid and true?" but: "In what way does this material, whether doctrinal, narrative, or moral, fit in with the problem of faith in Jesus Christ and the doing of his will, and in what way does it serve the upbuilding of faith and the learning of that obedience?"[7]

Spiritual reading presupposes the Bible as God's Word calling us to make a decisive response and thus trains us in a certain spiritual attitude—openness to God, humble listening, willingness to obey. These basic dispositions are the fertile ground from which the seeds of virtue sprout. Unlike ordinary reading, spiritual reading is done to affect the heart, not to gain information. This is why it is sometimes called meditative or affective reading, of which Henri Nouwen has given us a succinct description.

To take holy Scriptures and read them is the first thing we have to do to open ourselves to God's call. Reading the Scriptures is not as easy as it seems since in our academic world we tend to make anything and everything we read subject to analysis and discussion. But the word of God should lead us first of all to contemplation and meditation. Instead of taking the words apart, we should bring them together in our innermost being; instead of wondering if we agree or disagree, we should wonder which words are directly spoken to us and connect directly with our inmost personal story. Instead of thinking about the words as potential subjects for an interesting dialogue or paper, we should be willing to let them penetrate into the most hidden corners of our hearts, even to those places where no other word has yet found entrance. Then and only then can the word bear fruit as seed sown in rich soil. Only then can we really "hear and understand."[8]

For an example of spiritual reading, William Temple's *Readings in St. John's Gospel* is still one of the finest specimens.[9] In his own words,

We shall read the Gospel, then, in order to enter into the Evangelist's and the Beloved Disciple's communion with the Lord, not asking at each point precisely what was spoken or done, but knowing that as we share the experience, historical and spiritual, from which the Gospel flows we shall come nearer to the heart and mind of Jesus our Lord than ever our own minds could bring us by meditation upon the precise words that He uttered.[10]

At each point of his commentary, Temple masterfully leads us into a meditative reading of the text, using powerful images to evoke fresh visions and affective insights. What we see is, to use Temple's own imagery, not just the flat truth of a still photograph but the deep truth that only a master artist could portray.[11] Commenting on John 1:14 ("And the Word became flesh . . . and we beheld his glory"), Temple notes,

Not all who set eyes on Him did that. "We" does not mean all who ever met Him. Caiaphas and Herod and Pilate did not behold His glory. But His true disciples did. His glory was not something left behind to which one day He would return—as St. Paul had sometimes suggested. . . . Of course the Pauline doctrine is true. The Incarnation was an act of sacrifice and of humiliation—real however voluntary. But that is not the last word. For the sacrifice and humiliation *are* the divine glory. If God is Love, His glory most of all shines forth in whatever most fully expresses love. The Cross of shame *is* the throne of glory.[12]

We see here a constant moving back and forth between the text and the whole of Scripture that constitutes its context (Johannine glory is linked to the Pauline doctrine and to the cross motif, for example). Spiritual reading is essentially reading in the light of the whole story and putting ourselves in it.

Obstacles to spiritual reading. The modern mindset does not find it easy to cultivate the kind of skill described by Nouwen. This is why practical help in this area is necessary.[13] As modern Christians, we face a number of formidable obstacles when we try to cultivate the habit of spiritual reading. First, our educational system has trained us almost solely to read for information and skills acquisition. Furthermore, the busy world we live in leaves us with hardly any time for inspirational or recreational reading. Any reading we do after completing our formal education tends to be confined to instructional manuals, minutes and business reports. To read a book in a way that lets its message sink deeply into the heart is so foreign to us that a radical mental reorientation is required.

A second obstacle is that we tend to approach books, especially ancient books, with our historical pride and modern presuppositions. We find their imagery unappealing and even repulsive. Annette Muto remarks that we label books as "old fashioned," "archaic" or "conservative" and conveniently file them away.[14] We think that our scientific view is superior to the "mythological" view of the ancients, but we fail to realize that it is in fact a rather limited view that fails to take account of the larger world of nonobjectifiable reality.[15]

Third, we come with the scholar's attitude. Instead of letting the text speak to us, we analyze it. Instead of letting it tell us what we do not know, we judge the author by what he does not know, or by what he should have said, or by how he should have said it. Then we come away with an air of triumph. We treat an author more as a competitor than as a teacher.

A fourth hindrance that is more subtle than all the preceding ones is the expectation that every spiritual reading must be accompanied by good feelings or a powerful challenge. This attitude is symptomatic of our pragmatic reflex. Every book must have some immediate benefit; a spiritual book must yield some immediate effects or affects. If the reading does not produce the expected fruit of emotional stirrings, we conclude that it is "not the right book for me, since it does not speak to my condition."

Guidelines for spiritual reading. First, we need to develop the habit of regularly reading Scripture and other spiritual books. This is simply a commonsense ascetical principle: the first rung of the ladder of divine ascent must be low enough for anyone to step on. *The Way of a Pilgrim* includes this practical advice on beginning spiritual reading: "At the beginning be concerned only with reading it [the Gospel] diligently; understanding will come later."[16] For many who live in highly pragmatic societies, it is a case of re-forming the habit of reading, which they left behind after attaining the necessary academic qualifications to get on with the business of making a comfortable living. The church could be a vital re-forming agent, but it has to re-create itself as a reading-listening community. Such a community is not forthcoming if sermons continue to be patterned after instructional manuals that condition listeners to look out for only helpful tips and practical solutions. The spiritual reader must learn to approach a text as a disciple instead of as an information gatherer, a master or a critic. His attitude should emulate young Samuel's: "Speak, for your servant is listening" (1 Sam 3:10).

For most Christians in Asia, access to Christian books in their own language is limited and English may be a second or a third language. Reading an ancient text, even one that is well translated, is none too easy. They do well to begin with modern spiritual works and to proceed to the deeper spiritual resources of the Christian church later. For evangelical Christians, a few authors deserve special mention. The works of Richard Foster and A. W. Tozer are highly readable and are steeped in the Christian tradition.[17] Although Sadhu Sundar Singh has written few books, they faithfully reflect the best in the Christian spiritual tradition and are full of highly original and illuminating illustrations that will suit the Asian reader. An example is his *At the Feet of the Master*.[18] Traditional Asians with a penchant for stories may find spiritual biographies a fruitful way to begin their spiritual reading.[19] But one must not just remain with so-called devotional works. Even theological works can be read spiritually, once one has achieved enough proficiency. Theology and spirituality make up two sides of the same coin. They are different ways of attending to the same reality.

Spiritual reading is sometimes called superslow reading. If our aim is to go beyond acquiring facts to letting the truth speak to us, then we need to read slowly, savoring every word, mulling over it and digesting it, so that it begins to affect the heart deeply. The Collect for the second Sunday in Advent aptly captures this mood:

> Blessed Lord, who hast caused all holy Scriptures to be written for our learning: Grant that we may in such wise hear them, read, mark, learn, and inwardly digest them, that by patience and comfort of thy holy Word, we may embrace and ever hold fast the blessed hope of everlasting life, which thou has given us in our Savior Jesus Christ. Amen.[20]

Meditating on the Word

In ancient times both books and literacy were limited. Few had the privilege of retreating into the private world of reading. Reading was mostly a communal affair. The public nature of reading is also seen in an oral-aural culture, which characteristically reads, prays and even meditates aloud in private.[21] For most Christians, the Word came through listening. Hearing trained the mind to retain what was heard. Memorization was the foundation of learning in an oral-aural culture. It was only when "devocalization" had taken place through increasing dependence on the printed word that the amazing power of memory often seen in traditional societies began to wane.[22] The availability of the printed word obviated the need to memorize the spoken word in much in the same way that the electronic calculator has replaced the multiplication tables that every schoolchild used to learn by heart only a few decades ago. Chapter five referred to the need to retain this communal aspect of reading and listening so as to help us become more fully members of the community of the Scripture.

It was in this milieu that spiritual reading arose. For Christians, the practice was as old as the Bible itself. The first Christians naturally assumed the Jewish practice of hearing the Old Testament read in the synagogue. It was only later in monastic culture that spiritual reading was systematized. The *lectio divina* constitutes a vital part of the daily office, or *opus Dei*. What was remembered of the *lectio* would be ruminated on as the monks went about their daily chores. The rule of Basil encourages monks to pray unceasingly while they work. Thus reading and meditation became closely linked.

The use of aphorisms for meditation. To sustain the habit of praying and meditating while working, monks memorized short portions of biblical texts and sayings of the fathers called *florilegia*. The term *florilegium* literally means "flower-sipping." The imagery is derived from the bee drawing nectar from flower to flower and is one of the favorite emblems in the meditative tradition.[23] The collection of these short, aphoristic sayings for spiritual reading and meditation was an important feature not only of monastic practice but also of later Protestant devotional habit.[24] The logic of the aphorism is similar to the proverbs of ancient Israel or the *Analects* of Confucius. Unlike lengthier readings, the aphorism affects the heart by its succinct and arresting qualities. As the Puritan Richard Sibbes observed, "One seasonable truth falling upon a prepared heart, hath oftentimes a sweet and strong operation."[25] These "portable meditations," as another Puritan put it,[26] enable the meditator to focus on a quintessential truth distilled into a few words.

From here, we can trace the practice to the evangelical habit of memorizing verses of Scripture. (Unfortunately, this habit is increasingly falling out of use as the versified Authorized Version gives way to a plethora of paragraphed modern versions.) The mind immersed in Scripture selectively focuses on verses that sum up and distill the essential teachings of the whole Scripture.[27] Many ordinary Christians, who have little understanding of technical biblical criticism, spontaneously grasp these verses and commit them to memory. This phenomenon explains why certain verses and portions of Scripture (for example, Jn 3:16 and the psalms) seem to have a constant appeal to ordinary people reading the Scriptures and are more widely memorized than others.[28] Memorized texts are, therefore, not contextless, as many nurtured in the historical-critical method would like us to think. Rather, they presuppose the whole context of Christian Scripture. Just as the Jesus Prayer may be said to encapsulate the whole gospel,[29] a memory verse captures what is most essential in Christian tradition. Like the little "nosegay" (to use a well-known image from Francis de Sales's *Introduction to a Devout Life*) that we gather from our garden, the posies of meditation remind us of the larger garden of Scripture.

The memorization of Scripture is crucial to the well-being of the modern church, if not its survival. First, it is probably our last link to an oral-aural culture in which communal listening to Scripture can take place. The rhythm of hearing Scripture read and explained and then memorizing key portions of it gradually assimilated the community into the Christian story. Second, there is evidence to show that memorization is one of the most basic ways by which the unschooled deeply imbibe the Christian faith and gain real theological competence, that is, real sanctity.[30] This counters a dubious but commonly held notion regarding the relationship of the intellect to spiritual life. In our highly intellectualized age, we often equate theological competence with technical competence, the ability to apply the right rules of interpretation and to manipulate the latest critical tools. If indeed theological competence depends on technical competence, then we would have to assume that the more highly educated person has the potential to become more saintly than the less educated. The assumption that great saints are *necessarily* more learned is obviously false. As is often the case, the learned do not always put their vaster knowledge into practice and so remain spiritual dwarfs, while the virtual illiterates who actualize what meager knowledge they acquire, surpass them in sanctity.

But the assumption is also false in principle, because the more educated cannot even be said to have more theological knowledge than the less educated. What the former have more of is *explicit* theological knowledge, while the latter hold theirs *implicitly*, which is potentially no more or less than what the better educated possess. If "we know more than we can tell,"[31] then the uneducated saint knows *much more* than he or she can tell.

The fact that memorization of Scripture hardly goes on among Christians today indicates more than just a change in devotional habits. It is symptomatic of a basic failure in the traditioning process. The story is received superficially in the form of clichés and abstract principles for living rather than as transforming event that is deeply (often subconsciously) embedded in the individual's and the collective memory. A sign of hope comes from a lowly and unexpected source. I am referring to the phenomenon of chorus singing among Pentecostal-charismatic believers. "Solid" evangelicals and "high-brow" mainline types share a suspicion, if not disdain, of what appears to be an uncouth practice. There may be reason for concern if singing these little ditties begins to displace the solid hymns of the church (which has already happened in some churches), or if they are sung for recreation, or if they become a tool for psychological manipulation (which has happened). To the extent that the criticism of choruses is directed at their content and at the misuse of them, it is largely justified. But the criticism is misplaced if it is directed at their "boringly repetitive" nature. For it is precisely in the repetition that the chorus provides a vital function. A good short chorus is like a good ejaculatory prayer/meditation and functions like the Jesus Prayer or the *florilegium*. It aids continual prayer by letting a truth run through our minds over and over again so that it becomes a true part of us. Chorus singing could well be a critical mode of empowering the modern church's collective memory. Singing a chorus together may enable the modern church to remember in perhaps the only way that it can learn to remember.[32]

For chorus singing to serve its true purpose well, the content of the choruses needs to be improved. Unfortunately, with a few exceptions (such as the Taizé choruses), most contemporary choruses are shallow in content and/or dubious in theology. If they are to effectively encourage devotional habits, they should concentrate on three areas: (1) key portions of Scripture, so that they can be meditated on and memorized, (2) the great mysteries of the faith—God the Trinity, creation and redemption—for they constitute the basic facts of the Christian story, and (3) key expressions of the faith—the creed, the commandments and the Lord's Prayer—which make up the main content of ancient and modern catechisms.[33] These key concepts and expressions must be skillfully distilled into "ready-to-eat mouthfuls of different sizes, never too large and suited to any taste."[34] If the church as a colony of bees is to gather quality honey, it has to feed on the right flowers.

Methodical meditation. Once the usefulness of what began as a spontaneous habit has been proven, further reflection, refinement and systematization would inevitably follow to make it more readily available to others.[35] This was how the informal habit of ruminating on Scripture and other spiritual texts was eventually formalized into the "art" of methodical meditation.[36] We may define methodical meditation as a systematic way of engaging the whole person—the mind, emotions and will—in effective interaction with divine truth. It is a structured way of internalizing the gospel so that it affects the totality of one's being. Meditation is the intensification rather than the extensification of the Word. It is like bringing the diffused rays of the sun to a focal point with a convex lens so that the heat can be felt in all its intensity. It is not enough to have a cursory understanding of the truth. It must fire our imaginations and affect us so deeply that we are restless until it is put into effect. Most traditional methods employ a three-part scheme in meditation. First, the truth is read and assimilated by the intellect or understanding. Then it is made to affect the heart or, to use a traditional expression, "raise the affections." Finally, the truth that has deeply affected the heart moves the will to make a resolution. Meditation is therefore the main link between theology and praxis. It is the way to make truth come alive as it courses from mind to heart to daily living. Seen in this way, meditation plays a critical role in forging the integration of heart and mind in the spiritual life. Meditation, notes Pourrat, forms the main link of the chain that binds together all the other spiritual exercises.[37] This may explain why it features prominently in many popular devotional manuals. Francis de Sales's *Introduction* is a typical example. Meditation is the chief means for accomplishing the purgation of the soul and the formation of virtues. The function of meditation is aptly captured in these words:

> We see that little children by hearing their mothers speak and prattling often with them, do come to learn their language, and so we continually conversing with our Savior by meditation, observing and pondering reverently his words, his works and his affections shall soon by the help of his grace, learn to speak, to work and to will and desire as he did.[38]

But the real goal of meditation is to enable Christians to experience afresh their corporate life in Christ. As Merton puts it, "To enter into the mysteries of the faith by meditation . . . is to renew in oneself the Church's experience of those mysteries by participating in them."[39] For example, when we meditate on the great mystery of the incarnation (as Ignatius encourages us to do in his *Spiritual Exercises*), we see and experience that reality. The truth of the incarnation is made present to us. We see ourselves as part of God's greater work of forming the church through Christ's incarnation, life, death, resurrection and ascension. This is why the gospel story should constitute the central subject of all our meditation.

Among evangelical Christians methodical meditation began to enjoy a measure of acceptance only in relatively recent times, especially after the publication of Richard Foster's *Celebration of Discipline* in 1978.[40] Many would be surprised if informed that systematic meditation was as much a part of the Protestant spiritual tradition as it was of the Roman Catholic tradition.[41] The doctrine of meditation is rooted in John Calvin's understanding of the Christian life. Central to Calvin's conception is the doctrine of union with Christ in his death, resurrection and ascension, in that order. The Christian life is in a sense consummated with participation in Christ's ascension. This participation becomes possible by means of "true and holy thinking about Christ which forthwith bears us up to Heaven, that we may there adore him."[42] Calvin devoted a whole chapter in his *Institutes* to the theme of meditation on the heavenly life (3.9). Puritans in the late sixteenth and seventeenth centuries developed it into a full-fledged art. One of the earliest definitions of meditation came from Richard Greenham (1535?-1594?), who explained it as "the exercise of the mind, whereby we calling to our remembrance that which we know, do further debate of it and apply it to ourselves, that we might have some use of it in our practice."[43] Greenham lays down some simple rules for meditation, such as the need to read the Word first before meditating and to "sequester" oneself and choose a proper time and place to meditate.[44]

The "godly"[45] bishop Joseph Hall devised what is probably the first systematic exposition of the "art of divine meditation."[46] Hall's method is so complex that it is doubtful whether it was ever successfully implemented. The main body of the meditation consists of ten different ways of elaborating a subject in the "understanding" part and seven ways of raising the affections.[47] Later writers like Richard Baxter simplified the method considerably. This brief historical excursus shows that Christian meditation has a long and distinguished history in Protestantism and should neither be regarded as a recent innovation nor confused with the Hindu and Buddhist variety—an association that has alienated many Protestants from their own history and has prevented them from taking the practice of meditation more seriously.[48]

The following summary of the Salesian scheme of meditation shows how methodical meditation is intended to work. The method consists of three parts: the preparation, the main body of the meditation consisting of rational considerations, the raising of the affections and resolution, and the conclusion.

The Salesian Method of Meditation[49]

I. Preparation

A. Of the presence of God

(One is to place "thyself in the presence of God" by one of these four means.)

    1. "A lively and attentive apprehension of the omnipresence of God"

    2. "To think that not only is God in the place where you are, but that he is in a very special manner in your heart and in the depth of your spirit"

    3. "Consider our Saviour, who in his humanity looks from heaven upon

all persons . . . but particularly upon Christians . . . more especially upon those who are in prayer"

4. Using the imagination, "representing to ourselves the Saviour in his sacred humanity, as though he were near to us"

B. Of the invocation

(Having placed oneself in the presence of God, the next thing is to acknowledge our unworthiness and call on God for assistance.)

C. Setting forth the mystery

(This involves presenting to the imagination the subject of the meditation.)

II. The body of the meditation

A. Considerations

(Here the meditator thinks deeply on the subject, using imagination if the subject is sensible [for example, the crucifixion] or affective thought if it is not perceptible by the senses [our creation].)

(For example, if we are to meditate on our creation [1.9], we may consider the following: the world has been in existence long before we were born; God brought us into the world even though he has no need of us; and yet God bestows on us a nature which is "the chiefest and most excellent in this visible world," namely, our capacity to live eternally and be united with his divine majesty. This consideration should deeply humble us.)

B. Affections and resolutions

(After the consideration of his or her own creation, the meditator proceeds to "raise the affection" of humility by means of affective soliloquies [prayers addressed to oneself].)

"O Lord before thee and in comparison of thy majesty, I am just nothing. And how was thou then mindful of me to create me? Alas, my soul, thou was hidden . . . in the abyss of nothing; and in this abyss of nothing shouldst thou have remained until the present, if God had not drawn thee forth from thence. And what couldst thou have done, within this nothing?"

(With this deep sense of humility, the meditator gives thanks to God. But as he does so, he is again driven back to greater humility as he meditates on his own unfaithfulness to God.)

"Alas, my Creator, instead of uniting myself unto thee by pure love and loyal service, I have always been rebellious by my unruly affections, separating and withdrawing myself from thee, to join and unite myself unto sin and iniquity, doing no more honor to thy goodness, [as] if thou hadst not been my Creator."

(Thus thoroughly humbled, the meditator then makes this resolution:)

"O God, I am the work of thy hands. I will then no more henceforth take pleasure in myself, since in my self and of my self I am truly nothing. . . .

Wherefore, to humble myself, I will do such and such a thing. . . . I will change my life, and hereafter follow my Creator, and do myself honor with the condition and being which he hath given me, employing it wholly in the obedience of his blessed will, by such means as shall be taught me, and as I shall be informed by my spiritual father [director]."

III. The Conclusion

(The meditation closes with three acts.)

A. Thanksgiving

B. Oblation, or an act of consecration of oneself to God

C. Petition for grace to carry out the truth learned in practice

(But before the meditator leaves off the set exercise, he or she gathers the main thoughts and binds them together into a little "nosegay" [similar to the monastic *florilegium*] to carry through the rest of the day.)

The Salesian method represents but one method of meditating on the Word.[50] It may be noted that in their method of raising the affections, the teachers of methodical meditation like Francis show themselves to be master psychologists. To intensify the affections they encouraged rhythmic oscillation between a negative emotion and a positive emotion: from humility to thanksgiving to greater humility. If meditation is to function effectively in the modern context, adaptations are needed. But not everyone will find methodical meditation practicable. Even in Baxter's day, the methodical meditation he recommended in *The Saint's Everlasting Rest* (1650) was criticized for being too rigid. One Puritan bitterly complained that Baxter's method, which required as much as a full hour of "unmixed thoughts" on the "joys of heaven," was a practical impossibility for "many poor Christians . . . oppressed with sad thoughts arising from debts, debasements, unequal yoke-fellows, long sickness and pains" and would only aggravate their problems rather than alleviate them.[51]

Someone with a mind as methodical as Baxter's (who was a self-confessed "unfeigned lover of method" and for whom nothing could be effectively done unless reduced to "distinction and method"[52]) would find such a scheme immensely helpful. But for others (and in the modern world they are by far the majority), methodical meditation may offer a stumbling block instead of a means of grace unless they are first trained in the more basic skills such as spiritual reading. Bonhoeffer recommended that his seminarians spend half an hour each day meditating on a text of ten to fifteen verses for at least a whole week: "It is not good to meditate on a different text each day, since we are not always equally receptive."[53] This is how it should be done:

Just as you would not dissect and analyze the word spoken by someone dear to you, but would accept it just as it was said, so you should accept the Word of Scripture and ponder it in your heart as Mary did. That is all. That is meditation. Do not look for new thoughts and interconnections in the text as you would in a sermon! Do not ask how you should tell it to others, but ask what it tells you! Then ponder this word in your heart at length, until it is entirely within you and has taken possession of you.[54]

For Asian Christians, cultivating the meditative habit of mind is not as formidable as it at first appears. Many have come from religious backgrounds that instill such a habit. Unfortunately, evangelical Protestantism with its rational approach to Scripture and its negative attitude toward non-Western culture has either explicitly or implicitly discouraged the use of the meditative approach to Scripture.[55]

Conclusion

Within the Christian tradition meditation on Scripture or some scriptural truth forms one part of a larger scheme to promote progress toward union with God. What is called discursive meditation (the kind we have considered in this chapter) leads to deeper contemplation. A classic example of this schema is Bernard of Clairvaux, who sees spiritual perfection as a process involving progressive degrees of contemplation. One begins by meditating on the wounds of Christ to effect compunction of heart, then progresses to placing oneself before the crucified Christ, to a mental gaze of the glory of the saints, to contemplating the divine will and culminating in the rapt beholding of the divine glory.[56]

Progress in meditation is evident when discursive thought (usually accompanied by vocal prayers, colloquies, soliloquies and so on) are gradually replaced by "wordless" prayer, rapt attention, awe and silence before God. The end is Christian perfection or union with God, the realization of "man's chief end" (see chapter four). We develop the meditative habit of mind through spiritual reading, which grows out of simply being diligent in reading the Word: "At the beginning be concerned with reading it diligently; understanding will come later." This is the first rung of Jacob's ladder. It is within every Christian's reach, which is, ascetically speaking, the same as "the technique of going to church."

9

SPIRITUAL EXERCISES
FOCUSING ON
THE WORLD

· · · · · · · · · · · · · · · · · · · ·

W E REFER TO THE "WORLD" AT THREE LEVELS: THE WORLD OF INTERPER-
sonal relationships, the world of God's creation and the world of human
activities (the sociopolitical, religiocultural world). Part of Christian spiritual
development involves a growing consciousness of the larger world. Christian
spirituality has always encouraged Christians to look beyond themselves. It
sees the world as the place where God's significant actions occur. These acts
of God culminate in the coming of Jesus Christ.[1] Hindu and Buddhist
spiritualities by contrast are dominated by a sense of the eternal. The primary
concern of Buddhists and Hindus is their eternal destiny, which they try to
enhance through self-cultivation and self-improvement. The Christian life of
fellowship with the Father and the Son by the power of the Spirit, however,
does not find its fulfillment in some ethereal realm. It is already realized,
albeit in part, in the world of people, creation and history. There is an element
of truth in Chesterton's caricatures of the Christian saint and the Buddhist
saint. The Buddhist saint has a well-contoured body and sits serenely with
eyes closed or gazing at his navel. The Christian saint possesses a scrawny
body, but his eyes are wildly alive to the world around him.[2]

This chapter looks at three basic expressions of the social dimension of
Christian spirituality. The Christian life is expressed in the world of interpersonal relationships through the cultivation of spiritual friendship. It is
expressed in the world of creation through the practice of occasional

meditation. In the world of human activities we need a social spirituality involving a distinct kind of spiritual awareness.

Spiritual Friendship

Some contemporary discussions conflate spiritual direction and spiritual friendship.[3] The reason for this lies in the Western fixation on egalitarianism, preference for a "nonthreatening" and nonhierarchical relationship and fear of authoritarianism.[4] In the traditional East the master-disciple relationship or the practice of serving as an apprentice to a more experienced person is an acceptable way to learn. Thus taking direction from a spiritual master is not viewed negatively. In the Indian tradition, friendship and direction are quite clearly distinguished. For instance, intellectual discussion (prominent in the Aristotelian conception of friendship) takes place between gurus and their disciples, seldom between friends.[5] There is a significant difference between friendship and direction. Although there is an element of friendship in spiritual direction, the main focus is on helping another person grow. While the director and directee are fellow pilgrims, spiritual direction presupposes that one of them has traveled farther along the road and can serve as a guide to the newcomer. This is why a spiritual director must have certain qualifications, training (formal and informal) and experience.[6] Direction is by nature a relationship involving unequal partners. Spiritual friendship, on the other hand, as seen in Aelred of Rievaulx (1110-1167) or Francis de Sales,[7] stresses mutuality. "It is . . . a law of friendship that a superior must be on a plane of equality with the inferior," says Aelred.[8] In a friendship guidance is usually of a mutual kind. The qualities needed to be a friend are the same qualities needed to be found in the befriended person.

Contemporary discussions of friendship. The historian Martin Marty notes that little attention was given to a serious discussion of friendship in the past.[9] Perhaps there was not much talk about friendship because it was simply lived out, as can still be observed in rural settings and small villages. Perhaps it is only in a world characterized by alienation, distrust and, at best, functional relationships that the call to a reconsideration of friendship is increasingly heard.[10] But it is highly questionable whether friendship will serve its intended purpose as long as certain modern assumptions remain entrenched in Western thinking. One such assumption is the emphasis on inclusiveness. Moltmann, in keeping with his universalistic egalitarianism, advances the concept of "open friendship" or "cosmic friendship."[11] Similarly, Eliot Deutsch argues for a "creative friendship" based on certain common human qualities like creativity, apart from what he sees as the constrictive nature of traditional moral virtues or duties. What counts is the creative relationship in a friendship so that the question of what is morally right or wrong no longer comes into play.[12]

Feminism has produced a greater gender consciousness in contemporary discourse, so that it is no longer sufficient to speak in generic terms about friendship.[13] Some have come to see friendship as providing a new paradigm for understanding the basic structure of human relationships.[14] Radical feminist Mary Hunt has argued for putting friendship first, since it is "fundamentally more suited to the complex needs of our society" while "permitting, even encouraging, marriage as well." Prioritizing relationships around friendship opens the door for other structures of relationship (including homosexual ones) to be considered legitimate or even better alternatives to the traditional family.[15] While Hunt is aware that simply co-opting lesbian and gay friendships into the existing norm of marriage does not necessarily solve the problem of violence and abuse, she believes that relationships are better served by the friendship norm.[16] Such radical revisioning of human relationship requires a new set of criteria. Indeed, Hunt's criteria for human relationship are no less radical: they are qualitative, not quantitative. For example, longevity "is never the ultimate criterion for friendship."[17] This means, ostensibly, that relationships that do not last long can still be considered qualitatively good.

Walter L. Williams has observed that Asian and other traditional societies characterized by strong extended families and complex kinship networks are able to meet the emotional needs of individual members of those societies much better despite (or perhaps because of) the absence of any romantic concept of marriage so characteristic of modern Western culture.[18] Williams is right in asserting that "the American ideal of individual freedom and progress" has left behind "a legacy of individual alienation and loneliness."[19] It is doubtful, however, whether the problem of human relationships is better served by "a new rhetoric of friendship" as long as Western culture continues to operate on the principle of individual rights, in this case, the right to have one's emotional needs met. As long as this principle goes unchallenged, a relationship modeled on friendship will be no less fragile and vulnerable. No relationship can hope to endure when its value lies in whether or not it satisfies my personal right to and need for intimacy, my right to be the individual I want to be or "to build an emotionally satisfying future."[20] The aim of complex social arrangements in traditional societies, on the other hand, is not primarily to satisfy individual emotional needs but to ensure the stability of the larger community, be it the family, village or tribe.

In modern societies friendships, to use Aristotle's categories, are based on utility and pleasure (business friends) rather than virtue. Thus the friendship has no transcendent reference point. In Aristotle's terms, what counts as perfect friendship is "the friendship that is between the good, and those who resemble each other in virtue."[21]

This idea that friends exist for something beyond themselves unites the various traditions of both East and West and distinguishes them from modern culture, which sees friendship as ultimately serving to enhance the self. Here the church is one with the classical tradition. Aelred's work on friendship does not differ substantially from the classic treatment of the same subject in the Western tradition, namely, Aristotle's *Nicomachean Ethics,*[22] except that Aelred sees it in the context of faith. In this relationship the two friends help each other grow in grace and virtue while eliminating vice and weakness.[23] In the Platonic tradition friendship is not static but based on a drive toward a common transcendent goal.[24] Friendship serves a higher, instrumental end, namely, to make the individual more virtuous, to bring the individual closer to the ideal of the Good.[25] This Platonic view is a part of monastic spirituality, which sees spiritual friendship as developing one's individual character as a Christian. Aristotle's "perfect friendship" of virtue is exclusive and is possible only with a few people. Only friendship based on virtue can be considered true friendship; friendships based on utility and pleasure do not qualify.[26] This belief that true friendship is only possible among people of virtue runs in the Confucian and Indian traditions as well.[27]

Eastern and Western traditions of friendship differ in regard to nonbiological, voluntary, informal and noninstitutional relationships between two individuals. The Confucian and Hindu traditions presuppose the basic hierarchical structure of human relationship, while the Western tradition stresses the mutuality of the relationship.[28] In Confucianism, friendship is the most horizontal of the "five relationships," but even here "seniority of age demands a certain respect."[29] It "is based on appreciated differences between oneself and another person which present themselves as specific occasions for one's character development, rather than upon perceived commonalities with the other person."[30] Thus Confucius advised, "Take as friends only those who are better than yourself."[31] Similarly, a certain inequality exists in friendship in the Hindu tradition. This is exemplified in the mythic friendship between Krishna and Arjuna. Even though their relationship is "relaxed, informal and easygoing," Krishna is the senior partner who guides, instructs and admonishes the younger.

> Both depend on each other, but one depends a little more. Only such a relationship is believed to be inherently noncompetitive and nonconflictual, and free of the traces of jealousy and comparison deemed to be characteristic of the relations between equals. In such a relationship neither feels threatened by the other, for each derives a distinct kind of fulfillment from it.[32]

The difference between Eastern and Western traditions illustrates the cultural diversity of friendship (which may explain why crosscultural friendship is one of the most difficult to develop).[33] But it is remarkable that the two traditions hold the moral basis of friendship in common. Contemporary attempts at exploring friendship as a new paradigm for restructuring human relationships will not get anywhere if the basic concern continues to rest on the personal satisfaction of individuals whose "inalienable rights" are defined without any reference to an objective or transcendent goal.

The meaning of holy friendship. Spiritual friendship in the Christian tradition, while sharing many features with the classical traditions both East and West, has its own distinctive elements. Recognizing the existence of *holy* friendship suggests that a natural association can be consecrated, set apart, in the body of Christ. A holy friendship is not any less a friendship. Like any other friendship, it includes an element of exclusivity. As Francis recognizes, we must love all but befriend only a few.[34] In baptizing a human relationship, the church puts friendship on a surer and sounder footing: a friendship that is cultivated "in Christ" manifests "a certain likeness to eternity"[35] and can transcend its natural barriers. These include social classifications that have become increasingly determinative of modern human relations. The so-called enlightened world, while paying lip service to the principle of human equality, the dignity of the human race and so on, has thrown up new and deep divisions based on jobs, professional qualifications and wealth. Friendship in Christ breaks down all such barriers. Even a free person and a slave can become friends (an impossibility, according to Aristotle).

In a world starved for companionship, it is hardly necessary to extol the importance and value of having friends. A true friend is an intimate confidant to whom we can open the heart and receive counsel. We appreciate firm but gentle correction from someone who can point out our faults. We feel the firm pillar of support from a friend in times of sorrow. We wonder longingly at the friendship between Gregory Nazianzen and Basil the Great, of which the former said, "It seemed that in either of us there was but one soul dwelling in two bodies."[36]

Dangers of friendship. Precisely because there is such a thing as spiritual friendship, we need to guard against unspiritual ones. "The carnal springs from mutual harmony in vice; the worldly is enkindled by the hope of gain; and the spiritual is cemented by similarity of life, morals, and pursuits among the just."[37] Aelred in his classic treatment on the subject gives severe warnings about the dangers of false friendships. In fact, they should not even be called friendship at all.

Falsely do they claim the illustrious name of friends among whom there exists a harmony of vices; since he who does not love is not a friend, but he does not love his fellow-man who loves iniquity. "For he that loves iniquity" does not love, but "hates his own soul" [Ps 10:6]. Truly, he who does not love his own soul will not be able to love the soul of another.[38] A spiritual friendship can degenerate into a sensual one. This change has three leading characteristics. First, the friendship becomes exclusive. Two friends withdraw from the company of others and become jealous of each other in the presence of a third party. Second, the friendship becomes possessive. Neither friend can tolerate the absence of the other, or one begins to dominate the other. Third, the friendship becomes obsessive. One friend becomes preoccupied with the other. This preoccupation intrudes into the imagination and becomes a distraction even in prayer.[39]

Francis gave some very sound and practical advice on ending false friendships (3.21). We need to withdraw ourselves from a false friendship, including sometimes physically removing ourselves from the presence of the other (3.21.5). Failing that, cut off communication (3.21.6). The scars caused by breaking off a friendship do not last forever (3.21.7). Francis is all too aware of the common objection to his proposal: is it acceptable to break off a friendship so violently? But if it is false friendship, breaking it off releases both persons from bondage to it. Thus the other person is benefited rather than hurt (3.21.8).

The art of spiritual friendship. A condition for friendship is "autonomy," which "recognizes various dependencies—social, economic, cultural—and transforms those dependencies into care-filled relationships where one's own autonomy is seen to be realized only as one promotes as well the autonomy of others."[40] Autonomy is roughly the modern equivalent of what Aristotle called "virtue" and Christians call "charity." These terms suggest that a certain character is required if a friendship is to be forged. Thus we are back to the same ascetical situation that we encountered in prayer: in order to develop the ideal of being *good* friends (in the Aristotelian sense) we need to have at least the disposition or character for being a friend. Prayer, the first ascetical principle, is also the first principle of friendship. Moltmann is right when he says, "Prayer and answer are what constitute human friendship with God and divine friendship with human beings."[41] Through prayer we learn the meaning of friendship with God, which sets the condition for friendship with others.

Aelred speaks of four stages of friendship: selection, probation, admission and perfect harmony.[42] It is important to select the right kind of friend. A person who is prone to certain kinds of vices, especially the five vices mentioned in Sirach 22:27, does not make a good friend. "For there may be a reconciliation with your friend except in the case of upbraiding, reproach, pride, disclosing of secrets or a treacherous wound; for in all these cases a friend will flee away."[43] There are certain kinds of vices that are especially destructive of true friendship. For example, "disclosing of secrets" by its very nature undermines the trust necessary for friendships to flourish. Next, the friendship must be tested. There should be a gradual opening up to each other, a sharing of counsels and common concerns.[44] The potential friend must be tested with regard to "loyalty, right intention, discretion, and patience."[45] Only then is one "admitted" as a friend. Aelred does not explain what admission entails. Ostensibly it involves some kind of mutual recognition so that "from then on [the other is] treated as a friend deserves."[46] For Aelred, the cultivation of spiritual friendship is a conscious, deliberate act of the will rather than finding the right "mental chemistry." Aelred's method of cultivation suggests that a practical *askesis* for friendship can be developed if a few prerequisites are kept in focus.

First, friendship can develop only if there is a willingness to risk opening up to others. It may begin with just learning to be friendly. Proverbs 18:24 in the Authorized Version gives sound advice: "He that would have friends must show himself friendly." Someone who always waits for the other person to make the first move is not likely to have a friend. Even if the other person does initiate the move, an active response is necessary if the initiative is to become effective communication. As Francis recognized, "Friendship requireth great communication between friends, otherwise it will neither grow nor continue."[47]

Second, a small beginning can be made by discovering areas of common interest, even inconsequential ones. The friendship deepens as the area of mutual interest deepens and widens. The idea is from Aristotle, who believes that the quality of friendship is inversely proportional to the quantity of friendship. The more intense the friendship and the more extensive the area of common interest, the fewer the friends.[48] Aelred recognizes the possibility of growth in a friendship. A friendship may begin with a profit motive but over time change to a higher purpose.[49] The principle of discovering "another self" or alter ego in a friend, incidentally, explains why it is difficult for men and women to be friends. Gender differences make it difficult to maintain the common notion of friendship, that "like is the friend of like,"[50] unless they first relegate those differences to the background and meet each other strictly as individual persons. Sexuality "must . . . be bracketed for such friendship to be possible."[51] Thus it is probably only within a marriage that intimate friendship between a man and a woman can exist.

Third, the principle of common interests naturally implies that friendship includes some people and excludes others. We cannot be friends with too many people. There is perhaps some truth in the New International Version rendering of Proverbs 18:24: "A man of many companions [friends] may come to ruin." But exclusivity in friendship raises a serious problem. Will it not undermine the all-encompassing nature of the Christian fellowship and the Christian concern for the larger world? The answer is no, for two reasons. First, friendship becomes problematic only when it is made the all-embracing paradigm for human relations. This is a purely a modern, democratic view that finds support from neither Scripture nor tradition. In Scripture the inclusive way of relating is love, not friendship. We are to love even our enemies, who by definition are not friends. Thus the exclusivity of friendship is not a problem if we recognize that from the Christian perspective it represents one aspect of our total relationship with God and with each other. An all-inclusive friendship succeeds only in losing any distinctiveness. Second, exclusive friendships in the Christian community can be inclusive if the community is conceived of as a series of concentric circles or small interlocking circles of friends. Each Christian has circles of friends of varying degrees of intensity. At some point these circles intersect one another, linked together by common friends. Thus everyone has some exclusive friends.

The church should be characterized by exclusive friendships in which everyone has a share. Jesus practiced both exclusive and inclusive friendship. He was a "friend" of tax collectors and sinners in that he ate and drank with them and showed them love (Lk 7:34). But he was not on intimate terms with them as he was with his twelve disciples. With them he shared the secrets of the kingdom of God (Mt 13:11). An even narrower circle of three disciples—Peter, James and John—was given the privilege of seeing his glory on the Mount of Transfiguration. Jesus' friendship both embraces and excludes by arranging friendship in a series of concentric circles. In this way exclusive and inclusive friendships can coexist. Moltmann's concept of "open friendship" fails to clarify these different dynamics of relationship. To speak of a friendship that embraces all means either that it is confused with God's universal *agape* or that the friendship loses its distinctive character and degenerates into fussy acquaintanceship.[52]

Christian friendship is exclusive in another sense as well. No matter how "open" we may want friendship to be, it cannot be an unqualified openness. There is a higher interest around which holy friendships are forged—the will of God. In the Christian context, friendship must take the friends beyond themselves to some greater, more profound reality in God. And as long as some people exclude God's will from their lives, there cannot be real friendship that includes all people—at least not in the sense in which friendship is understood in the classical and Christian traditions.

Meditation on the Creature (Occasional Meditation)

Many ancient Christian writers refer to three books of meditation. The first is the Bible and is dealt with in the various methods of meditation; the second, the book of the heart, is read in self-examination; the third is the book of God's creation. Meditation on the creatures is sometimes called occasional meditation because it is not practiced according to set times and places. It suggests itself in the ordinary run of life. The "occasions" giving rise to a meditation are diverse. A threatening experience like sickness[53] or a trivial event like the unprovoked barking of a dog or the sight of a lark flying directly heavenward may evoke a spiritual lesson.[54] Brother Lawrence began his spiritual journey when he meditated on the sight of a tree in winter.

Many of these ancient writers appealed to the biblical doctrine of revelation in creation. "The heavens declare the glory of God; the skies proclaim the works of his hands" (Ps 19:1). "When I consider your heavens, the work of your fingers, the moon and the stars, which you have set in place, what is man that you are mindful of him?" (Ps 8:3-4). To a keen observer every creature yields a spiritual lesson. The slothful are directed to observe ants (!) to learn about industriousness (Prov 6:6), while the doubtful are to "consider" the lilies and sparrows and learn the lesson of trust (Mt 6:28; Lk 12:27). The universe, according to Calvin, is like a mirror before which we can contemplate God, who is otherwise invisible.

> Wherever you cast your eyes, there is no spot in the universe wherein you cannot discern at least some spark of his glory. You cannot in one glance survey this most vast and beautiful system of the universe, in its wide expanse, without being completely overwhelmed by the boundless force of its brightness.[55]

If creation reveals the glory of God, how does it do that? This question has been differently answered. Hugh of St. Victor was one of the earliest to incorporate creation into the spiritual quest. He encouraged meditation on creation, which is a mirror of God. It was "a disciplined contemplation of some creature in order that grace may guide us to see deeply into its message and purpose in the mind of God."[56] Francis of Assisi took his creation spirituality beyond that of the Victorines. While Hugh sees creation as a "mirror" of God that in some way implies an idealist philosophy, Francis sees it as "real" brothers and sisters, because they too were created by God and will, too, be taken up in the final restoration. Precisely because he loved the creatures of God, he would not seek to possess them selfishly; hence his vow of poverty. In his famous *Canticle of the Sun* (1225), all the creatures, including "Sir Brother Sun," "Sister Moon" and "Mother Earth," are alive to God in their own respective ways. Each serves the other, and all render praise to God.[57] It is no wonder that Francis of Assisi has been hailed as the patron saint of ecology.

The Franciscan view of creation greatly influenced Bonaventure, whose *Itinerarium Mentis in Deum* (1259) set the trend for subsequent thinking on the subject. The practice of meditating on the creatures is highly commended in this work:

> Whoever, therefore, is not enlightened by such splendor of created things is blind; whoever is not awakened by such outcries is deaf; whoever does not praise God because of all these effects is dumb; whoever does not discover the First Principle from such clear signs is a fool. Therefore, open your eyes, alert the ears of your spirit, open your lips and apply your heart so that in all creatures you may see, hear, praise, love and worship, glorify and honor your God lest the whole world rise against you.[58]

The soul's journey to God consists of six steps grouped into three sets of two stages. The first two stages contemplate creation, the next two contemplate the soul, the last two stages, God. The three pairs correspond to the three books of meditation. These six progressive stages coincide with the six faculties of the soul, namely, "the senses, imagination, reason, understanding, intelligence, and the summit of the mind or the spark of conscience."[59] Here we are primarily concerned with the first two stages, which deal with the contemplation of creation. The first stage involves contemplating God "*through* his vestiges in the universe." By looking at the seven properties of things, namely, their origin, magnitude, multitude, beauty, fullness, activity and order, the mind rises to consider the power, wisdom and goodness of God reflected in these things. For example, the *origin* of things reminds us of divine *power,* the *magnitude* of things reveals "the immensity of the power, wisdom and goodness of the triune God," and so on (1.14).

The first stage reveals God *through* the world, while the second stage sees God's "vestiges" *in* the world. Bonaventure's elaborate epistemology explaining how the soul, the microcosm of the universe, receives the macrocosm through the five senses need not detain us here.[60] The point of our interest is the distinction he makes between the first stage and the second stage of knowing God in creation. In the first stage divine knowledge is derived from comparing certain qualities of the world with what we know of God, while the second stage presupposes a sacramental relationship between things and God. God is in some way present in the creatures; the creature "has the character not only of a sign in the general sense but also of a sacrament."[61]

In the history of occasional meditation, Bonaventure's first stage of ascent has been the more predominant form in the Western tradition. With the Jesuit Robert Bellarmine this was systematically elaborated into fifteen steps in *The*

Mind's Ascent to God by the Ladder of Created Things (1614). Most of the meditations are highly structured and contrived. They would be what Perry Miller calls the "allegorist" rather than the "imagist" way of reading the book of creation.[62] A typical example can be seen in the fourth step of Bellarmine's *scala*, "the consideration of waters and especially fountains," which is part of the meditation on the world's four basic elements.

> Water is moist and cool and, therefore, has five characteristics. For it washes and cleans away stains, it puts out fires, it refreshes and restrains burning thirst, it brings together many diverse things into one, and finally it descends to the depths just as it ascends on high. All these are clear symbols of the footprints of God, the Creator of all things. Water washes away physical stains, God washes away spiritual stains.[63]

Among the Puritans, too, the "allegorist" way of reading the book of creation was widely practiced. They wrote "centuries" and "storehouses of similes."[64] These are stock emblems that set the ground rules for reading the book of creation. They train the individual living in ordinariness to look at the world with a certain devout consciousness. This approach derives lessons from the similarities that exist between creatures and spiritual realities as well as from the differences that exist between them. By *comparing* the similarity between the earthly and the heavenly, the meditator is led to appreciate God's earthly gifts. By *contrasting* the earthly with the heavenly, one learns to detach oneself from the world. Through this art the soul develops a proper relationship with creation. For example, the cleansing property of water is compared with God's washing away sins, but its limitation is contrasted with the unlimited power of "uncreated water" to clean all spiritual stains.[65] Other writers offered books for people in specific vocations, apparently to enable them to maintain a spiritual frame of mind in the midst of their daily work. Such were John Flavel's *Navigation Spiritualized* (1663) and *Husbandry Spiritualized* (1669) and Edward Bury's *A Husbandman's Companion* (1677).

There is a remarkable similarity between the two approaches of occasional meditation and the two ways of reading Scripture, the "Bible study" approach and the spiritual reading discussed in chapter eight. In the "allegorist" way we gather facts about the creatures and draw out appropriate lessons. This is like the "Bible study" approach. In the "imagist" we see creation as a medium of God's revelation. Just as the text carries the word of God, creation conveys the presence of God. Creation does not just remind us of God but sacramentally presents God to us. This corresponds to spiritual reading. Both are legitimate ways of understanding God's relation to the world. The first is seen in passages like Proverbs 6:6 and in the vast number of similes that compare physical objects to spiritual things, as can be seen in books on the meditation on the creatures such as Bellarmine's. The second is exemplified in passages like Psalm 104 and 148. Psalm 104 sees God as actively involving himself in creation. Nature is not an independently existing process. Its varied movements and phenomena are in a very real sense the actions of God. In Psalm 148, creation is alive to God and responds to God.

This sacramental understanding of creation was spontaneously expressed by Francis of Assisi but systematically developed in Bonaventure's second stage. It is also found in the Eastern Orthodox tradition, which sees the human race functioning as a priest of creation, mediating between God and God's world. As Gregory of Sinai puts it, "The man who makes the ascent to God sees all creation luminous."[66] Gregory's words find an echo in Celtic spirituality, which encounters God in things, as the prayer of Columba clearly shows:

Delightful I think it to be in the bosom of an isle
on the crest of a rock,
that I may see often
the calm of the sea.
That I may see its heavy waves
over the glittering ocean
as they chant a melody to their Father
on their eternal course.[67]

A sacramental view of creation must not be confused with natural theology, which teaches that nature can be an independent avenue to God. Reading creation spiritually requires a prior knowledge of God and a personal relationship with God; otherwise we end up with nature religions that worship and glorify creation itself rather than God.

Contemporary Christianity leans more toward the "imagist" understanding of creation.[68] This is because a sacramental understanding of creation, compared with creation understood simply as presenting object lessons of eternal things, is thought to provide stronger theological underpinnings for a positive appreciation of creation, since it links God to the world more closely. This bias is understandable in view of the severe ecological crisis in our world. If the world is to be saved from further destruction, the people who live on it must learn to love it and care for it.

It is important not to exaggerate the difference between the two views, since ultimately it is one of degree rather than kind. Even the most far-fetched allegorization is never completely arbitrary but recognizes some essential connection between the creature and the spiritual lesson drawn from it. Even if our reading of the book of creation is purely "didactic" rather than "symbolic,"[69] it will not (indeed, it cannot) escape the implication that creation is in some way related to God and is therefore to be valued as *God's* creation.

We need to stress the continuity of these two ways for ascetical reasons. Creation may remain a closed book for some people if the didactic method of reading is not made available to them. It is, following Bonaventure, the first stage of the soul's journey and is probably the most logical place to begin.

How to meditate on the creatures. For many young people growing up in sprawling urban centers, developing a meaningful relationship with the natural world may prove difficult. Take the case of six-year-old Johnny from a typical middle-class family in Singapore. For games Johnny has his computer. His heroes are Ninja Turtles or some futuristic creatures dressed in robotic suits who also serve as his constant companions, thanks to strategic marketing, which ensures that the icons of TV heroes are already available in the stores when the show is on. When Johnny's mother suggested a vacation in the country, Johnny expressed a preference for Disneyland instead. Johnny lives in a world where the gadgets of production lines are more real than streams, trees and birds. Increasing urbanization is producing people for whom nature is a stranger rather than a friend. Johnny's isolation is voluntary, but in some urban contexts the isolation people experience is involuntary. Poverty has created physical immobility as well as social immobility.[70] In either case, people need to be reintroduced to God's world. There are a few practical ways of making a friendly introduction.

First, we need to make contact with God's creation more often. It is not always lack of opportunity that blinds us to the beauty of God's world; we are preoccupied with other things. Our hectic life makes it almost impossible to be attentive to other matters in a leisurely way. Appreciating creation is like appreciating a work of art; it cannot be rushed. It requires a new habit of mind that in turn may require a new habit of movement. The *itinerarium mentis* of Bonaventure may have to begin with a new physical itinerary. It may mean breaking our old routine and incorporating a new one to include regular walks in the city park.

Second, if we live in the city and do not have the privilege of natural surroundings, we can nevertheless exercise responsible stewardship by bringing a bit of nature into our environment. Perhaps "a simple window-box may provide that vital link with other living things which is an essential basis for a growing sensitivity to God's good creation."[71] It is amazing to see how a small intrusion of nature into the concrete jungle can begin to effect important changes in the way we perceive our world. We become more sensitive to the growth of living things, to the sun and rain that affect their growth, to the invasion of insects and caterpillars. A whole microcosmic symbiosis opens up before our eyes.

Third, we need to cultivate an eye for the intricacies and beauty of the larger world. We need to look at it appreciatively rather than pragmatically. Often we look at things in terms of what benefit they have for us. If the sight of a stately tree elicits the thought that it would make a nice table to adorn the living room, then we are looking at creation too pragmatically. A tree must be appreciated for being a creation of beauty. Then creation will be an open book. We need to listen to sounds, feel textures, crunch dry leaves and twigs under our feet, breathe in the scents, taste the fruits.

Fourth, we need to read books on nature, animals, plants and so on in order to heighten our sensitivity to God's world. Once we can identify a creature by its name, we are more likely to encounter it on our nature walks.

These are some simple ways that can heighten our sensitivity to our Father's world. A person who has an increased appreciation of God's world will love the Giver of all good gifts better and will develop a sense of ecological responsibility. But while meditation on the creatures may have important ramifications for ecology, the practice of occasional meditation has a wider scope and purpose within the Christian tradition. Some of Hall's meditations were occasioned by events like the sight of a beggar or the sound of a cracked bell.[72] These events and situations, while not normally regarded as a part of "nature," are nevertheless within the order of divine providence and are no less the avenues of divine revelation—a revelation that deepens our spiritual awareness as well as our ecological awareness, as Francis of Assisi and many others since have taught us.

A Spirituality of Social Involvement

This discussion will be brief, since some of the issues related to social involvement have been dealt with in previous chapters.[73] My main concern is to highlight various possibilities of social involvement in the Asian contexts and to underscore the ascetical principle of involvement through prayer.

Options for social engagement. The nature of our spiritual commitment is to a great extent affected by the context in which we live. Some Christians in Third World countries seem to see spirituality almost exclusively in terms of a commitment to making radical structural changes in society. They propose to use the same tools that were used to create the structures they seek to replace. The theological basis undergirding this approach can be traced to the various theologies of hope represented by Moltmann, Pannenberg and the liberation theologians. The common thread that runs through them is the central place they give to eschatology. A consideration of their particular eschatological orientation vis-à-vis traditional eschatology will promote an appreciation of their significance for social engagement.

Traditional eschatology stresses hope as a purely future reality.[74] Such a hope can lead to a "pie in the sky" detachment from the world, as seen, for example, in the dispensational eschatology popularized by the Plymouth Brethren. But a world-denying tendency is not the necessary outcome of this form of eschatology. It could just as well inculcate a deep sense of spiritual watchfulness and freedom from worldly entanglements (compare Mt 24:42) that motivates us to live sacrificially and to serve the world without selfish regard. The example of George Müller, who founded an orphanage in Bristol (and was a dispensationalist, no less), comes readily to mind here.[75]

Modern eschatology stresses the *presence* of the future as the basis for social and political involvement. Christians are to be socially committed to this world because the world to come is already in some way present. Hope is neither purely transcendent nor purely future. The presence of the future shows what God intends to do for the world—transform it, not destroy it. The present historical process is in a very real sense continuous with the future kingdom of God. Commitment to the world is based on attachment to the kingdom of God present in the world rather than on detachment from the snares of the world. Understanding the presence of the kingdom means taking a more structured view of reality and being committed to structural rather than piecemeal changes in society. The theologies of hope provide a stronger basis for social commitment than traditional eschatology provides. But they also create the problem of uncritical commitment. The temptation is to view attractive ideologies as signs of God's kingdom. The result is enslavement to current ideology, be it liberal democracy, feminism or green politics. The most influential form that the theologies of hope take is probably the Moltmannian model of sociopolitical engagement, which purveys Western ideologies as universal norms.

The "theological politics" of John Howard Yoder, Stanley Hauerwas and others represents a coherent alternative that serves the Asian context better than the Moltmannian model, whose hegemony has sometimes blinded people to other viable options.[76] Theological politics stresses the separation of church and world rather than the diffusion of the church in the world. The church influences the world precisely by being distinct from it. It eschews the ways of the world, such as violence and power politics, in pursuing biblical objectives. Character formation of individuals and of the Christian community is essential to making a decisive impact.

In the political theology of Moltmann, by contrast, the very intensity of the involvement itself is constitutive of spirituality. One is spiritual by being full of spirit, not necessarily by being full of the Holy Spirit. Theological politics stresses the necessity of theological norms in giving the church its distinctive identity and basis for action in the world. The church is defined by a distinctive story that cannot be reduced to general moral principles, whereas the norms of political theology are thought to be universally valid principles, which usually turn out to be values defined by the Enlightenment culture such as individual rights and liberal democracy. There is no question that each model in its own way has the potential of making an impact on the world. But if the question is, Which is able to do it better while maintaining the theological integrity of the church in the varied contexts of the world? The choice must fall to the theological politics model.

The life and work of Vishal Mangalwadi from India illustrates what happens when scriptural norms and the Asian context are taken seriously. Mangalwadi's work embodies a spirituality that finds expression in a world of poverty, systemic corruption among government officials and exploitation of the peasantry by the higher caste. There is nothing unique about the biblical and spiritual basis of his social concern. What is peculiar is his combining social reform with evangelism and exorcism.[77] One who knew him describes him as "an evangelist and preacher who speaks in tongues and believes in the supernatural and interventionist God of Love and Justice."[78] Mangalwadi believes that if we cannot change the evil structure of society in places where oppressors are too powerful to be overthrown, then we need to change the oppressed through evangelism. "Evangelism liberates by spreading truth i.e. by undercutting the theological foundations of an exploitative system and by creating an alternative social structure which seeks to live out the truth."[79] Evangelism, the proclamation of the good news that Jesus is Lord, implies that there is to be no absolute human ruler who is above the law. That conversion and change can take place implies that one need not feel hopeless under an oppressive system. That there is a new creation coming implies that the present evil world is not the final reality. What we see in Mangalwadi are evangelical and charismatic components of spirituality combined with elements of the theological programs of Moltmann and Hauerwas—a rare combination indeed!

The asceticism of social engagement. It is one thing to discuss the relevance of various theories of social engagement and quite another to put one of them to work. Ultimately it is only as spiritualities that the real effects of these models will be felt. That is to say, only when it is put into practice will it become convincing. Even a spirituality whose theological basis is less than adequate looks attractive when it is actively engaged in human concerns. As the Hindu follower of Jesus[80] Prabhu Guptara has rightly pointed out,

> Whenever religiosity and spirituality become sources of dissent and of action on behalf of justice, peace and love, then even those who disagree

with that form of spirituality—or indeed with all forms of spirituality—must concede that at least its practical outworking is beneficial. Without such action on behalf of what is right, all forms of spirituality, whatever their theoretical validity, are so much escapism, so much noise.[81]

For theories of social engagement to become lived realities, they must finally descend to the level of practical *askesis*. If our starting point is the distinctive Christian ethics of the kingdom of God rather than some common ethical premise on which both Christian and non-Christian can build, then it is possible to develop a biblical *askesis* of engagement, beginning with such direct acts as freely offering food and water to the hungry and thirsty, clothing the naked, visiting prisoners, even if they are our enemies (Mt 25:35-36; Rom 12:9-21), or remitting our debtors in accordance with Jesus' declaration of jubilee.[82] These acts call for simple obedience and fidelity to grace, not rationalizations and casuistry (under what circumstance must I observe them? who is my enemy? when is one really poor?). They are observed not as acts for the promotion of personal virtue but as part of the "politics of Jesus," which identifies us as the community belonging to him.

These acts have their force if they are linked to the first ascetical principle of prayer. Prayer is a highly political act. When Jesus taught his disciples to pray "Thy kingdom come," he was showing them that in the ultimate analysis the rule of God on earth is to be accomplished through those who pray—those who live by the realization that God is at the center of the universe and at the center of their lives.[83] Without prayer there can be no true spiritual involvement in the world because there is no permanent center to which all things can be related. Revelation 8:3-5 vividly portrays the effects of the prayers of the saints on the world. The prayers of the saints along with the heavenly incense are borne by an angel into God's presence. Then, as if in response to the prayers, "the angel took the censer, filled it with fire from the altar, and hurled it on the earth; and there came peals of thunder, rumblings, flashes of lightning and an earthquake." Prayer does have cosmic effects even if we do not clearly perceive them to be the direct result of prayer.

Along with prayer we need a larger vision of reality. We need to bring the situation of our world into our conscious thought and prayer. If our vision is narrow, confined strictly to "spiritual" matters, then our prayer tends to revolve around a narrow area of concern. The social and political world does not feature in some people's prayer, even though they may be praying earnestly. But we must not suppose that such people's prayers are not real and sincere. In their own small way they are effecting changes, even if the changes are largely in themselves. We must beware of evaluating anyone's spiritual life by a particular theory of social involvement. These people are within their limits rendering acceptable sacrifices to God. As long as the people of God pray, there is hope for the world.

Even though the spirituality of social engagement takes on many forms (black, feminist) and methods (confrontational, consensual, critical coopera- tion) depending on the differing contexts, it must be impelled by the same Spirit of God who guides the church aright in these different situations as it prays. Only then is spirituality authentically Christian.[84]

10

THE RULE
OF LIFE

· ·

T HIS CHAPTER CONSIDERS THE INTEGRATION OF THE VARIOUS SPIRITUAL EXER-
cises that were discussed in preceding chapters. These exercises can be used
to reorder our pattern of life from a basically non-Christian existence to one
that is basically Christian. Embracing a rule of life means allowing our lives
to be reconstituted by this new pattern.

The Nature of the Rule of Life

A rule of life is not about observing a set of rules in order to make ourselves
good and acceptable before God—that would be legalism. Rather, it is about
living a life under a certain pattern of discipline in order to achieve ascetical
proficiency. Such a life is not as unnatural as it may appear at first glance.
Those of us who hold any kind of regular work, whether it be an eight-to-five
job in an office or a dawn-to-dusk job in the field, establish a certain rhythm
of life over time. The problem is not that we lack rule, but that over the years
we have evolved a bad one. For example, we may have become quite
proficient at making a comfortable living for ourselves but not at being
Christians. As noted previously (see pp. 137-38), a rule of life maintains the
basic orientation of our lives as Christians. As Christians, we need to fit secular
work into our rule rather than the other way around, which is what we often
do. Our work comes first, and then we try to work a small religious component
("when and where we can afford it!") into a basically secular existence. Having

a rule does not mean that a greater part of our time is taken up with performing religious duties. Rather, the rhythm that a good rule establishes helps us maintain our spiritual focus.

Embracing a rule means that we have decided to become "regular" Christians, and we reorder our lives accordingly. Along the way we may experience lapses and failures, but that does not make us any less "regular," as long as the rule remains intact. An overscrupulous concern with keeping the rules can lead to Pharisaism and can undermine our status as Christians. The parable of the Pharisee and the publican is instructive here. Like the Pharisee, we can feel smug about keeping all the rules and miss the heart of Christianity, namely, our relationship with God. The publican went away justified in spite of having broken many rules. Rules can make us or break us. They break us if we pursue them as ends in themselves, and they make us if we see them as means to an end. They have their place, as long as we recognize their fundamental status.

The Advantages of Rule

The Christian tradition has long recognized the importance of rule. Perhaps the best-known rule is the rule of Benedict. It is a classic example of common rule that covers every aspect of life in a monastic community. The rule revolves around the rhythmic cycle of common prayer, daily work and study.[1] Many spiritual writers devised personal rules for lay Christians. The Anglican divine Jeremy Taylor (1613-1667) wrote an "agenda," or "a rule to spend each day religiously." The rather comprehensive rule incorporates a wide range of spiritual exercises that cover all waking hours, including prayer, reading, meditation and self-examination at the end of the day. It includes reciting the Lord's Prayer, the Ten Commandments and the Apostles' Creed and meditating on the four last things (death, judgment, heaven and hell).[2] Many Puritans compiled extensive "guides to godliness" that direct the Christian on moral issues and on their entire life with God, relationship with others and conduct of their "special calling," or vocation. Richard Baxter's massive *A Christian Directory* (1674) is an example of such a guide.

A good rule of life has all the advantages that come with good ascetical practice. It ensures constancy, regularity and proficiency. Some people with exceptional abilities may experience occasional flashes of creative insight and accomplish prodigious undertakings. But as the story of the race between the tortoise and the hare reminds us, overall efficiency is found among average people who are willing to work at cultivating their skills systematically. Rule enables such people to plod along at the "slow and steady" pace to accomplish far more spiritually than those who rely on unpredictable, sudden spurts of inspiration. To embrace a rule is to make a commitment to a certain pattern of living that helps reinforce desirable habits in the long term. One indication of having reached a degree of proficiency is observing the rule without thinking too much about it. It becomes second nature. It fits like a pair of comfortable shoes, serving its intended function inconspicuously.

In a broader sense, a rule of life helps us see spiritual life as a holistic integration of various elements. A pattern of discipline implies the use of various spiritual disciplines in an integrated way. The spiritual exercises discussed in chapters seven, eight and nine function as resources that can be customized to meet individual needs. For example, someone making a concerted attempt to develop a closer walk with God needs to deal with a besetting sin like lack of temperance in the matter of food. That person might resolve to forgo supper or a late-night snack and donate the savings to a charity. Such a resolution is more likely to succeed if it is carried out as part of an integrated rule that includes daily prayers and spiritual direction.

Rule also functions as a "canon" that sets a true standard for measuring the adequacy of our spirituality. Traditional definitions of rule, like Aumann's, sometimes tend to restrict the rule of life to "practices of piety."[3] But a good rule embraces a great deal more. It should enable one to measure up against certain objective norms. It should include exercises that pertain to both the individual and the corporate dimensions of life as well as to the personal and the social dimensions.

The Daily Devotion and the Rule of Life

Many evangelical Christians consider their daily devotions or "quiet time" fundamental to their spiritual life. These times can serve as the linchpin for constructing their personal rule of life. Most set aside a regular time each day for some form or prayer and Bible reading. The practice can be improved upon to increase spiritual proficiency by bearing a few things in mind. First, as far as possible, it is best to develop a plan in accordance with the body's natural rhythm. For example, it makes sense for early risers to have a more extended regular morning devotion. Someone who functions better at night should focus mainly on evening devotions. In short, we must choose a time when we are most fresh and least likely to be rushed. I say "more extended" and "focus mainly" because some form of spiritual exercise should mark the beginning and the end of each day. They are the two focal points of most people's natural daily rhythm.

Second, start with a realistic plan. Begin with, say, twenty minutes of daily devotions, and then gradually increase the time when the habit has taken hold. Many beginners bite off more than they can chew, probably the result of mere intellectual conversion to the potential of a new and exciting idea. On learning of what a rule of life can do, they embark on an optimal plan that includes two hours of prayer and four chapters of Bible reading a day. Needless to say, the rule quickly becomes an insupportable burden. Third, besides observing the plan regularly, fixing it at a particular time and place will ensure that the devotional habit is more readily formed.

The following plan for set devotions incorporates a number of spiritual exercises.

A Suggested Plan for Set Devotions

I. Preparation

Ask the Holy Spirit to quiet your mind and remove all distractions.

Ask God to search your heart and bring to remembrance any known sin. (prayer of confession and self-examination)

Ask the Holy Spirit to illumine your mind as you reverently read Scripture or some other book. (prayer for illumination)

II. Spiritual reading

A Bible reading guide such as Robert Murray M'Cheyne's or the Scripture Union's daily Bible reading contains systematic readings that cover the entire Bible over a given period.

III. Meditation

This follows naturally from our spiritual reading. Use a traditional or modern method that suits you. There is no one best method of meditation. The best method is one that you can use effectively.

IV. Thanksgiving

We must thank God for helping us understand his Word, and beyond that, if we make it a habit to "count our blessings, name them one by one" we will begin to have a very different perspective on the world around us.

V. Petition

For many, petitionary and intercessory prayers are haphazard. We promise to pray for someone we meet in church and then forget about it until the following week when we meet again. The only sure way to remember to pray (and keep our promise) is to write it down. We can efficiently organize our prayers for others and the world by keeping a simple book of personal prayer, a small notebook that we keep together with our devotional paraphernalia. On top of each page of the book write down the day of the week. In this way we spread out our petitions evenly through the week. Praying for someone or something once a week might not seem much, but it is better than failing to pray at all.

Enlarging the Context and Time Frame of the Rule of Life

A rule of *life*, by definition, must cover the whole of life. It must "spiritualize" the whole of our existence. Daily set devotions are only one part of a personal rule. Other rules govern various contexts of life or pertain to various time frames. Enlarging the contexts ensures a balanced rule, one that is not restricted to "acts of piety" but embraces the larger world. While it is quite natural for people to be more inclined toward a rule that is either "life orientated" or "prayer orientated,"[4] a balanced rule must include both orientations. Some of the contexts we need to consider are personal relations (cultivating spiritual friendship), rule for the family (family devotions and grace before meals), participation in the life and worship of the church, life in the world in terms of social involvement (for example, a commitment to visit the hospice twice a month). We need to consider enlarging our rule to include other time frames. Some regular activities follow a weekly cycle, like Sunday service; others monthly, perhaps the Lord's Supper; still others annually, such as a family vacation and a personal retreat that may include, among other things, taking a spiritual inventory of the past year.[5] Harold Miller offers many helpful suggestions in his book *Finding a Personal Rule of Life.*[6]

Embracing a rule that is comprehensive in context and time frame may seem daunting. But if we bear in mind the first ascetical principle of prayer (see chapter six), the task becomes manageable. Some of the most valuable parts of our rule may not require much time at all, but they "sanctify" a greater part of our working day. Various acts like ejaculatory prayers or short recollections (discussed in chapter seven) can be incorporated into our rule at certain fixed times of the day—for example, a short prayer before beginning work in the office and a thanksgiving before leaving the office in the evening. These small acts reinforce habitual prayer and remind us of the living testimony we bear at work, at our meeting with the senior citizens on Wednesday evenings or with the check we promised to the drug rehabilitation center. All of these acts, bound together by habitual prayer, form a self-reinforcing rhythm of life.

Discovering Our Personal Rule

When developing a personal rule, first, we need to prayerfully decide what to include. The decision may require many weeks to make. A good rule of thumb is to devise a rule that is as close as possible to an existing routine. Take note of the major activities of each day over a two- or three-week period. This will enable us to identify our present pattern of life. Decide on the main devotional exercises for each day. These will serve as the main markers for the daily pattern of living. They will be the most important (though not necessarily the most time consuming) parts of the daily routine. It is advisable to work this out with a spiritual director.

Second, we need to strike a balance between flexibility and perseverance, especially at the beginning of the implementation of our rule. Flexibility is needed in the initial stages when we are still trying to find our rhythm. Some changes or adjustments may be necessary. On the other hand, we should not be too quick to make changes just because our scheme does not seem to work initially. We need to give ourselves some time to try out the scheme before deciding whether certain parts need to be changed. Developing a new habit, especially if it is a good habit, takes time.

Third, we need a rule that is simple, easy to remember and within reasonable reach. A rule that includes too many meticulous details is more likely to frustrate than to help. But if it does not stretch us beyond our present limits, it is not likely to result in the formation of new habits. If it is to guide us progressively up Jacob's ladder, it should strike a balance between making no demands at all and making too many demands. Thornton's suggestion is reasonable:

> Rule should be such that it is invariably kept without strain but *occasionally* makes a definite demand on the will. It should normally be kept with no fault occasionally, a few faults frequently, and if it goes all to pieces very rarely there is little to worry about.[7]

What would be considered a simple rule? There are a few essentials such as morning and evening prayers or set devotions, worship and communion, and some kind of rule related to our family and vocation.

The Relation Between Personal and Common Rule
It may be helpful in the beginning to embrace a common rule. There are a few well-known common rules. One is the rule of the Third Order of St. Francis designed for laypersons. The aims of the order are "to make our Lord known and loved everywhere," "to spread the spirit of brotherhood" and "to live simply."[8] To realize these aims, the rule focuses on several areas of duty, such as the Eucharist, penitence, personal prayer, self-denial, retreat, study, simplicity of life, work, obedience and fellowship.[9] Another is "The General Rules of the United Societies," which John Wesley drew up for the Methodist societies.[10] It revolves around three main areas of life. First, "avoiding every kind of evil." This is a list of personal and social evils that includes drunkenness and holding slaves. Second, "doing good of every possible sort to all men." Concern for others is expressed in terms of their bodies (for example, feeding the hungry, clothing the naked, visiting the sick) and their souls (instructing, reproving and exhorting). Third, "attending upon the

ordinances of God," which includes public worship, the ministry of the Word read or expounded, the Lord's Supper, family and private prayer, searching the Scriptures and fasting.

Common rules are in their own way highly focused and comprehensive. Common rules like that of the Third Order seek to inculcate a certain type of spirituality. Others, like Wesley's, are aimed simply at helping those who embrace it to "continue to evidence their desire of salvation," or, simply put, to become better Christians without specifying any distinguishing characteristics.

A common rule can be approached in two ways. First, it can be used as a guide for constructing a personal rule. Second, it can be embraced as such, that is, publicly. The latter option may turn out to be an effective way of making a decisive start, especially for those who are indecisive or poorly disciplined, since it involves placing oneself under some kind of direction or external accountability. In whatever way a common rule is used, the knowledge that one is traveling along a well-trodden path is always reassuring.

Another form of common rule is a "covenant group."[11] This is a small group within the local church that offers its members monitoring of individual progress. Mutual checking is one effective way of getting stabilized in a habit. The group must not become a score-keeping agency that keeps track of the number of successes or failures that its members experience and that marks spiritual progress by how many times members keep or fail to keep the rules. What counts, in the final analysis, is whether members remain committed to the principle of rule itself. As long as they persist in embracing rule they will make progress in the long term, failures notwithstanding. The covenant group is but one small step from the creation of the remnant (discussed in chapter five) as the agents of renewal in the church.

A common rule implies that we are not alone in the spiritual exercises. No personal rule is strictly private. It is an extension of corporate rule by which we subject ourselves to the rhythm of the church year and the daily office.[12] Our personal rule, therefore, should not be developed apart from the common rule of the church. Herein lies the answer to one of the most critical problems commonly observed in Protestantism: its lack of spiritual discipline. Bloesch says, "If anything characterizes modern Protestantism, it is the absence of spiritual disciplines or spiritual exercises."[13] Evangelicals often have difficulty with personal discipline because they have difficulty with corporate discipline: the regularity and sameness of the worship. If in the church they are always clamoring for variety and relevance, it is no wonder that in private devotions they quickly get bored with one method and are constantly switching to new and more exciting ways of having "quiet time" with God. Without a regular routine, there is no discipline.

Evangelicals tend to underestimate or ignore the power of the corporate life of the church to shape and reorder our private lives. They usually think of the church as depending on the collective input of individuals: individuals not only make up the church but make the church. The greater truth is the opposite: it is mother church existing through space and time that birthed us. It is we who depend on its life, which finds its highest expression in acts of corporate worship. As Thomas Howard discovers, the repetitive cycles of set prayers observed in the daily office, far from making worship dry, were like "gracious tutors and wise old sages [speaking] gravely and magisterially to me, settling me, reordering my topsy-turvy priorities, and leading me once more back to the center where the human soul is at home."[14] Our personal inner life is more closely tied to the life of the church than we realize. The first step in ascetical discipline is to learn the "technique of going to church." But here is where the modern church has failed its children. By constantly changing its format of worship to make the service more interesting the church is not helping them develop the rhythm necessary for their own personal discipline. Mother church, like many a modern parent, finds it easier to yield to the whims of her spoiled children than to maintain unpopular but necessary discipline.

Regularity is not to be confused with ironclad rigidity. A good rule must allow for breaks and relaxation. There will be days when rule cannot be kept assiduously, during times of serious illness or unforeseen and unpreventable schedule mixups. Even the rule of the desert solitary was probably broken by the intrusion of an earnest inquirer arriving unannounced (it could not have been otherwise). But he saw in the interruption an opportunity to apply his rule of hospitality and thereby demonstrated a larger rule—a rule with a place for the exceptional.[15] Besides giving space for God's surprising work, a certain concession to the weakness of the flesh may be necessary to encourage sagging spirits to keep rule. After all, "the human being cannot bear too much reality," and liturgical worship may have suffered not from too little but from too much of it. But some churches may have switched to charismatic worship as a concession to young Christians who are looking for just the right excuse to abandon spiritual discipline. Charismatic worship can be a tremendous aid to the rule of life, but it can also become the best excuse for liturgical slackness and an overall loss of discipline in the church and in the lives of its members.

The one danger in living under rule is formalism. Rule can degenerate into lifeless, humdrum routine. But if we keep in view the end to which our rule is directed, we will remain sensitive to the need for enlarging and revising our rule every few years in order to make room for progress. While a good rule should fit as well as a pair of comfortable shoes, we need to qualify the analogy here. Shoes have to be discarded when they become worn out or too small. Progress in the Christian life is evidenced in the regular small changes that we make to our rule. But how can we tell if a seeming lack of progress is due to a rule whose usefulness has been outgrown or to the "dark night" period that every Christian encounters in the course of life? This question raises a host of other questions. How long have we been under the present rule? Has the rule served us well up to this point? Are there other possible reasons why we are feeling restive? Changing jobs or moving into a new home—or any major transition in life—can upset our established rhythm of life. Answering these questions requires skills in discernment, understanding the place and nature of trial in spiritual progress, and above all, a mature spiritual guide to help us work through them.

11

THE DISCERNMENT
OF SPIRITS
· ·

C HRISTIAN DISCERNMENT HAS ALWAYS BEEN REGARDED AS A NECESSARY SKILL IN overcoming the common obstacles to spiritual progress. The need was most acutely felt in the monastic culture, where the focus on spiritual life had a flip side: the dark forces that threatened its nurture. Without discernment no one can hope to make much spiritual progress. According to one desert father, discernment is what transforms physical asceticism into virtue.

> An old man was asked, "How can I find God?" He said, "In fasting, in watching, in labours, in devotions, and, above all, in discernment. I tell you, many have injured their bodies without discernment and have gone away from us having achieved nothing. Our mouths smell bad through fasting, we know the Scriptures by heart, we recite all the Psalms of David, but we have not that which God seeks: charity and humility."[1]

This point is especially recognized in John Cassian's (d. 435) famous *Conferences*. An entire conference is devoted to a discussion of discernment. Discernment is the "eye and lamp of the body" (compare Mt 6:22-23) without which the whole body is plunged into total darkness (2.3).

There are two major contexts in which we need to exercise discernment. One is external, the other is internal. The first concerns the veracity of events, situations and people. When the early church was faced with the Gnostic heresy, it was told to "test the spirits to see whether they are of God" by the criterion of whether the spirit "acknowledges that Jesus Christ has come in the flesh" (1 Jn 4:1-2). Here we see discernment involving the application of a basic truth to an external problem. Such forms of discernment are relatively straightforward. A more difficult area concerns the discernment of alleged signs of the manifestation of God, including extraordinary phenomena. The very nature of the spiritual life contains an irreducible dimension of the extraordinary. Thus a need to interpret the significance of these phenomena has always been felt. Another aspect of external discernment concerns the sociopolitical context. The Christians' historical existence requires discerning what God is doing in the world and raises questions about one's active participation in it. Is this movement a work of God? What is God saying to us in this given situation? These questions voice concerns that are important to Christians throughout the world.

The greatest difficulty of all involves discerning God's will for one's own life in a particular situation. What is God telling *me* to do in this situation? How can I be sure that this urge, impulse or feeling coming in response to an external situation is from God and not just my self or from some malevolent agent? For the modern Christian the problem is further compounded by the modern consciousness, which raises questions that cannot be answered with simple certainties. Depth psychology, with its probing into the unconscious, hidden motives, unconscious desires and so on, has made it more difficult for modern people to apply traditional criteria in a straightforward manner such as this Ignatian rule: "Spiritual comfort with no previous occasion giving rise to it comes from our Lord God alone."[2] There is always a nagging doubt that a good action may be motivated by selfish concerns, that underlying a good impulse may be an undetected ulterior motive. That sudden urge to give up one's career to go into "full-time ministry" may be an unconscious desire to escape unbearable responsibility. Things are not always what they seem. The more we learn about human nature, the more difficult it is to make a judgment about the nature and source of a spiritual experience. How can we be sure that the sense of peace is from God and is not the result of a good meal or Satan lulling us into a false sense of security?

Determining the real source of inner impulses has always been difficult. This may be the reason why most of the work on discernment in the Christian tradition has concentrated on this area. For in the final analysis the work of discernment boils down to one question: How do I know that I am in God's will in this particular situation? It is generally recognized that we do not really know God's will until we are already in it or at least desire to be in it. The question of discernment cannot be dealt with apart from the question of spirituality.

Discernment and Spiritual Maturity

Discernment is knowing God's will in particular situations. And knowing God's will, as we learned earlier, is not just a matter of grasping a piece of information. It has to do with our whole attitude toward God and ourselves, with an ongoing relationship with God and loving him. Discernment, therefore, is more than just the scientific application of principles to particular situations. It requires practical wisdom that no amount of formal study can impart, that is, a kind of spiritual sensitivity that comes with long experience. Perhaps this is what Paul has in mind when he prays for the Philippians that "your love may abound more and more in knowledge and depth of insight, so that you may be able to discern what is best and may be pure and blameless until the day of Christ" (Phil 1:9-10). "Depth of insight" here refers to a kind of "feeling for the actual situation at the time." This increasing knowledge and tact will enable them to "distinguish the really important issues in their lives together."[3]

The ability to discern implies a degree of maturity or spiritual proficiency. Spiritual sensitivity is honed through constant training in listening to God and obeying his voice. One who does so becomes skilled in distinguishing between right and wrong (compare Heb 5:14), between the ordinary and "what is best" (Phil 1:10). "A solid personal spirituality is the only consistent ground for distinguishing good and bad impulses, tendencies, aspirations, and decisions."[4] Thus the more important issue in discernment has to do with the *process* of discerning rather than the *products* of the activity.[5] Specific questions involving vocation, marriage and so forth may turn out to be less significant in the long term than the way we go about making those decisions. The *how* is far more important than the *what* when it comes to the question of God's will.

For many overscrupulous Christians, the *what* continues to be the source of the most intractable difficulty. They worry themselves sick about missing God's "perfect will" and settling for God's "permissive will." What they usually mean is that at one point in their lives they felt sure that God wanted them to go into "full-time" ministry or some such calling, but they became lawyers and stockbrokers instead. A few things need to be said about this commonly encountered "case of conscience." First, a person who is really concerned about God's will is probably already in it. The willingness and desire after God *is* the will of God. Second, making a mistake in one choice does not mean forever missing out on God's perfect will. God's will for one's life is found in the process of living in love and obedience, not in one crucial choice we made or failed to make. Third, the wrong choice may be the very means that God is using to bring the Christian to the place of contrition and humility that enables him to be the honest stockbroker that he is now. God's will is better served by an honest stockbroker than by a bad pastor!

What is crucially needed is to develop a certain spiritual attitude as a prerequisite to genuine discernment.[6] We need to ask ourselves questions like, Do we decide out of a trusting relationship with God and out of humble acknowledgment that God is fully in charge of our lives (Prov 3:5-6)? Do we honestly will to do God's will? Do we seek counsel from others, or do we think that our personal integrity alone is an adequate basis for taking certain actions? These questions cannot be readily answered without, first, a true knowledge of our selves in relation to God. It is when we see ourselves as God sees us (compare the self-examination exercise in chapter seven) that we obtain true self-knowledge and are able to see through the process of discerning God's will in a particular situation to its proper conclusion. An *explicit* desire to know God's will in a given situation is not always an indication of a surrendered will. Rather, the opposite may be the case. We may be seeking divine sanction for our own secret wishes (compare Ezek 14:7-8). We may be hiding an inner insecurity or an inability to trust people. Ironically, it may even indicate a desire to control our own destiny instead of letting God take charge of our lives. In our efficiency-minded society, there is a real danger of treating God's will in such a way. If I can find out exactly what God wants me to do over the next five years, I can live efficiently and not have to worry henceforth. All hidden motives, repressed urges, unacknowledged fears, hatreds and so on need to be brought to light when we examine ourselves in the presence of God.

The rules of discernment. The totality of our relationship with God, not the individual choices we make, determines whether we are in God's will or out of it. There is also a cognitive content involved in knowing God's will. Growing in discernment includes learning objective principles, which represent the collective wisdom of the community. At the beginning of our spiritual lives, they may be our only means of avoiding serious error. It is like learning to play chess. The first thing we do is learn the ground rules of the game. Knowing the ground rules of chess does not make anyone a good chess player, but it gets a person into the game. Both Scripture and Christian tradition furnish us with some ground rules for discernment, which beginners would do well to heed if they are to grow into discerning Christians. For example, a genuine spiritual experience must manifest moral qualities such as truth, gravity, submissiveness, humility and Christ-centeredness. A counterfeit experience is accompanied by pride and vanity, morbid curiosity, confusion and depression, false humility expressed in an all-too-ready eagerness to talk about it, and extremes of either presumption or despair.[7]

The Old Testament gives certain objective criteria that help distinguish true prophets from false.[8] One criterion is the fulfilment of prophecy (Deut 18:20-22). Micaiah (1 Kings 22:28) and Jeremiah appealed to this criterion (Jer 28:16-17) in their opposition to the false prophets. Another is their orthodoxy. Even if the prophet's prediction should come to pass, if he induces the people to seek after false gods, he is a false prophet (Deut 13:1-5). A third criterion is the content of the prophet's teaching. False prophets were accused of preaching "peace" when there was no peace (Jer 6:14). This does not mean that a true prophet always preaches doom. Many true prophets also spoke of restoration, such as Ezekiel and Isaiah (Ezek 37; Is 40). These false prophets were giving false assurances to people who were obviously not living up to the demands of the covenant. In other words, a moral and spiritual presupposition underlies the true prophet's message. This moral dimension of the prophetic message is matched by the morality of the prophet's own life. False prophets often live questionable moral lives. They deal falsely (Jer 6:13), they get drunk (Is 28:7), they divine for money (Mic 3:5, 11), they plagiarize from others (Jer 23:30).

Jesus seemed to have this pattern of discernment in mind when he said, referring to false prophets who came in sheep's clothing: "By their fruit you will recognize them" (Mt 6:15-16). Their way of life and their character reveal them for who they are. Similarly, Paul exposed the false apostles who insinuated themselves into the Corinthian church by pointing out their questionable character, namely, their overweening pride. They did not hesitate to use their authority based on vaunted claims about their own accomplishments (2 Cor 11:18) to ride roughshod over the Corinthian Christians (v. 20).

The character that reveals truth is primarily seen in a life that is directed wholly to glorifying God, not in a display of spectacular signs and wonders. The latter are no proof of truth, for they can be counterfeited by the enemy (Col 2:8; 1 Tim 4:1-2; 2 Tim 4:3). Jesus exemplifies this discernment pattern in his own life. The miracles he performed were done to glorify God (Jn 7:18). The whole thrust of Jesus' own ministry was to bring honor to the Father rather than to himself (Jn 12:27-28; 17:4). Another sign of truth is unity. The genuine work of the Spirit characteristically brings greater unity to the body of Christ rather than division, since his work is always consonant with what is deep within the heart of the Father and the Son: "that they may be one as we are one" (Jn 17:11). This biblical pattern of knowing a tree by its fruit is the ground rule of discernment, which the Christian tradition further elaborated.

Ignatius's "rules for distinguishing between different spiritual influences," which are found at the end of his *Spiritual Exercises,* is considered one of the classic documents on discernment. The rules covering the first week of the spiritual exercises are actually quite straightforward. He begins with a broad principle. Those who are not in right relationship with God go "from mortal sin to mortal sin." The enemy will give them "illusory delights" and "sensual pleasure and enjoyments," while the good spirit will do the opposite, inducing compunction and remorse (314).[9] But the works are reversed when they are in right relationship with God: the evil spirit will try to bring distress, while the good spirit will bring comfort (315).

"Spiritual comfort" comes from the Lord, while "spiritual distress" is from the evil spirit. By the former term Ignatius is referring to experiences that direct the soul to love God, to love the creatures only in God (for God's sake) and to love experiences leading to increase in faith, hope and charity (316). Christians may experience spiritual distress in the form of temptations, aridity and such like. During the period of distress they should not alter any decision or resolution made previously as they are more likely to be mistaken (318).

The signs associated with the second week of exercises appear to be more subjective: "lightness of heart," "spiritual joy," "spiritual comfort with no previous occasion giving rise to it" and so on (329-30). But Ignatius is presupposing a higher level of maturity at this stage, marked by an ability to recognize certain subjective impressions produced by the Spirit. "When souls are advancing from good to better, the touch of the good angel is soft, light and gentle" (335). The soul is able to distinguish the quality of affections because it has now developed a certain "feel" for spiritual things. Ignatius, however, warns that the evil spirit can produce good impulses that seem like spiritual comfort, but we can tell their source if we follow them to their end. If they do not end well, they do not have their source in God (333-34). This rule implies that discernment takes time. We must examine inner urges and feelings carefully and always in the light of our relationship with God.

One of Ignatius's most insightful observations is the experience of the "afterglow":

He must distinguish exactly the specific time of the actual comforting from the subsequent stage when the soul is still glowing with the favour conferred on it, a sort of afterglow from the comforting which is now over. In this second stage the soul often makes different resolutions and plans which are not the direct result of the action of God our lord. They may be due to the soul's own activity, based on established habits of mind or the implications of ideas or judgements previously formed; they may be the result of the action of the good or the evil spirit. So they have to be very carefully scrutinized before we can give them complete credit and put them into effect. (336)

One might have a genuine experience given by God, but it does not follow that all decisions made subsequently are divinely sanctioned. Ignatius's teaching on the "afterglow" needs to be reemphasized today. There are many examples of "afterglow" effects coming from what may originally have been a genuine spiritual experience. People who have a "baptism of the Spirit" go on to make some disastrous mistake; a preacher who exercises what looks like a "gift of (fore)knowledge" follows it up with some misleading counsel.[10]

It is important to note the Ignatian pattern of discernment. It *begins* with objective moral and theological criteria. It's bad to feel good (and good to feel bad) when we are not right with God; we must suspect the divine origin of any impulse, however good, unless it leads to an increase in faith, hope and charity. It leads us to recognize certain subjective impulses as we grow in spiritual proficiency. Unless one is given a *charisma* of discernment (1 Cor 12:10), which is probably not given to all nor operative all the time, we need to develop the skill of discernment, but it cannot be done apart from living a life of intimate relationship with God.

Rules are helpful, but our ability to apply them to any specific situation is limited. There are three reasons for this. First, the rule of knowing a tree by its fruit is more readily applicable to a bad tree than to a good one. Evil works are clear signs that God is not present. One bad fruit may establish a certain experience as false, but it does not follow that one good characteristic in isolation will vindicate a religious experience. It is noteworthy that in Galatians 5, the *works* of the flesh are contrasted with the fruit (singular) of the Spirit. "The fruit of the Spirit" (Gal 5:22) refers to inner dispositions or attitudes. It is possible to do good without *being* good. This is why good actions alone are not a sure sign of the workings of God. It is the conjunction of a number of characteristics or dispositions that constitutes a single "fruit" of the Spirit and serves as a pointer to (rather than a sort of litmus test of) that which is good. Each good work taken separately cannot be determinative. It is when they are evident in more or less their totality that we can discern a pattern of existence that could be said to comport with the truth. Discerning a person's character is far more difficult than determining whether an act per se is right or wrong.

Second, spiritual counterfeits are sometimes difficult to distinguish from their genuine counterparts because, as the literature in this field often reminds us, Satan can disguise himself as an angel of light. Third, someone who is living "in the flesh" rather than "in the Spirit" can easily deceive herself into thinking that an experience is real. Only the spiritual person can properly discern spiritual things (1 Cor 2:14-15). The main problem is the weakness within ourselves, our lack of depth of personal relationship with God.

The character of a discerning Christian. What makes a discerning Christian is a loving relationship with God. Specific qualities are also particularly relevant to discernment. One is *humility*. Discerning Christians are humble because they know that they cannot pry open the secret counsels of God to discover his will. Ultimately it is God who decides and reveals; the Christian simply obeys. Cassian lays great emphasis on the need for humility in learning discernment (2.16).

> True discernment is obtained only when one is really humble. The first evidence of this humility is when everything done or thought of is submitted to the scrutiny of our elders. This is to ensure that one trusts one's own judgment in nothing, that one yields to their authority in everything, that the norms for good and bad must be established in accordance with what they have handed down. (2.10)

The need to submit to the counsel of more experienced people is especially acute for someone who has extraordinary experiences. The one who rejects such counsel may act presumptuously and as a result fall into delusion. Cassian observes that even old, experienced monks had been deceived on this account (2.5). Humble confession of faults before others is a sure way of dealing with hidden sins that give occasion for demonic deception. "An evil thought sheds its danger when it is brought out into the open, and even before the verdict of discernment is proferred the most foul serpent which, so to speak, has been dragged out of its dark subterranean lair into the light by the fact of open avowal retreats, disgraced and denounced" (2.10). Yet we need to be discerning when subjecting ourselves to the judgment of others. Not any old men will do, warns Cassian: "Our enemy, who is very cunning, uses the white hair of age to fool the young" (2:13). The importance of this insight should not be lost to us who live in the Asian context, where there is a strong tendency toward unquestioning deference to the elder. Cassian's counsel on humility is especially appropriate in the modern charismatic context. Curiosity in regard to the supernatural realm is often coupled with a lack of accountability, gross ignorance of the Christian tradition and open rejection of institutional authority.

A second quality is courage[11] or boldness.[12] An element of risk taking is involved in seeking to know what God would have us do in a specific situation because we have no objective basis to act with complete certitude. This was what many Pentecostal pioneer missionaries meant when they talked of launching out "by faith." Humanly speaking, there was little basis for doing what they did. All the odds were stacked against them. Yet beyond all human reckoning they possessed another kind of certainty that gave them the courage to step out under the "leading of the Spirit."[13] Not all "Spirit-led" endeavors succeeded.[14] For some, it may be due to the failure to develop other qualities of discernment, like humility; for others, it may be a failure of courage itself. But without the boldness to step out "based on a deeply felt sense that things are right,"[15] often little of God's will would actually be done on earth as it is in heaven. Missions would not expand beyond the comfort and security of familiar surroundings. Justice would not "roll on like a river and righteousness like a never-ending stream" (Amos 5:24) into the danger zones of poverty and oppression.

The courage to take risks does not require taking on a big one all at once. In our asceticism of small steps it may begin with nothing more than the risk of going beyond our normal routine to call on someone we don't normally visit, where the worst possible result may be some minor embarrassment. Through these small acts of courage we gradually sensitize our spiritual instincts to discern God's voice until one day our faith is challenged like Abraham's once was when he was told: "Take your son, your only son, Isaac, whom you love, and sacrifice him as a burnt offering on one of the mountains I will tell you about" (Gen 22:2). The test of Abraham's faith did not begin on Mount Moriah but on a humbler plane when he was given a call that must have seemed undramatic to people used to a nomadic existence: "Leave your country, your people and your father's household and go to the land I will show you" (Gen 12:1).

Another major quality of a discerning Christian is the ability to strike a certain poise between opposing errors. Cassian has once again helped us see the importance of this virtue. The discerning Christian avoids vacillating between zeal and sluggishness.

So, then, we must seek in all humility to acquire the grace of discernment which can keep us safe from the two kinds of excess. For there is an old saying: "Excesses meet." Too much fasting and too much eating come to the same end. Keeping too long a vigil brings the same disastrous cost as the sluggishness which plunges a monk into the longest sleep. Too much self-denial brings weakness and induces the same condition as carelessness. Often I have seen men who could not be snared by gluttony fall, nevertheless, through immoderate fasting and tumble in weakness into the very urge which they had overcome. Therefore life must be lived with due measure and, with discernment for a guide, the road must be traveled between the two kinds of excess so that in the end we may not allow ourselves to be diverted from the pathway of restraint which has been laid down for us nor fall through dangerous carelessness into the urgings of gluttony and self-indulgence. (2.16)

Extremes are a sign of a lack of discernment. They do not promote the personal wholeness needed for real spiritual progress. But with discernment it is possible to reach the utmost heights with the minimum of exhaustion. Without it there are many who despite the intensity of their struggle have been quite unable to arrive at the summit of perfection. For discernment is the mother, the guardian, and the guide of all the virtues. (2.5)

The concept of spiritual poise is also discussed in the eleventh sign of Edwards's *Religious Affections*.[16] Because Christians have the whole image of Christ stamped upon them, the beauty, symmetry and proportion in the image is also revealed in their affections. "A holy hope and a holy fear go together in the saints." Joy and comfort are present with "godly sorrow and mourning for sin" (p. 293). In the "hypocrites," however, affections are manifested "in a monstrous disproportion." They tend to exercise their affections in extreme and partial ways. Their zeal fluctuates wildly, or if they are zealous against sin, they will be vehement against some sins and totally ignore others (pp. 297-98).

In our modern context, spiritual poise must be maintained against another set of extremes. On one end of the scale is a prejudicial attitude of rejecting everything that does not conform to our preconceived ideas. We dismiss out of hand any experience that appears strange, especially one that unsettles our comfortable routine. The opposite extreme is gullibility. Naiveté is widespread and is perhaps the greater danger in our world today. In the past, tradition reinforced prejudice, but nowadays television and modern marketing strategies have conditioned people to accept changes without questioning. And Christians are no exception. They are all too easily awed by anything that looks extraordinary, be it "holy laughter," an extraordinarily large church or a preacher with an extraordinarily large ego. If Christians today were to learn discernment in large numbers, most television evangelists would go out of business!

Corporate Discernment

So far I have emphasized that the work of discernment grows out of a life of deep relationship with God. This life in God is rooted in the redemptive community through baptism. It is in that living organism called the church that we receive our true identity. Discernment, therefore, is ultimately a communal undertaking, based not on some private revelation that gives us access to privileged information about ourselves, others and the world but on the corporate reality that shapes our identity. In short, the church is the locus of all discernment because God's will is truly revealed there.

Protestant Christians who believe in the priority of Scripture in all matters of faith and practice have often taken this principle to mean that Christians can come to the Scripture on their own to discover God's will for their lives. Scripture functions as a resource book for private interpretation. Fortunately, they are mostly spared the hazards of an implicit gnosticism because they also recognize the need to check out their interpretation with more mature Christians. Reading and listening to Scripture as a traditioning process in the church was mentioned earlier (see chapter five). It is within this process that we can understand Scripture as a regulative principle. We know God's will in Scripture not because it is a quasi-magical book that objectively sets forth God's will for private individuals to discover but because we belong to a community shaped by the authoritative Word. The knowledge of God's will resides in the church, which is supremely the hearer and the bearer of the Word. Therefore individual Christians can come to know God's will only in a living relationship with the community.

Scripture is the apostolic tradition, that is, it contains truth handed down by the apostles to the church. It is as tradition that it is alive in the church, and the church is made alive by it. When the apostle Paul urges the Thessalonian church to "test" or discern the prophetic utterances (1 Thess 5:19-21), he does so on the basis of the apostolic traditions "passed on to you" (2 Thess 2:15).[17] When he instructs the Christian community in Corinth to judge a prophecy (1 Cor 14:29), he places the responsibility of discernment not on the shoulders of a particular individual nor even on a class of professional prophets but on the corporate body.[18]

We see this pattern of discernment in the book of Acts when Paul and Barnabas were sent out by the church in Antioch. The will of God was discerned after the church had fasted and prayed together (Acts 13:2). Similarly, when the church needed to determine the status of the Gentiles, although there is no mention of the church fasting and praying as at Antioch, the community was open to God. They listened to the testimonies of Peter, Paul and Barnabas and in the end confirmed their stories in a decision summed up in James's speech (Acts 15:1-21). It is no wonder that the Christian tradition has also insisted on the need to discern together with others. Cassian taught that in order to be discerning one must be humble, and humility means submitting oneself "to the scrutiny of our elders."[19] The Quaker "silent meeting" is another example of corporate discernment at work. The group waiting in silence before God seeks to discern God's will for the group or a particular individual. They recognize that while each individual may have the inner light, it "is often obscured by sundry forms of inner and outer interference."[20] Discernment, therefore, is irreducibly an effort of the community. Ultimately, even the most private decision is made in and with the community of which one is a part.[21]

One important consequence of seeing discernment in the context of the church is that it displays the real role of church leaders. Certain charismatic leaders today claim a spiritual authority far surpassing that of any pope or church council. The leader, they claim, is the specially "anointed" person through whom God reveals his will to the church through a "prophetic word."[22] Although this may have been the case in the Old Testament where only certain people were anointed for special tasks, including the work of discernment (Num 27:21), the critical difference in the New Testament is that all are filled with the Spirit (Acts 2:17). The real leader is Christ, the head who communicates his will to the entire body, not just to a special class of leaders. The leader's role is to make explicit what God is saying implicitly to his people. In practical terms, this means that no Christian leader has the right to lead unless he or she first learns to humbly listen to what God is saying in and through the ordinary members of the flock.

Discerning the Problems of the Spiritual Life

Discernment is frequently needed in the area of personal growth. The moment we begin to take our life with God seriously, we begin to encounter problems (as noted in chapter six in connection with growth in the prayer life). Some of these problems are generated in the process of trying to undo long-standing habits and cultivate new ones. Withdrawal symptoms may occur as old habits are stripped away. Spiritual growth, for its part, frequently is accompanied by growing pains. A failure to understand this process has led some to experience severe setbacks. Perhaps a few common symptoms need to be mentioned briefly at this point.

Distraction and aridity. The ascetic, like the professional athlete, may have occasional bad days when she performs poorly despite her best intentions. But these common problems of the spiritual life must be understood for what they are. They may cause us to loosen up on our rule of life, but they are not sins. "Cheating, dishonesty, the deliberate foul; these are sins. Playing badly is not."[23] Understanding and knowledge are essential to dealing with such problems, which are often involuntary. It is best to avoid paying too much attention to them, especially when one is praying or meditating. When we just get on with our meditation and prayer, presently we find ourselves really praying and meditating.

Scrupulosity. Thornton regards scrupulosity as "a serious spiritual disease in which the soul is perpetually oppressed by moral quibbles exaggerated out of all proportion."[24] Being overly scrupulous about minor details may well indicate a loss of nerve. The apostle Paul in Romans 14 describes such Christians as those who have a "weak conscience." If these were Jewish

Christians, as some commentators believe, we might wonder why they were reduced to a purely vegetarian diet. Could it be due to overscrupulosity arising from their aversion to the diet of their Gentile fellow Christians? Whatever the reason, the scrupulous Christian is always feeling the need to be on the safe side. When uncertain about what constitutes unclean meat, she eliminates meat from her diet altogether. When he is not sure about which day is holy, to be on the safe side he decides to make every day holy. She is always building another hedge around the law just to make doubly sure that she keeps within its bounds. While the Christian life is marked chiefly by reverence, it is also reverence tempered by holy familiarity. Propriety must be observed, but it ought to be spontaneous rather than forced. It is this holy familiarity and spontaneity that the overscrupulous Christian lacks.

New Christians often display symptoms of scrupulosity that are similar to symptoms displayed by new drivers: nervous and rigid, both hands clamped stiffly on the steering wheel and eyes fixed on the road. But the new Christian outgrows that scrupulosity just as the new driver gradually becomes more relaxed with experience. The new Christian's weak conscience is strengthened by the acquisition of new knowledge. Sometimes, however, the scruples are reinforced (especially in ultraconservative churches) and over time become a crippling disease—the same disease that afflicted the Pharisees.

Delusion. It is not uncommon for young believers embarking on an earnest pursuit of God to confuse zeal for spiritual things with the attainment of them or to mistake extraordinary experiences for advanced spirituality. They fail to realize that they are experiencing the "honeymoon" phase of the Christian life—that the dramatic experiences are actually the extra "sweetmeats" and props given in the initial phase of growth. Without proper guidance, self-deception easily sets in at this stage. It is a very real problem that dogs every Christian seeking to make spiritual advance. The monastic tradition offers many tragic examples. Cassian recalls the warning of Anthony, who told of a monk who was so engrossed in prayer that he refused to join others for communal meals, even on an important festival like Easter. Convinced of the merit of his own virtues, he was deluded by the devil to jump into a deep well and died two days later (2.5). Cassian cites several examples of monks who were deluded by the devil who came as an angel of light (2.6-8). It is noteworthy that it was precisely at the point when monks felt most secure in their acts of piety that they were in the greatest danger of self-delusion. Here is a warning that modern Christians, fired with fresh enthusiasm after experiencing some kind of "spiritual renewal," would do well to take heed.

It is important to understand the nature of growth. The Christian life includes a phase that is analogous to puberty, with all the upsets that can attend dramatic change. But if our theological schema does not recognize these problems, it is hardly surprising that they are then misdiagnosed as "oppression" or "demonization" in need of "deliverance." Spiritual aridity may be due to a genuine dark night or backsliding or cleverly disguised worldliness. Here again, we see that ground rules for discernment are useful to a point. Beyond that we have to learn to discern out of a life of intimate acquaintance with God. We must finally, in love, humility and courage, act on the best available knowledge, trusting that as we carry out the decision in the right spirit, God is working out his own will in our very acting (Phil 2:12-13). In such a situation the help of a spiritual guide or mentor is crucial. Learning to subject our experience to the scrutiny of another and especially the larger Christian community helps us develop qualities that will make us more proficient in discernment.

Discerning the Spirit in the World

The work of discerning the Spirit in the world has become rather prominent in modern theological discussions, especially among advocates of a strong eschatological view of history. If God is working in our world, how do we discern that working? For some, discernment is less a matter of knowing what God is doing in the world and more a matter of praxis, following Jesus' way of discernment, which has to do with the way he affirms God's yes and no to history. And God's yes and no in history relate to the place of the poor and oppressed in history. Liberation theologian Jon Sobrino declares quite categorically that the criterion for judging between true and false prophets is "whether or not they are building the kingdom for the poor."[25] Some Asian theologians, however, perhaps more concerned with development rather than revolution, are more cautious about identifying a particular historical movement with God's revelation.[26] The repeated failures of utopian movements on which the masses have previously pinned their hopes have led to the realization that discerning God's hand in history is not so simple after all. Christians are right in affirming their belief in divine providence. What they are not certain is how it works. This is why the doctrine of providence has always generated the problem of evil.

Perhaps we do not fully understand what God is doing in our history. The question of what God is saying to us or wanting us to do in a particular moment and context of history has the same logical status as the question of God's will in a particular circumstance of life requiring a particular decision. It may be that some are called to make one form of response, some another. In the end there may be no one right answer to a given historical situation.

But like the question of God's will for a particular life circumstance, the appropriate response to the mystery of providence always involves a right spiritual attitude.

The Scriptures identify this attitude as watchfulness, a stance that Jesus enjoins in connection with the signs of the times (Mt 24:42; 25:13). Watchfulness is not very different from praying (Mt 26:41). Spiritual alertness comes through prayer, "the loving relationship between the soul and God" that sensitizes heart and mind to the presence of God in the world. Living in this loving relationship, we begin to discern God's action in the world, God's person in the stranger, the hungry, the thirsty and the naked (Mt 25:34-46). And we act accordingly. Thus we can speak of discernment as "the meeting point between prayer and action."[27] Watchfulness does not come naturally. It requires the straining of all our senses: seeing, hearing, smelling, tasting, touching. Only bird watchers can discern the song of oriole or thrush from among a cacophony of sounds. Why? Because their ears are tuned to no other sounds but the singing from the birds. Discerning God's voice in the world requires no less. We must train our ears to listen and obey.

If we encounter a situation involving a beggar at our doorstep or a refugee fleeing a war half a world away and are not moved to ask, "Lord, what will you have me do?" then we have not yet learned to listen to God's voice in the world. It does not mean that God's answer will always come in the form of a call to a specific action (it may!), but we cannot be too often asking before we are ineluctably "led" to make a certain response.

Discerning Extraordinary Phenomena
The discerning of spirits has always included an evaluation of extraordinary phenomena.[28] Even in the New Testament church there were problems associated with the exercise of the *charismata:* How can we tell a true prophecy from a false one? Paul laid down guidelines in some early letters. The community is to judge a prophecy (1 Cor 14:29). Prophetic utterances are to be neither accepted unquestioningly nor rejected outright. Rather, they are to be tested (1 Thess 5:19-22).

The need for discernment has taken on added significance in recent times with the growing influence of the charismatic movement.[29] Human nature has a weakness for extraordinary phenomena. It treats them with either extreme awe or extreme skepticism. This tendency toward extremes makes discernment in this area especially urgent. A recent assessment of charismatics showed a number of noted Christian leaders in the United Kingdom succumbing to extreme naiveté in assessing spiritual gifts, especially prophecy.[30] By the biblical criterion of prophecy, those whose prophecies have obviously failed are false prophets (Deut 18:20-22), yet some of these self-styled prophets continue to enjoy broad acceptance and very "successful" ministries. Within the Asian context, where religiosity is often expressed in primitive animism, the main issue is distinguishing between Christian and non-Christian phenomena. Many Asian Christians tend to evolve a rather undiscerning attitude toward extraordinary phenomena occurring in a Christian context. There is a general reluctance to question even the most dubious "manifestations" as long as they are performed by Christian ministers.[31]

The Christian tradition has generally accorded a much more modest role to extraordinary phenomena. Paul G. Hiebert has rightly noted that "[t]he history of human faith is often a progression from belief rooted in God's work to belief rooted in God himself."[32] According to John of the Cross, spiritual phenomena like "ecstasies, raptures, and dislocation of bones" belong to a preliminary phase of spiritual development when one has only a limited capacity for "spiritual communications."[33] Within a different theological framework, Jonathan Edwards comes to basically the same conclusion, that is, that spiritual phenomena are not a certain sign of true, saving affections. Modern charismatics should heed their spiritual forebears and avoid putting too much weight on ecstatic experiences as a truth criterion.

Edwards's discussion of religious affections is especially important in light of a common modern phenomenon. Someone has a genuine spiritual experience that does not result in any abiding or "saving" fruit. In part two of his *Religious Affections* Edwards examines "what are no certain signs that religious affections are truly gracious or that they are not." There are many affections that may be good in themselves but may or may not be "gracious" affections. Unless they are accompanied by other, more abiding affections, they are not true. They may mislead someone into the impression that he or she has the truth. While they may not be outrightly false, they are inadequate.

The phenomena of "holy laughter" and being "slain in the Spirit" that grew out of the "signs and wonders" movement are but two of the more popular ones that have captured the imagination of many charismatics in recent times. What makes the movement as a whole problematic is its tendency to fixate on God's extraordinary works to the point of preferring them to his ordinary works in the natural order. Natural working is even regarded as a sort of concession to human weakness. For example, anyone who has *real* faith expects a supernatural healing. Someone who lacks faith takes medication. Theologically, such a mindset creates a false disjunction between nature and grace. Thus they perpetuate the same dualism that "signs and wonders" people often accuse other evangelical Christians of falling into. This fascination with the extraordinary represents a failure to appreciate a true biblical holism, which sees God's works of providence as no less special than his miraculous works.[34]

In view of the widespread naiveté of many modern Christians regarding extraordinary phenomena, a study of Edwards's discussion of these uncertain signs is in order. Edwards discussed ten such signs. Many of them are present in the modern renewal movement and unfortunately are given more weight than they deserve.

In part one of *The Religious Affections* Edwards shows from Scripture that there is a relationship between true religion and its manifestation in such affections as love, joy and so on (1 Pet 1:8). "True religion, in great part, consists in holy affections."[35] The affections are not essentially different from the will. The inclination or disinclination of the will involves some degree of affections such as love and hatred. Again, the affections are distinguished from the passions in degree. Passion is more sudden and affects the body with sufficient force that the mind is overpowered and loses command (pp. 26-27). Affections are the "moving springs in all the affairs of life, which engage men in all their pursuits; and especially in all affairs wherein they are earnestly engaged, and which they pursue with vigor."

In modern terms, affections may be regarded as basic dispositions that incline a person to act in a certain way more or less consistently. They are the manifestations of character. Religion consists largely in affections, but true religion consists in affections of a certain quality. Edwards tries to show what kind of affections qualify as true religion. His basic thesis carries two important implications. First, we must avoid identifying any religious affection as a sign of true grace, such as religious zeal that leads to error or short-lived affections. But it would also be wrong to exclude all affections and sensible emotions from the religious life. What we need is to distinguish between true and false affections and between "gracious" and natural affections.

Bodily effects (2.2) are the first sign that Edwards names as an inadequate measure of gracious affections. Any kind of affection, whether religious or natural, has effects on the body. This is due to the natural "laws of the union of body and soul" (p. 26). This implies that physical effects are no sure sign of gracious affections. But at the same time bodily manifestations are not incompatible with true religion. Bodily signs like trembling, groaning, fainting and so on, which in Scripture are sometimes associated with people whose affections are gracious, show that they are not satanic in themselves. Even if we are to regard these signs as "figures" of gracious affections, they are still, Edwards argues, "suitable" figures.

A religious experience may be accompanied by great fluency of speech (2.3). But even if it comes on suddenly and with great affections, that alone does not prove either that it is gracious or that it is satanic. Fluency is like the leaves on a tree. They are essential to the tree but do not indicate that the tree is good or bad. The real quality of the tree is demonstrated in its fruit. Edwards's second sign reminds us of one of Bunyan's characters in *Pilgrim's Progress,* "Mr. Talkative."

The next two signs deal with what might be called extraordinary experiences. Sometimes certain emotions arise quite suddenly and independently of our own endeavors (2.4), but that does not necessarily indicate that they are gracious. God's Spirit may work suddenly on the soul or secretly and silently. We must not suppose that one or the other way is the only legitimate way of God's working. Or a person may recall texts of Scripture in a "sudden and unusual manner" and these texts occasion religious feelings such as joy, hope, sorrow or fear (2.5). Edwards's description of the experience has a contemporary ring to it:

> There were such and such sweet promises brought to my mind: they came suddenly, as if they were spoken to me: I had no hand in bringing such a text to my own mind; I was not thinking of anything leading to it; it came all at once, so that I was surprised. I had not thought of it a long time before; I did not know at first that it was Scripture; I did not remember that ever I had read it. One Scripture came flowing in after another, and so texts all over the Bible, the most sweet and pleasant, and the most apt and suitable which could be devised; and filled me full as I could hold: I could not but stand and admire: the tears flowed; I was full of joy and could not doubt any longer. (p. 70)

Theologically, there is nothing to indicate that such experiences *must* be from God. If Satan, argues Edwards, "was permitted to put Christ Himself in mind of texts of Scripture to tempt *Him,* what reason have we to determine that he dare not, or will not be permitted, to put wicked men in mind of texts of Scripture to tempt and deceive *them?"* (p. 71).

Edwards observes that a person may experience a momentary affection of love for God and others (2.6), different kinds of affections (2.7), a right order of affections such as contrition followed by joy (2.8), great zeal (2.9), ability to praise God (2.10) and great confidence in religious matters (2.11). But we cannot on the basis of these "outward manifestations and appearances" (p. 110) conclude that they are a sign of godliness. For instance, a person exuding great confidence may actually be in a "bad frame" and living in Pharisaic hypocrisy. On the other hand, a weak Christian may be motivated by divine fear, which actually keeps him committed to his Christian duty. Therefore, confidence alone is no sure sign of grace.

Edwards's main thesis (pt. 1) that true religion in great part consists of affections and his discussion of certain ambivalent affections (pt. 2) enable him to give a legitimate place to feelings in religion without thereby validating every kind of religious feeling. This takes him beyond the pragmatic criterion of William James. Edwards insists that true religion must go beyond immediate practical results to combine good effects with theological truths, as he elaborates in part three of *Religious Affections*. Edwards's approach is set squarely within the Calvinistic framework that presupposes the doctrine of perseverance. Even a non-Calvinist has to agree that salvation must be evidenced by a certain degree of permanence. A person does not just fall in or out of grace easily.

Because of the ambivalent nature of these "outward manifestations," the discerning Christian must judge with extreme caution. In fact, they are "but poor judges and dangerous counsellors in soul cases, who are quick and peremptory in determining persons' states, vaunting themselves in their extraordinary faculty of discerning and distinguishing in these great affairs, as though all was open and clear to them" (2.12). Such a cautionary attitude is not the same as being cynical toward any form of "enthusiasm." By recognizing the reality of these uncertain signs, we can properly relate to all who differ from us in their experience. We avoid the extremes of cynical rejection and naive acceptance and begin to adopt the stance that Edwards himself recommends: "When there are many probable appearances of piety in others, it is the duty of the saints to receive them cordially into their charity, and to love them and rejoice in them, as their brethren in Christ Jesus" (p. 111).

The theological criterion of discernment. The two great works on discernment by Ignatius and Edwards place strong emphasis on the theological criterion as the ultimate test of any religious experience. Ignatius identifies it as growth in faith, hope and charity—the three theological virtues. Edwards has a much more developed concept of the theological criterion, which he elaborates in part three of his treatise.

Edwards gives us twelve signs of "truly spiritual and gracious" affections. It should be noted that while these signs are "certain and infallible" in themselves, their application to actual situations is not, for two reasons. First, we cannot be absolutely certain about the spiritual condition of others. The prerogative does not belong to us "to make a full and clear separation between sheep and goats." Second, true saints who are "low in grace" are often incapable of judging their own estate (pp. 120-21). Weak Christians can usefully employ these signs "to remove many needless scruples" and to "establish their hope." They can also be used "to convince the hypocrites," although some of them, Edwards concedes, are probably beyond convincing. But these rules can possibly prevent others from becoming hypocrites.

The first sign describes the source of spiritual affections. "Affections that are truly spiritual and gracious, do arise from those influences and operations on the heart, which are *spiritual, supernatural,* and *divine*." By "spiritual" Edwards means "sanctified by the Holy Spirit." But this immediately raises a question. What is the difference between the "sanctifying influence" of the Spirit and the "ordinary influence"? Edwards has two answers. First, the Spirit imparts to the true believer a *permanent principle* of new life that is not found in "temporary" believers. Second, the Spirit's indwelling the true saints also produces effects that are consonant with his own nature, namely, holiness. This quality is unique, having no parallel in nature. The Spirit "communicates Himself to them in His own proper nature" (p. 129). It is *entirely different* from natural goodness, not an improvement of the natural. This is what Edwards means by "supernatural" (p. 132). Grace produces an "entirely new kind of principle" in human nature, which in turn produces "an entirely new kind of perception or sensation" in the mind. This is not a new faculty "but a foundation laid in the nature of the soul, for a new kind of exercise of the same faculty of will" (pp. 133-34).

Edwards concedes that practically it is difficult to distinguish between a natural affection that has been raised to a high degree and a gracious affection that is just beginning (pp. 137-38). Natural things can impress themselves on the imagination and excite it to a high degree, but the affections so raised are still natural. The false prophet Balaam had such a natural impression made on his mind and accordingly prophesied about Christ, but he remained a natural man (p. 143). Edwards's caveat here is crucial for discernment. The real work of God is not determined by what a person does—"works," "manifestations" and so on—but by who one is, one's character, or what the Scripture calls "fruit."

A supernatural operation distinguishes itself in three ways. First, by the *Christ centeredness* of the experience. True extraordinary impressions of Scripture on the mind must occur in the context of faith in Christ and dependence on him (p. 150). Second, by the *God relatedness* that results when a truth is spiritually applied. A Christian who receives a promise from Scripture in an extraordinary way does not see just the excellency of the promise but also "the holy excellency of the *promiser* . . . thus drawing [his] heart to embrace the promiser and thing promised" (p. 153). Third, by the *objectivity* of the Spirit's witness. It is not just an inner subjective thought but "a gracious principle" that overflows in humble love to God (p. 164).

Edwards's first sign points to the deep, life-transforming quality of a saving operation of the Holy Spirit. He is describing a theological reality that he believes is present uniquely in those who are truly renewed by the Spirit. Subsequent signs are essentially elaborations of the first. The second sign is an inclination directing one to love God for God's sake and not for what benefits accrue to oneself. This sign is reminiscent of Bernard's third degree of love (loving God for God's sake). The third sign clarifies this love: "a love to divine things for the beauty and sweetness of their moral excellency." The God whom we love for his own sake is qualified as primarily moral goodness. The true saint is awed by the vision of God as holy and sees holiness as an intrinsic and primary beauty in God. The fourth sign says that gracious affections "do arise from the mind being enlightened, rightly and spiritually to understand or apprehend divine things." Affections that arise from (say) a vision that does not *inform* the understanding in "the nature of instruction" cannot be gracious. This understanding must be *spiritual,* having for its object the supreme beauty and excellency of divine things as they are in themselves. Spiritual understanding "consists primarily of the sense of the heart of the supreme beauty and sweetness of holiness or moral perfection of divine things."

The first four signs are integrally related to each other. True affections must arise from a spiritual understanding (sign 4) of the moral beauty and excellency of divine things (sign 3) for their own sake (sign 2). The cause of these affections are the sanctifying influence of the indwelling Spirit (sign 1). The rest of the signs reinforce in different ways the theological criteria. The fifth sign describes true saints as those who "have a solid, full, thorough and effectual conviction of the truth of the great things of the gospel" (p. 217). The sixth sign discusses "evangelical humiliation," which is distinct from "legal humiliation." The former arises from "a discovery of the beauty of God's holiness and moral perfection." It is humility "under a disposition of grace" (p. 238). In true affections there is to be found a continual change in a person's nature (seventh sign), "the spirit and temper of Jesus Christ" (eighth sign), "a Christian tenderness of spirit" (ninth sign), poise and orderliness (tenth and eleventh signs) and finally consistency in Christian living "to the end of life" (twelfth sign).

How useful are these signs as a practical guide to discernment in our present-day context? As Edwards himself reminds us, they are not intended to serve as foolproof tests, since it is difficult to tell the difference between "natural works" and "supernatural fruit." Yet the "ground rules" of Ignatius and Edwards have relevance for us. First, the "no certain signs" should make us cautious in accepting claims made on the basis of extraordinary experiences. We need to approach these experiences with a truly open mind. Knowing that a phenomenon may or may not be from God causes us to look for additional confirming or disconfirming evidences. In short, we begin to develop the spiritual poise needed for sound discernment. A work of discernment that lacks spiritual poise tends to overreact to excesses and then create excesses of its own.[36] Second, *The Religious Affections* forces us to focus on character as a mark of truth, not on experience. While it is true that we cannot determine with absolute certainty a person's character, we do obtain a fair idea of who a person is through close acquaintance. Discerning the integrity of a person and the phenomenon associated with him or her cannot be done hastily, as Ignatius' *Rules* implies (333).

Third, the power of discerning is derived from the total impact of the "distinguishing signs" on the larger context of a phenomenon. Applying an individual sign to an isolated phenomenon is not sufficient. A common mistake in discernment today is to treat phenomena in isolation. Questions like, Is being slain in the Spirit biblical? How about holy laughter? and Are claims to having the gift of healing valid? miss the heart of the issue. They imply that certain phenomena in and of themselves can be right or wrong, whereas such phenomena are better classified as "no certain signs." They can be true or false, depending on the larger context.

It is not sufficient to evaluate an experience solely in terms of its psychological or numerical benefits. The fact that a person has a sense of well-being after experiencing holy laughter or that some churches grow numerically is not an adequate test of its ultimate truthfulness. The decisive question is, What impact does holy laughter exert on the character of the people who experience it? Here is where Edwards's theological criteria (and to a lesser extent Ignatius's) are immensely helpful. His detailed description of the "distinguishing signs" can help us create something like a "character profile" of a true Christian. On the basis of these signs we can ask a different sort of question about any spiritual phenomenon: How does the experience promote or destroy Christian character? Some experiences (possibly holy laughter) may be meant to serve as catalysts for change rather than as regular means of growth. To regularize such phenomena is to turn them into potentially character-destroying agents. Applying the character test makes questions regarding the origin of the experience quite irrelevant in most cases. Many good gifts come originally from God but are subsequently abused. To put them to their proper use (which may mean abandoning their use altogether) is the work of discernment.

Edwards would probably have understood the situation differently. As a good Calvinist, he could not have conceived that humans would abuse God's good gifts *intended* for their salvation. That would be tantamount to frustrating God's sovereignty. A religious experience that produces no lasting character is understood as a gift of "temporary faith." If Edwards's doctrine of perseverance is understood as a moral imperative rather than an indicative (if saints are people who *ought* to persevere in order to be known as saints), then Edwards's teaching on the uncertain signs helps answer the question, Can someone misuse God's gifts and yet be right with God? Most Christians nowadays tend to be quite generous when it comes to giving "the benefit of the doubt." They will probably answer with something like "A person can be wrong in the head and right in the heart" rather than give a flat no. But if we accept the view that true Christianity is defined by a certain permanence of character ("gracious affections"), then a more nuanced answer to the above question would have to be "yes, but not for long."

A person who has a true religious experience can misuse it so that it does harm to herself and others instead of using it rightly and turning it into a "gracious affection."[37] Would her continuing misuse not turn the experience into a character-destroying agent? We are not talking here about weaknesses in the sanctified person (in Edwards's words, one who is "low in grace") but about an "affection" that turns one either decisively toward God or decisively away from God. This is the significance of Edwards's idea of temporary faith or nonsaving affections understood phenomenologically. In summary, Edwards's understanding of the "no certain signs," which eventually turn out to be nonsaving, implies that extraordinary phenomena that are wrongly used can have a soul-destroying effect on people who so use them and on those they influence. Clearly, discernment in this area is urgently needed.

Understanding the nature of extraordinary phenomena. We need to put extraordinary phenomena into proper perspective for a world that demonstrates a steadily growing penchant for the unexplainable. The following principles are meant to address some of the more common misconceptions about religious phenomena.

First, extraordinary phenomena are not necessarily "spiritual" or supernatural. Many of them may originate in the paranormal realm. The term *paranormal* describes experiences that cannot be readily explained by the principles of conventional science. Many of these phenomena occur in contexts that cannot be understood as coming from either God or the devil,[38] at least not without careful qualification,[39] which leads us to question whether the traditional religious explanations are adequate. They can also be called psychic phenomena inasmuch as they are believed to stem from functions of the mind that are only poorly understood.[40] Theologically, it is possible to understand certain supernatural gifts like miraculous healing and foretelling as the work of spiritual agents, whether divine or demonic, that use faculties already existing in the human mind. But some people may be able to induce psychic phenomena on their own even if they are not aware that they are doing it. The line between supernatural and paranormal operation cannot be clearly drawn, which may help explain why the success rate of "divine healing" is rather low, compared to the complete healing that Jesus performed on *all* who came to him.[41] There is probably more of the human than the divine at work in present-day "signs and wonders."

A more pertinent question in regard to the paranormal is whether Christians should tap it as a resource. Could it be that supranormal abilities belong to a different order of existence, which Christian tradition has always maintained is the Christian's final destination? Some make the mistake of assuming that if something is there it is free for us to use. It does not occur to them that manipulating something that God may not have intended for our use *now* is to go against God's will.

Sometimes extraordinary experiences are induced by ordinary means. People with certain types of temperament are more prone to certain types of extraordinary experiences. Melancholics and depressives are prone to hallucinations and visions. People with lively imaginations are prone to similar experiences. Some illnesses can produce hallucinatory experiences that are remarkably similar to spiritual visions. In other words, some people are *naturally* predisposed to visionary experiences. This fact does not rule out the possibility of God's using such people to communicate his will through visions, but we must always bear in mind that visions can result from natural causes. Psychologically induced experiences can appear very supernatural, and Edwards in his first sign considers at length many such experiences, such as the experience of having ideas and biblical texts come to mind suddenly and extraordinarily.[42]

Second, the test of a phenomenon is not whether it can be found in Scripture but whether it comports with the moral and theological criteria. Saints have had many strange experiences that have no parallel in Scripture, but they are not false for that reason alone. Two better-known examples are the flames of love experienced by Philip Neri (1515-1595), founder of the Congregation of the Oratory, and the stigmata of Francis of Assisi. Other experiences like bilocution (being in two places at the same time), levitation, mystical aureoles and sweet (or foul) odors have been reported.[43] They should not be ruled out a priori just because they are not found in the Bible. Protestants are sometimes too quick to reject an experience because it is not found in the Bible and are just as quick to accept another mainly on the basis of some biblical precedent (for example, prayer handkerchiefs, Acts 19:11-12). We must judge the phenomena in terms of the total life of the individual who experiences them. Is the *person* a godly, balanced, mature person, one not given to extremes? An experience, no matter how strange it may appear, is more likely to be true if it occurred in a person whose life generally manifests truth. It is possible that some of these phenomena are an anticipation or a foretaste of the glorified state.

Third, we need to distinguish between private and public revelations. It should be clear by now that God does reveal his will to a person who earnestly seeks it. It would not be inappropriate to call such an experience a private revelation. The whole tradition of discernment is unanimous on this point. Sometimes a private revelation may extend to a group or a community. A congregation may sense a need to ascertain what God is wanting it to do in a given situation. But this is the work of corporate discernment. Christ is the head and the church is his body. We can expect the head to lead the church forward. When a congregation prays together over matters for which it seeks God's guidance, we can expect something significant to happen. The mind of Christ begins to pervade the whole body, and a consensus that was not there before begins to emerge.

Many claims to revelation, the revelations usually coming through an individual "prophet," are meant to be a source of specific guidance for the whole church.[44] In an animistic Asian context a claim that something was supernaturally revealed to someone would almost certainly secure that person a sizable hearing. The basic mistake of these "prophets," leaving aside the question of their character, is to regard their revelations as public truths.

There are indications in Scripture that some revelations are strictly of a private nature and are never meant to be made public. The apostle Paul's experience of being caught up in the third heaven appears to fall into this category. What he heard, the "inexpressible things," he was not permitted to tell (2 Cor 12:1-4). We see the same reticence in the best mystics of the church, including John of the Cross. He knew firsthand the things of which he wrote. But like many other mystical theologians, he was more interested in guiding others in the way of union with God through sound teaching than in relating his own experience with God. In his two treatises on mystical experience, *The Dark Night of the Soul* and *Ascent of Mount Carmel,* he tells us hardly anything about his own experience. This is very unlike many modern visionaries. Lacking the conceptual tools to reflect theologically on their spiritual experiences, they are nonetheless quick to talk about what they have seen and heard in the third heaven or the netherworld. One such example is seen in Mary K. Baxter, *A Divine Revelation of Hell.*[45] The trouble with publishing such private revelations (even granting that it was a genuine experience from God)[46] is that it communicates an implicit theology that is crude and unreflected and often disturbing to young Christians because it gives the false impression of being divinely sanctioned. Such private revelations are best kept private. If they help the recipients to live and serve their Lord better, this is as much as we can expect private revelations to accomplish.

Discernment is a process that grows out of our life in the body of Christ and helps deepen that life. Through discerning we grow, and as we grow we become more discerning. If we may adapt the words of an Eastern theologian, a mature Christian is one who discerns, and one who discerns is a mature Christian.[47] Many Christians today are told that to question any spiritual manifestation is to "touch the Lord's anointed" and to quench the Spirit. They are never taught to discern, and consequently they are consigned to a perpetual childhood.

12

THE ART
OF SPIRITUAL
DIRECTION

· ·

I N THE MODERN CHURCH THE ROLE OF THE PASTOR IS NO LONGER CLEAR-CUT. THE
pastor is expected to do a lot of things but is not sure which is "the one thing
needful" (Lk 10:42), the essential duty. The recovery of spiritual direction in
recent years has once again drawn attention to the main focus of pastoral
care, namely, to help Christians develop their prayer life and discover the
will of God. For much of the history of the church, the work of the pastor
was quite unambiguous: the "cure of souls." The shepherd is to help the
sheep assimilate and live out the spiritual life. In short, the pastor is essentially
a spiritual theologian and a guide to godliness. It is this work and nothing
else that gives the pastoral vocation its distinguishing mark.[1]

The nature of the Christian life is such that no one grows spiritually without
some help from others. Strictly speaking, there are no self-taught saints. To
think that we can teach ourselves is the worst sort of self-deception. "If
anyone makes himself his own master in the spiritual life," warns Bernard,
"he makes himself scholar to a fool."[2] This learning process extends
throughout life. Even the most mature Christian needs help from others from
time to time. Spiritual direction is simply the formalization of this basic fact
of life.

The aim of this discussion is to look at spiritual direction as an integrative
art that brings the study of spiritual theology to its proper conclusion, not to
offer practical help on the direction of souls.[3] Spiritual direction is integrative

at many levels. First, it seeks to bring spiritual theology to the level of actual experience by integrating theory and practice. Second, it integrates the personal and corporate dimensions of the directee's life in God. Third, it brings two persons together into a dynamic traditioning process. Finally, it is an art that calls for integrating knowledge and character in the person of the director.

The Nature of Spiritual Direction

Spiritual direction is a dynamic relationship that exists between two persons as one helps the other grow in the Christian life. Spiritual direction is understood variously in contemporary writings on the subject. Some try to avoid the authoritarian connotation of the traditional expression, preferring the term *spiritual friendship*. But the implied egalitarianism of this term makes it less than adequate in certain social contexts. Further, spiritual friendship, as traditionally understood, has its own distinct focus, which cannot be equated with direction.[4] The concept of mentoring does not connote excessive authority, even as it does not suggest equality in the the mentor-learner relationship. But its association with academia makes it less than ideal in the pastoral context.

The nature of spiritual direction could be clarified from the standpoint of the one being directed. But Thornton has shown how elusive that relation can be.[5] He settles for a "director-client" relationship. But in some contexts the word *client* suggests a business-type relationship. It misses the interpersonal dynamic that is essential to spiritual direction. Since attempts to replace this traditional term have produced no particular advantage, it is best to stick with it. The spiritual life that is the subject of this direction in a very real sense is the total life of a person, not just one aspect of it (as suggested substitute terms implied).[6]

The intricacy of spiritual direction is suggested by the various practices associated with it. In most Protestant churches some form of general spiritual direction takes place through preaching and teaching. But direction in its specialized sense is a one-to-one relationship. The director offers the directee personal help in achieving full maturity in Christ. This mode of direction does not recognize the existence of the "average Christian." Between the rather impersonal approach of preaching and the highly personalized one-on-one approach lies group direction.[7] There are advantages in group direction. The richness and diversity in a group contribute to the spiritual development of each individual. Group direction is less likely to encourage dependency than is a highly personalized approach. In group direction the goal of realizing our communion in the body of Christ can become an intensely felt and practical reality. As Dougherty has aptly noted, the "group has become a spiritual community which celebrates the uniqueness of each individual's desire for God yet the commonality of that desire."[8] But group direction has limitations. It cannot deal as specifically with individual needs, and individual self-disclosure is more difficult. Finally, there is less individual accountability.[9] Asian people are generally less open in group situations. They are more inclined to ask the most important questions in a one-to-one relationship.

If the full ramifications of spiritual direction are to be realized, the relationship between director and directee must be viewed from a number of perspectives, namely, doctor-patient, coach-athlete and parent-child. The first analogy describes spiritual direction as a process that must be approached with some degree of clinical precision, as the "cure of souls." According to Thornton, the director must analyze and respect the peculiar character or basic inclination of the directee. Just as a psychologist tries to determine the personality type of each client, the spiritual director seeks to understand the basic spiritual type of the directee. This understanding determines the appropriate approach for each directee.[10] Is she basically the affective type or the speculative type?[11] Each type responds differently to the same spiritual things. The coach-athlete approach highlights the ascetical feature of spiritual direction. The director may have to help the directee decide, based on an intimate understanding of the latter's temperament, whether discursive or silent prayer is preferable, whether the rule of life should be tightened or relaxed, and so on. Modern manuals on spiritual direction prefer to let the directee make his or her own self-discovery. The athletic approach to spiritual development has generally given way to softer and less directive options. The parent-child analogy offers the greatest flexibility, depending on how the relationship is conceived. The abba of the desert tradition is generally more authoritarian than most modern directors. The latter are likely to stress the gentler side of fatherhood and motherhood, for example, by comparing spiritual direction to the work of a midwife in assisting in the birth process through "cleansing, aligning, resting."[12]

Direction and psychotherapy. One way of clarifying the nature of spiritual direction is comparing it with psychotherapy and counseling. The social sciences, particularly sociology and psychology, have contributed immensely to understanding human nature and to clarifying biblical concepts like sin and spiritual maturity from a phenomenological point of view. Psychology offers a rich vocabulary for exploring spiritual concepts. For example, the similarity between spiritual maturity and psychological self-integration means that we can expect a spiritually mature Christian to manifest what psychology recognizes as a well-integrated personality, such as the ability to exercise self-control in interpersonal relationships and in basic drives like sex.[13] What psychologists identify as neurotic behavior, such as slavish dependence on an external authority and reluctance to make independent decisions, has parallels in certain truncated forms of Christianity. Secular challenges to the faith are swept aside by wild rhetoric and caricature ("That is of the devil!") rather than engaged in a serious and thoughtful way. Theological difficulties are met with all kinds of exegetical artifice. For example, fundamentalists defend their theory of inerrancy by ingeniously harmonizing difficult passages of Scripture. A mentality of defending the faith and prosecuting heretics indicates an overprotectiveness and hides an inner insecurity. Psychoanalysis helps us to see that what sometimes passes as robust Christianity may actually be spiritual immaturity, or worse, an arrested form of spirituality.

But spiritual direction and psychoanalysis are not to be equated. This clarification is needed because there is a modern tendency to identify the two. For example, Rogerian "incongruence" of personality is sometimes equated with the Christian idea of sin.[14] If the phenomenological is equated with the theological, a psychological goal like personal integration may be identified with spiritual maturity.[15] Psychological wholeness may be *structurally* similar to spiritual wholeness but is *essentially* quite different. Spiritual direction cannot occur apart from the Christian story. The goal of direction is to learn to live in congruence with the Christian story, and therefore it cannot simply be identified with personal integration. It is integration of a specific kind, namely, union with God. Spiritual maturity involves a person's relationship with God, while psychological integration does not. A psychologically well-adjusted person is not necessarily a saint. On the other hand, it is possible that a saint may not be psychologically well adjusted. For example, mental retardation is no obstacle to sainthood. Saints, as Frankl reminds us, can well be concealed in the "miens of idiots." True saints may seem foolish in the eyes of the world; they are the "clowns of God."[16]

A person receiving spiritual direction may or may not have psychological problems. Spiritual direction should not be confused with the "ambulance syndrome," although the spiritual director may have to help solve some psychological problems along the way.[17] Furthermore, the quality of relationship between director and directee is inconceivable in counselor-client terms. The work of a spiritual director goes beyond merely providing a professional service; in fact, it goes beyond what we are accustomed to calling work. It is sharing a way of life with another. As Thornton puts it in his characteristically crisp way, "director-client eventually becomes father-child and finally brother-brother."[18] Unlike psychotherapy, spiritual direction may involve self-disclosure on the director's part. The director is aware of being a fellow pilgrim on the same journey. Part of that awareness is translated into a willingness to share from his own experience his weaknesses, failures and struggles in life. Although this must be done judiciously, neither in a way that overwhelms the directee nor gives him or her a grossly inflated picture of the director's ability or sanctity, yet it forms an important part of the dynamics of direction.[19]

Discerning the will of God. Spiritual direction may be understood as the application of spiritual theology to individual growth in the body of Christ. It is using doctrines as tools to assist the one being directed to grow in grace and in the knowledge of our Lord Jesus Christ.[20] While spiritual theology with its principles and exercises discussed in the preceding chapters provides the general framework for growth, direction aims at helping the individual grow to be uniquely the person God wants him or her to be. Edwards calls it "unique attentiveness to your naked soul."[21] It is "help given by one Christian to another which enables that person to pay attention to God's personal communication to him or her, to respond to this personally communicating God, to grow in intimacy with this God, and to live out the consequences of the relationship."[22] Although there are broad principles undergirding direction, there are no pat answers. A person must be helped, for instance, to discover her own rule of life in accordance with her own individual need and temperament. In this connection the role of women as spiritual directors must be more fully explored and incorporated into the work of direction of the whole church. Women are often able to bring a distinctive perspective to the cure of souls.[23]

Helping each person discover his or her own story implies that much of the work of direction has to do with discernment. The spiritual director is "a teacher of discernment"[24] who helps another distinguish between the workings of grace and contrary movements. Without clear discernment, no one can hope to make spiritual progress. But not only must the director help the directee discern, the director himself must have the ability to discern the workings of grace in the directee's life. Discernment may be in the form of a charism or an acquired skill. The first type of discernment is best exemplified in the desert fathers. Their guidance often consisted of a spontaneous counsel inspired by the Spirit—a "prophecy." For them, spiritual direction is ultimately a gift of the Spirit rather than a skill to be learned. It comes from being completely open to the Spirit of God.[25] This charismatic type of spiritual direction is retained in the Orthodox tradition in the person of the staretz.[26] In our modern context the need for such direction is often overlooked. Yet the very nature of *spiritual* direction requires it. As Tildern Edwards puts it, "We are dealing with the subtlest, most integrative dimension of a person's life in spiritual direction, and this always remains to a large extent an area of mystery and awe." Therefore,

> to attempt its reduction to some clinical technical model would be to defy the very heart of spiritual direction awareness. That awareness points to the necessity of patient waiting for healing sight. It means willingness to sit beside a person with words and methods and support, yet clearly aware that you wait outside his or her chamber of awareness for the Spirit to open heart and mind.[27]

Similarly, Gratton notes:

> People live not just according to the convictions in their rational minds, but also by the feelings in their hearts and in their guts. Spiritual guidance can help people to anchor those feeling hearts and guts in spiritual foundations. It can help people to accept life changes, even painful ones, as doors opening on to new life: to becoming more serving, more honest, more humble, more alive.[28]

What these contemporary spiritual directors highlight is that in direction we are working in a level of personal awareness—the human spirit's communion with God—where rational analysis becomes inadequate. The director may find himself falling back on hunches and intuition in her attempts to grasp the mysterious workings of grace. Thus a comprehensive approach to spiritual direction must include the charismatic model of direction as exemplified in the desert tradition.[29]

In order to exercise the ordinary gift of discernment, the director needs to cultivate an understanding of the directee's basic personality type—what Thornton calls his "attrait" or Edwards "the dominant spiritual path."[30] Only then can he give wise counsel. For example, specific temptations should be addressed specifically with a clearly laid out course of action in accordance with the nature and capacity of the directee. An overly scrupulous person may experience more "temptations" than there actually are. For that person a wise director might advise relaxing the rule. On the other hand, the hard-driving Chinese businessman is hardly aware of facing temptations at all. The director may have to prod him firmly about the seven deadly sins. To sum up, the director must be sensitive to the spiritual level of the person she is directing. Beginners in particular should not be expected to do too much.

The social context of spiritual direction. Social context is important in spiritual direction because, first, knowledge of other social contexts can enrich our own. Edwards has highlighted the need to learn from the apophatic[31] and Asian traditions in such areas as bodily disciplines (as seen in the practice of yoga in the Indian tradition and in the art of Tai Ji Quan in Taoism), intuitive insights and practical wisdom. The most profound questions are answered not by logical analysis but with an aphorism, with bodily movements, physical demonstrations and acted parables. He notes that these features are largely lost in the rationalistic and analytical approach so characteristic of the West.[32]

Second, if we are to take people's individual uniqueness seriously, we need to be sensitive to contextual differences. Each Christian exists in a social milieu that produces distinctiveness in outlook, attitude and habits. While we must not exaggerate contextual differences (all Christians share a common tradition), we cannot minimize them either, especially when we are dealing with a concern in which the distinctiveness of an individual is a determining factor. Knowledge of the person being directed is not just knowledge of him or her as an individual but as one who lives in and is shaped by the surrounding culture. "No spiritual guide can afford to despise a person's actual, functioning culture."[33] Margaret Guenther observes that people "can talk easily about sex, somewhat less comfortably about death, and only with the greatest difficulty about their relationship with God."[34] But hers is the Western world. Spiritual directors in the Asian church are likely to find an almost completely opposite type of character. Asian Christians are often chatty about their personal relationship with God and tend to be quite ambivalent about death (depending on their cultural upbringing),[35] but sex is almost always a taboo subject.

Thornton's client on the "cold slab," for example, is clearly the average modern Anglican, generally disciplined and well read. The Eucharist is more or less a dominant feature of his or her spiritual experience.[36] The typical urban, affluent Protestant in Asia, by contrast, is likely to be ill disciplined in spiritual matters, has probably never heard about a rule of life (much less observed it) but is extremely aggressive and single-minded in his business dealings.

The relationship between director and directee in the East (the *shifu-mentu* [master-disciple] relationship in Chinese culture; the guru-follower relationship in Indian culture[37]) is almost always hierarchically ordered. Urban Asia is coming to recognize the value of counseling. Many counselors are trained in the West and soon discover a need to adapt what they have learned to the Asian situation. Characteristically they shift from an individualistic, nondirective approach to a family-oriented, directive approach. The counselor becomes a director. As one Asian counselor notes, Asians "are more familiar with an authoritarian social system and family relationships tend to be less democratic. The family and other social networks play an important part in a person's life and problems."[38] One danger in such a context is that direction can turn into brainwashing sessions in the hands of a patriarchal pastor who molds the whole church after his own image.

Spiritual Direction and the Christian Community

Spiritual direction considers each Christian as a unique individual, but it also recognizes an equally important fact: that individual is a member of the body of Christ. Every Christian has a unique story, but each person's story forms part of the larger Christian story. And it is the larger story that authenticates each person's own individual stories. This larger story is not just a model for individual growth; it is also a single tapestry to which each individual contributes his or her unique strand. To sum up, spiritual direction seeks to realize individual growth within a social reality by helping the individual conform to the basic pattern of growth and contribute to the ongoing Christian tradition.

A pattern of growth. The Christian life is defined by a distinctive common pattern revolving around the story of Jesus Christ. This was the concerted testimony of the Christian tradition when it formulated the three ways. While the concepts that make up the three ways remain foundational to growth, modern directors have sought contemporary terms to express the same reality. Thornton, for one, feels that the old terminology is too closely tied to a substantive view of graces and virtues to be of much help to modern people, who tend to think of progress in existential terms, including attitudes, habits and dispositions. In his view, the biblical category of covenant-en-counter-incorporation may be better for understanding progress in contemporary culture. *Covenant* refers to the relationship that demands a response of obedience, *encounter* refers to the whole person meeting the person of Christ, and *incorporation* states the theological fact that we are united with Christ.[39] There is relational improvement as we move from merely obeying orders (covenant) to getting personally acquainted (encounter) to a relationship of some measurable depth (incorporation).

Tildern Edwards has developed a similar approach to spiritual direction based on a pattern of growth that stresses the personal-existential dimension of progress. The pattern is called "cleansing, aligning and resting." The whole process is called the "healing process," but it could just as well be called sanctifying, divinizing or unfolding.[40] Spiritual direction is undertaken in this broad framework of growth. In the "cleansing" phase the directee is encouraged to go into God's presence, learn confession, experience cleansing through silence and develop a three-way conversation (director-directee-God) that includes listening to God's voice together. Cleansing should lead to "alignment," the coming together of a fragmented life. This integration comes through "interior awareness." The director can promote growth in self-awareness by asking the directee to reflect on his or her pictures of God, self-image, prayer life and so on. How a person thinks of God, images self and prays reveals much.[41]

Alignment also includes "vocation." Interior awareness should lead us to the recognition of our calling in life. We progress from the inner world to the outer world. This calling is not something that once laid hold of becomes our fixed possession. Rather, it is an unfolding awareness based on a continuing relationship with God.[42] Edwards has identified four levels by which the discernment of one's vocation can proceed.[43] It begins with the foundational covenant—the basic relationship that the Christian has with Christ. A person needs to be brought to an awareness of it, which in evangelical parlance would be called "conversion."

The second level is to discern the "human covenant state," the basic, "long-term commitments that provide a general framework for our living and caring." Here the director helps the Christian resolve basic questions regarding his or her basic state of life: marriage or celibacy, ordained or lay state, questions of career and work. In a world that is increasingly moving from lifetime commitments (marriage and ordination) to long-term commitments, and from long-term commitments in work and human relationships (such as friendship) to temporary arrangements, it is most important that directees are impressed with the seriousness of life's basic *covenantal* structure.

One area that deserves special mention is the issue of our covenantal relationship with one another and with the Lord Jesus within the church ratified by water baptism. The continuing movement of Christians from church to church observed in urban contexts reflects a lack of ecclesial covenantal faithfulness. It is true, as Edwards points out, that some churches do not possess the basic infrastructure for spiritual development.[44] Thus seeking spiritual guidance in extraecclesial institutions like a retreat house or a monastery may be necessary, but it still does not justify removing oneself from the covenant community to which one is committed by baptism. The spiritual life of an individual will always remain in flux if there are no stable structures of church, family, friendship and work through which one expresses one's covenantal relationships.

The third level is discerning the person's gifts for ministry. How can we best serve and in what capacity, especially in the light of basic commitments made at the second level? The evangelical-charismatic church emphasizes this level of vocation—discovering your "giftings," as it is often called. One moves straight from personal relationship with Jesus to service for the Lord with only a vague awareness of covenantal responsibilities. In discovering our gifts, we need to develop deeper spiritual awareness. We need to understand our true self. Why have I chosen this form of work? Why am I seeking a change of work at this time? The Ignatian pattern of discernment under the guidance of a spiritual director may be one way for Christians to discover their true selves. We must avoid making decisions based on a desire to satisfy our superficial ego or a desire (probably unconscious) to escape a current difficulty or boredom. Proper self-examination reveals any hidden motives.[45]

A problem at this third level of vocation is tension between the desire to fulfill a calling and the necessity of remaining at an unfulfilling job in order to support a family. Many Christians find themselves in such a situation because they never really began their lives in a planned way. This is why spiritual direction should begin as early as possible for children in a Christian family. It is never too early to begin discerning the basic direction of one's life. This will ensure that every level of vocation is planned. Many Christians go through life never asking themselves such basic questions as, How should my life with God be best lived in the world? What sort of work am I best suited for? Should I get married or should I remain single? If married, should we have children or not? If we decide to have children, how many? They simply find the best-paying job, get married, have children, more or less by default! Then they find themselves trapped in a no-win situation, hating work intensely but needing it to support a certain kind of lifestyle. A planned life under direction, while it does not guarantee complete satisfaction or freedom from life's drudgeries, can give us the freedom to make choices that fulfill what we deeply sense to be God's calling for our lives.

The fourth level has to do with what Edwards calls "immediate callings," also known as the "sacrament of the present moment" or "fidelity to grace." First the unexpected crops up, and then a call comes to fulfill our duty to God. "They are signs of the open-endedness, the surprising quality of life's daily passing."[46] This level highlights the charismatic dimension of life. The spiritual director should help the directee open up to the unexpected. Sometimes such a "surprising work of God"—an unexpected visitation, a chance encounter, a call to visit a hospital patient—could become the decisive turning point in one's life.[47]

The "resting" phase of growth may be compared to the convalescing period of the healing process. Between the times of spiritual direction, the directee needs to develop his or her own spiritual disciplines such as journaling and personal prayer to continue the "unfolding" process.[48] A rule of life can serve as the means of developing a spiritual rhythm.

For the most part, there is nothing very esoteric about the growth process with which spiritual direction is concerned. Growing awareness of God and self is mostly realized, as Merton reminds us, through simplicity, "the recovery of a simple and wholesome ordinary life, lived at a moderate and humanly agreeable tempo."[49] The Christian life is better lived by attending to the ordinary, simple ways of development than by esoteric methods and extraordinary *charismata*. A Christian receiving direction and observing a sensible rule is more likely to experience solid spiritual advance over time than one who is constantly seeking new spiritual experiences and experimenting with the latest techniques of prayer, Bible study and group dynamics.

A traditioning process. Spiritual direction is by nature a traditioning process. The directee learns from or is discipled by the director, who is working within a given framework. The director's wisdom is a funded wisdom, drawn from the common pool of the Christian tradition. No matter how individually customized the direction may be, it also presupposes a shared life in a community. Our own personal stories as Christians make sense only as part of the larger Christian story. The individual Christian life is nourished by and in the Christian tradition; it is not just "my personal relationship with God." The real danger of the church's becoming a collectivity of individualists comes not from those who are properly guided by a director but by self-taught saints. As Thornton notes, "It is those without competent guidance who are liable to be driven into a holy corner."[50]

It is important that we see direction in the context of the church. Otherwise it may just become a process for self-improvement. This is why it should be undertaken within the context of sacramental life. Leech notes that the sacraments have always played a central role in the work of spiritual direction.[51] If spiritual life is essentially life in the body of Christ, then spiritual direction must help individuals grow within the spiritual organism of the body. This means first being initiated into the body by baptism and then feeding on the shared life in Christ through the sacrament of Communion. Whether or not other rites like marriage and laying on of hands for ordination or healing (including exorcism and prayer of deliverance) are to be regarded as sacraments, there is no doubt that they have a sacramental value. They are means of grace to draw us more fully into the life in the body of Christ. In the case of prayers for healing and deliverance, there is a very real danger of distortion and sensationalism in our present day. It is all the more needful to see these works within the life of the church and within the normal channels of ministry like prayer, fasting, confession of sin and Communion.[52] The spiritual director uses these resources for guidance to help the individual personally discover the path of progress.[53]

Spiritual direction is an *oral* traditioning process that engages the individual in a one-to-one personal encounter, unlike, for instance, preaching, which is oral but addresses a group. There is something in oral exchange that other forms of communication cannot replace, say, the difference between reading a book and meeting a person. Edwards points out the special need that such a process fills:

> Today we are almost totally dependent on books and scholarship for reminding us of the depths and nuances of human interior development that have been known in the light and path of Christian experience. We have been largely missing the careful, chastened, long-term, faith-grounded, tested, and intuitive person-to-person conveyance of the heart of Christian awareness.[54]

The crucial question is, Can spiritual direction be carried out in the modern church context? The fact that the modern church tends to model itself after the giant business corporation hinders its ability to undertake spiritual direction. Even if the megachurch is broken down into cell groups, its tightly controlled structure does not leave room for the freedom that individual spiritual direction needs. In spiritual direction personal knowledge of the one being directed is essential if the director is to lead the directee effectively and efficiently to spiritual maturity. Such knowledge does not come from the mass-production factory of the megachurch. It can only come, to use an image from Thornton, from "dissecting" the person on a cold slab.

For spiritual direction to be possible, a radical reconception of the church is needed. Such attempts have been made from time to time. Late seventeenth-century pietists conceived the idea of the *ecclesiola in ecclesia,* a small church within a larger church. This became the basis of Wesley's "class meeting," a development that accounted for the success of the early Methodist movement. More recently the United Methodist Church in North America has resurrected the class meeting to form the "Covenant Discipleship Group."[55] It "consists of two to seven people who agree to meet together for one hour per week in order to hold themselves mutually accountable for their discipleship. They do this by affirming a written covenant on which they themselves have agreed."[56] As noted in chapter ten, a covenant group is a method of embracing common rule,[57] and its dynamic coincides to some extent with group direction.[58]

Among these alternative ecclesiologies, perhaps the most explicit link to be found between spiritual direction and church renewal is the remnant idea proposed by Thornton. If the church is to be the alternative polis that witnesses effectively to the world, the pastor will have to seek out a remnant within the church for spiritual direction. It is one way to ensure that the church is led by mature Christians who understand the spiritual nature and mission of the church, are capable of discerning God's will, and have within them the spiritual resources to carry out God's will in the church and in the world.

Qualities of a Spiritual Director

What about formal training for spiritual directors? Tildern Edwards, who directs an institution that trains spiritual directors, reminds us that "the reality of dealing with the spiritual lives of real people takes it out of the realm of guinea-pig experimentation. This is no game." For this reason the Shalem Institute did not offer a "qualifying certificate" to those who completed its course. It seems incongruous to formalize a qualification in an area that by its very nature is unformalizable, namely, "the mystery of the growth process."[59] The danger always exists that the training program could eventually turn into a regular "school." Perhaps we need to go back to the model of the desert father whose "directorship" was recognized by those who came to him rather than conferred through formal training.[60] The guru in the Indian tradition becomes one by learning from another guru.[61] In spiritual direction the learning process is quite different from academic learning; it is more "caught" than taught. What is learned goes infinitely beyond facts and information. Learning is imbibing a way of life that the director embodies. The director seeks to create a "space" for the Spirit to teach and for the learner to experience personal insights into the truth. This requires more the "apophatic" rather than the "kataphatic" approach.

Such a form of learning implies that the guide must know the way personally and intimately in order to lead others in it. This is why traditional spiritual direction has always placed the greatest emphasis on the personal quality of the director. First, he needs to know himself, and to do this he needs to cultivate intimacy with others through spiritual friendship. A director is not merely a resource person who provides information for others. He must be a fellow traveler along the way.

Second, he must be humble. A director is constantly tempted to bask in directees' adulation. In his desire to be well liked, he wants to appear nice to people and to conceal any anger he may feel. But even as he needs to be humble, he needs to be aware of the anger within him. As one desert father warned, "A man who is angry, even if he were to raise the dead, is not acceptable to God."[62] Abba Ammonas spent fourteen years "asking God night and day to grant me the victory over anger."[63] Honesty is another essential quality. The director must be prepared to speak the hard truth at times, as Jesus spoke the truth to the rich young man who asked, "What must I do to inherit eternal life?" The man had the right question, but he was not prepared for the hard truth that Jesus delivered in love (Mk 10:21). Some of the desert fathers exemplify this pattern of direction. Their answers to earnest inquirers may sometimes seem harsh or even irresponsible, but as Kallistos Ware has observed, behind the seeming indifference lies a deep love for others and the ability to take the sufferings of others upon themselves.[64]

But preparation for directing others is not necessarily ad hoc. First, a director needs be well versed in systematic and spiritual theology. Spiritual direction is *ultimately* concerned with spiritual realities and their basis in theology, not psychological problems. Thornton emphasizes the need to ground direction in solid dogma, beginning with the doctrine of creation, the Trinity, Christology and so on. The director must be able to use these doctrines as "directional tools" on the "patient." Take the doctrine of creation, for instance. Humankind is "lord of the known world, possibly of the universe, but certainly not of the creation which contains cherubim, seraphim, angels and archangels, the whole company of heaven embracing the saints of the Church triumphant and the inhabitants of paradise." Without locating human beings in their right place in creation, we might bring God down to our familiar level and lose the sense of divine mystery. Theologically, we would have overstressed divine immanence at the expense of transcendence.[65] Dogma to a spiritual director is like a map to a traveler. It charts a safe path for travelers to their final destination. It does not matter that the one being guided does not know how the tool functions, but it is imperative that the guide know.

Some knowledge of counseling techniques, psychology and abnormal psychology is immensely useful because spiritual development is closely tied to psychological development. An understanding of human psychological development can shed light on someone's spiritual condition. For instance, a spiritual director needs to have some understanding of the dynamics of midlife crisis, which signals a time in life when people become deeply aware of their mortality. The body begins to show signs of wear and tear. Children are growing up as their middle-aged parents are winding down. For the first time they realize that they are no longer in full charge. But it is also a time when people are more likely to open up to a more enduring reality—the spiritual dimension of life.[66] A basic grounding in these social disciplines, besides providing insights into the psychospiritual condition, will furnish the spiritual director with tools for distinguishing between spiritual and psychological problems, such as demon possession and schizophrenia, aridity and psychosomatic illness. Both skills and character are required in a spiritual director.

We have been looking at spiritual direction as an integrative process. We see how spiritual theology finds its eventual application in individual Christians who are uniquely guided into a living organism, the church, by a personal process of traditioning in which something more than ideas is transmitted. Spiritual theology finds its fulfillment in direction just as biblical study finds its true end in the preaching of the Word.[67] One is not complete without the other.

Conclusion

The Christian spiritual tradition has often employed the image of mountain climbing, since the spiritual life is a life of toil and progress that includes struggles, dangers and joy. The mountain-climbing image lends itself well to the asceticism of small steps. We have learned that virtues are formed by repeated acts. But for many modern Christians, repeating an act often enough to form a habit is not easy. The conflicting demands of modern living soon erode their best intentions. The answer to this dilemma does not lie in reducing the demands of discipleship and discipline. It would be downright dishonest to offer a "stairway of divine ascent" that reaches only partway up the mountain on the assumption that a short route is more attractive. This is what the gospel of cheap grace does. But offering a stairway with such high steps that only a few spiritual athletes can scale it will not do either. Some modern spiritual guidebooks (and not a few ancient ones) are like that. The would-be climber is told to undertake many spiritual disciplines but is not told how one exercise leads to another. What we need is a pathway with many small steps, especially at the bottom, so that no one is excluded from making the climb for lack of skill.

Suggesting such a finely graded spiritual apparatus does not preclude the surprising action of God (which does sometimes happen) whereby some saints are catapulted several steps upward without much effort on their part. But this is by definition not God's normal way of working and remains a mystery. New Christians beginning the spiritual journey will find it less daunting if they are shown an ascetical stairway of small steps: the "technique" of prayer (essentially the same as the "technique of going to church," chapter six), the simple acts of recalling the presence of God and of obedience (chapter seven), the acts of reading (chapter eight), the acts of befriending, of taking nature walks, of giving a cup of cold water to a stranger (chapter nine). No spiritual theology can be successfully implemented without an asceticism of small steps.

Above all, the new climber needs a guide, an experienced climber who can lead the way, point out the dangers, suggest the best equipment and offer a helping hand. The challenge seems less formidable in the reassuring presence of an experienced guide, who is the spiritual director—parent and companion.

Notes

Preface

[1] See T. F. Torrance, *The Trinitarian Faith* (Edinburgh: T & T Clark, 1993), chap. 2.

[2] John Zizioulas, *Being as Communion* (Crestwood, N.Y.: St. Vladimir's Seminary Press, 1985), p. 19. Author's emphasis.

[3] Ibid., pp. 130-32.

[4] For the use of the masculine pronoun for God, see Donald D. Hook and Alvin F. Kimel Jr., "The Pronouns of Deity: A Theolinguistic Critique of Feminist Proposals," *Scottish Journal of Theology* 46, no. 3 (1993): 297-323.

[5] This point is made by Hook and Kimel (ibid., pp. 318-23) and, from a very different background and perspective, by an Asian woman writer, Delia Kang-Oakins, "In for a Rude Awakening," *Asia Magazine,* June 5, 1994, p. 30.

Chapter 1: Christian Spiritual Theology

[1] Robert Wuthnow, "Small Groups Forge New Notions of Community and Sacred," *The Christian Century* 110, no. 36 (1993): 1236-40; Paul Stevens, *Marriage Spirituality: Ten Disciplines for Couples Who Love God* (Downers Grove, Ill.: InterVarsity Press, 1989); Susan Muto, *Celebrating the Single Life: A Spirituality for Single Persons in Today's World* (Garden City, N.Y.: Doubleday, 1982).

[2] For a helpful description of some of these subjective types, see James M. Houston, *The Holy Spirit in Contemporary Spirituality* (Bramcote, Nottingham, U.K.: Grove, 1993), pp. 4-7.

[3] I am indebted to Stanley Hauerwas on this.

[4] For a translation and a philosophical analysis of Anselm's argument, see M. J. Charlesworth, *St. Anselm's "Proslogion"* (Notre Dame, Ind.: University of Notre Dame Press, 1979).

[5] Cited by Andrew Louth, *Theology and Spirituality* (Oxford: SLG Press, 1981), p. 16.

[6] This is the opening sentence of William Ames's highly influential work *The Marrow of Sacred Divinity,* published in 1642.

[7] For an account of the process of theological disintegration since the Enlightenment, see Edward Farley, *Theologia: The Fragmentation and Unity of Theological Education* (Philadelphia: Fortress, 1989).

[8] Martin Thornton, *English Spirituality: An Outline of Ascetical Theology According to the English Pastoral Tradition* (London: S.P.C.K., 1963), p. 20.

[9] Ibid., pp. 24, 21.

[10] Joseph de Guibert, *The Theology of the Spiritual Life* (New York: Sheed & Ward, 1953), p. 11.

[11] K. E. Kirk, *Some Principles of Moral Theology* (London: Longmans, Green, 1921), p. 2.

[12] Jordan Aumann, *Spiritual Theology* (London: Sheed & Ward, 1984), p. 22.

[13] John Cassian, *Conferences* (Paris: La Tour-Maubourg, 1955), 2:26.

[14] Thomas Aquinas, *Summa Theologiae* (London: Eyre & Spottiswoode, 1976), 2a.2ae

Q.24; Teresa of Ávila, *The Interior Castle,* ed. Allison Peers (Garden City, N.Y.: Image, 1961); Bernard of Clairvaux, *On Loving God* (Kalamazoo, Mich.: Cistercian Publications, 1995), and *The Steps of Humility* (Cambridge, Mass.: Harvard University Press, 1940).

[15]For a brief discussion of these differences, see de Guibert, *Theology of the Spiritual Life,* pp. 4-12.

[16]If we may apply an important epistemological principle from Michael Polanyi, systematic theology attends *from* the nonrational *to* the rational, while spiritual theology attends *from* the rational *to* the nonrational. *The Tacit Dimension* (London: Routledge & Kegan Paul, 1966), p. 10.

[17]Richard Lovelace, *Dynamics of Spiritual Life* (Downers Grove, Ill.: InterVarsity Press, 1979), pp. 229-37.

[18]The question of which is prior, word or spirit, has been differently understood. It used to be thought that spirituality began with some kind of primal, instinctual experiences of a religious nature that were subsequently reflected on and rationalized. Compare Rudolf Otto, *The Idea of the Holy* (London: Oxford University Press, 1925). It is now more widely recognized that the relationship between experience and rationalization of experience is much more complex. We are all born into a cultural-linguistic framework that predefines our experiences so that it is difficult to conceive of a purely primal or uninterpreted religious experience. Each individual experience occurs within a community and draws its significance from that community. The cultural-linguistic framework is not a static reality but grows and develops in response to novelties from individual experiences. For a discussion of the cultural-linguistic understanding of faith, see George Lindbeck, *The Nature of Doctrine* (Philadelphia: Westminster, 1984).

[19]Thus it is not without significance that the Faith and Order Commission of the World Council of Churches has produced an important study on the Nicene-Constantinopolitan Creed, *Confessing the One Faith,* rev. ed. (Geneva: WCC, 1991), as the foundation of Christian unity.

[20]Thornton, *English Spirituality,* pp. 48-52. This may explain why Puritanism was at best a passing phase in England. It was much closer to the Ignatian spirit and did not quite fit the English temperament.

[21]Aumann, *Spiritual Theology,* p. 34.

[22]Thomas Merton, *Contemplation in a World of Action* (London: George Allen & Unwin, 1971), p. 164.

[23]See Watchman Nee's *Love Not the World* (London: Victory, 1976). Nee believes that in such fields as politics, education, literature, science and so on we are dealing with a "world-system" that will reach its zenith in the kingdom of antichrist (p. 14).

[24]For a recent discussion of the common heritage of Protestants, Catholics and Orthodox see James S. Cutsinger, ed., *Reclaiming the Great Tradition: Evangelicals, Catholics and Orthodox in Dialogue* (Downers Grove, Ill.: InterVarsity Press, 1997).

[25]Noted by de Guibert, *Theology of the Spiritual Life,* p. 148.

[26]According to Rowan Williams, paradox lies at the heart of Christian spirituality. The Christian is one who experiences life through death. Union with God is always through Christ in the world with all its sufferings, temptations and weaknesses. Knowledge of God is a knowledge that "wounds" rather than a knowledge that gives a sense of superiority or control over things. *The Wound of Knowledge,* rev.

ed. (Cambridge, Mass.: Cowley, 1990), esp. pp. 180-82. G. K. Chesterton earlier in the twentieth century made the point that "whenever we feel there is something odd in Christian theology, we shall generally find that there is something odd in the truth." Christianity is paradoxical because it detects the oddities that make up the fabric of real life. *Orthodoxy* (New York: Lane, 1909), pp. 150, 181.

[27]One of the early landmark documents produced by evangelicals reflecting their critical self-understanding known as the Chicago Call (1977) noted "a neglect of authentic spirituality on the one hand, and an excess of undisciplined spirituality on the other." It also included a call to "sacramental integrity." For the full text and exposition of the Call, see Donald Bloesch and Robert E. Webber, eds., *The Orthodox Evangelical* (New York: Thomas Nelson, 1978).

[28]The concept is borrowed from the theory of religious language of Ian Ramsey, who sees religious language as functioning to "evoke" an essentially religious vision. *Religious Language: An Empirical Placing of Theological Phrases* (London: SCM Press, 1957).

[29]The basis for this affirmation is our belief that Christianity is a historical faith grounded in the incarnation.

[30]A biblical parallel may be noted here. There is one basic Christian story (the gospel) but four different, contextually grounded Gospels; four different ways of telling the story, yet each is authentic in its own way. Similarly, the evangelical movement as we know it today is but one expression of the evangelical faith that has always existed in Christianity.

[31]Philip Sheldrake's *Spirituality and History: Questions of Interpretation and Method* (New York: Crossroad, 1992) is a typical case in point. The whole interpretive framework is based on the assumption of historical relativism and pluralism. See especially chapter four.

[32]William C. Placher, *Narratives of a Vulnerable God: Christ, Theology and Scripture* (Philadelphia: Westminster/John Knox, 1994), pp. 6-7.

[33]See William Dyrness, *Invitation to Cross-Cultural Theology* (Grand Rapids, Mich.: Zondervan, 1992), pp. 51-55. Interestingly, Placher finds the God of Israel "a more complicated case" (*Narratives of a Vulnerable God*, p. 5), and quite understandably so, since it is difficult to force the Old Testament narratives into a single motif of divine vulnerability.

[34]Wagner's understanding of the spiritual world appears to be an overreaction to Western secularism and as a consequence borders dangerously on animism. See my critique in "Pentecostalism, Social Concern and the Ethics of Conformism," *Transformation* 11, no. 1 (January/March 1994): 29-31.

[35]Dyrness notes that Western influences have deeply affected liberation theology's view of God's action in history, which leaves little or no room for divine transcendence. *Learning About Theology from the Third World* (Grand Rapids, Mich.: Zondervan, 1990), p. 110.

[36]Jon Sobrino, *Spirituality of Liberation* (New York: Orbis, 1988), pp. 19-24.

[37]Virginia Fabella et al., eds., *Asian Christian Spirituality: Reclaiming Traditions* (Maryknoll, N.Y.: Orbis, 1992), pp. 53-56.

[38]For example, Emerito Nacpil and Douglas Elwood, eds., *The Human and the Holy* (Manila: New Day, 1978), p. 4.

[39]This is the way M. M. Thomas sees "traditional" culture. According to him, it lacks

the historical orientation that makes progress possible. See *The Christian Response to the Asian Revolution* (London: SCM Press, 1966). Aloysius Pieris, however, has pointed out the limitation of a purely historical (or, in his term, *cosmic*) approach in Asia. *An Asian Theology of Liberation* (Maryknoll, N.Y.: Orbis, 1988), pp. 80-81.

[40]Arne Rasmusson, *The Church as "Polis": From Political Theology to Theological Politics As Exemplified by Jürgen Moltmann and Stanley Hauerwas* (Notre Dame, Ind.: University of Notre Dame Press, 1995), chap. 8, esp. p. 294. It is amazing that Western Christianity agrees with Western secularism in its valuation of the democratic-egalitarian ideal. Both assume its universal validity. But in recent years this ideal has been subjected to systematic critique and has been found wanting. See Tage Lundblom, *The Myth of Democracy* (Grand Rapids, Mich.: Eerdmans, 1996).

[41]Simon Chan, "*The Spirit of Life*: An Asian Review," *Journal of Pentecostal Theology* 4 (1994): 35-40.

[42]According to Pieris, in a metacosmic religion like Buddhism, the cosmic dimension of life (wealth, technology) is made subservient to metacosmic concerns like eternal salvation. *Asian Theology of Liberation*, pp. 74-80.

[43]Placher, *Narratives of a Vulnerable God*, p. 55.

[44]Compare George Newlands, *God in Christian Perspective* (Edinburgh: T & T Clark, 1994), p. 139.

[45]Jürgen Moltmann, *The Trinity and the Kingdom of God* (San Francisco: Harper & Row, 1981), p. 191.

[46]Walter Kasper, *The God of Jesus Christ* (London: SCM Press, 1984), p. 239.

[47]This explains why in many Asian contexts, the Old Testament has played a much more significant role in the preaching and self-understanding of the church.

[48]See Dyrness, *Learning About Theology*, pp. 121-62; Pieris, *Asian Theology of Liberation*, p. 69.

[49]Ng Kam Weng, "Dialogue and Constructive Social Engagement: Problems and Prospects for the Malaysian Church," *Trinity Theological Journal* 4 (1995): 39-40.

[50]Eka Darmaputera, "The Roles of Christians in Nation Building in Indonesia," *Trinity Theological Journal* 4 (1995): 51-58.

[51]Stanley, Hauerwas, *A Community of Character: Toward a Constructive Christian Social Ethic* (Notre Dame, Ind.: University of Notre Dame Press, 1981), p. 26.

[52]Anthony Price, *Reconsidering the Rosary* (1991), and Mark Morton, *Personal Confession Reconsidered* (1994), both published by Grove Books, an evangelical publisher in Bramcote, U.K.

[53]A. M. Allchin, *The Dynamic of Tradition* (London: Darton, Longman & Todd, 1981), p. 2.

[54]Ibid.

[55]Matthew Fox, *Western Spirituality: Historical Roots, Ecumenical Roots* (Santa Fe, N.M.: Bear, 1981), p. 2; *Original Blessing* (Santa Fe, N.M.: Bear, 1983), pp. 11, 18-19, 21-22.

[56]The example that comes most readily to mind is Mary Daly. See the various editions of *The Church and the Second Sex* (Boston: Beacon, 1965).

[57]For example, Elisabeth Schüssler Fiorenza, *In Memory of Her: A Feminist Theological Reconstruction of Christian Origins* (New York: Crossroad, 1984).

[58]Margaret Miles, *Practicing Christianity* (New York: Crossroad, 1988), pp. 10-11.

Miles operates on an assumption that will always prove her case: "I assume that it will *never* be known if, or to what extent, biological differences of women and men determine behavior; we will never find individuals who have not received gender conditioning because there is no society that has not developed a host of strategies for training individuals to gender roles and expectations" (p. 11, emphasis mine). If some scientist should discover sexual differences behind behavioral differences, Miles could still argue that it was due to the social conditioning of the scientist, since we already know that whatever has to do with behavioral difference must be due to social conditioning, not sexual difference.

[59]See Rasmusson, *Church as "Polis,"* p. 290.

[60]But so far Asian feminists appear to adhere to the Western feminist agenda and modus operandi, as a work like Virginia Fabella and Sun Ai Lee Park, eds., *We Dare to Dream: Doing Theology as Asian Women* (Maryknoll, N.Y.: Orbis, 1990) seems to bear out. The Western feminist model of society with its language of rights, power and struggle (disguised as the biblical vision of the church) is used as a supracultural principle to critique the worst features of Asian patriarchalism. In this approach, Asian feminist theologians may be able to challenge the sinful structures of Asian societies, but in its place is a version of Western egalitarianism that is not true to the Asian spirit, which prefers change through consensus rather than confrontation. No genuine Asian liberation or feminist theology can hope to emerge without first giving due recognition to the Asian "ordered society" as an ideal type. Only then can a meaningful comparison be made with the Christian vision of a community in Christ.

[61]This is the subject of an interesting study by John R. Levison and Priscilla Pope-Levison, "Toward an Ecumenical Christology for Asia," *Missiology: An International Review* 22, no.1 (January 1994): 3-17.

[62]Dyrness, *Learning About Theology*, pp. 175-84.

[63]The classic example is Raimundo Pannikar, *The Unknown Christ of Hinduism* (London: Darton, Longman & Todd, 1968).

[64]M. M. Thomas, who is more favorably disposed toward the historical approach, is well aware of this danger but thinks that it is "a risk Christians have to take" (*Christian Response*, p. 24).

[65]Levison and Pope-Levison, "Toward an Ecumenical Christology," p. 7.

[66]Peter K. H. Lee, "Hong Kong: Living in the Shadow of the Third World," in *Asian Christian Spirituality*, pp. 106-20.

[67]Ibid., p. 109.

[68]Ibid., p. 110. Emphasis mine.

[69]Ibid., p. 9.

[70]M. M. Thomas, "The Struggle for Human Dignity as a Preparation for the Gospel," in *What Asian Christians Are Thinking: A Theological Sourcebook*, ed. Douglas J. Elwood (Manila: New Day, 1976), p. 273.

[71]Vinay Samuel and Chris Sugden in a conference of evangelical mission theologians held in Bangkok in 1982 were right in seeing that the presence of Christ in other religions must be acknowledged as a prerequisite to genuine dialogue. But they also posed a pertinent question: "Our agenda is to discern how [Christ is present]." Vinay Samuel and Chris Sugden, eds., *Sharing Jesus in the Two Thirds World* (Grand Rapids, Mich.: Eerdmans, 1983), pp. 138-40.

[72]It is ironical that Thomas's historically oriented theology did not achieve the practical relevance that we have come to expect from such an emphasis. The Hindu Prabhu Guptara has observed, "Thomas may be regarded as trying to understand and to present the relevance of Christianity in the light of contemporary, secularizing, urbanizing, industrializing, India. He wishes to campaign to provide all people with conditions in which they can live with human dignity. However, his achievement, respectable at the intellectual level, has remained at that level." *Indian Spirituality* (Bramcote, Nottingham, U.K.: Grove, 1984), p. 22.

[73]Pieris, *Asian Theology of Liberation*, p. 3.

[74]Ibid., p. 5.

[75]Ibid., pp. 9-10.

[76]Ibid., p. 9. Author's emphasis.

[77]Such a commitment can be seen in deontological ethics and in Confucianism.

[78]Pieris, *Asian Theology of Liberation*, pp. 59-60.

[79]Ibid., pp. 11-12.

[80]For example, David Wells, *No Place for Truth: Or, Whatever Happened to Evangelical Theology?* (Grand Rapids, Mich.: Eerdmans, 1992), and Mark Noll, *The Scandal of the Evangelical Mind* (Grand Rapids, Mich.: Eerdmans, 1994).

[81]Donald Bloesch, *Essentials of Evangelical Theology* (San Francisco: Harper & Row, 1978), 1:8. Bloesch can speak of a "true evangelicalism [which] is at one with a true Catholicism" (p. 12).

[82]Ibid., pp. 16-17.

[83]Francis de Sales, *An Introduction to a Devout Life*, facsimile reprint (1613; London: Scolar, 1976), 2.2.

[84]This does not imply that there are no other components in evangelical spirituality or that its spirituality could not be differently expressed. Insofar as a "catholic evangelicalism" (to use an expression from Bloesch) has many historical expressions, this essential element is configured differently.

[85]C. S. Lewis, *The Pilgrim's Regress* (Glasglow: Fount, 1977), pp. 13, 9.

[86]B. H. Streeter and A. J. Appasamy, *The Message of Sadhu Sundar Singh: A Study in Mysticism on Practical Religion* (New York: Macmillan, 1921), p. 8.

[87]The most recent and thorough evaluation of Hauerwas has been done by Rasmusson, *Church as "Polis."* It also contains the most up-to-date bibliography.

[88]Stanley Hauerwas and William H. Willimon, *Resident Aliens* (Nashville: Abingdon, 1989).

[89]It is interesting to note that Ng, speaking from the Malaysian context, also emphasizes the need for the church to "serve as a counter-community in the world" and to have "morally robust individuals who are schooled in the art of community living." "Dialogue," pp. 36-37.

[90]See, for example, Sobrino, *Spirituality of Liberation*, and Gustavo Gutiérrez, *We Drink Water from Our Own Wells* (Maryknoll, N.Y.: Orbis, 1984).

[91]Quoted in Rasmusson, *Church as "Polis,"* p. 291. Compare Hauerwas, *Community of Character*, p. 78.

[92]Dyrness has indicated the significance of the "testimony" in Chinese house churches. *Invitation to Cross-Cultural Theology*, pp. 53-56. It is a common joke in English-speaking churches in Singapore that Chinese-educated preachers don't preach; they tell stories!

[93]Elsewhere Hauerwas has strongly argued that being Christian is not equivalent to being human, since to be Christian is to be part of a specific story that gives specific shape and character to our humanity. *The Peaceable Kingdom: A Primer in Christian Ethics* (Notre Dame, Ind.: University of Notre Dame Press, 1983), pp. 55-64. In this connection he is highly critical of much of modern Catholic thinking, which has reduced Christianity to anthropology (pp. 55-56).

[94]R. A. Knox, *Enthusiasm: A Chapter in the History of Religion* (Oxford, U.K.: Clarendon, 1959), is a good case in point.

[95]See, for example, Kilian McDonnell and George Montague, *Christian Initiation and Baptism in the Holy Spirit: Evidence from the First Eight Centuries* (Collegeville, Minn.: Liturgical, 1991).

[96]For example, de Guibert, *Theology of the Spiritual Life*, p. 76.

[97]Donald Gelpi, "Two Spiritual Paths: Thematic Grace vs. Transmuting Grace, Pt. 1," *Spirituality Today* 35, no. 3 (Fall 1983): 241-55; pt. 2: *Spirituality Today* 35, no. 4 (Winter 1983): 341-57.

[98]Joyce Hugget's widely read *Listening to God* (London: Hodder & Stoughton, 1986) is an example of such a practical integration.

[99]See Stanley M. Burgess and Gary B. McGee, eds., *Dictionary of Pentecostal and Charismatic Movements* (Grand Rapids, Mich.: Zondervan, 1988), s.v. "baptism in the Holy Spirit," "glossolalia," "spirituality, Pentecostal and charismatic."

[100]Hauerwas, *Peaceable Kingdom*, pp. 105-6.

[101]We see this, for example, in Moltmann's soteriology. He sees mystical union as occurring at the end of the *ordo salutis*. *The Spirit of Life: A Universal Affirmation* (Minneapolis: Fortress, 1992), chap. 10.

[102]As in Francis Schaeffer, *True Spirituality* (Wheaton, Ill.: Tyndale House, 1972), p. 15, and Laurence Richards, *A Practical Theology of Spirituality* (Grand Rapids, Mich.: Zondervan, 1988), pp. 54-55.

[103]R. S. Wallace, *Calvin's Doctrine of the Christian Life* (Grand Rapids, Mich.: Eerdmans, 1959), pp. 17-21.

[104]John Calvin *Institutes of the Christian Religion* 3.1.1.

[105]Howard L. Rice, *Reformed Spirituality: An Introduction for Believers* (Louisville, Ky.: Westminster/John Knox, 1991).

[106]R. T. Kendall in *Calvin and English Calvinism* (Oxford: Oxford University Press, 1981) calls Cotton "the first in his tradition to allow for the immediate witness of the Spirit" (pp. 175-83). It is likely, however, that earlier Puritans like Richard Sibbes had already developed similar ideas. Paul Coolidge is perhaps more to the point when he calls Cotton "the first consistent and authentic Calvinist in New England." *The Pauline Renaissance in England* (Oxford: Oxford University Press, 1970), p. 138.

[107]Sibbes's enthusiastic pneumatology can be found in many of his works, including "Bowels Opened: Or, A Discovery of the Neare and Deare Love, Union and Communion Betwixt Christ, and the Church" (1641); "The Bruised Reed and Smoking Flax," 5th ed. (1635); "A Glance of Heaven: Or, A Pretious Taste of a Glorious Feast" (1638); "The Soules Conflict with Itself" (1635), in *Works*, 7 vols., ed. A. B. Grosart (Edinburgh: James Nichols, 1862). Owen's pneumatology is best seen in *The Holy Spirit, His Gifts and Power; "Sunesia Pneumatik": Or, The Causes, Waies & Means of Understanding the Mind of God As Revealed in His Word* (1678) and *Pneumatologia: Or, A Discourse Concerning the Holy Spirit* (1674).

[108]Statistics from the American Assemblies of God show that a sizable number of its adherents either do not speak in tongues or have stopped doing so, even though glossolalia remains a central doctrine. This phenomenon is characteristically explained in terms of Max Weber's "routinization of charisma." Margaret M. Poloma, *The Assemblies of God at the Crossroads: Charisma and Institutional Dilemmas* (Knoxville: University of Tennessee Press, 1988), p. 40.

Chapter 2: The Christian Doctrine of God

[1]The question of whether Confucius himself believed in a supreme divine being is a matter of debate among Confucian scholars. But it is clear that the general orientation of Confucius (more so for Mencius) is toward an ethical rather than a religious absolute. This agnosticizing tendency eventually led to the denial of God in later Confucianists like Hsün-tzu (fl. 238 B.C.) and Wang Ch'ung (A.D. 27-100?). See Julia Ching, *Confucianism and Christianity: A Comparative Study* (New York: Kodansha International, 1977), p. 124.

[2]Kenneth Leech, *Experiencing God: Theology as Spirituality* (San Francisco: Harper & Row, 1985).

[3]For a helpful summary and discussion of major trinitarian views and issues, see Ted Peters, *God as Trinity* (Philadelphia: Westminster/John Knox, 1993), and John Thompson, *Modern Trinitarian Perspectives* (Oxford: Oxford University Press, 1994). Peters takes a position closer to Rahner, while Thompson's is closer to Barth's and Torrance's.

[4]Wolfhart Pannenberg, *Systematic Theology*, trans. Geoffrey Bromiley (Grand Rapids, Mich.: Eerdmans, 1991), 1:287.

[5]The term *immanent Trinity* refers to the Trinity in their essential relationship from all eternity. This relationship is sometimes described as the *ad intra* life of God. *Economic Trinity* refers to God in his relation to the world, especially in the work of salvation. God's relationship to creation is sometimes designated by the term *ad extra*.

[6]For a cogent restatement of the need to maintain the distinction between the immanent Trinity and the economic Trinity, see Paul D. Molnar, "Toward a Contemporary Doctrine of the Immanent Trinity," *Scottish Journal of Theology* 49, no. 3 (1996): 311-57.

[7]Another notable example is Catherine Mowry LaCugna's *God for Us: The Trinity and the Christian Life* (San Francisco: HarperCollins, 1991), a work that is at once characterized by a refusal to speculate about the inner trinitarian life as it is emphatic about the *ad extra* life of God. In his review of LaCugna's book Joseph Bracken has criticized her dropping the distinction between the immanent and economic Trinity. Bracken is right that "this distinction guarantees that the reality of God will not be absorbed into the reality of history even when the latter is presented as the progressive revelation of the triune God." *Theological Studies* 53, no. 3 (1992): 559. Along similar lines, Paul D. Molnar's review of Colin Gunton's *The Promise of Trinitarian Theology* (Edinburgh: T & T Clark, 1991) has noted that the latter's overemphasis on the Cappadocian view borders on tritheism. *Theological Studies* 53, no. 3 (1992): 560.

[8]George Newlands, *God in Christian Perspective* (Edinburgh: T & T Clark, 1994), pp. 84, 85, 190-94.

[9]According to Henri Blocher this position owes more to Hegel than to the biblical faith. See "Immanence and Transcendence in Trinitarian Theology," in *The Trinity in a Pluralistic Age: Theological Essays on Culture and Religion,* ed. Kevin J. Vanhoozer (Grand Rapids, Mich.: Eerdmans, 1997), pp. 104-23.

[10]Ibid., pp. 171-72.

[11]For example, when we speak of God's work of miracles as distinguished from his works of providence, an interventionist model is probably the best way to speak of a direct divine action from outside the natural order. But divine intervention is not even confined to what we normally regard as "extraordinary" works of God. See the examples cited in William Alston, "How to Think About Divine Action," in *Divine Action: Studies Inspired by the Philosophical Theology of Austin Farrer,* ed. Brian Hebblethwaite and Edward Henderson (Edinburgh: T & T Clark, 1990), pp. 51-57. See also Thomas F. Tracy, "Narrative Theology and the Acts of God," pp. 173-80.

[12]This is the last line of defense in all theodicies. In order for the theist to maintain the compatibility of the existence of God and the existence of evil, the ultimate explanation is that God has his own reason for permitting evil in the world, even if *we* cannot specify a reason for it. The "freewill defense" could also be postulated, but in the final analysis an element of real mystery still remains because we cannot explain why God permitted a freedom that could result in such horrendous evil in our world. For one of the latest in the tradition of this essentially Augustinian theodicy, see R. Douglas Geivett, *Evil and the Evidence for God: The Challenge of John Hick's Theodicy* (Philadelphia: Temple University Press, 1995), p. 62.

[13]Ted Peters, for instance, does not seem to discern any logical oddity when he groups together cancer, AIDS, earthquakes, storms and floods as "natural evils." *Sin: Radical Evil in Soul and Society* (Grand Rapids, Mich.: Eerdmans, 1994), p. 280. The case of AIDS is interesting because it is one problem whose moral dimension many moderns seek consciously to tone down or eliminate altogether. The reason (and here I am speaking as a non-Westerner) is probably because it is closely associated with what is increasingly regarded as simply an "alternative lifestyle" that must be defended on the basis of individual human rights. Individual rights is the bottom line for determining moral and natural evil.

[14]This criticism can also be leveled against Karl Rahner and the so-called "Rahner's rule," which says, "The 'economic' trinity is the 'immanent' trinity and the 'immanent' trinity is the 'economic' trinity." See Thompson, *Modern Trinitarian Perspectives,* pp. 26-27.

[15]For example, in Pannenberg's conception of the Trinity the divine personalities are dependent on the kingdom, which is realized eschatologically. But since the kingdom has provisionally come with the resurrection of Christ, history can contain novelty and surprises because it is God's history (*Systematic Theology,* esp. 1:310-13).

[16]David Suh and Lee Chung Hee, "Liberating Spirituality in the Korean Minjung Tradition," in *Asian Christian Spirituality,* pp. 31-43.

[17]Ibid., p. 39.

[18]Noted by Peters, *God as Trinity,* pp. 105-6.

[19]Compare Julia Ching, *Confucianism and Christianity,* p. 117.

[20]In this connection, Jung Young Lee's Asian perspective of the Trinity, which uses

the Taoist yin-yang category to underscore the nonsubstantial, relational nature of God, does not differ materially from the basic thrust of much of modern trinitarian thinking. *The Trinity in Asian Perspective* (Nashville: Abingdon, 1996), esp. chap. 3.

[21]Colin Gunton, *The One, the Three and the Many* (Cambridge: Cambridge University Press, 1993), pp. 6-7.

[22]Walter Kasper, *The God of Jesus Christ* (London: SCM Press, 1984), p. 315. Kasper insists that the Trinity is "the Christian form of monotheism" (p. 295) or "concrete monotheism" (pp. 307, 314, 315).

[23]For a discussion of the dynamic between worship, popular devotion and the development of doctrine, see Geoffrey Wainwright, *Doxology: The Praise of God in Worship, Doctrine and Life* (New York: Oxford University Press, 1980), pp. 51-56.

[24]For a brief and helpful discussion of these types of spiritualities and their integration, see Peter Adam, *Living the Trinity* (Bramcote, Nottingham, U.K.: Grove, 1986).

[25]John Baggley, *Doors of Perception: Icons and Their Spiritual Significance* (London: Mowbrays, 1987).

[26]On the basis of the universal fatherhood of God, John Hick, for instance, calls for a "Copernican revolution" of the theology of religion in which the center shifts from Christ to God. *God and the Universe of Faiths* (London: Macmillan, 1973), pp. 120-32.

[27]It should be said, however, that a more biblical understanding of what it means to be "in Christ" would actually undermine this individualistic emphasis.

[28]Seventeenth-century congregationalism may be regarded as a happy compromise between free associationism on the one side and iron conformism on the other. It posits a view of the church that stresses personal holiness but extends the concept of faith to "believers and their seed."

[29]According to the Assemblies of God "Statement of Fundamental Truths," no. 7.

[30]Pentecostals inherited a theological framework from the Wesleyan-holiness movement in which entire sanctification is regarded as the "second work of grace." But their Reformed orientation led them to identify salvation and sanctification as a single divine work and baptism in the Spirit as a second work.

[31]Frank Macchia, "Sighs Too Deep for Words: Toward a Theology of Glossolalia," *Journal of Pentecostal Theology* 1 (1992): 47-73.

[32]Peter Hocken, "The Meaning and Purpose of Spirit-Baptism," *Pneuma* 7, no. 2 (Fall 1985): 133.

[33]H. H. Farmer, *The World and God* (London: Nisbet, 1946), p. 6.

[34]One such instance is the dramatic founding of the Assemblies of God in Brazil by two simple Swedish immigrant workers in America. See Walter Hollenweger, *The Pentecostals* (London: SCM Press, 1972), p. 75.

[35]Del Tarr, "Transcendence, Immanence and the Emerging Pentecostal Academy," *Pentecostalism in Context* (Sheffield, U.K.: Sheffield Academic Press, 1997), p. 211.

[36]Ibid., p. 199.

[37]One example is Benny Hinn. While Hinn encourages spiritual disciplines like mortification and prayer, they are performed with one end in view: to obtain power. See *The Anointing* (Nashville: Thomas Nelson, 1992).

[38]Assemblies of God, "Statement of Fundamental Truths," no. 7.

[39]John Wimber, for instance, may pay lip service to the "has come" and "not yet"

tension, but in practical terms it is the "has come" that is all decisive. See *Power Healing* (San Francisco: Harper & Row, 1987), pp. 169-70. A similar position is taken by Peter Wagner, *How to Have a Healing Ministry Without Making Your Church Sick* (Ventura, Calif.: Regal, 1988), p. 96, 109-11.

[40]The logical priority of the Father does not mean that our starting point is an undifferentiated oneness in God. Rather, the starting point is the trinitarian God whose inner life is constituted by the eternal generation of the Son and the procession of the Spirit from the Father. This is generally the Eastern way of understanding perichoresis. For a helpful summary of the Eastern and Western approaches to the Trinity, see Kasper, *God of Jesus Christ,* pp. 296-99.

[41]Yves Congar, *I Believe in the Holy Spirit* (New York: Seabury, 1983), 3:165-71.

[42]It must be noted that the perichoresis described here is one way, albeit a very ancient way, of understanding the relationship between the persons of the Trinity. Some contemporary trinitarian conceptions have emphasized the "social analogy of the Trinity" (for example, Moltmann in works already referred to) or the mutually constitutive nature of the Father, Son and Spirit as in Wolfhart Pannenberg, *Systematic Theology,* 1:310-12.

[43]Compare Thornton, *English Spirituality,* pp. 16-20.

[44]I suspect that the introduction of inclusive language into the liturgy of some Western churches is more often than not another case of fashionable innovation that is poorly thought out. The convoluted language that results from, for instance, eliminating the masculine pronoun for God and substituting the reflexive with a contrived word like *Godself* succeeds more at irritating and distracting hearers than promoting the cause of equality between men and women. But more than just being an irritation, these ideologically motivated attempts at linguistic reform will have drastic consequences for the church and theology. For a critique of this feminist proposal, see Donald D. Hook and Alvin F. Kimel Jr., "The Pronouns of Deity: A Theolinguistic Critique of Feminist Proposals," *Scottish Journal of Theology* 46, no. 3 (1993): 297-323.

[45]Peters, *God as Trinity,* pp. 184-85.

[46]Donald Gelpi, *The Spirit in the World* (Wilmington, Del.: Michael Glazier, 1988), p. 114. Compare Gelpi, *The Divine Mother: A Trinitarian Theology of the Holy Spirit* (Lanham, Md.: University Press of America, 1984), pp. 9-11.

[47]Jürgen Moltmann, *History and the Triune God: Contributions to Trinitarian Theology* (New York: Crossroad, 1992), p. xiv.

[48]Rosemary Radford Ruether, *Sexism and God-Talk: Toward a Feminist Theology* (Boston: Beacon, 1983), p. 60.

[49]Peters, *God as Trinity,* p. 186.

[50]Both Fee and Barrett in their commentaries agree that "head" has the sense of origin or source of life, not having authority over. Conzelmann, however, seems to think that a certain subordination is involved. Fee strenuously avoids the word *hierarchy,* but this is understanding hierarchy only in the sense of having authority over. The word admits of other meanings, as any good dictionary will bear out. But even if *origin* or *source* is meant here, some such concept as order or priority cannot be avoided. Gordon Fee, *The First Epistle to the Corinthians* (Grand Rapids, Mich.: Eerdmans, 1987), pp. 50-105; C. K. Barrett, *The First Epistle to the Corinthians* (Peabody, Mass.: Hendrickson, 1968), pp. 248-49; Hans Conzelmann, *1 Corin-*

thians, trans. James W. Leitch (Philadelphia: Fortress, 1975), pp. 183-84.

[51]Compare Moltmann, *History and the Triune God,* pp. xv-xvi: "The fellowship of the triune God is thus the matrix and the sphere of life for the free community of men and women, without domination and without subjection, in mutual respect and in mutual recognition."

[52]This view is found in the Greek fathers such as John of Damascus and Gregory of Nazianzus. Cited by Pannenberg, *Systematic Theology,* 1:311. See also Kasper, *God of Jesus Christ,* p. 296.

[53]The importance of the father-son relationship is demonstrated in the fact that Confucius sees filial piety as the overriding virtue that supersedes even the conjugal relationship. Society, for Confucius, is hierarchically ordered around the five relationships: king-subject, father-son, husband-wife, older brother-younger brother, friend-friend. Even in the relationship between friends, "seniority of age demands a certain respect, as also with brothers." See Ching, *Confucianism and Christianity,* pp. 97-98.

[54]According to Lucian Pye, Asian hierarchicalism in the political realm has often been misinterpreted by the West as mere dictatorship. *Asian Power and Politics: The Cultural Dimensions of Authority* (Cambridge, Mass.: Harvard University Press, Belknap, 1985), pp. 50-51. For an account of how it works in various Asian countries, see chapter eleven.

[55]Ching, *Confucianism and Christianity,* p. 97.

[56]According to the Confucian scholar Tu Wei-Ming, the golden rule is essentially an extension of the principle of reciprocity. For an analysis of the moral dynamics of reciprocity in the five relationships, see Tu Wei-Ming, *Centrality and Commonality: An Essay on Confucian Religiousness* (Albany: State University of New York Press, 1989), pp. 102-7.

[57]Pannenberg's conception of the Trinity could be interpreted in such a way. For he sees, first, Jesus' submission and obedience as itself constitutive of his eternal sonship in relation to the Father (*Systematic Theology,* 1:310) and, second, his eternal generation from the Father as an "irreversible" relationship (p. 312). These facts could constitute the "hierarchical" pole of the Trinity. But then Pannenberg quickly goes on to stress "reciprocity" based on the fact that "the relativity of fatherhood that finds expression in the designation 'Father' might well involve a dependence of the Father on the Son" (p. 312). Like most Westerners, Pannenberg seems to have difficulty reconciling hierarchy with reciprocity, so much so that any suggestion of hierarchy must be offset by, in this case, a kind of quid pro quo reciprocity.

[58]For a brief analysis, see John L. Gresham Jr. "Three Trinitarian Spiritualities," *Journal of Spiritual Formation* 15, no. 1 (1994): 21-24.

[59]There is a remarkable conjunction between the modern Pentecostal experience of tongues and the experience of union with God in the contemplative tradition. See Richard Baer Jr., "Quaker Silence, Catholic Liturgy and Pentecostal Glossolalia: Some Functional Similarities," in *Perspectives on the New Pentecostalism,* ed. Russell P. Spittler (Grand Rapids, Mich.: Baker, 1976), pp. 151-64.

[60]Baer refers to the "element of playfulness" and "childlike delight" in glossolalia. Ibid., p. 158.

[61]François Fénelon, *Christian Perfection* (New York: Harper & Brothers, 1947), p. 123.

[62]The term *inebriated* is often used by Bernard to describe a mystical experience.

[63]Hans Küng, "The World Religions in God's Plan of Salvation," in *Christian Revelation and World Religions,* ed. Joseph Neuner (London: Burns & Oates, 1967), p. 52.

[64]Ibid., p. 55.

[65]The criticism raised here is not meant to invalidate the inclusivist theory of religion as a whole but to show that if inclusivism is to commend itself as a better alternative to pluralism or exclusivism, it has to incorporate within it a more consistently Christian view of salvation.

[66]The nature of this sharing, or "theosis" as the Eastern Orthodox would call it, has been variously conceived. But because it involves the whole people of God participating in the "social" relationship between the Father, Son and Spirit, it gives to our corporate life its own distinctive character. For examples, see Gresham, "Three Trinitarian Spiritualities," pp. 26-27.

[67]Gunton, *The One, the Three and the Many,* p. 168.

[68]Ibid., p. 170.

[69]Ibid., p. 172.

[70]Samuel Huntington, "The Clash of Civilizations?" *Foreign Affairs* 72, no. 3 (Summer 1993): 22-49.

[71]It should perhaps be noted that the common Western criticisms (especially those represented by the mass media) of the "human rights record" in Asia have not always been nuanced. The difference between the two civilizations is not that one upholds human rights and the other does not; the real difference, rather, is that the West promotes *individual* human rights as the highest good, while in Asia (at least in Confucian societies) the human rights of the larger society are seen as more important than those of individuals.

[72]Gelpi, *Spirit in the World,* pp. 113-14.

[73]It must be emphasized that this analogy is intended only to highlight one aspect of the divine economy. It does not imply sexual distinctions in God. It is of interest to note that the motherly function of God is not always identified with the Spirit. In Julian of Norwich, for instance, it is consistently identified with the second person of the Trinity. In her *Revelations of Divine Love* (Harmonsworth, U.K.: Penguin, 1984) Jesus is regularly decribed as "our beloved Mother," "our Mother, Brother, and Saviour" and so on (chaps. 57-63).

[74]The blurring of family identities and roles in modern societies is not helped by Moltmann's conceptualizing (no doubt, from egalitarian interest) in which *each* person of the Trinity possesses male and female characteristics (*History of the Triune God,* pp. xiv-xv).

[75]This is Gresham's third model of trinitarian spirituality, which he terms the "sacramental, not charismatic" ("Three Trinitarian Spiritualities," pp. 26-31).

[76]Ibid., p. 29.

[77]John F. MacArthur Jr. is one such case. *Charismatic Chaos* (Grand Rapids, Mich.: Zondervan, 1992), p. 224.

[78]It would be ridiculous to suppose that the basic father-son relationship in Confucianism, in which the son renders filial piety to the father, is a relationship of domination and oppression. In such a society the vocabulary that functions meaningfully in an egalitarian context is no longer adequate.

Chapter 3: Sin & Human Nature

[1]Thus Edward Farley in his book *Good and Evil: Interpreting a Human Condition* (Minneapolis: Fortress, 1990) attempts to develop a "philosophy of the human reality." The human reality is identified in three overlapping spheres: the interhuman, the social and individual agents.

[2]See, for example, Colin Brown, ed., *The New International Dictionary of New Testament Theology* (Grand Rapids, Mich.: Zondervan, 1986), s.v. "man."

[3]This view goes back to the Old Testament, where the concept of God as the unconditioned lawgiver and initiator of the covenant gives rise to a sense of individual responsibility before God. See Walther Eichrodt, *Man in the Old Testament*, trans. K. Gregor Smith and R. Gregor Smith (London: SCM Press, 1959), p. 16.

[4]As seen, for example, in a classic work like Reinhold Niebuhr's *The Nature and Destiny of Man*, 2 vols. (London: Nisbet, 1941).

[5]Viktor Frankl, *Man's Search for Meaning: An Introduction to Logotherapy*, trans. Ilse Lasch (Boston: Beacon, 1970).

[6]Niebuhr, *Nature and Destiny*, 1:12-18.

[7]For example, Peter Wagner, ed., *Wrestling with Dark Angels* (Ventura, Calif.: Regal, 1990).

[8]Niehuhr, *Nature and Destiny*, 1:161-78.

[9]Quoted in Donald F. Tweedie, *Logotherapy and the Christian Faith* (Grand Rapids, Mich.: Baker, 1961), p. 65. Frankl's observation reminds us of the hauntingly Christlike figure in Dostoevsky's *The Idiot*.

[10]The *possibility* of such an existence can be seen in some of Scott Peck's case studies in *People of the Lie: The Hope for Healing Human Evil* (New York: Simon & Schuster, 1983). The fact that they came for help, however, indicates that the conscience was not completely dead and was therefore curable, as the subtitle of the book shows.

[11]Francis de Sales *An Introduction to a Devout Life* 3.23.4. The spelling has been modernized. Francis here is simply echoing what was a piece of standard monastic advice. Compare Cassian *Conferences* 2.23.

[12]Aumann, *Spiritual Theology*, p. 148.

[13]R. Garrigou-Lagrange, O.P., *The Three Ages of the Interior Life*, trans. S. M. Timothea Doyle, (Rockford, Ill.: Tan Books, 1947, 1989), 1:275.

[14]More recent Catholic discussions of sin have given more attention to the personal-relational dimension. See, for example, Patrick McCormick, C.M., *Sin as Addiction* (New York: Paulist, 1989), chap. 5. Two remarks, however, need to be made about this new Catholic conception. First, when interpreted in an individualistic context, the personal comes to be equated with the private. This problem has led McCormick to call for further reform in Catholic moral theology (pp. 81-82). Second, the relational character of sin is interpreted in such a way, namely, as interpersonal and social alienation, that its religious character is obscured. Compare Hauerwas's critique below.

[15]Garrigou-Lagrange, *Three Ages*, 1:287-88. Modern Catholic conceptions have not changed considerably. If anything, they have weakened. For example, in Francis Kelly Nemeck and Marie Theresa Coombs, *The Way of Spiritual Direction* (Wilmington, Del.: Michael Glazier, 1987), sin is seen in the context of a natural

cosmic process of entropy: "regression into matter, scatteredness, the multiple. In the human sphere, entropy is selfishness, self-centeredness, the sin of the world" (p. 29). Sin is regression into matter as salvation is the process of being transformed from matter to spirit or "trans-matter" (p. 31).

[16]Mark O'Keefe, "The Three Ways," *Studies in Formative Spirituality* 13, no. 1 (February 1992): 74.

[17]Ibid., p. 75.

[18]Ibid., p. 76.

[19]O'Keefe refers to Rahner for this distinction. See Karl Rahner, *Theological Investigations* (New York: Crossroad, 1982), 6:178-96.

[20]Augustine's doctrine of the bondage of the will is found extensively and is frequently referred to by Calvin (*Institutes* 2.2). But from the perspective of spirituality the most important portrayal of sin is to be found in his *Confessions*.

[21]Martin Luther, "Preface to Romans," in *Martin Luther: Selections from His Writings*, ed. John Dillenberger (Garden City, N.Y.: Doubleday, 1961), p. 22.

[22]This is why Hauerwas is highly critical of modern Catholic moral theology, which reduces Christian ethics to human ethics. See *The Peaceable Kingdom* (Notre Dame, Ind.: University of Notre Dame Press, 1983), pp. 55-64. Compare Hauerwas, *Community of Character*, p. 130.

[23]A classic Puritan example of preparationism can be found in Thomas Hooker, *The Soules Preparation for Christ: Or, A Treatise on Contrition* (London, 1632). But John Bunyan's *Grace Abounding to the Chief of Sinners* is perhaps a better known example. For a discussion of this Puritan practice, see Norman Pettit, *The Heart Prepared: Grace and Conversion in Puritan Spiritual Life* (New Haven, Conn.: Yale University Press, 1966).

[24]James Torrance, "Contemplating the Trinitarian Mystery of Christ," in *Alive to God*, ed. J. I. Packer and Loren Wilkinson (Downers Grove, Ill.: InterVarsity Press, 1992), pp. 144-45.

[25]Ibid., pp. 142-44.

[26]Ibid., p. 142.

[27]Ibid., pp. 145-46.

[28]Martin Thornton, *Christian Proficiency* (London: S.P.C.K., 1964). Thornton has strongly argued that proficiency in Christian devotion and discipline, far from being just a matter of practical expediency, is strictly based on Christian doctrine, namely, the Trinity, the incarnation and the church (chap. 2).

[29]Brown, ed., *New International Dictionary of New Testament Theology*, s.v. "grace, spiritual gifts." *Charisma* sometimes has the sense of *charis* (Rom 4:2, 25) and vice versa (Eph 4:7).

[30]In Reformed theology conversion may be understood in the passive and in the active sense. In the passive sense it refers to the work of regeneration whereby the Spirit implants the principle of new life. In the active sense it refers to the regenerated person's response to the Spirit's work. It is in the second sense that we can speak of conversion as a process. Noted by Peter Toon, *Born Again: A Biblical and Theological Study of Regeneration* (Grand Rapids, Mich.: Baker, 1987), p. 123. I shall have more to say about this in the next chapter.

[31]Against the backdrop of missionary exigencies, Paul Hiebert has proposed a view of conversion using the category of a "centered set," which integrates the decisive

event with continuous growth. Conversion involves both a basic reorientation of one's belief toward a center (Christ) and a continuous movement toward it. "Conversion, Culture and Cognitive Categories," *Gospel in Context* 1, no. 4 (October 1978): 215-20.

[32]It is not the case that there was no Protestant asceticism as such. But its development has generally been ad hoc and piecemeal rather than systematic, except possibly among the late sixteenth- and seventeenth-century English Puritans. See Charles E. Hambrick-Stowe, *The Practice of Piety: Puritan Devotional Disciplines in Seventeenth-Century New England* (Ann Arbor, Mich.: University Microfilm International, 1981).

[33]Richard Foster, *Celebration of Discipline* (San Francisco: Harper & Row, 1978).

[34]The parable of the sower (Mt 13:1-23) shows that not everyone who receives the word of God (some even joyously) is decisively transformed by it.

[35]*Martin Luther: Selections from His Writings,* p. 25.

[36]Lovelace, *Dynamics,* pp. 86, 92-93.

[37]An influential work of casuistry entitled *Conscience with the Power and Cases Thereof* (1639) was written by the Puritan theologian William Ames.

[38]Richard Baxter's massive tome *A Christian Directory* (1674) is essentially a work of casuistry dealing with such diverse subjects as how to control one's thought and speech and a wide range of practical issues from usury to family life.

[39]*The Autobiography of Richard Baxter,* abridged by J. M. Lloyd Thomas (London: J. M. Dent, 1925), p. 25. A similar incident was recorded in Augustine's *Confessions* 2.9. It is possible that Augustine's experience came to represent a sort of archetype in Christian conversion that may have influenced the way others experienced theirs.

[40]The early Christians' perception of pagan immorality was derived from their Jewish roots. God's sovereignty over the whole person undermined what Peter Brown calls the "benevolent dualism" of the pagan world. It was a dualism involving, on the one hand, a carefully coded public sexual ethic that sought "to absorb marriage into the greater order of the city" and, on the other hand, "a marked degree of tolerance . . . accorded to men, both on the matter of homosexuality and in their love affairs before and outside marriage." *The Body and Society: Men, Women and Sexual Renunciation in Early Christianity* (New York: Columbia University Press, 1988), pp. 23-29.

[41]The contextual sensitivity of the early Christians may be seen in the prohibitions enjoined on Gentile Christians at the Jerusalem council (Acts 15:20, 29). Two of them, food offered to idols and things strangled, seem rather morally incongruous until we realize that they were probably for the purpose of making table fellowship between Jewish and Gentile Christians possible. Compare Romans 14:15, where Paul warns against eating meat that causes a fellow Christian to stumble.

[42]McCormick, *Sin as Addiction,* pp. 104-5.

[43]Peters, *Sin,* chap. 1. Cornelius Plantinga, *Not the Way It's Supposed to Be: A Breviary of Sin* (Grand Rapids, Mich.: Eerdmans, 1995), discusses sin along a similar line. For a brief but helpful historical perspective of sin that includes the major psychological theories of evil, see Hans Schwarz, *Evil: A Historical and Theological Perspective* (Minneapolis: Fortress, 1995).

[44]For example, Aumann, *Spiritual Theology,* pp. 165-67.

[45]In Hinduism, too, there is no real place for a doctrine of sin. Hindu philosopher Swami Vivekenanda charges that it is a sin to call a man a sinner. Noted by Sunand Sumithra, *Holy Father: A Doxological Approach to Systematic Theology* (Bangalore: Theological Book Trust, 1993), pp. 276-78. One must be sure, however, that the contrast between Christianity and Confucianism is not made against an over-wrought doctrine of sin found in certain strands of Puritanism and Pietism that tends to induce morbid introspection. See Wolfhart Pannenberg's criticism of what he calls "penitential piety" in *Christian Spirituality* (Philadelphia: Westminster Press, 1983), chap. 1.

[46]Christopher Chou, "A Theological Dialogue between Christian Faith and Chinese Belief in the Light of 'Sin,'" S.T.D. diss., Lutheran School of Theology at Chicago, 1977, p. 73.

[47]Ibid., pp. 82, 89-92.

[48]Ibid., pp. 106-7. Julia Ching has challenged the commonly held assumption that Chinese culture is dominated by shame consciousness rather than guilt conscious-ness. There is a strong awareness of moral evil, but it is defined in social and interpersonal terms. *Confucianism and Christianity,* pp. 74-79.

[49]The difficulty with Confucianism illustrates the general difficulty that Christianity encounters with the metacosmic Asian religions. It is nearly impossible to challenge large systems of thought; it is at the level of daily living where traditional spiritualities began to break down in the face of other challenges such as modernization that Christian mission in Asia has been more successful.

[50]Peters, *Sin,* pp. 28-31.

[51]M. Scott Peck has analyzed this problem and attributes it to the way modern societies and their large institutions are organized. "Whenever the roles of individuals within a group become specialized, it becomes both possible and easy for the individual to pass the moral buck to some other part of the group" (*People of the Lie,* p. 218).

[52]These are F. P. Harton's categories of worldly people. *Elements of the Spiritual Life* (London: S.P.C.K., 1964), pp. 111-12.

[53]As in Aumann, *Spiritual Theology,* pp. 163-64.

[54]Kevin F. O'Shea, C.SS.R., "The Reality of Sin: A Theological and Pastoral Critique," in *The Mystery of Sin and Forgiveness,* ed. Michael J. Taylor, S.J. (New York: Alba House, 1971), pp. 94-95. Quoted by McCormick, *Sin as Addiction,* p. 114.

[55]The most extensive discussion of the subject may be Walter Wink's trilogy: *Naming the Powers: The Language of Power in the New Testament* (Philadelphia: Fortress, 1984); *Unmasking the Powers: The Invisible Forces That Determine Human Existence* (Philadelphia: Fortress, 1986); and *Engaging the Powers: Discernment and Resistance in a World of Domination* (Minneapolis: Fortress, 1992).

[56]Plantinga, *Not the Way It's Supposed to Be,* pp. 75-76.

[57]Calvin devotes a whole chapter in the *Institutes* (3.9) to a consideration of the vanity of this present world and the glory of the life to come.

[58]Thus Francis de Sales reminds us that at death "there shall be no more world for thee . . . for then the pleasures, the vanities, the worldly joys, the fond affections will seem unto us like flying shadows and fading clouds" (*Devout Life* 1.13).

[59]For example, Peters, *Sin,* pp. 284-86. Calvin, however, is quite clear that "contempt of the present life" should not engender "hatred of it or ingratitude against God," since it is from the right use of the things of this world that we come to appreciate

the benevolence of God and, by analogy, the greater good in the life to come (*Institutes* 3.9.3).

[60]*Contemptus mundi* is but one short step from the ancient baptismal ritual in which the candidate was asked to renounce the world, the flesh and the devil. For a history of this ritual, see Henry Ansar Kelly, *The Devil at Baptism* (Ithaca, N.Y.: Cornell University Press, 1985).

[61]Calvin *Institutes* 3.9.2.

[62]C. S. Lewis, *The Screwtape Letters* (New York: Macmillan, 1943), p. 9.

[63]I shall have more to say about this in chapter twelve.

[64]See, for example, the lucid discussion in Harton, *Elements of the Spiritual Life*, pp. 117-18, 123-26.

[65]Peck, *People of the Lie*, chap. 5.

[66]R. B. Russell, *The Prince of Darkness: Radical Evil and the Power of Good in History* (Ithaca, N.Y.: Cornell University Press, 1988), pp. 274-77.

[67]C. S. Lewis, *The Weight of Glory and Other Addresses* (New York: Macmillan, 1949), p. 15.

[68]Søren Kierkegaard, *Fear and Trembling/The Sickness unto Death*, trans. Walter Lowrie (Garden City, N.Y.: Doubleday, 1954), p. 153.

[69]Russell, *Prince of Darkness*, p. 273.

[70]Peters, *Sin*, p. 18.

[71]One obvious modern instance is the identification of the United States of America as "the great Satan" by the ayatollahs of Iran. But according to Robert C. Fuller, America also has a history of "obsession with naming the Antichrist" whatever it regards as threatening. *Naming the Antichrist: The History of an American Obsession* (New York: Oxford University Press, 1995), p. 5.

[72]The problem of "false memory" related to alleged child abuse is a good case in point. In a spurt of zeal to eliminate this horrendous evil (the image of an innocent child being ruthlessly abused is bound to evoke strong emotions), the new witch hunters unwittingly implanted ideas of sexual abuse into the child's mind in the course of questioning.

[73]Peters, *Sin*, pp. 20-21.

[74]Cassian *Conférences* 5.2. Cassian's list includes eight principal vices: gluttony, fornication, avarice, anger, melancholy, sloth *(acedia)*, vainglory *(vana gloria)* and pride *(superbia)*.

[75]Gregory the Great *Moralia in Job* 31.45, followed by Aquinas *Summa Theologiae* 1a.2ae Q.84.4.

[76]*Summa Theologiae* 2a.2ae Q.84.3. Compare Garrigou-Lagrange, *Three Ages*, 1:300.

[77]Donald Capps, *Deadly Sins and Saving Virtues* (Philadelphia: Fortress, 1987), p. 2.

[78]Seward Hiltner, *Theological Dynamics* (Nashville: Abingdon, 1972), p. 94.

[79]As the word *radical* is a derivative of the Latin for root, I shall retain its use for modern descriptions of evil and use *root* with reference to the deadly sins.

[80]Karl Menninger's *Whatever Became of Sin?* (New York: Hawthorn, 1973) discusses the seven deadly sins from the perspective of personal life (chap. 8). Capp's *Deadly Sins and Saving Virtues* seeks to correlate them with the developmental psychology of Erik Erikson.

[81]Stanford M. Lyman, *The Seven Deadly Sins: Society and Evil* (New York: St Martin's, 1978), uses the traditional category to discuss what he calls "the sociology of evil"

(p. 1).

[82]A recent example is Plantinga's *Not the Way It's Supposed to Be*.

[83]Mary Daly, *Gyn/Ecology: The Metaethics of Radical Feminism* (Boston: Beacon, 1978), p. 30.

[84]Bo Yang, *The Ugly Chinaman and the Crisis of Chinese Culture*, trans. Don J. Cohn and Jing Qing (St. Leonards, N.S.W.: Allen & Unwin, 1992), pp. 11-14.

[85]Plantinga, *Not the Way It's Supposed to Be*, pp. 81, 82-83.

[86]Capps, *Deadly Sins*, p. 15.

[87]Such as Aumann, *Spiritual Theology*, chap. 7; Harton, *Elements of the Spiritual Life*, chap. 9.

[88]Dorothy L. Sayers, "The Other Six Deadly Sins," in *The Whimsical Christian* (New York: Collier, 1987), pp. 157-79.

[89]Augustine *City of God* 14.13. The quotation is from Ecclesiasticus 10:15. Thomas Aquinas also refers to it (*Theologiae* 2a.2ae Q.84.3).

[90]Augustine *City of God* 14.13.

[91]Plantinga, *Not the Way It's Supposed to Be*, p. 10.

[92]John Milton, *Paradise Lost and Regained*, ed. Christopher Ricks (New York: Signet, 1968), 2:11, 263. Compare Calvin *Institutes* 2.2.10-11.

[93]Karl Barth, *Church Dogmatics* (Edinburgh: T & T Clark, 1958), 4:405-7. Barth devotes some eighty pages to the sin of sloth (pp. 403-83).

[94]Herbert Waddams, *A New Introduction to Moral Theology* (London: SCM Press, 1964), p. 126.

[95]Eugene Peterson, *The Contemplative Pastor: Returning to the Art of Spiritual Direction* (Grand Rapids, Mich.: Eerdmans, 1993), p. 19.

[96]Lyman, *Seven Deadly Sins*, p. 27.

[97]It is at the time of the day when the sun is hottest that the mind begins to wander and sloth sets in. Lyman observes that the "boring tedium of the intense desert sun at midday initiated the drama of the long dark night of the soul" (ibid., p. 25).

[98]According to Lucian Pye, the Asian concept of deference to the person means that politics (or any other power structure) is essentially a function of personal status and therefore comes in the form of consensual paternalistic authoritarianism in which "patrons and clients seek each other out for different but equally compelling reasons." This sort of authoritarianism, however, must be distinguished from Western concepts of dictatorship, since "the spirit of dependency is quite different from the Western expectation that the bonds which tie superiors and inferiors are likely only to allow the former to manipulate the latter for their own interests." *Asian Power and Politics: The Cultural Dimensions of Authority* (Cambridge, Mass.: Harvard University Press/Belknap, 1985), p. 51. We might add that in this arrangement reciprocity is represented by mutual manipulation rather than top-down manipulation only. The subordinate who defers unquestioningly to the superior often succeeds in wheedling as much from the superior as he gives. The classic example Pye gives is Japanese society (pp. 286-91).

[99]Compare the nature of Chinese *guanxi* relationship (personal connections) in ibid., pp. 291-99.

[100]Calvin *Institutes* 2.2.11.

[101]*Martin Luther: Selections from His Writings*, p. 26.

[102]*The Rule of St. Benedict,* trans. Justin McCann (London: Sheed & Ward, 1976), chap. 7. This is the longest chapter in the entire rule.

Chapter 4: Salvation & the Life of Spiritual Progress

[1]The most thoroughgoing example can be seen in Buddhism, which developed a concept of perfection embodied in the *arahant,* or one who has moved beyond the conditioned world and beyond rebirth. See Nathan Katz, "Perfection Without God: A View from the Pali Canon," *Studies in Formative Spirituality* 14, no. 1 (February 1993): 11-21.

[2]Williams, *Wound of Knowledge,* p. 32. "The Christianity of the first century is sharply distinguished from other contemporary cults chiefly by this concern with historical reality, and so with growth and conflict in human experience" (p. 22).

[3]Most modern theologians tend to avoid using the term *eternity* to describe the "beyond" of present history because of its association with the Platonic concept of timelessness and absolute discontinuity with history. There is, however, no reason to drop it as long as it is remembered that in Christianity eternity embraces both a transcendent pole and a historical pole. The Christian story includes the incarnation, the coming of God in human history, the ascension and the assumption of humanity in the Godhead. It is a story of strange happenings, where, in Lewis's words, myth became fact. For a helpful summary of modern eschatological views, see Brian Hebblethwaithe, *The Christian Hope* (Grand Rapids, Mich.: Eerdmans, 1984), chap. 10.

[4]Augustine *Commentary on Psalm 118.* Cited by Williams, *Wound of Knowledge,* p. 88.

[5]G. C. Berkouwer, *Faith and Sanctification* (Grand Rapids, Mich.: Eerdmans, 1952), pp. 86-87.

[6]Ibid., pp. 88, 90.

[7]Helmut Thielicke, *Theological Ethics* (Philadelphia: Fortress, 1966), 1:11-12.

[8]Ibid., pp. 53, 61.

[9]Ibid., pp. 84, 87.

[10]Ibid., p. 89.

[11]Ibid., pp. 65-66.

[12]See Geoffrey F. Nuttall, *Studies in Christian Enthusiasm* (Wallington, Penn.: Pendle Hill, 1948).

[13]The classic exposition is found in Hannah Whithall Smith, "The Christian's Secret of a Happy Life," in *The Devotional Writings of Robert Pearsall Smith and Hannah Whithall Smith,* Higher Christian Life Series 43 (New York: Garland, 1984), pp. 43, 50, 55.

[14]Calvin *Institutes* 3.9 and 21.

[15]Ibid., 3.1.1.

[16]Ibid., 3.1.3.

[17]Ibid., 3.2.7.

[18]The guide to godliness is one of the most popular genres of Puritan devotional literature. It was patterned after popular Catholic spiritual directories such as Luis de Granada's *Of Prayer and Meditation* (1582) and Gaspare Loarte's *The Exercise of a Christian Life* (1579). More than twenty separate titles of such guides were published in the seventeenth century, and many of them went through multiple

editions. Lewis Bayly's *The Practice of Piety*, 3rd ed. (1613) and Richard Baxter's *The Saints' Everlasting Rest* (1650) are but two of the better-known ones.

[19]William Ames, *The Marrow of Sacred Divinity* (London, 1642), pp. 4-5. The spelling has been modernized.

[20]Henry Scudder, *The Christian's Daily Walk in Holy Security and Peace*, 7th ed. (London, 1637), pp. 773-74.

[21]Baxter, *The Saints' Everlasting Rest*, p. 608.

[22]Thornton, *English Spirituality*, pp. 71, 74.

[23]Calvin regards the teaching of the "Schoolmen" that love is prior to faith and hope as "mere madness" (*Institutes* 3.2.41).

[24]Faith lays hold of the promises of God. "But," Calvin asks, "how can the mind be aroused to taste the divine goodness without at the same time being wholly kindled to love God in return?" (*Institutes* 3.2.41).

[25]The Wesleyan tradition seems to take a mediating position. The spiritual life is understood as denoting a quality in the Christian such as "perfect love." But the focus is not on sins as individual acts but on the principle of sin that needs uprooting. To be sure, the Wesleyan concern could entail a more precise devotional methodology. When the uprooting is understood to be an instantaneous "entire sanctification" of the soul that happens "by faith" rather than a progressive work, the response, as evident in the holiness movement, is one of passivity rather than activity. See J. Kenneth Grider, *Entire Sanctification: The Distinctive Doctrine of Wesleyanism* (Kansas City: Beacon Hill, 1980), pp. 11-25.

[26]Interestingly, the Anabaptist conception of grace is much closer to the second. According to Robert Friedman, the Anabaptists eschewed any theological explanation. Theirs was just an existential awareness of a divine power at work, which is identified as "grace." Grace is "an inner, spiritual illumination" or "charisma" similar to the Quaker's "divine principle" or "divine love." *The Theology of Anabaptism* (Scottdale, Penn.: Herald, 1973), p. 98.

[27]The term *prevenient grace* as used here must be distinguished from Wesley's more technical usage that refers to the grace given to all to enable them to respond to the call to salvation.

[28]Augustine *On Grace and Free Will* 17.33. Cited by Thomas C. Oden, *The Transforming Power of Grace* (Philadelphia: Abingdon, 1993), p. 52. Oden's book is an attempt to recover the doctrine of grace, which he claims is largely lost in modern Western spirituality (pp. 15-20). It is interesting to note that Oden's recovery (see esp. chap. 2) goes back to sources that many ancient and most modern Protestants are reluctant to accept. For them, the idea of cooperating grace smacks too much of semi-Pelagian synergism.

[29]Thornton, *English Spirituality*, pp. 73-4.

[30]Terms like *justification* and *sanctification* are a kind of shorthand for telling different facets of the Christian story. As Hauerwas puts it, sanctification "is but a way of reminding us of the kind of journey we must undertake if we are to make the story of Jesus our story. 'Justification' is but a reminder of the character of that story—namely, what God has done for us by providing us with a path to follow" (*Peaceable Kingdom*, p. 94).

[31]See, for example, Louis Berkhof's *Systematic Theology* (Grand Rapids, Mich.: Eerdmans, 1941), p. 418.

[32]Salvation in the perfect tense is found in Ephesians 2:5, 8; in the present in Acts 2:47; 1 Corinthians 1:18; 2 Corinthians 2:15; and in the future in Acts 2:21; Romans 13:11; 1 Corinthians 5:5; Hebrews 9:28; 1 Peter 1:15.

[33]At this point, we are interested in the ramifications that the Protestant doctrine of justification by faith has for spiritual theology rather than how it is actually understood in Scripture. According to Krister Stendahl, Paul's understanding of justification has to do with more objective concerns: the place of the law after the coming of Christ and the relationship between Jews and Gentiles in the new covenant community. "The Apostle Paul and the Introspective Conscience of the West," in *Paul Among the Jews and Gentiles and Other Essays* (Philadelphia: Fortress, 1976), pp. 78-96. If Stendahl is correct, the Pauline doctrine would have important implications for ecclesiology, a subject for the next chapter.

[34]Cited by Alistair McGrath, *Christian Theology: An Introduction* (Cambridge, Mass.: Basil Blackwell, 1994), p. 382.

[35]Calvin *Institutes* 3.11.1.

[36]Ibid., 3.1.1.

[37]John Cotton, *The Way of Life* (London, 1641), p. 11.

[38]Ibid., pp. 255-300.

[39]Richard Sibbes, "The Glorious Feast of the Gospel," in *Works* (Edinburgh: Banner of Truth, 1973), 2:466-467. Italics mine.

[40]John Ball, *A Treatise of Faith*, 3rd ed. (London, 1637), p. 14.

[41]Thomas Hooker, *The Soul's Preparation for Christ* (London, 1632), p. 2.

[42]Ibid., pp. 12-13.

[43]Calvin *Institutes* 3.11.2.

[44]Ibid.

[45]Harton, *Elements*, p. 15.

[46]Craig Dykstra, *Vision and Character: A Christian Educator's Alternative to Kohlberg* (New York: Paulist, 1981), p. 94. According to Dykstra, repentance is one of the three disciplines (the others being prayer and service) needed for the formation of Christian character (pp. 89-94).

[47]As seen in Berkouwer, *Faith and Sanctification*, chap. 5.

[48]Harton, *Elements*, p. 21.

[49]Pope John Paul II, *The Gospel of Life* (New York: Random House, 1995), pp. 146-53.

[50]In Catholic moral theology such workings of grace are understood in a special category of virtues called the "gifts of the Spirit" (Is 11:2). They are "special divine interventions" distinct from the infused virtues. They "constitute specific kinds of divine mediation designed to aid the moral virtues." See Romanus Cessario, *The Moral Virtues and Theological Ethics* (Notre Dame, Ind.: University of Notre Dame Press, 1991), p. 52. They seem to approximate, or at least they would not be averse to, the Pentecostal understanding of the surprising interventions of God but should be distinguished from the Pentecostal gifts of the Spirit based on 1 Corinthians 12.

[51]The virtues are usually classified broadly as infused and acquired. Under the category of infused virtues, three kinds are identified: the theological, the moral and the gifts of the Spirit. For a theological interpretation of these virtues, see Cessario, *Moral Virtues and Theological Ethics*.

[52]Augustine, "On the Morals of the Catholic Church," in *A Select Library of the Nicene and Post-Nicene Fathers of the Christian Church*, ed. Philip Schaff, vol. 4 (Grand Rapids,

Mich.: Eerdmans, 1956), chap. 6. The same idea is put differently in Bernard, who sees progress in the Christian life in terms of the four degrees of love, the final degree being "loving self for God's sake." It is only "for God's sake" that it is possible to love self without becoming selfish. "To love oneself, once one knows oneself to be a divine likeness, is to love God in oneself and to love oneself in God." Etienne Gilson, *The Mystical Theology of Saint Bernard,* trans. A. H. C. Downes (Kalamazoo, Mich.: Cistercian Publications, 1940, 1990), p. 118.

[53]Thomas Aquinas *Summa Theologiae* 2a.2ae Q.2.a.3.

[54]Bernard of Clairvaux, *On Loving God* (Kalamazoo, Mich.: Cistercian Publications, 1995).

[55]John Wesley, *A Plain Account of Christian Perfection* (London: Epworth, 1952), p. 42.

[56]Augustine *On the Morals of the Catholic Church* 11.12.20.

[57]It is noteworthy that the Catholic moral theologian Cessario has called for greater emphasis on the theological virtues. "Moralists formerly took such 'dogmatic' questions for granted, but the difficulties many people experience in living according to the virtues requires that today we emphasize the life of faith, hope and charity lived in the Church of Christ" (*Moral Virtues and Theological Ethics,* p. 48). At the same time he concedes that "few [Catholic authors] have developed the full implications which the mystery of the blessed Trinity along with those of the economy of salvation hold for Christian moral development" (p. 50).

[58]Katz, "Perfection Without God," pp. 13-14.

[59]Augustine *On the Morals of the Catholic Church* 15.

[60]Aumann, *Spiritual Theology,* pp. 298-305.

[61]Augustine *On the Morals of the Catholic Church* 19.

[62]Ibid., 11.12.20.

[63]According to Cessario, "Faith unites the believer to God the First Truth; hope to God who is Highest Good for me; and charity to God who is Highest Good for himself" (*Moral Virtues and Theological Ethics,* p. 95).

[64]This is what we find in a work like Aumann's *Spiritual Theology,* p. 304.

[65]Augustine *On the Morals of the Catholic Church* 19-20.

[66]Cessario, *Moral Virtues and Theological Ethics,* p. 95.

[67]Most notably Stanley Hauerwas, whose theological ethics is drawn from Iris Murdoch, *The Sovereignty of Good* (New York: Schocken Books, 1970) and Alistair MacIntyre, *After Virtue* (Notre Dame, Ind.: University of Notre Dame Press, 1981). See especially Hauerwas's *The Peaceable Kingdom: A Primer in Christian Ethics* (Notre Dame, Ind.: University of Notre Dame, 1983), chap. 1. From the same perspective, Dykstra has found the concept of justice in Lawrence Kohlberg's moral developmental psychology wanting. Dykstra, *Vision and Character,* pp. 7-29.

[68]Hauerwas has argued that the distinctiveness of Christian theological virtues entails its own unique concept of justice (*Peaceable Kingdom,* pp. 103-6).

[69]The Thomistic way of putting these matters across is to say that acquired moral virtues in themselves "constitute the natural perfection of manhood" and "cannot make man an 'adopted son of God.'" But they could be "an instrument of infused virtues." See Reginald Garrigou-Lagrange, O.P., *The Theological Virtues* (St. Louis: B. Herder, 1965), p. 28. Garrigou-Lagrange is here commenting on the *Summa Theologiae* 2a.2ae Q.63.a.3.

[70]Bernard T. Adeney, *Strange Virtues: Ethics in a Multicultural World* (Leicester, U.K.: Apollos; Downers Grove, Ill.: InterVarsity Press, 1995). See especially chap. 5.

[71]It should be noted that the concept of filial piety as a form of justice is not entirely absent in the West. It is at least formally recognized in spiritual theology texts such as Aumann's (*Spiritual Theology*, p. 287).

[72]Not only is morality the basis for the proper relationship between the ruler and the ruled, Harvard Confucian scholar Tu Wei-Ming in his study of the Confucian doctrine of the mean (*zhong yong*) has gone further to argue that morality is ultimately grounded in some transcendent reference point. *Centrality and Commonality: An Essay on Confucian Religiousness* (Albany, N.Y.: State University of New York Press, 1989), pp. 67-70. This gives to Confucian ethics a certain independent status and frees it from the whims of dictators.

[73]Aquinas *Summa Theologiae* 2a.2ae Q.51.a.2.

[74]C. S. Lewis, *Mere Christianity* (Glasgow: Fount, 1980), p. 114.

[75]M. Scott Peck, *Further Along the Road Less Traveled: The Unending Journey Toward Spiritual Growth* (New York: Simon & Schuster, 1993), p. 22.

[76]Aquinas *Summa Theologiae* 2a.2ae Q.63.a.3-4.

[77]Ibid., 1a.2ae Q.51.a.4.

[78]Quoted in F. N. Flew, *The Idea of Perfection in Christian Theology* (London: Oxford University Press, 1934), p. 395. Flew notes the same idea going back to Luther: "In the place of the possibility of a present deliverance from sin, Luther sets a doctrine of progress. And this progress is primarily progress in faith" (pp. 250-51).

[79]See Alister E. McGrath, *Spirituality in an Age of Change: Rediscovering the Spirit of the Reformers* (Grand Rapids, Mich.: Eerdmans, 1994), pp. 106-12.

[80]A good example of this Reformed-evangelical aversion may be seen in the way perfection and perfectionism are lumped together in Sinclair B. Ferguson and David F. Wright, eds., *New Dictionary of Theology* (Downers Grove, Ill.: InterVarsity Press, 1988), s.v. "perfection, perfectionism." Compare the much more balanced discussion of perfection by Gordon Rupp in *A New Dictionary of Christian Theology*, ed. Alan Richardson and John Bowden (London: SCM Press, 1983), s.v. "perfection."

[81]Flew, *Idea of Perfection*, p. 397.

[82]William Penn, *A Testimony to the Truth of God* (1698), p. xi. Cited by Flew in *Idea of Perfection*, p. 287.

[83]Wesley, *Plain Account*, p. 72.

[84]Asa Mahan, *Scripture Doctrine of Christian Perfection* (Boston: D. S. King, 1839), p. 11.

[85]François Fénelon, *Christian Perfection* (New York: Harper Brothers, 1947), p. 118.

[86]Ibid., p. 140.

[87]Mahan, *Scripture Doctrine of Christian Perfection*, pp. 9-10.

[88]See, for example, George Allen Turner, *The Vision Which Transforms: Is Christian Perfection Scriptural?* (Kansas City: Beacon Hill, 1964), pp. 112-13.

[89]It is of interest to note that the Protestant vision of life begins with the relational dimension and ends with the moral dimension, while the Catholic view begins with the moral dimension and ends with the perfection of a relationship of mystical union.

[90]Thomas à Kempis, *Imitation of Christ*, trans. William C. Creasy (Macon, Ga.: Mercer

University Press, 1989), 2:4.

[91]C. S. Lewis, "The Weight of Glory," in *Transposition and Other Addresses* (London: Geoffrey Bles, 1949), p. 31.

[92]Studies on Christian mysticism are extensive. For a critical summary of significant secondary sources, see Bernard McGinn, *The Foundations of Mysticism*, vol. 1 of *The Presence of God: A History of Western Christian Mysticism* (New York: Crossroad, 1991), pp. 265-343.

[93]Fénelon, *Christian Perfection*, p. 135.

[94]Joseph Hall, "Holy Raptures," in *Works: The Third Tome* (London, 1662), p. 626.

[95]Joseph Hall, "The Soul's Farewell to Earth and Approaches to Heaven," in *Works: The Third Tome*, pp. 927-28.

[96]Baxter, *Reliquiae Baxterianae*, vol. 1 (London, 1696), sec. 6.

[97]Nathaniel Ranew, *Solitude Improved by Divine Meditation* (London, 1670), p. 56. According to Gilson, the mystical union in Bernard is often designated by terms like *excessus* and *raptus* (*Mystical Theology of St. Bernard*, pp. 104-8).

[98]Lewis, "Weight of Glory," p. 22.

[99]Kenneth Kirk, *The Vision of God: The Christian Doctrine of the* Summum Bonum (London: Longmans, Green, 1956), p. 444.

[100]McGinn, *Foundations of Mysticism*, p. 78.

[101]Bernard *Sermons on the Song of Songs* 12.5. Cited by Kirk, *Vision of God*, p. 349.

[102]Jürgen Moltmann, "Theology and the Future of the Modern World," Occasional Papers (Pittsburgh: Association of Theological Schools, 1995), pp. 3, 7. To see Christian perfection as the larger category for interpreting our historical vision implies a doctrine of divine aseity and the priority of the vertical over the horizontal dimension of existence.

Chapter 5: The Church as the Community of Saints

[1]*Sayings of the Desert Fathers: The Alphabetical Collection*, trans. Benedicta Ward, S.L.G. (Kalamazoo: Cistercian Publications, 1975), p. 104.

[2]*The Wisdom of the Desert Fathers, Apophthegmata Patrum*, trans. Benedicta Ward, S.L.G. (Oxford: SLG Press, 1975), p. 42.

[3]Louis Bouyer, *History of Christian Spirituality: The Spirituality of the New Testament and the Fathers* (New York: Seabury, 1960), 1:314-17.

[4]See Hauerwas and Willimon, *Resident Aliens*, p. 71. Compare Rasmusson's comment, *The Church as "Polis*," pp. 196-98.

[5]Hauerwas has considered how the dynamic of patient hope might look in a violent world: "Patience . . . is one of the most needed virtues if we are to live amid this violent world as a peaceable people. Though we have learned to look on the present and future as God's kingdom and know that the kingdom has come in Jesus and is present in the breaking of bread, it is still to come. Sustained by its having come and fueled by its presence, we hope all the more in its complete fulfillment, but such a hope must be schooled by patience. Otherwise our hope too easily turns to fanaticism or cynicism" (*Peaceable Kingdom*, p. 103).

[6]See chapter two.

[7]Two decades after the Chicago Call (1977) was issued, the problem of ecclesiology dealt with in two of the eight points remains. Evangelicals appear to be no nearer to overcoming the problems of church authority and disunity.

[8]Thomas Howard, *Evangelical Is Not Enough: Worship of God in Liturgy and Sacrament* (San Francisco: Ignatius, 1984).

[9]Ibid., p. 60.

[10]David Lim renews an earlier call from another Asian, Saphir Athyal, for a "theology of the visible church." "Beyond Success: Another 'Great Awakening' Through US Evangelicalism Soon?" in *Emerging Voices in Global Christian Theology*, ed. William Dyrness (Grand Rapids, Mich.: Zondervan, 1994), pp. 171-72.

[11]See Robert Wuthnow, "Small Groups Forge New Notions of Community and the Sacred," *The Christian Century*, December 8, 1993, pp. 1236-40; *"I Come Away Stronger": How Small Groups Are Shaping American Religion*, ed. Robert Wuthnow (Grand Rapids, Mich.: Eerdmans, 1994).

[12]Such as Bob and Win Couchman, *Small Groups: Timber to Build God's House* (Wheaton, Ill.: Harold Shaw, 1982); Jeffrey Arnold, *The Big Book on Small Groups* (Downers Grove, Ill.: InterVarsity Press, 1992).

[13]For example, Julie A. Gorman, *Community That Is Christian: A Handbook on Small Groups* (Wheaton, Ill.: Victor, 1993), pp. 11-56.

[14]Leonardo Boff, *Ecclesiogenesis: The Base Communities Reinvent the Church*, trans. Robert R. Barr (Maryknoll, N.Y.: Orbis, 1986).

[15]Elton Trueblood, *The Incendiary Fellowship* (New York: Harper & Row, 1967), p. 27.

[16]Peterson, *Contemplative Pastor*, pp. 27-37.

[17]Trueblood, *Incendiary Fellowship*, p. 24.

[18]The term *singularity* (rather than a more normative term like *unity*) is used here descriptively to designate the Protestant view of the church as the one people of God, the one body of priests without stratification.

[19]Rodney Clapp, "Remonking the Church," *Christianity Today*, August 12, 1988, pp. 21-22.

[20]Martin Thornton, *Pastoral Theology: A Reorientation* (London: S.P.C.K., 1956). See especially chapters 4-5.

[21]In this way Thornton's concept is quite different from those that see the Christian life as developing in two or more stages that everyone in the church should undergo. The remnant are not theologically superior to the rest. They are there by way of a certain "calling" to embrace a common rule for the sake of the rest.

[22]Thornton, *Pastoral Theology*, p. 23.

[23]Ibid., p. 24.

[24]Thornton, *Christian Proficiency*, p. 67.

[25]Compare the classic text of the Higher Life movement, *The Christian's Secret of a Happy Life* (Old Tappan, N.J.: Fleming H. Revell, 1981) by Hannah Whitall Smith: "Do you, then, now at this moment, surrender yourself wholly to Him? You answer, Yes. Then, my dear friend, begin at once to reckon that you are His. . . . And keep on reckoning this. You will find it a great help to put your reckoning into words, and say over and over to yourself and to your God, 'Lord, I am thine; I do yield myself up entirely to thee, and I believe that thou dost take me. I leave myself to thee.' Make this a daily, definite act of your will. . . . Confess it to yourself" (pp. 48-49).

[26]Thornton, *Christian Proficiency*, p. 69.

[27]Ibid., p. 19.

[28]According to Krister Stendahl, "Once the Messiah had come, and once the faith in Him—not 'faith' as a general religious attitude—was available as the decisive

ground for salvation, the Law had done its duty as a custodian for the Jews, or as a waiting room with strong locks [Gal. 3:22ff.]. Hence, it is clear that Paul's problem is how to explain why there is not reason to impose the Law on the Gentiles, who now, in God's good Messianic time, have become partakers in fulfillment of the promises to Abraham (v. 29)." *Paul Among the Jews and Gentiles and Other Essays* (Philadelphia: Fortress, 1976), pp. 27-28, 86.

[29]The close relationship between justification and the working of the Spirit is discussed in Sam K. Williams, "Justification and the Spirit in Galatians," *Journal for the Study of the New Testament* 29 (1987): 97-98, and G. Walter Hansen, *Galatians,* IVP New Testament Commentary Series (Downers Grove, Ill.: InterVarsity Press, 1994), p. 88.

[30]Calvin *Institutes* 3.1.1.

[31]See Stendahl's essay "The Apostle Paul and the Introspective Conscience of the West," in *Paul Among the Jews and Gentiles,* pp. 78-96.

[32]Dietrich Bonhoeffer, *Life Together,* trans. John W. Doberstein (New York: Harper Brothers, 1954), pp. 32-33.

[33]Ibid., p. 33.

[34]Compare the story of the Vanaukens in Sheldon Vanauken, *A Severe Mercy* (San Francisco: Harper & Row, 1977). See especially C. S. Lewis's letter to the author in which he pointed out that a beautiful relationship that excluded God "had to die" (pp. 209-10).

[35]Thornton, *Christian Proficiency,* p. 18. Author's emphasis.

[36]Bonhoeffer, *Life Together,* pp. 38-39.

[37]Calvin *Institutes* 4.14.3-4.

[38]Pannenberg, *Christian Spirituality,* p. 32.

[39]Ibid., p. 38.

[40]Ibid., p. 40. What Pannenberg is calling for harks back to the Orthodox tradition. According to John D. Zizioulas, "the eucharist was not the act of a pre-existing Church; it was an event *constitutive* of the being of the Church, enabling the Church to *be.* The eucharist *constituted* the Church's being." *Being as Communion: Studies in Personhood and the Church* (Crestwood, N.Y.: St. Vladimir's Seminary Press, 1993), p. 21. Author's italics.

[41]The independence of the preacher's authority is tied to a view of Scripture as an independently authoritative *text* (rather than as the bearer of the authoritative Word) that can exist apart from the community from which it arises. The church is prior to the Scripture, which only makes any real sense to the community when it is read as the text of the community. See Stanley Hauerwas, *Unleashing the Scripture: Freeing the Bible from Captivity to America* (Nashville: Abingdon, 1993), chap. 2.

[42]Zizioulas has strongly argued that in the Eucharist "we draw together ecclesial being and the being of God, history and eschatology, without destroying their dialectical relationship" (*Being as Communion,* p. 20). Eschatology defines the transcendent dimension of the church's existence, which is distinguished from the merely historical (p. 19).

[43]C. S. Lewis, *Letters to Malcolm: Chiefly on Prayer* (New York: Harcourt, Brace & World, 1963), p. 66.

[44]Henri Nouwen, *Reaching Out: The Three Movements of the Spiritual Life* (Glasgow:

Collins, 1988), pp. 68-73.

[45]Kenneth Leech, *Soul Friend: A Study of Spirituality* (London: Sheldon, 1987), pp. 121, 123.

[46]Scott J. Hafemann, *Suffering and Ministry in the Spirit: Paul's Defense of His Ministry in II Corinthians 2:14—3:3* (Grand Rapids, Mich.: Eerdmans, 1990), p. 46. Author's italics.

[47]Ibid., p. 226.

[48]For a classic study of the nature of play see Johann Huizinga, *Homo Ludens: A Study of the Play-Element in Culture* (Boston: Beacon, 1955), pp. 1-13.

[49]Geoffrey Wainwright, *Doxology* (New York: Oxford University Press, 1980), p. 26.

[50]Eugene H. Peterson, *Working the Angles: The Shape of Pastoral Integrity* (Grand Rapids, Mich.: Eerdmans, 1987), pp. 74-83.

[51]Pannenberg, *Christian Spirituality*, p. 36.

[52]Theology, according to Diadochos of Photiki, is "the exact tracing of the glory of God" (Louth, *Theology and Spirituality*, p. 16).

[53]Psalms as a whole demonstrates a complex relationship between praise, pain and thanksgiving in the context of worship. For a brief discussion of this, see John Goldingay, *Praying the Psalms* (Bramcote, Nottingham, U.K.: Grove, 1993).

[54]Compare Bonhoeffer, *Life Together*, chap. 2.

[55]Ibid., pp. 44-50.

[56]Henri J. M. Nouwen, *Making All Things New: An Invitation to the Spiritual Life* (San Francisco: Harper & Row, 1981), p. 86.

[57]Walter Ong has done a rather engaging study of this shift from what he calls the verbal sensorium to the visual-tactile sensorium. Through this shift "a certain silencing of God may have been prepared for by the silencing of man's life-world. The ability to respond directly to the word enjoyed by early oral-aural man has been attenuated by objectifying the human life-world through hypertrophy of the visual and the obtrusion of the visual into the verbal itself as man has moved through the chirographic and typographic stages of culture." *The Presence of the Word: Some Prolegoumena for Cultural and Religious History* (New Haven, Conn.: Yale University Press, 1967), pp. 288-89.

[58]*Unleashing the Scripture*, p. 15. Hauerwas's point is that the Bible is church mediated and can properly be understood only within the communal life of the church.

[59]Peterson, *Working the Angles*, p. 99.

[60]Ong, *Presence of the Word*, pp. 69-70.

[61]Bonhoeffer, *Life Together*, p. 60.

[62]Peter Brunner, *Worship in the Name of Jesus*, trans. M. H. Bertram (St. Louis: Concordia, 1968), p. 271.

[63]Bonhoeffer, *Life Together*, p. 56.

[64]Brunner, *Worship in the Name of Jesus*, p. 272.

[65]See the study produced by the Faith and Order Commission on the Nicene-Constantinopolitan Creed *Confessing the One Faith*, rev. ed. (Geneva: WCC, 1991).

[66]Peter E. Gillquist, *Becoming Orthodox: Journey to the Ancient Christian Faith* (Ben Lomond, Calif.: Conciliar, 1992).

[67]Henri Nouwen, *Clowning in Rome* (Westminster, Md.: Christian Classics, 1992), p. 14.

[68]Nouwen, *Making All Things New*, p. 82.

[69]Bonhoeffer, *Life Together,* p. 77.

[70]Thomas Merton, *New Seeds of Contemplation* (New York: New Directions, 1961), p. 55.

[71]Ibid., p. 54.

[72]These will be elaborated in part two.

[73]*The Rule of St. Benedict,* chap. 52.

Chapter 6: The Theology & Life of Prayer

[1]Chapter five, pp. 107-8.

[2]For example, besides the various books focusing on specific exercises referred to in this chapter, the collection of essays Robin Maas and Gabriel O'Donnell, eds., *Spiritual Traditions for the Contemporary Church* (Nashville: Abingdon, 1990), includes practical helps on various spiritual exercises in a readily accessible format.

[3]See chapter two, pp. 45-50.

[4]Brother Lawrence, *The Practice of the Presence of God: The Best Rule of a Holy Life* (New York: Fleming H. Revell, 1895); Jean-Pierre de Caussade, *The Sacrament of the Present Moment,* trans. Kitty Muggeridge (San Francisco: Harper & Row, 1981).

[5]Sobrino, *Spirituality of Liberation,* pp. 14-20.

[6]P. T. Forsyth, *The Soul of Prayer* (London: Charles H. Kelly, 1916), p. 9.

[7]Thornton, *Christian Proficiency,* p. 71.

[8]*Writings from the "Philokalia" on Prayer of the Heart,* trans. E. Kadloubovsky and G. E. H. Palmer (London: Faber & Faber, 1951), p. 62. Quoted by Simon Tugwell, O.P., *Prayer: Living with God* (Springfield, Ill.: Templegate, 1975), p. ix.

[9]Tugwell, *Prayer,* p. xi.

[10]Thornton, *English Spirituality,* pp. 48-49.

[11]Hans Urs von Balthasar, *Prayer* (London: S.P.C.K., 1973), pp. 18-19.

[12]Ibid., p. 18.

[13]George Arthur Buttrick, *Prayer* (New York: Abingdon-Cokesbury, 1941), p. 16.

[14]St. Bonaventure, *The Soul's Journey to God,* trans. Ewert Cousins (New York: Paulist, 1978), 2:1.

[15]Diadochos of Photiki, *On Spiritual Knowledge and Discrimination,* vol. 1 of *The Philokalia,* ed. G. E. H. Palmer, Philip Sherrard and Kallistos Ware (London: Faber & Faber, 1979), p. 290.

[16]Eugene Peterson, *Earth and Altar: The Community of Prayer in a Self-Bound Society* (Downers Grove, Ill.: InterVarsity Press, 1985).

[17]Ibid., p. 49.

[18]Buttrick, *Prayer,* p. 32.

[19]Peterson, *Earth and Altar,* p. 129.

[20]St. Basil, "The Long Rules," in *Ascetical Works,* trans. M. Monica Wagner, vol. 9 of *The Fathers of the Church* (New York: Fathers of the Church, 1950), p. 308.

[21]Peterson, *Earth and Altar,* p. 142.

[22]Buttrick, *Prayer,* p. 163.

[23]Severally noted, for example, by Adolf Holl, *The Last Christian,* trans. Peter Heinegg (Garden City, N.Y.: Doubleday, 1980), p. 3.

[24]Austin Farrer, *The End of Man* (Grand Rapids, Mich.: Eerdmans, 1973), p. 78.

[25]Kenneth Leech, *True Prayer: An Invitation to Christian Spirituality* (San Francisco: Harper & Row, 1980), p. 61.

[26]It may of interest to note that unlike the classical Pentecostals, neo-Pentecostals or charismatics have discovered this type of intimacy usually later in life and therefore tend to interpret the charismatic dimension of prayer as part of a maturing process. No doubt, it helps to enlarge their spiritual life and vision. Still, what they have discovered, essentially, is a lost spiritual childhood!

[27]T. S. Eliot, *Murder in the Cathedral.* Quoted by Tugwell, *Prayer,* p. vii.

[28]Quoted by Thornton, *Christian Proficiency,* p. 95.

[29]Buttrick, *Prayer,* p. 27.

[30]Jean-Nicolas Grou, *How to Pray,* trans. Joseph Dalby (Greenwood, S.C.: Attic, 1964), p. 29.

[31]Ibid., p. 33. This is remarkably similar to François Fénelon's prayer: "O my God, O love, love thyself in me!" (*Christian Perfection,* p. 135). Grou, like many others before him, sees prayer simply as charity in action (*How to Pray,* p. 39). Thus his view of growth in prayer from self-attentive petition to God-directed adoration is broadly similar to Bernard's concept of the progression of love: from loving self and God for self's sake to loving God and self for God's sake.

[32]Grou, *How to Pray,* p. 31. Though not as systematically delineated, his view of the soul's progress in prayer falls broadly within the schema of Teresa's seven mansions of prayer. See Aumann's comments on the latter (*Spiritual Theology,* chap. 12).

[33]Diadochos, *On Spiritual Knowledge and Discrimination,* p. 271.

[34]Thornton, *Christian Proficiency,* p. 130.

[35]*The Collected Works of St. John of the Cross,* trans. Kieran Kavanaugh, O.C.D., and Otilio Rodriguez, O.C.D. (Washington, D.C.: Institute of Carmelite Studies, 1973).

[36]St. John of the Cross, *The Dark Night of the Soul,* bk. 1, deals with the night of the sense; bk. 2 addresses the night of the spirit.

[37]Grou, *How to Pray,* p. 39.

[38]Compare James Houston, *The Transforming Friendship* (Oxford: Lion, 1989), pp. 41-51.

[39]*A Life of Prayer by St. Teresa of Ávila,* ed. James Houston (Portland, Ore.: Multnomah, 1983), p. 2.

[40]Aumann, *Spiritual Theology,* p. 373.

[41]Thornton, *Christian Proficiency,* p. 47.

[42]Buttrick, *Prayer,* p. 76.

[43]Fredrick Heiler, *Prayer: A Study in the History and Psychology of Religion* (New York: Oxford University Press, 1958), pp. 241-42. It is not necessary to agree with Heiler in setting prophetic and mystical prayers in contrast. Properly understood, they occupy different segments of the same path of growth toward union with God. Heiler's approach is historical and psychological rather than theological.

[44]For an excellent discussion of these aspects of prayer, see Thornton, *Christian Proficiency,* pp. 59-107.

[45]C. S. Lewis, *That Hideous Strength* (New York: Macmillan, 1946), p. 418.

[46]I am referring to a traditional practice that still exists in rural Asia today. Excess fish that are not sold are usually laid out under the sun to be dried and preserved.

[47]Buttrick, *Prayer,* p. 77.

[48]Ibid., p. 115.

Chapter 7: Spiritual Exercises Focusing on God and Self

[1]See Robert Banks, *Redeeming the Routines: Bringing Theology to Life* (Wheaton, Ill.: BridgePoint, 1993).

[2]For a number of years, those applying to the theological college where I teach were asked if they had read through the Bible at least once. Three out of four had not. In some traditions this fact may not mean very much. But in a tradition that regards reading the Bible in "private devotions" as almost the sine qua non of spirituality, I find this quite alarming. It may well indicate a general breakdown of spiritual discipline due, perhaps, to the increasingly hectic nature of urban life. Statistics elsewhere are not too encouraging either. A recent survey of Presbyterian ministers and laity revealed that 62 percent of members and 56 percent of elders did not read the Bible or read it infrequently. A third of pastors and nearly half of specialized clergy had no daily Bible-reading habit. *Presbyterian News Service*, April 5, 1996, pp. 13-15.

[3]St. Basil, "The Long Rules," p. 308.

[4]Grou, *How to Pray,* pp. 80-81.

[5]Brother Lawrence, *Practice of the Presence of God,* p. 20.

[6]Ibid., pp. 23-25.

[7]Thornton, *Christian Proficiency,* p. 62.

[8]Francis de Sales *Introduction to a Devout Life* 2.2.

[9]Ejaculatory prayers have been used since very early times. They arise spontaneously from the heart of the believer who knows that God is present everywhere. See Irénée Hausherr, *The Name of Jesus* (Kalamazoo, Mich.: Cistercian Publications, 1978), p. 205.

[10]Nathaniel Ranew, *Solitude Improved by Divine Meditation* (1670), pp. 204-5.

[11]A good example of a contemporary application is found in Thomas A. Langford, *Prayer and the Common Life* (Nashville: Upper Room, 1984), esp. chap. 7.

[12]In the Eastern tradition, the Jesus Prayer has a comprehensive function in the growth of the spiritual life. It belongs to the category of formalized or "set" prayer. It cultivates the "memory of God" through continuous repetition or meditation. For a historical study of the Jesus Prayer, see Hausherr, *The Name of Jesus,* esp. chap. 4.

[13]Diadochos, *On Spiritual Knowledge,* p. 293.

[14]St. Hesychios, *On Watchfulness and Holiness,* in *The Philokalia* (London: Faber & Faber, 1979), 1:163, 169.

[15]*The Way of a Pilgrim,* trans. Helen Bacovcin (New York: Doubleday, 1987), p. 18.

[16]Ibid., pp. 31-33.

[17]Ibid., p. 22.

[18]M. Basil Pennington, *A Place Apart: Monastic Prayer and Practice for Everyone* (Garden City, N.Y.: Doubleday, 1983), pp. 89-90.

[19]Brother Lawrence, *Practice of the Presence of God,* p. 7.

[20]Langford, *Prayer and the Common Life,* pp. 32, 30-31.

[21]This habit among Chinese converts (although not exclusively confined to them) may go back to a popular Taoist practice involving fortune sticks. John and Angela Pearce have noted a similar practice among residents of inner London: "Perhaps because of the unwelcoming environment which pertains so widely in the inner city, it seems that God shows his hand more clearly and (dare we say it?) more

crudely in these places." *Inner City Spirituality* (Bramcote, Nottingham, U.K.: Grove, 1987), p. 11.

[22]Fénelon, *Christian Perfection*, p. 78.

[23]Ibid., p. 4.

[24]Ibid., p. 195.

[25]Grou, *How to Pray*, p. 48.

[26]M. Basil Pennington, *Centering Prayer: Renewing an Ancient Christian Prayer Form* (Garden City, N.Y.: Doubleday, 1980), esp. pp. 9-20.

[27]Diadochos, *On Spiritual Knowledge*, p. 167.

[28]*The Wisdom of the Desert Fathers: The Anonymous Series*, trans. Benedicta Ward, S.L.G. (Oxford: SLG Press, 1975), p. 47.

[29]Prologue, *The Rule of St. Benedict*, p. 1.

[30]Ibid., pp. 3, 4.

[31]Cited by Thornton, *Christian Proficiency*, p. 25.

[32]de Caussade, *Sacrament of the Present Moment*, pp. 15-16. For a contemporary example, see Joyce Huggett, *Listening to God* (London: Hodder & Stoughton, 1986), pp. 28-31.

[33]Fénelon, *Christian Perfection*, p. 8.

[34]Grou, *How to Pray*, p. 49.

[35]de Caussade, *Sacrament of the Present Moment*, p. 11.

[36]Augustine *Soliloquies* 2.1. Quoted by Pierre Pourrat, *Christian Spirituality in the Middle Ages* (London: Burns & Oates, 1924), p. 291.

[37]Thomas à Kempis *Imitation of Christ* 1.3.4.

[38]William Barclay, *Flesh and Spirit* (London: SCM Press, 1962), p. 72.

[39]Richard Rogers, *Seven Treatises* (1603), p. 316. The *Seven Treatises* was one of the earliest systematic spiritual directories produced by a Puritan.

[40]Ibid., p. 236.

[41]See Joseph de Guibert, *The Jesuits: Their Spiritual Doctrine and Practice* (St. Louis: n.p., 1972), pp. 126-27.

[42]*The Spiritual Exercises of Ignatius Loyola*, trans. Thomas Corbishley, S.J. (Wheathampstead, Hertfordshire, U.K.: Anthony Clarke), pp. 22-24.

[43]Ibid., pp. 28-29.

[44]Charles Hambrick-Stowe, *Practice of Piety* (Ann Arbor, Mich.: University Microfilm International, 1981), pp. 29-30.

[45]Francis de Sales *Introduction to a Devout Life* 5.1.2.

[46]For a discussion of journaling, see George F. Simons, *Keeping Your Personal Journal* (New York: Paulist, 1978); Ronald Klug, *How to Keep a Spiritual Journal* (New York: Thomas Nelson, 1982); Lawrence Osborn, *Dear Diary: An Introduction to Spiritual Journaling* (Bramcote, Nottingham, U.K.: Grove, 1988).

[47]Ignatius was not the only one to suggest keeping a record of self-examination. Some Puritans offered very practical help on "casting up" a spiritual account. For example, Isaac Ambrose, *Prima, Media, Ultima* (1654), chap. 7, and Thomas White, *A Treatise of the Power of Godliness* (1658), pp. 324.

[48]Jungian psychologist Ira Progoff has systematically enlarged this principle into what he calls the "intensive journal" approach to creativity and wholeness. See his *At a Journal Workshop* (New York: Dialogue House, 1975).

[49]Simons, *Keeping Your Personal Journal*, p. 11.

Chapter 8: Spiritual Exercises Focusing on the Word

[1]Richard Greenham, *Works* (1612), p. 41.

[2]Compare Simons, *Keeping Your Personal Journal*, p. 18.

[3]See, for example, the work of Brevard Childs, *Biblical Theology of the Old and New Testaments: Theological Reflections on the Christian Bible* (Minneapolis: Fortress, 1993).

[4]*Way of a Pilgrim*, pp. 131-32.

[5]Ibid., p. 131.

[6]This is what canonical criticism seeks to recover. See *Dictionary of Christ and the Gospels* (Downers Grove, Ill.: InterVarsity Press, 1992), s.v. "canon criticism."

[7]James Barr, *The Scope and Authority of the Bible* (London: SCM Press, 1980), p. 54.

[8]Henri J. M. Nouwen, *Reaching Out: The Three Movements of the Spiritual Life* (London: Fount, 1980), p. 124.

[9]William Temple, *Readings in St. John's Gospel*, 2 vols. (London: Macmillan, 1939-1940).

[10]Ibid., 1:xix.

[11]Ibid., 1:xvi-xvii.

[12]Ibid., 1:14.

[13]Susan Annette Muto, *A Practical Guide to Spiritual Reading* (Petersham, Mass.: St. Bede's Publications, 1994) is an excellent and comprehensive guide to spiritual reading. The book also includes reading lists from Scripture and spiritual writers organized around major and minor themes as well as a three-year cycle of readings.

[14]Muto, *Practical Guide to Spiritual Reading*, p. 29.

[15]For a critique of the modern scientific view, which is essentially the Cartesian view of reality, see Michael Polanyi, *Personal Knowledge: Towards a Post-Critical Philosophy* (Chicago: University of Chicago Press, 1958).

[16]*Way of a Pilgrim*, p. 31.

[17]Richard Foster: *Celebration of Discipline* (San Francisco: Harper & Row, 1978); *Freedom of Simplicity* (San Francisco: Harper & Row, 1981); *Prayer: Finding the Heart's True Home* (San Francisco: Harper, 1992). A. W. Tozer: *Of God and Men* (Harrisburg, Penn.: Christian Publications, 1960); *The Knowledge of the Holy* (New York: Harper & Row, 1961); *The Pursuit of God* (Harrisburg, Penn.: Christian Publications, 1948).

[18]Sadhu Sundar Singh, *At the Feet of the Master*, trans. Arthur and Mrs. (Rebecca Jane) Parker (London: Hodder & Stoughton, 1985).

[19]The stories of two outstanding Asian Christians, Sundar Singh and John Sung, are well worth noting. The best biography of Sundar Singh is still Bishop A. J. Appasamay's *Sundar Singh: A Biography* (Madras: Christian Literature Society, 1966). For John Sung, see Leslie T. Lyall, *John Sung* (London: China Inland Mission, 1961).

[20]Quoted by Muto in *Practical Guide to Spiritual Reading*, p. 18.

[21]Ong, *Presence of the Word*, p. 271; Hausherr, *Name of Jesus*, p. 177.

[22]Ong, *Presence of the Word*, pp. 69-70.

[23]See Jean Leclercq, *The Love of Learning and the Desire for God* (New York: Fordham University Press, 1985), pp. 182-84. Compare Francis de Sales *Introduction to a Devout Life* 2.5.

[24]Protestant devotional writers of the seventeenth century produced many collec-

tions of aphoristic sayings for the purpose of meditation. Robert Cawdry, *A Treasury or Store-House of Similies* (1600); Joseph Hall, *Meditations and Vows Divine and Moral* (1606); Richard Baxter, *Aphorisms of Justification* (1655).

[25]Sibbes, *The Soules Conflict with Itself* (1635), p. 197.

[26]Francis Rous, *The Arte of Happinesse* (1619), p. 71 (72).

[27]Bonhoeffer is right when he observes that "for the mature Christian *every* Scripture reading will be 'too long,' even the shortest one" (*Life Together,* p. 53).

[28]The psalms feature prominently in the divine office of the Benedictine rule. The entire psalter is chanted once a week (*The Rule of St. Benedict,* chap. 18).

[29]See *Way of a Pilgrim,* pp. 32-33.

[30]In his biography of Puritan John Bruen, William Hinde refers to an illiterate "godly" servant in Bruen's household known simply as "Old Robert" who amassed such a vast knowledge of Scripture by using certain markings on his leather girdle that he was constantly consulted as a walking concordance. William Hinde, *A Faithful Remonstrance of the Holy Life and Happy Death of John Bruen of Bruen-Stapleford in the County of Chester* (1641), pp. 56-57.

[31]According to Michael Polanyi, much of our knowledge is "tacit" knowledge (*Tacit Dimension,* pp. 3-25).

[32]The power of music to shape the community is seen most clearly in the spirituals and gospel music that are sung in North American black churches. See Kenneth Leech, *The Eye of the Storm* (San Francisco: HarperSanFrancisco, 1992), pp. 51-53.

[33]For example, Luther's *Short Catechism,* and the *Catechism of the Catholic Church* (Chicago: Loyola University Press, 1994).

[34]Hausherr, *Name of Jesus,* p. 177. Hausherr is describing the *florilegium,* but her description could apply just as well to a charismatic chorus.

[35]Ibid., p. 205.

[36]The earliest work of methodical meditation was the *Rosetum Exercitiorum Spiritualium et Sacrarum Meditationum* (Duaci, 1494) by Johannes Mauburnus, a canon regular of Mount St. Agnes (d. 1502). Methodical meditation culminated in the *Spiritual Exercises* of Ignatius Loyola in the second quarter of the sixteenth century.

[37]Pourrat, *Christian Spirituality,* 3:7.

[38]Francis de Sales *Introduction to a Devout Life* 2.1.

[39]Thomas Merton, *Spiritual Direction and Meditation* (Wheathamstead, Hertfordshire, U.K.: Anthony Clarke, 1975), p. 77.

[40]A number of practical guides on meditation written by evangelicals have followed Foster's *Celebration,* including Peter Toon, *Meditating upon God's Word: Prelude to Prayer and Action* (London: Darton, Longman & Todd, 1988); Peter Toon, *From Mind to Heart: Christian Meditation Today* (Grand Rapids, Mich.: Baker, 1987).

[41]Simon Chan, "The Puritan Meditative Tradition, 1599-1691: A Study in Ascetical Piety," Ph.D. diss., Cambridge University, 1986.

[42]Quoted by Wallace, *Calvin's Doctrine of the Christian Life,* pp. 87-92.

[43]Richard Greenham, *Works* (1612), p. 37.

[44]Ibid., pp. 40-41.

[45]The term *godly* was used regularly by Puritans to refer to those who approximated their ideal of the Christian life.

[46]Joseph Hall's *The Art of Divine Meditation* was first published in 1606.

[47]For a reproduction of Hall's *Art of Divine Meditation* and a study of the literary sources of the text, see F. L. Huntley, *Bishop Joseph Hall and Protestant Meditation in Seventeenth-Century England* (Binghamton, N.Y.: Center for Medieval and Renaissance Studies, 1981).

[48]Methodologically, the Asian genre is closer to what in Christian tradition would be called contemplation, but substantially they are diametrically opposed. The goal of Buddhist meditation, for instance, is the extinction of self, while the goal of Christian contemplation is the discovery of the true self in union with God. Some evangelicals remain suspicious of contemplation and mysticism and tend to settle for a practice of meditation involving general good thoughts. For example, Campbell McAlpine, *The Practice of Biblical Meditation* (London: Marshall, Morgan & Scott, 1986); Walter C. Kaiser Jr., "What Is Biblical Meditation?" in *Renewing Your Mind in a Secular World,* ed. John D. Woodbridge (Chicago: Moody Press, 1985), pp. 39-53; Dave Hunt and T. A. McMahon, *The Seduction of Christianity: Spiritual Discernment in the Last Days* (Eugene, Ore.: Harvest House, 1985). Hunt and McMahon's otherwise sound critique of cultural Christianity is somewhat vitiated by their undiscriminating criticism of imaginative meditation (chap. 11).

[49]Frances de Sales *Introduction to a Devout Life* 2.2-7.

[50]For a study of other methods, see Bede Frost, *The Art of Mental Prayer* (London: Alban, 1988).

[51]Giles Firmin, *The Real Christian: Or, A Treatise of Effectual Calling* (1670), pp. 314-19.

[52]Richard Baxter, *Aphorismes of Justification* (The Hague, 1655), sig. M6; *Reliquiae Baxterianae* (1690), 1:5.

[53]Dietrich Bonhoeffer, *Meditating on the Word,* trans. David McI. Gracie (Cambridge, Mass.: Cowley, 1985), p. 34.

[54]Bonhoeffer, *Meditating on the Word,* p. 33. Bonhoeffer suggests that a few persons meditate on a single text, which he terms "occasional meditation." "In such a meditation there is a narrow way that leads between false, pious talk and idle theological discussion" (p. 34).

[55]Conservative Protestantism often encourages what Niebuhr calls a "Christianity against culture" stance, with the result that even positive values like the meditative mindset found in Hinduism and Buddhism are repudiated. However, an Asian Christian minister who was converted from Buddhism once told me that the training in the meditative technique he had received in his previous religion had helped him greatly in meditating on Scripture.

[56]See Bernard of Clairvaux's commentary *On the Song of Songs* (Kalamazoo, Mich.: Cistercian Publications, 1971), sermon 62.4-7. Compare Pourrat, *Christian Spirituality,* 3:12-13.

Chapter 9: Spiritual Exercises Focusing on the World

[1]See chapter four.

[2]G. K. Chesterton, *Orthodoxy* (Garden City, N.Y.: Image, 1959), p. 131.

[3]For example, Kenneth Leech, *Soul Friend: The Practice of Christian Spirituality* (San Francisco: Harper & Row, 1977); Tildern Edwards, *Spiritual Friend: Reclaim-*

ing the Gift of Spiritual Direction (New York: Paulist, 1980).

[4]Kenneth Leech, *The Eye of the Storm: Living Spiritually in the Real World* (San Francisco: HarperSanFrancisco, 1992), pp. 204-5. Western nonhierarchical practices, such as children's calling their parents by their first names, are just as appalling to Asians as Eastern hierarchicalism is to Westerners.

[5]Bhikhu Parekh, "An Indian View of Friendship," in *The Changing Face of Friendship*, ed. Leroy S. Rouner (Notre Dame, Ind.: University of Notre Dame Press, 1994), p. 110.

[6]This will be discussed in chapter twelve.

[7]Aelred of Rievaulx, *Spiritual Friendship*, trans. Mary Eugenia Laker (Washington, D.C.: Cistercian Publications, 1974); Francis de Sales *Introduction to a Devout Life* 3.19-22.

[8]Aelred *Spiritual Friendship* 3.90.

[9]Martin E. Marty, *Friendship* (Allen, Tex.: Argus Communications, 1980), pp. 39-44.

[10]The friendship paradigm in contemporary discussion has been extended to include the social realm (as seen in Ninian Smart's essay "Friendship and Enmity Among Nations," in *Changing Face of Friendship*, pp. 155-68) and the animal realm.

[11]Jürgen Moltmann, "Open Friendship," in *Changing Face of Friendship*, pp. 38-41.

[12]Eliot Deutsch, "On Creative Friendship," in *Changing Face of Friendship*, p. 27.

[13]On women's friendship, see Pat O'Connor, *Friendships Between Women: A Critical Review* (London: Guildford, 1992). On male friendship, see Peter M. Nardi, ed., *Men's Friendships* (Newbury Park, Calif.: Sage, 1992).

[14]Mary E. Hunt, *Fierce Tenderness: A Feminist Theology of Friendship* (New York: Crossroad, 1991).

[15]Mary E. Hunt, "Friends and Family Values," in *Changing Face of Friendship*, pp. 171, 173.

[16]Ibid., pp. 179-81.

[17]Ibid., p. 174.

[18]Walter L. Williams, "The Relationship Between Male-Male Friendship and Male-Female Marriage: American Indian and Asian Comparisons," in *Men's Friendships*, pp. 186-99.

[19]Ibid., p. 196.

[20]Ibid., p. 199.

[21]Aristotle *Nicomachean Ethics* 8.3.

[22]The discussion on friendship is found in books 8 and 9.

[23]Aelred *Spiritual Friendship* 1.38. Compare Francis de Sales *Introduction to a Devout Life* 3.20.

[24]David L. Hall and Roger T. Ames, "Confucian Friendship," in *Changing Face of Friendship*, p. 79.

[25]Ibid., p. 81.

[26]Aristotle *Nicomachean Ethics* 8.6.

[27]In Confucianism, the goal of friendship is the cultivation of the all-important virtue of *jen* (see Hall and Ames, "Confucian Friendship," pp. 82-86). The moral basis of friendship in Hinduism is noted in Parekh, "Indian View of Friendship," p. 104.

[28]Aristotle also recognized friendship between unequal partners, such as a father and a son, but even here, he stressed the equalizing effect of friendship. Each

party in an unequal friendship should get an equally larger share from the other but of a different kind. For example, between a rich person and a poor person, the rich gets a larger share of honor from the poor, while the poor gets an equally large share of physical things from the rich (8.13.2). This is what Aristotle meant by rendering to each party according to one's desert. "In all dissimilar friendships, it is proportion . . . that establishes equality and preserves the friendship" (9.1). In this respect, the Aristotelian friendship is very similar to the Confucian concept of reciprocity (see p. 51).

[29]Ching, *Confucianism and Christianity,* p. 97.

[30]Hall and Ames, "Confucian Friendship," p. 84.

[31]Ibid., pp. 83, 91.

[32]Parekh, "Indian View of Friendship," p. 109.

[33]"There is a poignancy in the conclusion that Socrates and Confucius could not be friends," note Hall and Ames ("Confucian Friendship," p. 92).

[34]Francis de Sales *Introduction to a Devout Life* 3.19.

[35]Aelred *Spiritual Friendship* 3.6.

[36]Noted by Francis de Sales *Introduction to a Devout Life* 3.19.

[37]Aelred *Spiritual Friendship* 1.38.

[38]Ibid., 1.35.

[39]Aumann, *Spiritual Theology,* p. 379. Compare Francis de Sales *Introduction to a Devout Life* 3.20.

[40]Deutsch, "On Creative Friendship," p. 23.

[41]Moltmann, "Open Friendship," p. 38.

[42]Aelred *Spiritual Friendship* 3.8.

[43]Quoted in ibid., 3.23.

[44]Aelred *Spiritual Friendship* 3.130.

[45]Ibid., 3.61.

[46]Ibid., 3.55.

[47]Francis de Sales *Introduction to a Devout Life* 3.22.

[48]Aristotle *Nichomachean Ethics* 8.3-6.

[49]Aelred *Spiritual Friendship* 1.44.

[50]Aristotle *Nichomachean Ethics* 9.3.

[51]For a discussion of this problem, see Gilbert Meilaender, "When Harry and Sally Read the *Nicomachean Ethics:* Friendship Between Men and Women," in *Changing Face of Friendship,* pp. 190-92.

[52]Biblically, the category of friendship has a limited application to relationship with God. As Martin Marty has pointed out, "Friendship is a bonus that God throws into the deal, a gift that goes along with divine goodness but is not the basis for ties between humans and the divine. When friendship becomes religion, our picture of God is too small, our expectations of human life too large to endure the tests" (*Friendship,* p. 116).

[53]John Donne's *Devotions upon Emergent Occasions* (London, 1624) was occasioned by his own sickness.

[54]Joseph Hall, "Occasional Meditations," in *The Second Tome* (London, 1630-1634), pp. 127, 132.

[55]Calvin *Institutes* 1.5.1.

[56]Thornton, *English Spirituality,* p. 112.

[57]For the full text of the canticle, see Bonaventure, *The Soul's Journey into God; The Tree of Life; The Life of St. Francis,* trans. Ewert Cousins (New York: Paulist, 1978), pp. 27-28.

[58]Bonaventure *The Soul's Journey* 1.15.

[59]Ibid., 1.6.

[60]Ibid., 2.

[61]Ibid., 2.12.

[62]In Perry Miller's introduction to Jonathan Edwards's *Images or Shadows of Divine Things* (New Haven, Conn.: Yale University Press, 1948).

[63]Robert Bellarmine, *The Mind's Ascent to God by the Ladder of Created Things,* in *Spiritual Writings,* trans. John Patrick Donnely and Roland J. Tske (New York: Paulist, 1989), 4.1.

[64]For example, Robert Cawdry, *A Treasurie or Store-house of Similes* (1600).

[65]Bellarmine *Mind's Ascent* 4.1, pp. 86-87.

[66]Cited in Lawrence Osborn, *Meeting God in Creation* (Bramcote, Nottingham, U.K.: Grove, 1990), p. 15.

[67]Cited in ibid., p. 16. Compare Elizabeth Culling, *What Is Celtic Christianity?* (Bramcote, Nottingham, U.K.: Grove, 1993), p. 24.

[68]For example, Osborn, *Meeting God in Creation,* p. 17.

[69]The terms are Barbara Lewalski's. They approximate Miller's "allegorist" and "imagist" respectively. See *Protestant Poetics and the Seventeenth Century Religious Lyric* (Princeton, N.J.: Princeton University Press, 1979), p. 162.

[70]Once I met some social workers who organized a picnic for street children in the island of Cebu in the Philippines. I was told later that some of these children saw the sea for the first time!

[71]Osborn, *Meeting God in Creation,* p. 11.

[72]Huntley, *Bishop Joseph Hall and Protestant Meditation,* pp. 138, 151.

[73]Especially chapters one, five and six.

[74]I have in mind the futuristic schools of eschatology (both premillennial and dispensational) that are popular with evangelicals. Traditional eschatology also includes postmillennialism, but it is often criticized in modern eschatology for its naive utopianism.

[75]A number of books on George Müller's life and work have been written. Among them are Basil Miller, *George Müller, the Man of Faith: A Biography of One of the Greatest Prayer-Warriors of the Past Century* (Grand Rapids, Mich.: Zondervan, 1941); Arthur T. Pierson, *George Müller of Bristol and His Witness to a Prayer-Hearing God* (New York: Loizeaux Bros., 1944); Roger Steer, *George Müller: Delighted in God* (Wheaton, Ill.: Harold Shaw, 1975).

[76]For example, Leech's *Eye of the Storm: Living Spiritually in the World,* for all its noble effort to present a spirituality of social engagement, essentially presupposes the Moltmannian model and is therefore limited in its application.

[77]See Vishal Mangalwadi's *Truth and Social Reform* (New Delhi: Nivedit Good Books, 1986), chap. 2.

[78]Guptara, *Indian Spirituality,* p. 23.

[79]Mangalwadi, *Truth and Social Reform,* p. 25.

[80]Guptara is one of a number of Indians who are not formally identified with any Christian church but follow Jesus as their guru. For a study of this phenomenon,

see J. Paul Rajashekar, "The Question of Unbaptized Believers in the History of Mission in India," in *Debate on Mission: Issues from the Indian Context,* ed. Herbert E. Hoeffer (Madras: Gurukul Lutheran Theological College and Research Institute, 1979), pp. 323-41.

[81]Guptara, *Indian Spirituality,* p. 23.

[82]John Howard Yoder, *The Politics of Jesus: Behold the Man! Our Victorious Lamb,* 2nd ed. (Grand Rapids, Mich.: Eerdmans, 1994), chap. 3. Yoder, following the work of André Trocmé (*Jesus and the Nonviolent Revolution* [Scottdale, Penn.: Herald, 1973]), sees Jesus' proclamation of the good news as essentially the inauguration of the year of jubilee. As such it carries far-reaching sociopolitical implications.

[83]See pp. 129-30.

[84]Bernard Adeney presents an excellent case study of the relationship between spirituality and social involvement and analyzes the dynamics involved as well in *Strange Virtues,* chapter ten. He shows that in a particular African context, the usual Western approach to dealing with social evil may not work (pp. 233, 239, 244).

Chapter 10: The Rule of Life

[1]For a brief history of the rule of life, see *A Dictionary of Christian Spirituality* (London: SCM Press, 1983), s.v. "rules."

[2]Jeremy Taylor, *Selected Works* (New York: Paulist, 1990), pp. 418-25.

[3]Aumann, *Spiritual Theology,* p. 373.

[4]Harold Miller, *Finding a Personal Rule of Life* (Bramcote, Nottingham, U.K.: Grove, 1984), p. 10.

[5]See Francis de Sales *Introduction to a Devout Life* 5.1.

[6]Miller, *Finding a Personal Rule of Life,* pp. 13-23.

[7]Thornton, *Christian Proficiency,* p. 54. Author's italics.

[8]*Source Documents for the Living Tradition of the Society of St. Francis* (Society of St. Francis, 1987), pp. 56-59.

[9]Brother Ramon, S.S.F., *Franciscan Spirituality: Following Saint Francis Today* (London: S.P.C.K., 1994), pp. 107-9.

[10]*The Book of Discipline of the United Methodist Church* (Nashville: United Methodist Publishing House, 1992), pp. 71-73.

[11]See, for example, David Lowes Watson, *Accountable Discipleship: Handbook for Covenant Discipleship Groups in the Congregation,* rev. ed. (Nashville: Discipleship Resources, 1986), and "Covenant Discipleship at Wesley Theological Seminary," *Covenant Discipleship Quarterly* 3, no. 2 (January 1988): 2-6.

[12]See p. 146.

[13]Donald Bloesch, *The Crisis of Piety: Essays Toward a Theology of the Christian Life,* 2nd ed. (Colorado Springs: Helmers & Howard, 1988), p. 49.

[14]Howard, *Evangelical Is Not Enough,* p. 68.

[15]*The Wisdom of the Desert Fathers, Apophthegmata Patrum,* trans. Benedicta Ward, S.L.G. (Oxford: SLG Press, 1975), p. 42.

Chapter 11: The Discernment of Spirits

[1]*Wisdom of the Desert Fathers,* trans. Benedicta Ward, p. 29.

[2]*The Spiritual Exercises of Ignatius Loyola,* p. 330.

[3]See Peter T. O'Brien, *Commentary on Philippians,* New International Greek Testament Commentary (Grand Rapids, Mich.: Eerdmans, 1991), p. 77.

[4]Ernest E. Larkin, O.Carm., *Silent Presence: Discernment as Process and Problem* (Denville, N.J.: Dimension Books, 1981), p. 10.

[5]Larkin identifies four steps in this process: self-knowledge, self-acceptance, integration of self, and validation from the community where one interacts with the larger Christian community of teachers, counselors and spiritual directors. The sort of personal wholeness implied in these four steps is not just a psychological state of well-being but a wholeness that grows out of a depth relationship with God through various channels of grace (p. 42-59).

[6]Compare Thomas H. Green, *Weeds Among the Wheat: Discernment—Where Prayer and Action Meet* (Notre Dame, Ind.: Ave Maria; Manila: St Paul's Publications, 1984), pp. 58-63.

[7]Compare Aumann, *Spiritual Theology,* pp. 402-3, 412; Paul G. Hiebert, "Discerning the Work of God," in *Charismatic Experiences in History,* ed. Cecil M. Robeck Jr. (Peabody, Mass.: Hendrickson, 1985), pp. 147-63.

[8]See Martin McNamara, "Discernment Criteria in Israel: True and False Prophets," in *Discernment of the Spirit and of Spirits,* ed. Casiano Floristán and Christian Duquoc (New York: Seabury, 1979), pp. 3-13.

[9]Numbers refer to the sections of *The Spiritual Exercises.*

[10]The following tragic story was told to me by a close friend of a cancer victim. His sick friend had gone to a well-known local evangelist for prayer. The evangelist, whom he had not met previously, mysteriously disclosed the exact type of cancer he was suffering from and then went on to assure him of God's healing. Since the evangelist's "spiritual diagnosis" was correct, the man's hope was raised considerably. But he never recovered from his illness and died with serious doubts about God's failure to keep his promise. It is possible that the evangelist might have been endowed with a special "gift of knowledge" (1 Cor 12:8) in that instance, or it could have been a psychic phenomenon. But his foretelling of healing was his own idea (an afterglow effect) and had nothing to do with his "prognosis." The whole episode involved a misuse of either a special charisma or an innate psychic endowment.

[11]Green, *Weeds Among the Wheat,* p. 67.

[12]Courage is sometimes conceived of as the strength to endure hardship passively, whereas boldness is usually understood as a virtue that supports active participation in risky ventures. For a discussion of this virtue, see Daniel A. Dombrowski, "The Virtue of Boldness," *Spirituality Today* 37, no. 3 (Fall 1985): 213-20.

[13]A recent study on how the Pentecostal experience of the "leading of the Spirit" works itself out in the practice of discernment and decision-making observes that Pentecostals use "transrational" criteria in discernment. Stephen E. Parker, *Led by the Spirit: Toward a Practical Theology of Pentecostal Discernment and Decision Making* (Sheffield, U.K.: Sheffield Academic Press, 1996), pp. 11-12. Such "transrational" criteria are also recognized in other traditions. See Green, *Weeds Among the Wheat,* pp. 67-68.

[14]See Parker, *Led by the Spirit,* chap. 4.

[15]Ibid., p. 204.

[16]Jonathan Edwards, *The Religious Affections* (Edinburgh: Banner of Truth, 1984).

[17]So Gordon Fee, *God's Empowering Presence: The Holy Spirit in the Letters of Paul* (Peabody, Mass.: Hendrickson, 1994), pp. 60-61. True to his evangelical heritage, Fee equates the apostolic traditions strictly with the written text (p. 75).

[18]Ibid., p. 252.

[19]Cassian *Conferences* 2.10.

[20]Cited by Rose Mary Dougherty, *Group Spiritual Direction: Community for Discernment* (New York: Paulist, 1995), p. 12.

[21]Richard Foster has suggested some practical steps in this area (*Celebration of Discipline*, p. 226).

[22]We see this, for example, in the Kansas City prophets and in the self-styled Malaysian prophet Jonathan David. While they try to teach others to learn "revelation knowledge" (better, discernment), it is also quite clear that they see themselves as special channels of God's prophetic word to the church. Jonathan David's official textbook for his "school of the prophets" contains repeated statements like "let me prophesy to you," "the Lord allowed me to see a unique vision," and so on. *The Spirit of Wisdom and Revelation* (Malaysia: Jonathan David, 1988), pp. 17, 19. For the Kansas City prophets, see Nigel Scotland, *Charismatics and the Next Millennium* (London: Hodder & Stoughton, 1995), pp. 145-49.

[23]Martin Thornton, *Spiritual Direction* (Cambridge, Mass.: Cowley, 1984), p. 130.

[24]Thornton, *Christian Proficiency*, p. 134.

[25]Jon Sobrino, "Following Jesus as Discernment," in *Discernment of the Spirit and of Spirits*, ed. Casiano Floristán and Christian Duquoc (New York: Seabury, 1979), pp. 18, 23.

[26]Note, for example, the ambiguity expressed in the various attempts at understanding God's relationship to human history in "Theological Foundations of Modernization," in *What Asian Christians Are Thinking*, ed. Douglas J. Elwood (Manila: New Day, 1976), pp. 379-86.

[27]Green, *Weeds Among the Wheat*, p. 64.

[28]Aumann, *Spiritual Theology*, pp. 424-40.

[29]Concern over charismatic excesses is expressed in a recent spate of books and articles. For example, Edward N. Gross, *Miracles, Demons, and Spiritual Warfare: An Urgent Call for Discernment* (Grand Rapids, Mich.: Baker, 1990); *Power Religion*, ed. Michael Scott Horton (Chicago: Moody Press, 1992); David Powlison, *Power Encounters: Reclaiming Spiritual Warfare* (Grand Rapids, Mich.: Baker, 1995); Nigel Scotland, *Charismatics and the Next Millennium* (London: Hodder & Stoughton, 1995); Robert A. Guelich, "Spiritual Warfare, Paul and Peretti," *Pneuma* 13, no. 1 (Spring 1991): 33-64; Laurence W. Wood, "Third Wave of the Spirit and the Pentecostalization of American Christianity: A Wesleyan Critique," *Wesleyan Theological Journal* 31, no. 1 (Spring 1996): 110-41.

[30]Scotland, *Charismatics and the Next Millennium*, pp. 137-57.

[31]This explains why people whose ministries have been discredited elsewhere, such as Morris Cerullo, Vernon Falls, Benny Hinn (who is supposed to have recanted) and Rodney Browne, continue to enjoy wide acceptance in many parts of Asia.

[32]Hiebert, "Discerning the Work of God," p. 155.

[33]St. John of the Cross, *The Dark Night of the Soul*, trans. Benedict Zimmerman, O.C.D. (Cambridge: James Clarke, 1973), 2.1.3-4.

[34]See Hiebert's critique of the charismatics on this point in "Discerning the Work of God," pp. 158-60.

[35]Edwards, *Religious Affections*, p. 23. Compare Joseph Hall: "A man is a man by his understanding part, but he is a Christian by his will and affections" (*Art of Divine Meditation*, chap. 28). For a modern development of the same idea, see Robert C. Roberts, *Spirituality and Human Emotions* (Grand Rapids, Mich.: Eerdmans, 1982), esp. chap. 2.

[36]This is the case, unfortunately, with an otherwise useful book by Dave Hunt and T. A. McMahon, *The Seduction of Christianity* (Eugene, Ore.: Harvest House, 1985). The authors simply lump together all forms of "visualization" techniques as dabbling in the territory of the devil (pp. 112-31). It would be difficult to conclude prima facie that Christians who are engaged in practices involving the paranormal are influenced directly by the enemy.

[37]I am translating Edwards's "no certain signs" into the language of religious phenomenology. From Edwards's perspective both sanctified and unsanctified persons can experience an uncertain sign (for example, zeal). But a saint's zeal is marked by certain qualities that emerge over time and can never be lost. If we translated his theology phenomenologically, we would say that Christian formation takes place when the initial zeal develops into certain character-forming qualities, while de-formation occurs when zeal fails to develop those character-forming qualities.

[38]For example, when the so-called Kansas City prophet Paul Cain correctly predicted over the phone someone's sniffle and wet hair, he seemed to be engaging in what parapsychologists term prognostication rather than serious prophecy. See Scotland, *Charismatics and the Next Millennium*, p. 147.

[39]We could say that when Paul Cain trivialized prophecy (see preceding note), he was doing the devil's work in the sense that he brought the good gift of God into disrepute.

[40]See Marguerite Shuster, *Power Pathology, Paradox: The Dynamic of Evil and Good* (Grand Rapids, Mich.: Zondervan, 1987), pp. 43-63.

[41]Noted, for example, by Gross, *Miracles, Demons and Spiritual Warfare*, pp. 61-63.

[42]Edwards, *Religious Affections*, pp. 137-65.

[43]See Aumann, *Spiritual Theology*, pp. 424-40.

[44]See note 22.

[45]Mary K. Baxter, *A Divine Revelation of Hell* (Titusville, Fla.: Kathy Baxter Ministries, n.d.).

[46]Jonathan Edwards's highly nuanced discussion of "non gracious" ideas and visions that impinge mysteriously on the mind, including accurate prophecies, should alert us to the danger of giving too much credence to many modern claims.

[47]"If you are a theologian, you will truly pray. And if you pray truly, you are a theologian," says Evagrius. "On Prayer," in *The Philokalia* (London: Faber & Faber, 1979), 1:62.

Chapter 12: The Art of Spiritual Direction

[1]Thornton, *Spiritual Direction*, p. 5.

[2]Quoted in Thornton, *Christian Proficiency*, p. 25.

[3]The works of Tildern Edwards and Rose Mary Dougherty are particularly helpful

on the practice of individual and group direction, respectively. Thornton is strong on the relationship between spiritual theology and direction.

[4]As noted in chapter nine, friendship and direction carry different connotations in Asian cultures and should be kept separate. But if spiritual friendship is to be seen in terms of direction, it could be described as a kind of mutual direction.

[5]Thornton, *Spiritual Direction*, p. 22.

[6]Ibid., chap. 4.

[7]Tildern H. Edwards, *Spiritual Friend: Reclaiming the Gift of Spiritual Direction* (New York: Paulist, 1980), chap. 7. For a helpful example of group spiritual direction at work, see Rose Mary Dougherty, S.S.N.D., *Group Spiritual Direction: Community for Discernment* (Mahwah, N.J.: Paulist, 1995), chap. 4.

[8]Dougherty, *Group Spiritual Direction*, p. 55.

[9]See Shaun McCarty, "On Entering Spiritual Direction," in *Spiritual Direction: Contemporary Readings*, ed. Kevin G. Culligan, O.C.D. (Locus Valley, N.Y.: Living Flame, 1983), p. 112.

[10]See Thornton, *Spiritual Direction*, chap. 5.

[11]Note that these are the two major divisions in theology (ibid., pp. 32-35).

[12]Edwards, *Spiritual Friend*, pp. 210-11.

[13]See Leech, *Soul Friend*, pp. 113-16.

[14]For a critique of this position, see Robert C. Roberts, *Taking the Word to Heart: Self and Other in an Age of Therapies* (Grand Rapids, Mich.: Eerdmans, 1993), pp. 29-34. Roberts is surely right when he says, "Sin is not just a failure to be congruent with one's true self but a failure to be congruent with one's true self conceived in a very particular way—namely, *as before God*" (p. 33, author's italics).

[15]As when Kenneth Leech says, "The aim of spiritual direction is the achievement of wholeness of life, an integrated personality, in which the inner and the outer man are united." *Soul Friend*, pp. 108-9.

[16]Morris West, *The Clowns of God* (New York: Bantam, 1982).

[17]Thornton, *Spiritual Direction*, pp. 9-10.

[18]Ibid., p. 126.

[19]This point is clearly emphasized in Margaret Guenther, *Holy Listening: The Art of Spiritual Direction* (Cambridge, Mass.: Cowley, 1992), pp. 35-39.

[20]This point is especially marked in Thornton. See *Spiritual Direction*, chaps. 7-9.

[21]Edwards, *Spiritual Friend*, p. 118.

[22]William A. Barry and William J. Connolly, *The Practice of Spiritual Direction* (New York: Seabury, 1983), pp. 5, 8.

[23]Guenther, *Holy Listening*, chap. 4.

[24]Ibid., p. 43.

[25]Corcoran, "Spiritual Guidance," p. 450.

[26]Kallistos Ware, "The Spiritual Father in Orthodox Christianity," in *Spiritual Direction: Contemporary Readings*, ed. Kevin G. Culligan, O.C.D. (Locus Valley, N.Y.: Living Flame, 1983), pp. 21-23.

[27]Edwards, *Spiritual Friend*, p. 210.

[28]Carolyn Gratton, *The Art of Spiritual Guidance* (New York: Crossroad, 1992), pp. 41-42.

[29]It may be of interest to note that this charismatic model of direction has also been schematized in the classical Pentecostal doctrine of being "led by the Spirit." See

Stephen E. Parker, *Led by the Spirit: Toward a Practical Theology of Pentecostal Discernment and Decision Making* (Sheffield, U.K.: Sheffield Academic Press, 1996).

[30]Thornton, *Spiritual Direction*, chap. 5; Edwards, *Spiritual Friend*, pp. 112-16.

[31]The apophatic way of knowing is usually associated with the Eastern Church and refers to the way of knowing by negation *(via negativa)*. By focusing on what God is not, one is led beyond positive and rational affirmations into the very mystery of God's being. In this sense, apophatism represents a tradition stressing nonrational and intuitive insights into truth.

[32]Edwards, *Spiritual Friend*, pp. 164-72.

[33]Gratton, *Art of Spiritual Guidance*, p. 27.

[34]Guenther, *Holy Listening*, pp. 19-20.

[35]For some traditional Chinese who have reached a certain age, death is an event that is awaited with positive anticipation rather than dread, as seen in elaborate preparations, such as securing a coffin long before the event. The Singaporean writer Catherine Lim has poignantly captured this peculiar cultural trait in her story "The Old Man in the Balcony" in *They Do Return* (Singapore: Times Books, 1983), pp. 6-11.

[36]Thornton, *Spiritual Direction*, esp. chaps. 12-13.

[37]It should be noted that while spiritual formation in ashrams is still very much alive in India, the Chinese *shifu-mentu* relationship is hardly relevant in contemporary Chinese culture. For the function of the guru, see Mettina Bäumer, "The Guru in the Hindu Tradition," *Studies in Formative Spirituality* 11, no. 3 (November 1993): 341-53.

[38]Anthony Yeo, *Counselling: A Problem-Solving Approach* (Singapore: Armour, 1993), pp. 2-4.

[39]Thornton, *Spiritual Direction*, pp. 102-4.

[40]Edwards, *Spiritual Friend*, p. 251.

[41]Ibid., pp. 138-39.

[42]Compare the discussion on knowing God's will in the previous chapter.

[43]Edwards, *Spiritual Friend*, pp. 145-56.

[44]Ibid., p. 150.

[45]In more than fifteen years of interviewing candidates for the ministry, we have discovered that applicants want a change of vocation for a wide range of implicit reasons, including problems with people at work, boredom, lack of prestige and retrenchment, although the usual explicit reason given is "the call of God."

[46]Edwards, *Spiritual Friend*, p. 155.

[47]In J. R. R. Tolkien's *The Hobbit*, Bilbo Baggins's adventure began with "an unexpected party."

[48]Edwards, *Spiritual Friend*, pp. 156-62.

[49]Merton, *Spiritual Direction*, pp. 36, 38.

[50]Thornton, *Spiritual Direction*, p. 76.

[51]Leech, *Soul Friend*, p. 121.

[52]Ibid., p. 131.

[53]For a discussion of some of these resources for guidance, see Edwards, *Spiritual Friend*, pp. 94-99.

[54]Ibid., p. 101.

[55]David Lowes Watson, *Accountable Discipleship: Handbook for Covenant Disci-*

pleship Groups in the Congregation, rev. ed. (Nashville: Discipleship Resources, 1986).

[56]Ibid., p. 57. It might be of interest to note that the idea of covenanting was also practiced by English Congregationalists from the mid-seventeenth century in a manner not very different from the covenant discipleship group. The main difference is that in congregationalism the covenant group *was* the *ecclesia* rather than an *ecclesiola.* See G. F. Nuttall, *Visible Saints* (Oxford: Blackwell, 1957), pp. 75-84.

[57]See page 196.

[58]To the extent that spiritual direction includes finding and following a rule of life, the covenant discipleship group as described by Watson (*Accountable Discipleship,* pp. 63-68) is a form of group spiritual direction. Spiritual direction also pertains to matters such as the discernment of long-term and immediate vocations.

[59]Edwards, *Spiritual Friend,* pp. 214, 211, 212.

[60]Ware, "Spiritual Father in Orthodox Christianity," pp. 22-23.

[61]See Vandana Mataji, "Spiritual Formation in Ashrams in Contemporary India," *Studies in Formative Spirituality* 11, no. 3 (Nov. 1990): 355-79.

[62]*Sayings of the Desert Fathers,* p. 23.

[63]Ibid., p. 26.

[64]Ware, "Spiritual Father in Orthodox Christianity," p. 28; compare p. 32.

[65]Thornton, *Spiritual Direction,* pp. 73, 66-67.

[66]A point noted by Gratton, *Art of Spiritual Guidance,* p. 45.

[67]Compare Thornton, *Spiritual Direction,* p. 1.

A Select Bibliography

Adam, Peter. *Living the Trinity*. Bramcote, Nottinghamshire, U.K.: Grove, 1986.

Aelred of Rievaulx. *Spiritual Friendship*. Translated by Mary Eugenia Laker. Washington, D.C.: Cistercian Publications, 1974.

Appasamy, A. J. *Sundar Singh: A Biography*. Madras, India: The Christian Literature Society, 1966.

Augustine. *On the Morals of the Catholic Church*. In volume 4 of *A Select Library of the Nicene and Post-Nicene Fathers of the Christian Church*. Edited by Philip Schaff. Grand Rapids, Mich.: Eerdmans, 1956.

Aumann, Jordan. *Spiritual Theology*. London: Sheed & Ward, 1984.

Bacovcin, Helen, trans. *The Way of a Pilgrim*. New York: Doubleday, 1978.

Baggley, John. *Doors of Perception: Icons and Their Spiritual Significance*. London: Mowbrays, 1987.

Banks, Robert. *Redeeming the Routines: Bringing Theology to Life*. Wheaton, Ill.: BridgePoint, 1993.

Bernard of Clairvaux. *On Loving God*. Kalamazoo, Mich.: Cistercian Publications, 1995.

Boff, Leonardo. *Ecclesiogenesis: The Base Communities Reinvent the Church*. Maryknoll, N.Y.: Orbis, 1986.

Bonhoeffer, Dietrich. *Life Together*. Translated by John W. Doberstein. New York: Harper & Brothers, 1954.

———. *Meditating on the Word*. Translated by David McI. Gracie. Cambridge, Mass.: Cowley, 1985.

Buttrick, George Arthur. *Prayer*. New York: Abingdon-Cokesbury, 1941.

Capps, Donald. *Dead Sins and Saving Virtues*. Philadelphia: Fortress, 1987.

Caussade, Jean-Pierre de. *The Sacrament of the Present Moment*. Translated by Kitty Muggeridge. New York: HarperCollins, 1989.

Cessario, Romanus. *The Moral Virtues and Theological Ethics*. Notre Dame, Ind.: University of Notre Dame Press, 1991.

Chesterton, G. K. *Orthodoxy*. New York: Lane, 1909.

Congar, Ives. *I Believe in the Holy Spirit*. Translated by David Smith. 3 vols. New York: Seabury, 1983.

de Guibert, Joseph. *The Theology of the Spiritual Life*. New York: Sheed & Ward, 1953.

Edwards, Jonathan. *The Religious Affections*. Edinburgh: Banner of Truth, 1984.

Edwards, Tildern H. *Spiritual Friend: Reclaiming the Gift of Spiritual Direction*. New York: Paulist, 1980.

Fabella, Virginia, et al., eds. *Asian Christian Spirituality: Reclaiming Traditions*. Maryknoll, N.Y.: Orbis, 1992.

Fénelon, François. *Christian Perfection.* New York, London: Harper Brothers, 1947.

Flew, F. N. *The Idea of Perfection in Christian Theology.* London: Oxford University Press, 1934.

Foster, Richard. *Celebration of Discipline.* San Francisco: Harper & Row, 1978.

———. *Freedom of Simplicity.* San Francisco: Harper & Row, 1981.

———. *Prayer: Finding the Heart's True Home.* San Francisco: Harper & Row, 1992.

Francis de Sales, St. *An Introduction to a Devout Life.* 1613. Facsimile reprint, London: Scolar Press, 1976.

Garrigou-Lagrange, R. *The Three Ages of the Interior Life.* Translated by S. M. Timothea Doyle. 1947. Reprint, Rockford, Ill.: Tan Books, 1989.

Gorman, Julie A. *Community That Is Christian: A Handbook on Small Groups.* Wheaton, Ill.: Victor, 1993.

Grou, Jean-Nicholas. *How to Pray.* Translated by Joseph Dalby. Greenwood, S.C.: Attic, 1964.

Harton, F. P. *The Elements of the Spiritual Life: A Study of Ascetical Theology.* London: S.P.C.K., 1964.

Hauerwas, Stanley. *A Community of Character: Toward a Constructive Christian Social Ethic.* Notre Dame, Ind.: University of Notre Dame Press, 1981.

———. *The Peaceable Kingdom: A Primer in Christian Ethics.* Notre Dame, Ind.: University of Notre Dame Press, 1983.

———. *Unleashing the Scripture: Freeing the Bible from Captivity to America.* Nashville: Abingdon, 1993.

Hauerwas, Stanley, and William H. Willimon. *Resident Aliens: Life in the Christian Colony.* Nashville: Abingdon, 1989.

Hausherr, Irénée. *The Name of Jesus.* Kalamazoo, Mich.: Cistercian Publications, 1978.

Houston, James M. *The Holy Spirit in Contemporary Spirituality.* Bramcote, Nottinghamshire, U.K.: Grove, 1993.

Howard, Thomas. *Evangelical Is Not Enough: Worship of God in Liturgy and Sacrament.* San Francisco: Ignatius, 1984.

Ignatius, St. *The Spiritual Exercises of Ignatius Loyola.* Translated by Thomas Corbishley, S.J. Wheathamstead, Hertfordshire, U.K.: Anthony Clarke, 1973.

Lawrence, Brother. *The Practice of the Presence of God, the Best Rule of a Holy Life.* New York: Revell, 1895.

Leclercq, Jean. *The Love of Learning and the Desire for God.* New York: Fordham University Press, 1985.

Leech, Kenneth. *Soul Friend: A Study of Spirituality.* London: Sheldon, 1987.

Lewis, C. S. *Letters to Malcolm: Chiefly on Prayer.* New York: Harcourt, Brace & World, 1963.

———. *Mere Christianity.* Glasgow: Fount, 1980.

Lovelace, Richard F. *Dynamics of Spiritual Life: An Evangelical Theology of Renewal.* Downers Grove, Ill.: InterVarsity Press, 1979.

Lyman, Stanford M. *The Seven Deadly Sins: Society and Evil.* New York: St. Martin's, 1978.

Maas, Robin, and Gabriel O'Donnell, eds. *Spiritual Traditions for the Contemporary Church.* Nashville: Abingdon, 1993.

Marty, Martin E. *Friendship.* Allen, Tex.: Argus Communications, 1980.

McCann, Justin, trans. *The Rule of St. Benedict.* London: Sheed & Ward, 1976.

McGinn, Bernard. *The Foundations of Mysticism.* New York: Crossroad, 1991.

Merton, Thomas. *Spiritual Direction and Meditation.* Wheathamstead, Hertfordshire, U.K.: Anthony Clarke, 1975.

Miller, Harold. *Finding a Personal Rule of Life.* Bramcote, Nottinghamshire, U.K.: Grove, 1984.

Muto, Susan Annette. *A Practical Guide to Spiritual Reading.* Petersham, Mass.: St. Bede's Publications, 1994.

Nouwen, Henri. *Reaching Out: The Three Dimensions of the Spiritual Life.* Glasgow: Collins, 1988.

Oden, Thomas C. *The Transforming Power of Grace.* Philadelphia: Abingdon, 1993.

Osborn, Lawrence. *Meeting God in Creation.* Bramcote, Nottinghamshire, U.K.: Grove, 1990.

Palmer, G. E. H, Philip Sherrard and Kallistos Ware, eds. *The Philokalia: The Complete Text.* 4 vols. London: Faber & Faber, 1979-1995.

Peck, M. Scott. *People of the Lie: The Hope for Healing Human Evil.* New York: Simon & Schuster, 1983.

Peters, Ted. *God as Trinity: Relationality and Temporality in Divine Life.* Philadelphia: Westminster/John Knox Press, 1993.

————. *Sin: Radical Evil in Soul and Society.* Grand Rapids, Mich.: Eerdmans, 1994.

Peterson, Eugene H. *The Contemplative Pastor: Returning to the Art of Spiritual Direction.* Grand Rapids, Mich.: Eerdmans, 1989.

————. *Earth and Altar: The Community of Prayer in a Self-Bound Society.* Downers Grove, Ill.: InterVarsity Press, 1985.

————. *Working the Angles: The Shape of Pastoral Integrity.* Grand Rapids, Mich.: Eerdmans, 1987.

Pieris, Aloysius. *An Asian Theology of Liberation.* Maryknoll, N.Y.: Orbis, 1988.

Plantinga, Cornelius, Jr. *Not the Way It's Supposed to Be: A Breviary of Sin.* Grand Rapids, Mich.: Eerdmans, 1995.

Ramon, Brother, S.S.F. *Franciscan Spirituality: Following Saint Francis Today.* London: S.P.C.K., 1994.

Rouner, Leroy S., ed. *The Changing Face of Friendship.* Notre Dame, Ind.: University of Notre Dame Press, 1994.

Sayers, Dorothy L. *The Whimsical Christian.* New York: Collier, 1978.

Simons, George F. *Keeping Your Personal Journal.* New York: Paulist, 1978.

Singh, Sadhu Sundar. *At the Feet of the Master.* Edited by Halcyon Backhouse. London: Hodder & Stoughton, 1985.

Smith, Hannah Whitall. *The Christian's Secret of a Happy Life.* Old Tappan, N.J.: Revell, 1981.

Sobrino, Jon. *Spirituality of Liberation: Toward Political Holiness.* Maryknoll, N.Y.: Orbis, 1988.

Thornton, Martin. *Christian Proficiency.* London: S.P.C.K., 1964.

————. *English Spirituality: An Outline of Ascetical Theology According to the English Pastoral Tradition.* London: S.P.C.K., 1963.

————. *Pastoral Theology: A Reorientation.* London: S.P.C.K., 1956.

Trueblood, D. Elton. *The Incendiary Fellowship.* New York: Harper & Row, 1967.

von Balthasar, Hans Urs. *Prayer.* London: S.P.C.K., 1973.

Wainwright, Geoffrey. *Doxology: The Praise of God in Worship, Doctrine and Life.*

New York: Oxford University Press, 1980.

Ward, Benedicta, trans. *Sayings of the Desert Fathers: The Alphabetical Collections.* Kalamazoo, Mich.: Cistercian Publications, 1975.

———. *The Wisdom of the Desert Fathers, Apophthegmata Patrum.* Oxford: SLG Press, 1975.

Watson, David Lowes. *Accountable Discipleship: Handbook for Covenant Discipleship Groups in the Congregation.* Rev. ed. Nashville: Discipleship Resources, 1986.

Wesley, John. *A Plain Account of Christian Perfection.* London: Epworth, 1952.

Williams, Rowan. *The Wound of Knowledge: Christian Spirituality from the New Testament to St. John of the Cross.* Rev. ed. Cambridge, Mass.: Cowley, 1990.

Zizioulas, John. *Being as Communion.* Crestwood, N.Y.: St. Vladimir's Seminary Press, 1985.

Index of Persons

Index of Subjects